THE MODERN ERA OF

the Les Paul Legacy

1968–2009

THE MODERN ERA OF
L the
Les
Paul
Legacy
1968–2009

by Robb Lawrence

Hal Leonard Books • New York
An imprint of Hal Leonard Corporation

Cover photos by Robb Lawrence, except the photo of Les and Jimmy Page, by Chuck Pulin.

ISBN: 978-1-4234-5531-8

Published by:
Hal Leonard Corporation
7777 W. Bluemound Road
P.O. Box 13819
Milwaukee, WI 53213

Library of Congress Cataloging-in-Publication Data

Lawrence, Robb.
 The modern era of the Les Paul legacy, 1968-2009 / by Robb Lawrence. -- 1st ed.
    p. cm.
 Includes index.
 ISBN 978-1-4234-5531-8
 1. Electric guitar--History. 2. Gibson, Inc.--History. 3. Guitarists--Interviews. 4. Paul, Les. I. Title.
 ML1015.G9L392 2009
 787.87092--dc22
                    2009038468

Printed in U.S.A.

First Edition

Visit Hal Leonard Online at **www.halleonard.com**

Contents

Acknowledgements

This second volume is dedicated to the memory of Lester William Polsfuss, who shared his tremendous wisdom and great knowledge with me to make these books a reality for all of us to enjoy. It is also dedicated to the memory of luthier Chuck Burge, who wound Les Paul's special pickups and spoke with him almost every night of his later years.

My sincere appreciation goes to my family in San Diego, and to the hard-working folks at Hal Leonard in Milwaukee and New York who believed in my vision and helped bring it to fruition, including Brad Smith, Jackie Muth, Richard Slater, Linda Nelson, Tommy Haack, John Cerullo, and publicist Aaron Lefkove.

To the past and present Gibson employees who graciously shared their insights, time, and expertise—from the old guard, Bruce Bolen, Jim Deurloo, Tim Shaw, and Chuck Burge; and for sharing insight into Gibson's recent years, Henry Juszkiewiez, Dave Berryman, Mike McGuire, Rick Gembar, Ren Ferguson, Al Carness, Frank Johns, Pat Foley, Edwin Wilson, Tom Murphy, Danny Hoefer, and Mitch Holder—I am forever grateful.

Much thanks to the guitar stores who graciously allowed me to photograph their inventories, including the SoCal Guitar Centers in Hollywood, Sherman Oaks, Ventura, and San Diego. I also wish to acknowledge artist relations man Dave Weiderman, Justin "The Killer" Slater, the Burst Brothers Dave Belzer and Andrew Berlin, and Jeremy, Norman, and Jordan Harris, Nick Karakulos of Norm's Rare Guitars, Dan Duhren and David Swartz of California Vintage Guitars, Yuris Zeltins and DeForest of the Blue Guitar Workshop, David and Caroline Brass of Fretted Americana, Bob Page of Buffalo Brothers, Saul Frank at Centre City, and Music Ground in London. Thank you, Donna Lynn, for your photography assistance.

For their great inspiration through the years, I thank my friends Jeff Beck, Billy Gibbons, and Del Casher. Other artists I would like to thank for their interviews and portraits include Slash, Neal Schon, Warren Haynes, Sonny Landreth, Waddy Wachtel, Brad Whitford, Zakk Wylde, Joe Bonamassa, Frankie Sullivan, Jeff "Skunk" Baxter, Joe Satriani, Joe Perry, Steve Lukather, Robben Ford, and Pat Martino.

Special thanks goes to Jim Marshall for sharing his thoughts on Les Paul and the sound with his beloved amplifiers. Once again, pickup specialists Seymour W. Duncan, Bill and Becky Lawrence are such wonderful, caring friends and are deservedly thanked for sharing their expertise.

Extra photography was graciously supplied by Neil Zlozower, Chuck Pulin, Rick Gould, TJ McCann, Martin G. Miller (both cover guitars), Erol Reyal, and Cy White.

To the many player/collectors who let me photograph their beloved instruments—including Bill Feil, Chuck Kavooris, Jeff Lund, Don Breeze, Martin G. Miller, Mike Tilley, and Mikey Voltage—muchas gracias. Mike Slubowski's guitars were lovingly photographed by Steve Pitkin.

The present volume would be lacking several fine instruments without the enthusiastic help of Four Amigos guitar show promoters Larry Briggs and Dave Crocker, who appreciate a good book on their favorite guitars! Barry Cleveland of *Guitar Player* magazine is a compadre in great guitars and has gotten me back onboard writing articles.

Les's hit album wouldn't have been possible without the able help of Bob Cutarella, Fran Cuthcart, Marc Ursele, Rob Christie, and all the amazing musicians who created a Grammy Award-winning effort.

Much appreciation goes to Les Paul's family—Rusty and Gene Paul, Colleen and Gary Weiss, Bobby Paul, nephew Greg Carronna—as well as personal assistant and photographer Chris Lentz, manager Michael Braunstein, original bassist Wally Kamen, godson Steve Miller, Gail Bellows (Wally Jones's daughter), Suzie Manners, and Arlene Palmer, who took good care of Les for so long.

A family of extremely talented musicians ably backed up Les through the later years, including Lou Pallo, Gary Mazzaropi, Paul Nowinski, Nikki Parrott, Frank Vignola, John Colliani, Bucky Pizzarelli, John Paris, Stanley Jordan, Andrew Nimmer (tap dancer), and Sonya Hensley. They have my deepest admiration. Also deserving special mention is soundman extraordinaire Tommy Doyle, plus Ron Sturm and John, at the Iridium club.

I thank everyone who contributed to making this treatise on the magic of the Wizard of Waukesha a special book to celebrate Les Paul's marvelous life and incredible musical impact.

Introduction

As we continue through the wonderful world of Les Paul, this companion book picks up with his re-emergence in the late sixties—and Gibson's innovative efforts with their most famous model—and continues to the 50th anniversary of the famed original sunburst Les Paul Standard and the 2008 Rock and Roll Hall of Fame tribute event, finally ending with the memorials following Les's death in August 2009. The players tell appreciative stories of the instrument's musical influences and how its tone inspires them to great sonic heights. The Gibson designers and personnel explain their motivation and ideas for numerous models through the years.

As covered in the companion book, *The Early Years of the Les Paul Legacy*, the tradition blossomed during the fifties, when the world-renowned Gibson company and guitarist/tinkerer extraordinaire Les Paul created a landmark solid-body guitar, destined to further the greatness of tone, giving musicians a rich and robust voice for their expression of musicality and new trends. Les Paul and his wife and musical partner Mary Ford were the first to promote the signature guitars, but revered blues artists, like John Lee Hooker and Freddy King, soon embraced its tonal magic. Then, numerous Gibson jazz artists, including Jim Hall and Mickey Baker, found a new voice with the classy 1954 Les Paul Custom model's rich, solid tones for session work and live performances. And the rock 'n' roll craze hit with Bill Haley's "Rock Around the Clock," featuring Fran Beecher on the new Black Beauty. The great Carl Perkins played his rockabilly hit, "Blue Suede Shoes," with a golden solid Gibson model, too. The Les Paul guitar was now in motion.

When sales waned, Gibson dropped the single cutaway guitar in 1961. It was replaced by a sleek, comfortably sculpted silhouette model with a thinner all-mahogany body that resulted in a thinner voicing. The signature name was retained and gained some sales ground. Les stated at the time, though, that the subdued tone was less desirable for him. Then his second five-year contract expired in 1963, Les and Mary divorced, and he retired. The golden Les Paul era was gone. The renamed SG carried on bravely and the ES-355 semi-solid Custom model was king of the hill for Gibson electrics when that void was so apparent.

The Modern Era begins in the late sixties, as one of America's great guitar treasures surfaced. A young Chicagoan named Michael Bloomfield began experimenting with the original Les Paul guitars in a new context of American blues big bands. In *The Wizard of Waukesha* film (1979), he explained how he discovered the sunburst Standard's refined and articulate voicing for rock-flavored blues. Playing with the Paul Butterfield Blues Band, on Al Kooper's *Super Session* LP, and with the group the Electric Flag, we heard the sizzling tone of Bloomfield's single cutaway Les Paul with fervor and great taste. Our ears were tipped and our minds were wowed!

In England, things were stirring musically and sonically, too. A number of prominent British guitarists discovered the amazing Les Paul tonalities for a new flavor of rock-inspired blues, à la Keith Richards with the Rolling Stones, Eric Clapton with John Mayall and Cream, the Jeff Beck Group, Peter Green's Fleetwood Mac, Paul Kossoff with Free, Albert Lee, and Jimmy Page with Led Zeppelin. Instead of the bright Fender reverb amps powering the Les Paul, the English sound was magically transformed, matched up with the mighty Marshall amp. The stage was set with old Les Paul guitars, and we were all ears!

It was time to revive a once-heralded instrument, worthy of recognition to further the voice of the musician. Les got wind of all this and called Gibson. They set up a meeting to reinstate the original guitar and tossed around some new ideas. The Les Paul guitar was soon back on the map in 1968 and took off like wildfire. The music and musicians were ready for another go at it. This time, the single cutaway solid-body Gibson was here to stay.

In the last extended chapter on Les Paul's career, I share our times together since the seventies, serving as his guitar tech for many West Coast concerts. We enjoyed radio shows, visited concerts and recording studios to meet guitarists and producers, and had fun traveling the country with his son, Bobby. Covered herein are the amazing albums Les has done, the many awards and tributes, and his weekly gigs at Fat Tuesdays and the Iridium in Manhattan. As a man who lived 94 years, he did it all—and then some!

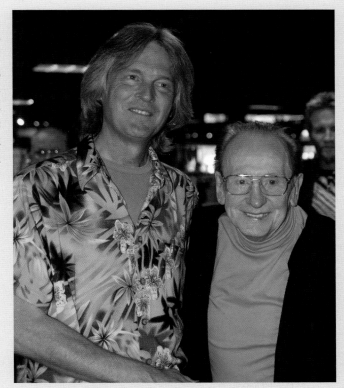

Les Paul and author Robb Lawrence, at a book signing for *The Early Years of the Les Paul Legacy*, Milwaukee, June 2008. *Photo courtesy Erol Reyal*

The Les Paul Guitar Is Reborn '68–'75

The Les Paul Guitar Is Reborn '68–'75

Years after production had ceased, the demand for these instruments continued, bringing about an unprecedented reissuing of these two models. Gibson is proud to announce its newly reborn affiliation with the man who has come to be known to millions of music lovers the world over as "Mr. Guitar"… Les Paul.

The famous Les Paul guitar returns!
Meet the new Les Paul Standard and Custom!

After a hiatus of over five years, the Gibson company proudly announced the reintroduction of the famed Les Paul series. The void created when the single-cutaway solid-body was discontinued eventually compelled a number of purists to search out the discontinued but coveted originals. This was especially apparent in England, as a number of young blues-rock artists championed the original Les Paul models for its big majestic tone. Many of their American blues heroes had played the original Goldtops.

One guitarist, Keith Richards of the Rolling Stones, had found a sunburst Standard while on tour in the U.S. He used it for TV shows and on their 1965 hit recording, "Satisfaction." According to Les Paul, a few years later both Keith and bassist Bill Wyman were attending a rare 1967 solo appearance by Les, and sat right in the front row. During the middle of the show, Les dedicated a song to "those gals" sitting in front—and the whole audience started laughing. Little did Les know that they were none other than the popular, long-haired young rockers from London. Afterward, when they all met backstage, Keith and Bill mentioned to Les that many guitarists back home still admired him and were beginning to collect the famed original 1950s Les Paul models.

This soon got Les to thinking that he should contact Gibson and see what's doing. A quick phone call to Maurice Berlin's office at CMI eventually led Les to find him already in Kalamazoo. Mr. Berlin was actually in the electric guitar area when Les asked, "What's going on over there?" He answered that things were "almost dead here," Les says. Gibson was becoming aware of their current electric guitar sales dropping—and the growing demand for the Les Paul guitars.

Gibsonite Bruce Bolen performing at a Gibson seminar. He became quite instrumental for numerous advancements in the Gibson line for many years, and ably performed at trade shows and Gibson events.

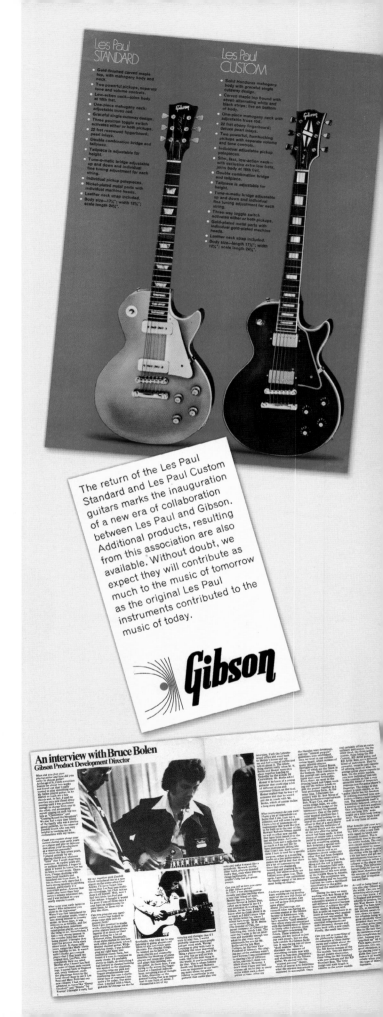

The return of the Les Paul Standard and Les Paul Custom guitars marks the inauguration of a new era of collaboration between Les Paul and Gibson. Additional products, resulting from this association are also available. Without doubt, we expect they will contribute as much to the music of tomorrow as the original Les Paul instruments contributed to the music of today.

A meeting was set up in Chicago with Berlin, Mark Carlucci (VP), and a young guitarist named Bruce J. Bolen. Bruce had just joined Gibson in 1967 as a traveling representative, after doing a few prior artist endorsements. He was quite excited to finally meet Les, and very enthused about the future possibilities. His valuable input got the new guitars right on track. Gibson was also becoming aware of their current waning electric guitar sales—and the growing demand for the Les Paul guitars. So another historic deal was made in order for Gibson to get back on track—a move that truly set the wheels in motion for the future of Gibson's flagship solid-body. Les agreed to a five-percent royalty on Gibson's sale price to CMI... and another lucrative artist/manufacture marriage was made in heaven.

"After a period of semi-retirement, [his] restless nature started again. Sitting around and doing nothing was going nowhere. So, in 1968, the action started again. Gibson already had a reputation for 'firsts.' And Les had some innovations both were eager to market. After a few conversations, both sides were ready. The Gibson/Les Paul affiliation was reborn!" (Gibson *Gazette*, Vol. 8, No. 2)

brand new release of the original Les Paul guitars . . . played by Les on his latest London Ph

The official unveiling of the next revolution! This large flier from June of 1968 brings back both "Mr. Guitar" and the Les Paul Standard and Custom for an unprecedented reissuing. Here's the Goldtop and Custom back on the scene with P-90s and twin humbucking in familiar attire. The return of these guitars kick-started a dramatic resurgence of Gibson solid-body popularity that still is going strong as ever.

GIBSON
and "Mr. Guitar" bring back the world's most sought after guitars / the instruments that launched a fretted revolution

Les Paul STANDARD
Les Paul CUSTOM

Once a few prototypes were built, Bruce took a new Custom Les Paul on the road with him to stores during late 1967 and 1968 in order to get some feedback. The guitar created a lot of interest wherever he went. Gibson was obviously on the right track already; both models were successfully launched at the trade show that summer in Chicago, with much anticipation. The Les Paul guitar had risen... like a phoenix from the ashes!

In this brief 1992 interview, Bruce recalls the first Les Paul models to remerge from Gibson:

RL: In 1967, you were in on the very first version of the reissue Les Paul.

BB: Yes, well, actually we introduced the Les Paul in late '68. They wanted 500 units [for the first shipment].

RL: At our music store in 1968, the Gibson rep said they were reissuing the Les Paul series that fall.

BB: We introduced the three guitars then. We had a couple of prototypes (with the low-impedance guitar) in 1968 at the trade show in Chicago. Then production started thereafter in October. In '67, though, we started on prototypes.

RL: Why did you decide to put a maple top on the Custom instead of all mahogany?

BB: Basically to put the two straight into production. The public wasn't going for the straight mahogany. The '68 Les Paul was almost a '58 Les Paul Custom; it wasn't about the '54…

RL: And you reverted back to the gold and single coils on the Standard. Then came the mini-humbucking Deluxe.

BB: Yes, that came the following year. We had to have new pickup covers [bezels]. We put in a hole by routing them out.

RL: Inside a P-90 cover.

BB: Yes. They are good pickups. They have the poles at the upper edge of the pickup.

RL: I remember some of the Goldtops had extra flat cream surrounds around the pickups.

BB: Those are the modified Deluxe bezels by Gibson.

Gibson's *Gazette* followed suit with a three-page article on "Mr. Guitar"… featuring our favorite guitarist's past career, his latest London Phase 4 Stereo LP *Les Paul Now* recording, a new teaching method, and the merits of the brand-spanking new 1968 Les Paul guitars.

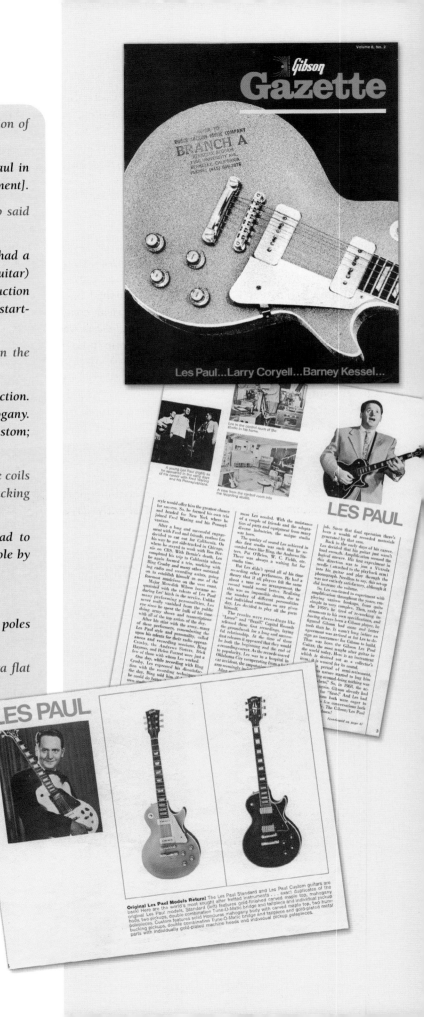

1968 Les Paul Standard

It's back! Gibson revived the original gold-finished wonder guitar! The new Les Paul Standard for 1968 was a fairly faithful (for those days) recreation of the 1956–57 Goldtop model. It featured the twin P-90 pickups, a Tune-O-Matic bridge, and a gleaming gold-finished top. Since the plan was to introduce two basic models, Gibson decided to equip one with the original P-90 pickup, and the upscale Custom model with the big humbuckings.

Gibson's new Goldtop Standard was similar in many respects to its earlier brethren, but certain details were changed. The beautiful, iridescent gold finish was resurrected after a ten-year hiatus. Its natural-finished back used a brown-beige filler paste prior to its clear coats. Some even had the darker stained brown backs. Gone was the nickel-plating and amber-colored selector tip in favor of chrome parts and a white (T12745) switch tip. The Tune-O-Matic bridge came with nylon saddles and was either stamped "GIBSON PAT. NO. 2,740,313" on the bottom (the actual patent number), or the old-style (but chrome-plated) "ABR-1." The P-90 pickups had black and white wires with a ground-wire lug anchored to one of the base screws. Coil forms were sometimes made of clear plastic. Cream-colored covers were thicker and taller as well. Its Kluson tuners still used the double-collared "Keystone" grips, and now had a slightly larger casing without the stem coming through—along with "Kluson Deluxe" printed on two rows across the back. The occasional, custom-ordered gold Klusons (NOS) still had the single-collar grips.

Other 1968 Standard differences included a slightly lighter, blueish color change of the crown pearloid inlays, the binding in the cutaway, the use of a different glue, and a new top carve, head angle, and headstock width. All the positive attributes, however, truly summed up the new guitar—great tone, looks, and playability. Plus, it earned historical significance as the first reissue of the single-cutaway Les Paul since 1961.

During the mid to late '60s, guitarists who were occasionally exposed to the defunct Les Paul models via some popular British and American artists started clamoring to find the older Gibson models. In the mid 1960s, this author witnessed the total void of Les Paul models available in local stores. I heard the rumors from older guitarists of how great the old Les Pauls sounded compared to the current SGs and 335s. Out of curiosity, we started searching them out in hopes of experiencing the original mystique ourselves. Those were exciting days when we located a nice Gibson Les Paul (for a few hundred dollars). We would bring it home, admire it in the original case, and plug it right in! We soon discovered why everyone was so enamored—its amazingly rich tones and blazing sounds that we heard when playing it with our rock band were incomparable. We were in seventh heaven! Many other guitarists were doing the same collecting around both America and England. Then Kalamazoo woke up to the fact that there was a void in the market—and now it was their turn to get the heralded Les Paul guitar back in gear.

In 1968, our Gibson rep from LD Heater mentioned the new guitars were coming out soon. Within a few short months, they arrived in boxes at La Jolla Music store where I taught guitar. What an exciting and historic moment for all of us that auspicious day, when we pulled out and played those special guitars for the first time!

Construction

During the first year, the one-piece neck, maple/ mahogany body construction, carved top, and small headstocks were retained as on the original '50s models. The neck-angle pitch was tilted farther back one degree to five, raising the overall height of the Tune-O-Matic bridge and pickups. By 1969, the carving template had been newly revised, resulting in less of a scooped-dish (concave) effect to the arching around the top. During that year, the headstock angle was also changed, from seventeen degrees to three degrees forward (in an effort for less breakage). A larger headstock was basically instated on the Goldtop during early 1969 (some are thought to be made in 1968). It measured 3¼" by 3⅜" wide (like the Custom), and gave the instrument slightly more mass and tone. Visually, the aesthetic of its larger profile was a subjective matter, according to what the beholder was accustomed to. The Custom's fancy binding created an illusion of similarity to the smaller head, respectively.

Other minor details differentiated the new Standard, such as the larger heel and almost squared neck-shaping by the body. Generally, larger headstock versions came with a more slender-profile neck. The binding was widened in the cutaway area to conceal the once-exposed maple top. This wide binding continued for many years on the Standard and Deluxe models.

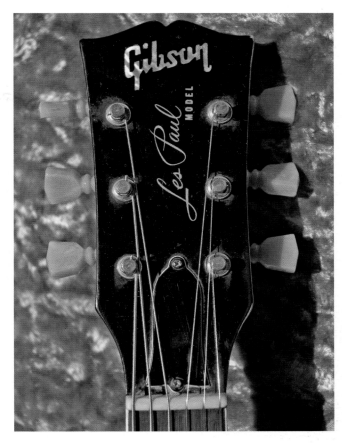

Early versions of the first reissue Standards used the classic crown headstock inlay with the Les Paul script name engraved into the truss cover. This second version still retains the original small head-stock of the '50s guitars, and reinstates the famed Les Paul Model silkscreen logo, but slightly thicker than before.

(Opposite and Above) A rare and beautiful example of a 1968 Les Paul Standard "Goldtop" #531901 with a walnut brown (filler stained) back. This guitar still shimmers! *Courtesy Albert Molinero, 2004*

The following is an excerpt from my interview with James Hutchins in 2003:

RL: *So what was your job at Gibson?*

JH: *I was a pattern maker. They never knew what to call us—a pattern maker, a luthier, or a tool-and-die maker—because we would take a whole guitar and make all the prototype parts for it, make all the fixtures needed. Back then, we didn't have CNCs and the like. They would come up with a new version of the Les Paul. They already had the shape formed, the outside shapes and what-not, but we had to make any necessary routing fixtures. We had to neck-fit them, make a pitch gauge for them, to tell what angle the pitch is for the neck. After we showed the prototype, we'd produce five out on the floor, and then the initial run would be 25. We had to go through all these steps with our new tooling to make sure there were no errors in them. If the production run went through without any problem, then the guitar went into production. We were done with it, but we had to get with the draftsman to make sure we had all our changes made. Pitches, angles, all that stuff was done by pencil back then. We didn't have a computerized system.*

RL: *Your work on the new Les Paul series began in '67?*

JH: *Yeah, right around '67. There wasn't a lot that had to be changed from this to the other one. The basic shapes were exactly the same. Somewhere around here we got the template to do it on a shaper. It's got a hardened steel bottom on it for the Les Paul body shape, so the shape could never change. It could vary a little bit in size according to who set it up, but that was because of all the hand work you had to do. It wasn't exactly a CNC or something like that, you know.*

RL: *So you started off with the P-90s in '68 and then went to the Deluxe pickups. You had to change the routing for the big humbucking, too.*

JH: *Right. Change the routing for the pickups. Had to make a new pickguard. That was all hand made. Then we made a new routing template. We have some templates back here. I still use the old routing templates for my carved top just like we used back in those days. And that was done on the old carving form back there.*

RL: *This carved top was different than the fifties guitar. They went through a few variations during the late sixties into the early seventies.*

JH: *Yes. It was changed here. So we would come up with a new carving form pattern.*

RL: *And the neck pitch was different on these. Tilted farther back than the '59s.*

JH: *Yes, because of the style of pickups you had. These pickups are much higher off the body on the Deluxe pickups than your P-90s. You had to have more clearance.*

Very rare 1968 black Standard with black pickup covers and chrome stop tailpiece. *Courtesy Jay Rosen, Pomona, 2008*

The Heavy Les Paul

During 1968, the new Gibson Les Paul guitars were most often of various weights, just as before, coming in somewhere between 8.5 to just over 9 pounds, with exceptions. 1969 saw the influx of denser building materials. Many of these new Les Paul guitars were intrinsically heavy in comparison to older versions. It seemed that the new guitars, over the next a few years, gained some serious weight. This was due to the supply and demand of available woods, since much of the earlier stocks of seasoned tonewoods were depleted during the first guitar boom of the mid '60s. Aged, lightweight Honduras mahogany was scarce then at Gibson, as well as being hard to find in the local lumber yards. The company settled for a denser mahogany that was available at that time (possibly an economically influenced corporate decision). During this era, Les Paul models often weighed somewhere between 9–11 pounds plus, compared to the 7¾ – 9½-pound weights of the dried-out wood of the vintage instruments. (As we know, lighter weight and density equates to good resonance and open vibration.)

This extra density, however, produced a strong, sustained tonality—great for the advent of heavy metal guitarists. At the time, it was somewhat in vogue. Many current players actually sought out a heavier guitar for its strong tone, regardless of their own sore shoulders. Some were lightweight, however, and consequently had a more open, bright tone.

A few early Standards were special-ordered with a full-sized humbucking pickup in a gold and sunburst finish—these models could be considered the other real reissues. They almost made it into the catalog and regular production. Overall, the return of this 1968 Gold Les Paul Standard was very well received, and began a new generation of the Gibson solid-body—a trend that continued into 1969 with relatively few changes, besides laminated necks and a "Made in USA" stamp. Production in 1968 saw 1,224 special orders filled, and in 1969, more than double at 2,751 (which included the upcoming Deluxe models).

This authentic catalog still of a humbucking-equipped Goldtop Standard is from Rem Wall, a Gibson employee's personal collection. It was intended to be included in an early seventies catalog to officially re-introduce the Standard as a humbucking guitar, but never quite made it in. It is the same pose as the 1970 Deluxe. Note the original Grover machines, 1968 arching yet laminated body construction. *Courtesy John Bernunzio and the author*

The 1968 Les Paul Custom

The new Les Paul Custom was truly a class act; the "Black Beauty" had triumphantly returned in all its glory—and with some important improvements. The elegant 1968 Les Paul Custom featured the beautiful ebony black finish that earned it the popular nickname "Black Beauty," but now, with the maple top construction and twin gold humbuckings—an actual improvement in many respects. Plus, since the jazz guitar impetus was not such a criterion, the sustaining maple cap finally graced this top-of-the-line solid-body. Gone was the late-'50s models' middle pickup, since so many complained that there was nowhere to pick between them. (They were available special-order, however, in limited numbers.)

Custom models still retained their pearl-inlaid ebony fingerboard (and those little frets that many replaced), fancy headstock inlays, multi-layered trim binding, and pickguard. Producing the guitar in white, like the prior sculptured SG versions, was considered and soon abandoned for contamination reasons. A few early Customs were painted white, and were quite striking with their gold hardware. A bright cherry sunburst and wine-red was available in later years. (Maple fingerboards, à la early Fenders, were even available in the late '70s.)

The quality craftsmanship of these early Custom models was quite respectable. I wouldn't be surprised at all if the first run of Customs were made using similar 1950s techniques, with the old-pattern jigs and fixtures prior to the high demand that implemented more efficient tooling and procedures. Gibson was back in the saddle and excited. Obviously, their workers truly took pride in building these new "Black Beauties"… and it shows.

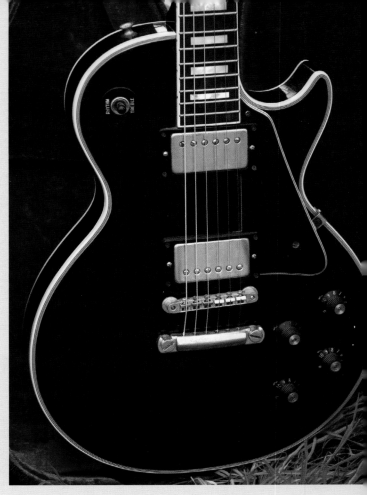

The incomparable Les Paul Custom "Black Beauty" in its majestic wonder! This exceptional guitar is a culmination of the best attributes rolled into Gibson's "Top of the Line" model—now with a maple top for enhanced sustain and highs, twin patent number humbucking pickups, and a fast-action sleek ebony neck. These guitars were indeed a superlative instrument for the discerning guitarist with a flair for excellence. *This prime 1969 version #35090 courtesy Steve Baird, Seattle, 2008*

An early 1969 Les Paul Custom #549257 in faded sunburst with cherry back. *Courtesy Bart Whitrock, 2005*

Technical Specs

Humbucking pickups still featured patent numbers (Gibson's deliberate misdirection tactic) with a large "T" imprinted on top of the black coils, M56 magnets, and featured either slotted or Phillips round-head, brass-coil screws. Early versions (begun in 1967) had the "T" on one coil only. The square porthole through which to see the copper wire was also deleted. Automated windings gave this era of humbuckings a general output of 7.5K. These "T-top" pickups still used the old black M-69 bezels, but were eventually changed to M8 70-style surrounds without corner supports. Control knobs were of the Fender amp-style, "witch hat" design that sort of cheapened the instrument compared to the nice '60s-style, see-through black-foil insert versions. (Many put those and speed knobs on their guitars anyway.) The gold patent-number "ABR-1"-labeled (ABR-2, technically) Tune-O-Matic bridges used the nylon inserts and a wire retainer. Gold-plated Kluson tuners were of the Sealfast variety as on the original '50s Customs, but with metal keystone buttons. The binding in the cutaway retained the normal equal width.

The 1968 and 1969 Les Paul Customs and Standards started off with fairly accurate, early-style appointments—one-piece mahogany neck (with the correct small headstock on the Standard), one-piece mahogany bodies with maple caps (many with center seam tops), and a normal-length tenon into the pickup cavity. Soon that same year, however, the dotted "i" on the Gibson logo would disappear. It's no wonder many of these first reissue Customs were much like the originals, having been constructed only seven years prior in the same plant by many of the same people.

The transition models of mid/late 1969 saw the intro of the first three-piece necks, with the Standard finally adopting the wider headstock by February. This would allow for the cutting out of the necks from the same standardized templates. The tri-laminate neck design strengthened the overall neck, due to opposing grain tensions, and gave more stabilization. During 1969, a medium-length (transition) neck tenon was instigated, while the one-piece body was still being built. Naturally some feel that the shortened tenon takes away from the contact resonation and overall tone. Gibson obviously felt that it didn't make that much of a difference, considering the length of mahogany contact already provided with the single-cutaway guitar. They sometimes added a curious mahogany insert near the short tenon that filled in the empty hole.

"The return of the Les Paul Standard and Les Paul Custom guitars marks the inauguration of a new era of collaboration between Les Paul and Gibson. Additional products, resulting from this association, are also available. Without a doubt, we expect they will contribute as much to the music of tomorrow as the original Les Paul instruments contributed to the music of today." (Gibson *Gazette*, 1968) Certainly, Les Paul's enthusiasm fueled Gibson, while Gibson's abilities fueled Les Paul's future ambitions.

The two instruments actually took off like wildfire that year. After the summer trade show, the original batch of 500 (400 Standards and 100 Customs) took three months to complete. Soon Gibson was making hundreds of them every week. The orders were pouring in from around the world, and Gibson was now in overdrive.

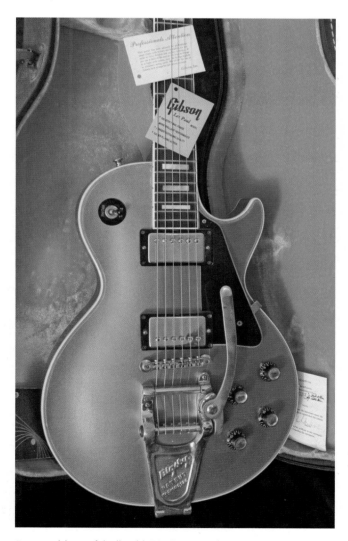

Rare and beautiful all-gold 1969 Les Paul Custom #585307 with Bigsby tailpiece. *Courtesy Sean Cummings, 2005*

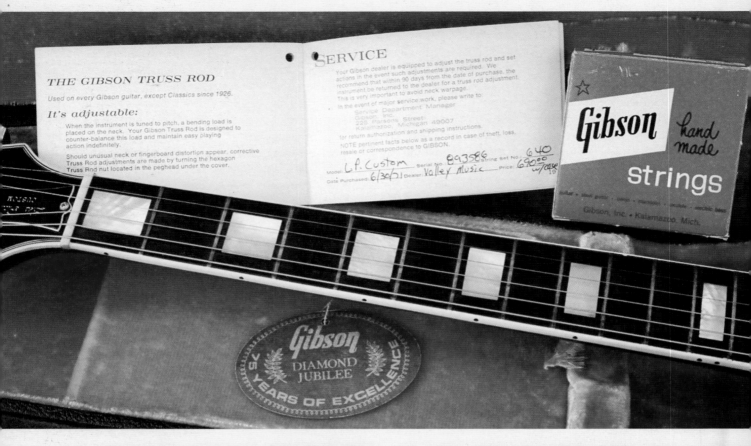

THE GIBSON TRUSS ROD

Used on every Gibson guitar, except Classics since 1926.

It's adjustable:

When the instrument is tuned to pitch, a bending load is placed on the neck. Your Gibson Truss Rod is designed to counter-balance this load and maintain easy playing action indefinitely.

Should unusual neck or fingerboard distortion appear, corrective Truss Rod adjustments are made by turning the hexagon Truss Rod nut located in the peghead under the cover.

SERVICE

Your Gibson dealer is equipped to adjust the truss rod and set actions in the event such adjustments are required. We recommend that within 90 days from the date of purchase, the instrument be returned to the dealer for a truss rod adjustment. This is very important to avoid neck warpage.

In the event of major service work, please write to:

Service Department Manager
Gibson, Inc.
225 Parsons Street
Kalamazoo, Michigan 49007

for return authorization and shipping instructions.

NOTE pertinent facts below as a record in case of theft, loss, resale or correspondence to GIBSON.

Model: *L.P. Custom*   Serial No. *893586*   String Set No. *640*
Date Purchased *6/30/71*   Dealer *Valley Music*   Price *690.00 w/case*

Gibson hand made **strings**

guitar • steel guitar • banjo • mandolin • ukulele • electric bass

Gibson, Inc. • Kalamazoo, Mich.

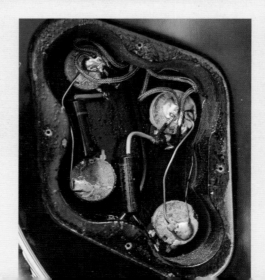

A very nice 1971 Les Paul Custom #893586 sitting in golden plush, built during Gibson's Diamond 75th Anniversary. This guitar has its tag and original booklet dating when it was purchased in June of 1971 from Cactus at Valley Music, El Cajon, CA—plus some original strings. Note the lack of a dot on the "i," the Kluson Sealfasts, and the Sprague "Black Beauty" capacitors. *Guitar courtesy Todd Stemmerman, 2003*

A 1971 sunburst Les Paul Custom, caught before our Ridgemont Allstars rehearsal, with sandwich body and sunburst back. *Courtesy Gene Rochambeau, 2004*

(Right) Customs were still "Fretless Wonders," and were available in ebony, sunburst, and white (cream) in this 1975 ad.

Keith Richards graced the cover of the 1975 Gibson catalog. He and Ron Wood had been visiting Gibson quite a bit during these years.

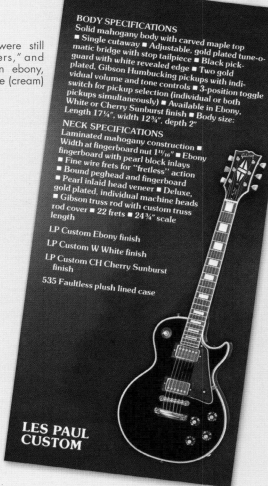

BODY SPECIFICATIONS
Solid mahogany body with carved maple top ■ Single cutaway ■ Adjustable, gold plated tune-o-matic bridge with stop tailpiece ■ Black pickguard with white revealed edge ■ Two gold plated, Gibson Humbucking pickups with individual volume and tone controls ■ 3-position toggle switch for pickup selection (individual or both pickups simultaneously) ■ Available in Ebony, White or Cherry Sunburst finish ■ Body size: Length 17¼", width 12¾", depth 2"

NECK SPECIFICATIONS
Laminated mahogany construction ■ Width at fingerboard nut 1¹¹⁄₁₆" ■ Ebony fingerboard with pearl block inlays ■ Fine wire frets for "fretless" action ■ Bound peghead and fingerboard ■ Pearl inlaid head veneer ■ Deluxe, gold plated, individual machine heads ■ Gibson truss rod with custom truss rod cover ■ 22 frets ■ 24¾" scale length

LP Custom Ebony finish

LP Custom W White finish

LP Custom CH Cherry Sunburst finish

535 Faultless plush lined case

LES PAUL CUSTOM

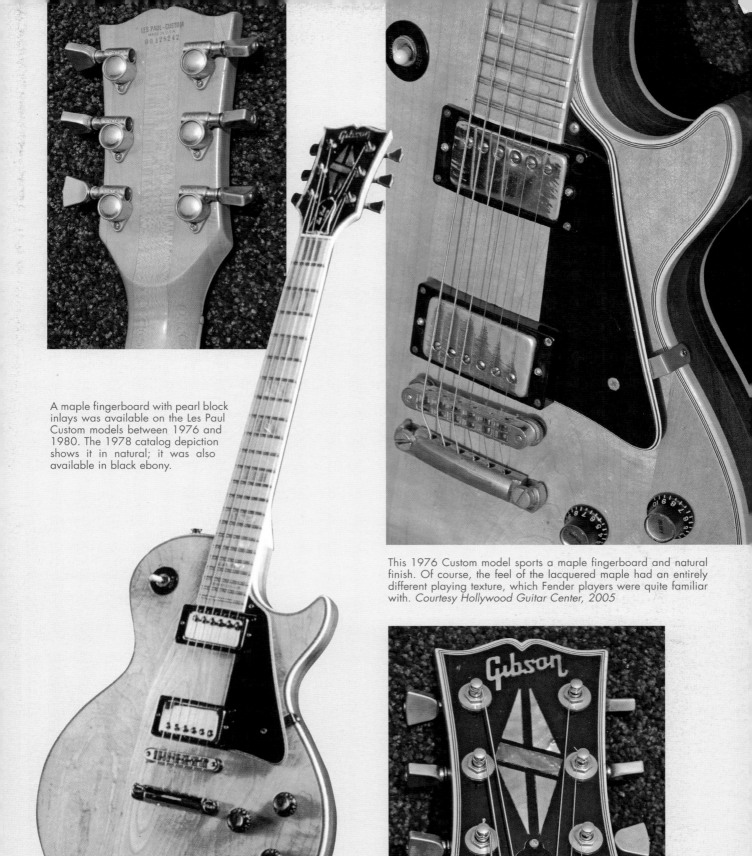

A maple fingerboard with pearl block inlays was available on the Les Paul Custom models between 1976 and 1980. The 1978 catalog depiction shows it in natural; it was also available in black ebony.

This 1976 Custom model sports a maple fingerboard and natural finish. Of course, the feel of the lacquered maple had an entirely different playing texture, which Fender players were quite familiar with. *Courtesy Hollywood Guitar Center, 2005*

The Deluxe Les Paul

In 1969, the new Goldtop Standard was transformed into the new "Deluxe" model, with slight changes soon to follow. A new style of pickup for the series was introduced, along with a whole different method of body construction and a neck volute. "This Les Paul Model is 'deluxe' in every way!" said the September 1970 catalog. The new Deluxe model did quite well during the entire 1970s through 1984.

The Mini-Humbucking Pickup

Players were asking for the old humbucking pickups to be incorporated once again on the Standard models. Gibson put Jim Deurloo, from their pattern shop, in charge of the switchover to a humbucking pickup—with the requirements that its production costs be low, and that it would fit into the existing routing fixtures. Jim figured that the simplest way to go was to use their "mini-humbucking" pickup, and slide them right in.

Seth Lover had previously designed a remarkably efficient, small humbucking pickup for the newly acquired Epiphone line during the early 1960s. The original New York-style pickups were small, and Seth felt that the new Gibson pickup was quite large. He therefore designed a trimmer pickup with enough clearance between the coils to maintain proper magnetic flux with the strings. Only 4,250 winds of 42-gauge copper wire would fit on the small nylon-coil bobbins, thus producing a brighter tonality. The 1/16" cylindrical polepieces were slotted on top as well as partially into the lower threaded portion. The other coil used a soft iron bar instead of slug polepieces. Measurements were 2⅝" by 1³⁄₃₂" by ⁹⁄₁₆". The old, erroneous "Patent No. 2,737,842" decal from earlier humbuckings was attached to the back. The base legs were only ½" deep with ⅜" flanges. They had a strong output, but with a lot more highs than the full-sized pickups.

These chromed units with small adjustable polepieces were fairly popular during the 1960s on many Epiphone guitars, including the Riviera and Wilshire models. Gibson conveniently still had an extra inventory of leftover Epiphone pickups by 1969. The sound of the Epiphones was cleaner and more articulate. On the Les Paul, their less over-modulated tone was especially apparent in the neck position compared to full-sized humbuckings. Gibson's innovative Firebird models previously adopted a similar pickup without polepieces.

LES PAUL DELUXE—High Impedance
This Les Paul model is "deluxe" in every way. Fine performance and outstanding styling. The attractive gold finished carved maple top is magnificently highlighted by two powerful chrome-plated humbucking pickups.

FEATURES: Gold finished carved maple top with laminated mahogany back and neck. Two powerful chrome-plated humbucking pickups. Fast, low-action neck joins body at 16th fret. Three-piece laminated mahogany neck with adjustable truss rod. Graceful single cutaway design. Three-position toggle switch activates either or both pickups. 22 fret rosewood fingerboard with pearl inlays. Double combination bridge and tailpiece. Tune-O-Matic bridge, adjustable up and down and individual fine tuning adjustment for each string. Individual pickup pole pieces. Nickel-plated metal parts with individual machine heads. 17¼" long, 12¾" wide, 2" deep; scale length 24¾".

Gibson simply took the cream P-90 casings and conveniently fit the small chrome pickups inside with two height adjustment screws. Early versions were slightly roughed out, but that was soon rectified. Attachment to the body was done with a tapped aluminum piece already secured with wood screws into the center of the cavity. Some were tapped for the narrower P-90 attachment, too. Occasionally, Deluxes were shipped with P-90s. Thin pickup surrounds were added around the mini-buckers to conceal any manufacturing flaws that might occur on the edges. The workers nicknamed them "goof hiders," which pretty well sums up the situation. These short-lived, cream-colored rings were held on with small Estacion brass nails. (Pickup chrome covers had the "Gibson" logo imprinted during the mid '70s.)

Electronics

CTS potentiometers (often 300K) and Sprague "Black Beauty" capacitors were installed during the first few years. Dating guitars by the pots' manufacture codes can be generally accurate, but can also be somewhat tricky at times. Often, an earlier CTS (137) code of 1376852 (52nd week of 1968) would be on a 1969 guitar months later, while at other times, it's way off in either direction (since the serial numbers jumped around). For example, if the container of pots was regularly topped before the original supply was depleted, those that ended up on the bottom were usually from an earlier manufacture. Gibson's attractive gold "bell" knobs with chrome inserts (as on the earlier '60s models) were standard on Deluxes during these years.

(Above) Good example of a 1970 Deluxe Goldtop with nylon-insert bridge and original case. A slight greening effect is apparent around the worn area. *Courtesy Cal Vintage, 2004*

(Opposite Top) This is the new Les Paul Deluxe model shown in the small 1970 catalog. Its departure from the previous Standard is the addition of quiet "mini" humbucking pickups and the "laminated mahogany back and neck" that was common in the furniture-making practice, but somewhat controversial with guitarists over the years.

(Opposite Bottom) 1974 Les Paul Deluxe in cherry sunburst, resting against a maple "Woodie" Junior amp. *Guitar courtesy Preston Smith, 2004*

(Bottom Right) Rare lefty Les Paul Deluxe #70089059. *Courtesy DeForest Thornburgh, Blue Guitar Workshop, 2008*

Construction

Although the first mini-humbucking Goldtops were one-piece neck/body models (some without the Deluxe truss cover), major changes were made during the next few years to strengthen the guitars' weak points and make some improvements as they saw fit. Both the neck and body were given multiple laminations as in fine furniture construction.

Other changes took place, such as neck tenons being shortened and round wiring channels instituted. Control cavities changed, from the "straight" rout being done before the maple top was glued on, to being routed afterwards (beginning in early 1969), as on 1950s guitars. A small lip is present around the base of the rout on later models. Also in 1969, the "Gibson" logo changed, with the dot on the "i" being omitted, and the "b" and "o" opened. More changes took place with overlapping features that year than any other, giving rise to the title "mutant Goldtop" ascribed to those guitars with odd combinations. It seems that Gibson consistently switched from one spec to the next during this high-demand production period. One fellow on the Les Paul forum said, "It's like they did something different every single day in '68–'69!"

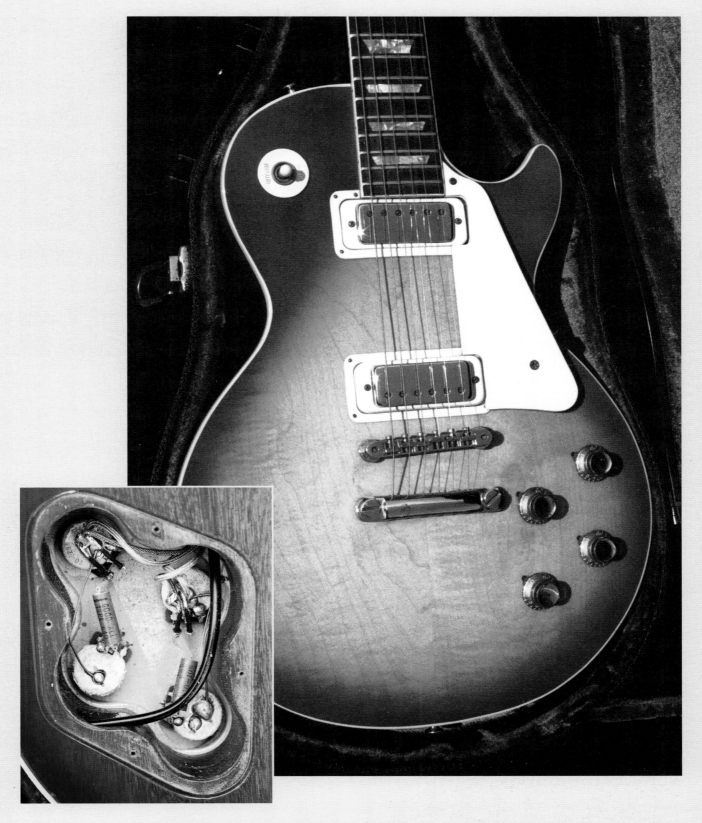

A cherry sunburst finish finally became a regular option for the new Deluxe Les Paul. The whole guitar is sunburst and uses a novel yellow filler stain on the mahogany back. This example #398655 sports the "goof hider" surrounds to hide the temporarily loose-fitting pickups. Note the now dotted "i" and closed "b" and "o" on the logo. Late model Kluson 320 tuners have the double-lined "Gibson Deluxe" brands and dual-collared Keystone grips. Its new "Made in USA" stamp is hard to miss. The side view shows the laminated body with its thin cross-grained strip. This steeper 5-degree neck angle was almost tall enough to work with Les's trapeze-bar tailpiece. Note the curved routing bit in the control cavity and extra later prepping for the back pickups potentiometer. Those "Good-All" 640 capacitors match the glorious purple plush nicely. *Courtesy Boe Stevens, 2004*

Necks

Three-piece maple necks were nothing new to Gibson. It was deemed necessary for balancing the natural tendencies of the wood. Mid- to late-1969 transition models saw the intro of the first three-piece necks (some with P-90s). The tri-laminate neck design strengthened the overall neck and gave more stabilization. Although not as critical for those made of maple, warping necks were always a concern for sales. Now Gibson was ensuring a more stable neck with mahogany. This would also allow for the cutting out of necks from the same standardized templates.

A medium-length (transition) neck tenon was also instigated during 1969, which eventually changed to a short tenon. Gibson would also add the mahogany insert near the short tenon (sometimes after finishing), filling in the existing gap for added body mass, and, of course, necessary for the mini-humbucking pickup attachment. They soon changed to a shorter neck slot rout. Although the change took place earlier, some full-length, long-tenon guitars were shipped as late December 1969. Some collectors today feel that the shortened tenon takes away from the contact resonation and overall tone.

In December 1969, a volute was added to give more support to the inherently weak area of the neck where it angles back. The raised portion on the back of the neck naturally stopped the hand in the first position. Violins had traditionally used a volute—they were also used to hang the instrument in days of old. The volute was considerably smaller during earlier years and became more pronounced for the later-'70s versions. Gibson volutes became quite reminiscent of the ones on early Epiphone Masterbilt De Luxe models of the 1930s.

During 1971, a large "Made In USA" stamp was placed on the back of the headstock under the serial numbers. Some were stamped "Not For Resale," signifying show and rep specials. Maple necks became standard during 1974 for most of Gibson's lineup. This hardwood saved many a cracked headstock, but gave a distinctively brighter tonality and sustain factor to the guitars—and some extra weight.

Body Laminations

A big change in body construction came in 1969, with the newly layered "sandwich" effect. Gibson thought this process of "cross-banding" the body would help counteract the wood's natural movements—somewhat like a technique that furniture-makers utilize. Many would call them "pancake" bodies.

During the development process of the first style of multiple lamination, a .06-inch strip of maple was glued directly to the bottom of the carved maple. The laminate grain was at a 90-degree angle to the grain of the top. You can clearly see the fine maple strip in the cutaways, and routed pickup cavities of those early guitars. Gibson's reasoning would have been that this process guarded against top-seam separation.

This was soon abandoned for the more common "cross-banded" mahogany versions that were the standard practice for a few years. The .060-inch (nearly 1⁄16") thin strip of maple was then glued between two pieces of mahogany. It is visually quite apparent along the sides of the Deluxe and the barely discernable lines of black Custom Les Paul models. Gibson's internal memos noted that this was to strengthen the body and prevent future cracking.

Possibly, there were difficulties obtaining large amounts of 8/4" mahogany stock, too. The inexpensive Norlin orders for thinner lumber gave the switch to the central strip a go-ahead. Evidently, protecting the maple top was a moot point when putting the lamination in the middle of the mahogany.

This laminating procedure was deemed more expensive to do and was finally discontinued, generally by 1975. Years later, you can see signs in the lacquer checking of slight stress and hygroscopic wood movement along the seams of weathered instruments. The mahogany

(Above) A beautiful red 1972 Deluxe. *Courtesy Apple Music, Portland, 2008*

(Below) When these flashy "sparkle" Les Pauls hit the scene, there was quite a buzz in our circle of guitar players. My favorite was this blue version, since I always liked it on speedboats. This example actually looks almost turquoise up close. These custom color Deluxe models came in yellow, red, and this cool blue sparkle for just a few years into 1975. Its finish was actually created with medium-sized reflective glitter fragments suspended in the tinted lacquer coats. Note the weather checking and mixed wood colorations on the back. *Courtesy Hollywood Guitar Center, 2003*

(known for its stability) kept the bookmatched maple tops intact quite adequately. Most Deluxe models were made with plain maple on their two- or three-piece tops. The return of the flamed, book-matched Les Paul was still a few years off.

Over the years, much has been said about the lack of tonal vibrancy of these extra-laminated "sandwiched" guitars—along with an increased neck pitch (producing too much string angle over the bridge), short tenons, decreased headstock pitch, and volutes (that could limit or dissipate the overall tone). Granted, multiple-piece mahogany bodies would not vibrate as freely, creating some varying tonal differences—but many sound quite vibrant regardless. More than any other post-1970 guitars, the original '68/'69 guitars retained the general "fifties build quality" of woods, yet these pitch variations actually create distinct tonal changes (or deficiencies, in some peoples' minds). Without major modifications to compensate for these weak points of angle and mass, some players simply revert to the wrap-over stopbar stringing, plus an addition of a quality-cut nut, more substantial tuners (Grovers) with deeper string winding that produce more angle over the nut—all to improve their favorite Les Paul guitar. Like vintage cars however, radical modifications can affect later values for the "original minded" buyer.

Finishes

Gold was still the main color, but the demand for sunburst was growing by numerous special orders. By 1970, the new Deluxe models were finally available in the cherry sunburst finish. Attractive sunburst shading was also introduced on the back of the body and necks. A yellow paste filler, left over in the grain, nicely accented the sunburst backs on these models. These were soon complemented with a new wine-colored, deep maroon red (not to be confused with the traditional cherry). A tobacco sunburst was done in later years with a brown to dark-brown outer coat. A run of beautiful, sparkle-finished Deluxes was released in 1973 and 1974. Their red, yellow, and blue fine-glitter sparkle finishes were a popular custom color item at the time. The mid-seventies era also produced original, natural maple-finished models. Both the Deluxe and Customs were the only guitars in the lineup available as left-handed models at no additional charge.

This fine-condition 1978 Deluxe #72098581 features the deep maroon-colored Burgundy finish. *Courtesy Hollywood Guitar Center, 2005*

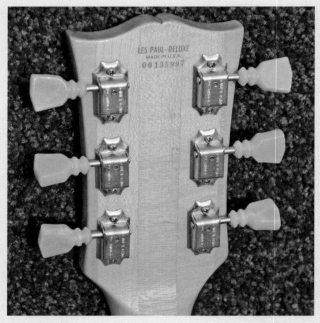

Mid-seventies maple neck construction with late-model Klusons and gold decal with eight-digit number and model designation. Prefix "00" refers to 1976.

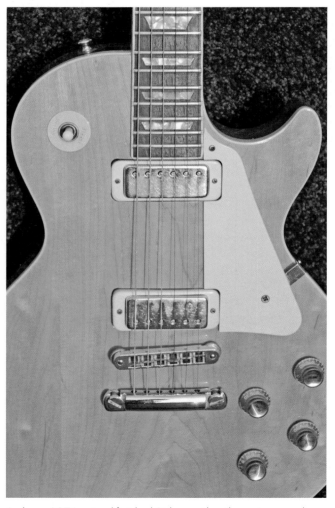

A clean, 1976 natural-finished Deluxe with a three-piece maple top and neck. *Courtesy Hollywood Guitar Center, 2005*

1978 imprinted Deluxe serial number and unusual Gibson metal tulip Klusons.

Standards

Meanwhile, the hidden Standard (1970 to 1975) was actually still alive as a Deluxe with factory-routed, full-sized humbuckings, but by special-order only. Humbucking-equipped Les Pauls were shipped in small quantities, yet remained a specialty item. They came in cherry sunburst, cherry, and gold as before, but with plain three-piece or mismatched two-piece tops, for the most part. Sometimes, a sticker is found (i.e., CSB) in the neck cavity determining the factory color. Some of their cherry-red finishes were actually quite light during these years compared to the '60s red colors. Sam Ash stores ordered 100 humbucking-equipped Deluxes in 1974 for their three East Coast stores. Fifty were in cherry sunburst, while the other 50 were brown sunbursted. The Standard wasn't officially marketed and revived until 1976 (in literature, anyway, although one was shipped in 1975). Even the full-humbucking Deluxe serial numbers had the "Deluxe" name on the headstock.

Original 1975 Les Paul Standard in chocolate-brown-shaded sunburst #509001, with slightly off-centered book-matched maple top. Gibson Kluson Deluxe tuners instituted a wider bezel by this time. *Courtesy Shane Gudlow, Time Warp Music, 2005*

Serial Numbers

Deluxe production reached unprecedented highs of 3,587 in 1969, 4,466 in 1971, 5,194 in 1972, and up to 10,484 in 1973. In 1974, 7,367 were built, in 1975, 2,561; then things dwindled down until 1978 with 4,450.

Les Paul serial numbers during 1968 began in the low 519,000 range and quickly jumped up to the 820,000 to 970,000 ranges, skipping many numbers into 1969 (earlier years had the higher numbers). Guitars shipped in 1969 with mid- to late-'68 pots can be in the 558,000 to 567,000 range. This lack of consistency created confusion for owners trying to ascertain the production dates of these few years. Serial numbers from this period are quite misleading, which makes the potentiometer codes a better source of determining the actual manufacturing date.

The numbers on most models were deeply imprinted into the wood before the filler and finish were done. Later models between 1975–77 were done with a gold transfer decal under the finish that included the model name, "Made in USA," and an eight-digit number. Numbers starting with "99" corresponded to 1975, while "00" was '76, and "06" was '77. Imprinted serial numbers were reinstated during 1977 with eight digits and the "Made in USA" stamp. The first and fifth digits would signify the last two digits of the year. This particular system has been successfully in use for many Gibson models since.

Later Deluxes, after 1975, were manufactured in Gibson's new facility in Tennessee. These models received a more substantial-sized Tune-O-Matic bridge—dubbed the "Nashville"—and soon had much sturdier posts imbedded into metal bushings. Maple necks and metal-mounted electronics were standard for the early Nashvilles. The original Deluxe Les Paul was continued into 1984, and enjoyed over a decade-and-a-half of popularity among many musicians worldwide.

Cases

In the late 1960s, Gibson gave guitarists their choice of the normal formed case or a new rectangular-shaped version with either rounded or squared corners. The new white "Gibson" logo was generally emblazoned on them as well. They were available in either the black formed (535 Faultless-shaped) for $73, with either yellow/orange (1968–69) or purple (beginning in 1970) velours, or the three-latch, black rectangular (1237 oblong-shaped) for $50, with yellow or purple (1969) plush and a little leather neck strap emblazoned with "Gibson." Of course, there were other shaped variations afterwards,

with a different type of plush, in red or violet (which can matt up with furballs). Many Standards were shipped in rectangular cases, and Customs in the shaped variants.

Strings

Gibson produced a multitude of very high-quality strings for their extended family of instruments for many years. The Les Paul guitar was often shipped with a Mona-Steel/GE-229/medium-gauge set (a GE-240 set with plain B and G that measured .0138, .0177, .0205, .033, .047 and .056 for the first to sixth strings). The February 1969 Gibson string catalog states, "If you play the electric guitar, you will find that the brightest sound comes from ferrous alloys, such as the one used in our medium-gauge Guitar Set, #GE-240." They also sold a Rock and Roll/GE-290/extra light-gauge set for the modern, flexible playing style (first to sixth sizes: .0106, .0145, .019 (wound?), .026, .035, .044) for $3.25. Their Rhythm & Blues Bender XL/GE-740XL/extra light-gauge set featured a plain G (with first to sixth sizes: .009, .0115, .0138, .022, .030, .0375), also for $3.25—quite bendy for a short-scale guitar. A more normal R&B Bender/light-gauge set was also standard on Les Pauls (.0106, .0122, .0157, .024, .032, .040), which was still fairly light by today's standards.

They also made flat-wound, polished stainless magnetic ribbon-wrapped, Hi-Fi G-040 strings for jazz playing, along with flat-polished strings that combined the tonal qualities of regular wound strings with flat strings. Their popular Sonomatic strings, for both electric and acoustic guitars, were available in a light gauge by this time, as a GE-340L (ranging .0106, .0122, .018 (wound), .0225, .0445, .056). Mona Steel acoustics were still available, along with Bronze Wound strings. Some older guitarists today don't play brass strings, and have to search for the nickel-steel variety. The in-between Gibson gauges were progressive for their time, and many players really didn't notice the fine differences.

During the early seventies, Gibson Artist Strings were introduced after consulting "many of today's most renowned performers," along with intensive research on materials. This resulted in the Rock and Roll Electric Guitar series—ranging from the medium gauge G5500 set (.012, .015, .024WD, .030, .040 and .050), to the popular light G5501 (.010, .012, .016PL, .026, .034 and .044), on down to the Extra Light G5502 (.008, .011, .014, .022, .030, .038) set. Flatwound Stainless sets included the medium G5100 (.012 to .057) and the hip G5101 Light gauge (.010 to .051) set.

1954 Les Paul Custom Reissue & 1954/1958 Les Paul Reissue

Getting back on track…

During the early '70s, Gibson decided to recreate two more early-'50s Les Paul guitars—namely, the first version of the Custom and the second Goldtop model. These models are nearly faithful recreations that lasted a few years, and were an honorable effort on Gibson's part to truly get back to basics.

This "1958/1954" 1972 Gold-top #678341 was Gibson's next effort for a reissue.

Goldtop Reissue '54/'58

A gallant effort to faithfully recreate the second version of the original Goldtop was begun in 1971. Gibson evidently named it a "1958 reissue," while, in fact, it was their knockoff of a 1953–1956 model. Bodies were identified as "'58" in production as well. It was back to the basics—no volute, twin P-90 pickups (early ones shipped with "goof hiders," and later with Norlin's "Gibson" logo emblazoned), just the McCarty stop/stud combination bridge tailpiece (in chrome), gold speed knobs and old-style, thin binding in the cutaway showing maple cross-banding between the maple and mahogany. The arching, however, still featured a more rounded, less dished '70s style. Large frets made it an easier guitar to play, too. An urban guitar myth began again, this time with the speculation that Gibson used up some old '50s bodies. One look at the size of the routing channel through the body revealed the telltale large width that was used on the new body. These early '71–'72 reissues are now quite collectable, and have those great, inherent, vibrant Les Paul tones.

Les Paul "Black Beauty" 1954 Reissue

Here's the most accurate recreation Gibson did in the 1970s. Alnico V rhythm and P-90 bridge pickups, small "Fretless Wonder" frets, all-mahogany body construction, and black speed knobs completed the new "Limited Edition" Les Paul Custom. Unlike the current early-'70s production Les Paul, this specially made model was true to form, with a one-piece mahogany neck, without a volute, and solid one-piece body. Both Kluson Sealfast Tulip or Pat. Pend gold Grovers machine heads were used. A "Made in USA" stamp, with the LE number (i.e., LE 7795xx) on the back of the head, were used to differentiate them from the originals. The white pickup selector switch tip and current electronics also set this apart from the oldies. Otherwise, this early reissue was a valiant effort by Gibson at the time, and commands a good premium today. Gibsonian folklore has it that leftover parts from the 1950s were used, which is, of course, not substantiated.

By late '72, Gibson logos saw both the "o" and "b" closed. The "i" was soon dotted near the "G" on these Gibson Customs. Production on the '54 LTD Custom was 60 the first year, and 1,090 in 1973. Just a few more were built—three in '75 and one in '77. People who collect and play these early RI rare birds love them.

Gibson faithfully recreated the 1954 Les Paul Custom in 1972 with this very accurate "Black Beauty" reissue. Minute details give it away, such as the exact top carve, white switch tip, and whiter numbers on the speed knobs. "LE" (Limited Edition) serial numbers and "Made in USA" stamps were intended to let everyone know it was a special issue. *Courtesy Sol Betnuns Music, 1973*

These are photos from my second tour through the Kalamazoo factory in August 1975. Julius Bellson mentioned that this machine was the same one used in the fifties to cut the arched Les Paul tops. The carved template on the right guides the double cutters across two bodies at once. Note the directed blowers to keep debris off the wide template. This is a loud machine that takes constant multiple swipes across the maple tops. Note the multi-laminated mahogany and maple constructed bodies during 1975.

The angled neck-slot routing jig is all in place as these workers share a cheerful moment before taking the plunge.

Preparing for the angled control-cavity routing.

This Custom Les Paul is wrapped up like a mummy to ensure that the multiple binding will adhere properly.

Preparing for final setup on a Les Paul Custom. Looks like most of the parts are there, as she prepares to screw down the pickups before soldering them to the controls.

Checking string height during final setup on a sunburst Les Paul Special.

Artists

Harvey Mandel is performing in his smooth, fluid style on a 1971 Les Paul '54/'58 reissue with Deluxe pickups in San Diego, circa 1973. He's doing an age-old classical hammer-on technique he learned a few years earlier from a fellow Chicago guitarist (long before the shredders copped it). After playing with blues harmonica great Charlie Musselwhite in Chicago and moving to San Francisco, Harvey had a memorable instrumental album, *Cristo Redentor*, which featured multi-layered guitars, in 1968. He later went on to play on and off with Canned Heat (one of America's greatest blues bands), and released another instrumental LP, *Shangrenade*, when this picture was taken.

Bill Conners, with his Custom Les Paul, performing with Chick Corea and Return to Forever on the *Hymn of the Seventh Galaxy* tour in La Jolla, CA, 1973. Bill's fiery fusion style perfectly complemented the rhythm section of Stanley Clarke and Lenny White for Chick's brilliant compositions. Conners's high-volume amplifier cabinet was miked and facing away from the audience that night.

Here's the great Latin rock virtuoso Carlos Santana playing his '70s Les Paul Sunburst Standard on the *Inner Secrets* tour in San Diego, circa 1977. Although he played SG Specials live (Fillmore & Woodstock), he recorded his first hit record in 1968 with an early Les Paul Special.

British rocker *par excellence* Stevie Marriot loved Gibson Les Paul guitars and had a number of unique Epiphones, Standards, and Customs, like this Black Beauty with cream parts. He's performing here with his popular Humble Pie group on the 1973 *Smokin'* tour at the Forum in Los Angeles.

Neil Schon is playing some soulful burning solos on his Les Paul Standard with the group Journey at San Diego State College, circa 1974.

Guitarist Les Dudek grew up in Florida and became a professional guitarist by the age of fifteen. His hot blues guitar playing was heard on the "Ramblin' Man" recording with Dickey Betts on the Allman Brothers' *Brothers and Sisters* album, Silk Degrees with Boz Scaggs, and live with the Steve Miller band. He's playing his favorite late-1967 Goldtop "Alma," with black Gibson parts he added back then. Gig circa 1977 with Boz Scaggs.

David Lambert, from the English group the Strawbs, with his Les Paul Custom, 1974.

Rick Derringer playing Dimarzio-equipped 1969 Les Paul Custom with Johnny and Edgar Winters in San Diego, circa 1974.

The Low-Impedance Series:
Les Paul Personal, Professional, Bass, Jumbo,
Recording, Triumph, and Signature Models

The Low-Impedance Series: Les Paul Personal, Professional, Bass, Jumbo, Recording, Triumph, and Signature Models

Striving for a purer guitar tone:
Les Paul's quest for fidelity and true tonal presence.

Shortly after Les Paul's astounding "New Sound" recordings stirred the public, he wanted to recreate that same sort of "hi-fi" idea with his guitar's electronics and overall sound for recordings. The modern reality of "full frequency response" became Les Paul's inevitable guitar goal during the mid 1950s, which is clearly apparent in his recordings from 1955 onward. Microphones had made the transition from high impedance (high-Z) to low impedance (low-Z), with crystal clarity and presence.

Les was now ready to unleash his advanced tone revolution on the world. He would do this with a new guitar sound via his "personal" guitar. What was this remarkable Les Paul sound and the secret behind it? Gibson had been asking Les how he got his trademark electronic tones all along. Many guitarists wanted to know, since they weren't quite able to achieve it from their production guitars. It was a mystery for many for years. Since he had finally come out of retirement, Les figured it was now time to unleash the secret of this breakthrough in guitar clarity.

Les speaks about low impedance in 1972:

LP: I'm on the road. Mary and I are performing, so all I know is the guitars are selling like mad, and they're good guitars. Now you realize that every one of those guitars, I immediately pulled out the electronics. I used that guitar, but with my electronics, which are low impedance.

RL: Did you use different pots?

LP: It's all different. We never used the standard Gibson pickup, we never claimed to. It was a Les Paul model guitar, and the agreement with Gibson was that I would not divulge this information to them because this is part of my sound that made me distinctive from anyone else, and I wanted to keep it.

RL: And the public couldn't get those sounds?

LP: You can't get it with the gold and the black, but you can with the Recorder. That guitar jumps right out at you. That's really tuff if it's plugged properly.

Again, this is how it is, looking into the pre-amplifier and what the speaker is saying, coming out of it or the console. But I go directly in the board with everything I do. I never use a speaker. So all my stuff, I just plug right in the board, and that's it. And those pickups are designed so you can get screaming highs (just like you just shattered a plate glass), all the way down to a Johnny Smith mellow sound, a real dark sound. So you have all these sounds. Then I also get sounds on the Recorder where you get the highs of an acoustical box and the depth of a jazz sound. So you have this Charlie Christian, Johnny Smith, whoever, this dark sound to combine together; you get a sound like an acoustical L-5 sound, or an Epi sound or whatever.

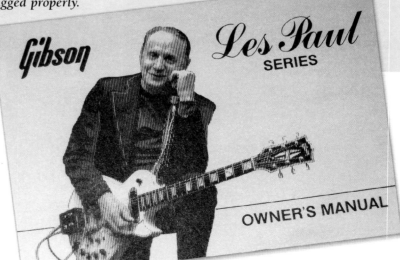

A Gibson owner's manual showing Les with his low-impedance modified '58 Custom with his mic and Paulverizer attachment.

Les playing his early '80s custom built "Recording/Heritage" model at the Strand in Hermosa Beach, circa 1989.

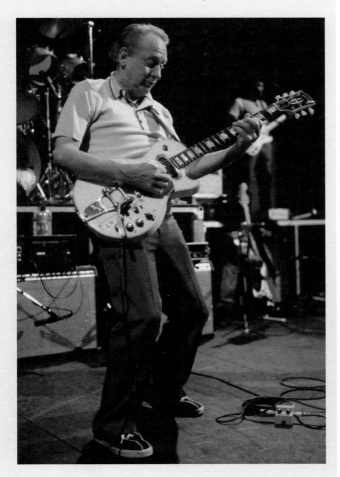

A warm-up session at Perkin's Palace, 1979. Les used this 1958 white Custom with various low-Z pickups for many years.

(Right) Les Paul's original Custom model modified by Wally Kamin into the first "Recording" model. It sports the first novel mic input and control by the toggle switch. Wally's hand-wound pickups sounded amazing in the studio through the big LP12 amp! It's quite the vintage recording machine. Mahwah, 1975.

Les's experimentation led him finally to perfect the true low-impedance guitar pickup in 1955. He knew that if a high output was desired, the overall frequency response (loss of dB highs and lows) was sacrificed. To achieve the extended response (true reproduction) desired, less output was the eventual result. Les worked on developing this new guitar sound to couple with his studio electronics. Its clear and distinctive tone is quite apparent, beginning with the mid 1950s *Time to Dream* album. On close listening, the bass strings really ring right off the vinyl.

The Les Paul Custom models that Gibson gave to him were the perfect test bed for these electronics. Les and his brother-in-law Wally Kamin wound pickup coils and installed them with extra electronics for their experiments. Wally, whom Les sometimes referred to as "my main chopper," would rough out big holes in the guitars that Gibson sent over. Some of these low-impedance pickup's coils were under blank, black plastic covers and others hidden beneath the extended pickguard.

Gibson sent three white-finished Custom models in 1958. Two of those were flattop versions, which facilitated easy mounting of the pickups and custom electronics. Les's remote-controlled "Paulverizer" unit (coined by Bea Manners) was regularly attached to the Bigsby tailpiece in order to produce his other multiple-track effects. Les and Mary performed with the white guitars for years, until the SG models arrived. During the seventies, Les continued using a white 1958 model with modern low-Z pickups until his 1979 Heritage/Personal sunburst guitar was constructed.

The following is from my 2001 interview with Les:

RL: Before the humbuckings came out, you went to low-impedance pickups. You can hear it on your recordings in 1955.

LP: From the very beginning I told Gibson, "You can have everything but my sound. Unless you find it, I'm not going to tell you." And so the sound that I had on the guitar was mine… I happened to be privileged to make my own studio and my own sound—and got it.

I was low impedance since time began. I got it from the Bell telephone. I got it right from the very beginning, when I did a hysterectomy on Mother's phone. And when I took it apart, I saw… and they did all the brainwork for me. All I had to do was put their earphone under my string. Bell Labs had done all the searching for me. That was years ahead of anybody else.

RL: When did microphones become low impedance?

LP: They started before me. You go to 1915, the carbon microphone was there, and the earphone was there. The telephone was there.

RL: So they had to develop low impedance to get the fidelity and use long cords.

LP: Yes. Anybody who does things the correct way would say, "If we're going to do this in a professional manner, they would go low impedance."

RL: Did you have the low impedance on your Epiphone "Clunker" in the '40s?

LP: I had both. It was more than just hearing it in the pickup. But anyway, those were all contributing factors. It's endless.

GIBSON SETS THE STAGE FOR PROGRESS IN SOUND

75th Anniversary Year Launched With New Sound . . . The cyclonic impact created by the new line of Gibson guitars and amplifiers sent dealers home anticipating greatly increased sales through these exciting new additions. The commotion started with the unveiling of the all-new Walnut finish Les Paul Guitar line, starting with the Les Paul Personal . . . the only guitar in the marketplace today having two, low impedance pick-ups, giving every player new found versatility of expression. The Personal is also equipped with a microphone attachment and microphone; Les Paul Professional, Les Paul Custom . . . with two humbucking pick-ups, ebony finishes, Les Paul Deluxe . . . featuring beautiful gold finish, rosewood fingerboard; Les Paul solid body Bass . . . with two, low impedance pick-ups, bass and treble roll-off control; and the new, Jumbo Flattop . . . with single cutaway, 1 low impedance pick-up and special controls for complete flexibility of performance. New Les Paul models give the player full control of the tonal spectrum right at the guitar with his never having to adjust his amp controls, once set. To enhance the new sounds of the Les Paul line, we added the versatile Les Paul low impedance amp, 190 RMS with 4, 12-inch speakers, and two, high frequency horns. New Special Effects make this the hottest amp on the market today at only $995.00.

In 1969, Les Paul's low-impedance revolution was unveiled with the initial model range shown at the NAMM display. This CMI flier page shows that display and acoustic Jumbo model, along with one of the prototype Personals with a normal-sized Les Paul guitar body.

A trio of Personals getting personal late one night. *Courtesy Mark Hays, 1994*

The Real Les Paul Sound

During the 1967 discussions with Mr. Berlin, Mr. Carlucci, and Bruce Bolen, Les and Zeke Manners earnestly promoted his earlier sonic breakthrough of high fidelity with low-impedance electronics. Zeke was a key factor in advising Les to promote his "magic pickup." Zeke remembers, "I was there with Mr. Berlin in 1967 for the second deal. I told him to use them on the other Gibson models. They made a deal and put the new pickups in the guitars. I talked them into giving Les a better percentage too. I spent the whole day with them."

Low impedance was—and is still—ahead of its time. The super-clean sound was quite advantageous for low-Z input, hi-fi recording equipment. You may have noticed the distinct change in tonality in Les's 1955 guitar recordings. (The sixth string, especially, would virtually jump out at you and sound as if your ear was right next to the string.) This widened frequency response in fidelity is like the sonic difference between AM and FM radio.

Telefunken's Neumann condenser microphone of the 1930s (with its 500-ohm output that became the standard) led the high-fidelity revolution in studios and sound systems. Les figured that if microphones and telephones gained great fidelity with low impedance, why couldn't he recreate the true dynamic tones of the guitar for recording and live performance? This special setup that Les had secretly used for the last ten years also enabled him to run longer cords with virtually no degradation in the signal; plus, it was totally quiet and free of electrical interference.

Everybody at CMI loved what they heard. Gibson soon began developing the first true hi-fi, low-impedance guitar—the Les Paul "Personal." This revolutionary guitar featured twin dual-coil (stacked) low-output humbucking pickups. They were also slanted for a broader string response, as on the old Sunburst L-12 that Mary used. The slanted fingerboard end also helped get the large pickup positioned into the neck for deeper tones.

As on Les's personal guitars, a master volume, bass, treble, and "decade" rotary switch (low-pass filter) controlled and shaped the tonalities of the guitar. It had his novel Cannon microphone input jack on the top edge with an extra volume control nearby. Also, Les could then easily address the audience with a handy Shure gooseneck studio talkback system.

The Les Paul Personal, Professional, and Bass Guitars

"Gibson engineers and 'Mr. Guitar,' Les Paul, spent endless hours of research and experimentation in producing this exceptional instrument. A revolutionary new design with low-impedance pickups. The Les Paul Personal is truly a giant step forward in musical electronics and tone reproduction." (Gibson, 1970)

According to the Gibson catalog, the guitar and bass models were constructed with the normal "three-piece laminated British Honduras mahogany neck construction. The laminations are quarter-sawn for maximum strength." The arched, three-piece body had the "center cross-band," and featured a beautiful, deep brown finish. "Clear walnut finish reveals all the fine grain-lined feature of the basic wood," said the brochure. All three models of the original series came in a natural, deep-brown walnut nitrocellulose finish, which was nicely polished like a piece of beautiful fine furniture. Some were done in cherry, too.

The Personal

The upscale Personal (named for Les's own modified Customs) was basically a more luxurious model with fancy Custom binding and the ever-so-small "fretless wonder" frets. They were used for a period and then replaced by the jumbo frets just before Gibson introduced their new volute neck. Gold-plated hardware gave this beautiful top-of-the-line instrument some extra class. In September 1969, its West Coast price was a whopping $650… $70 above the Les Paul Custom model.

The earliest prototype of the Personal was first seen in the CMI NAMM ad. The guitar combined a normal-sized, all-mahogany archtop custom LP with the new low-impedance setup and a Bigsby vibrato. Subsequent pre-production and actual production versions were slightly widened, nearly 1" to 13⅞" across at the lower

(Right Top) 1970 Les Paul model range catalog cover featuring the Personal headstock. Gibson had a whole series of smaller catalogs depicting the various styles of instruments that year.

(Right Bottom) LP Personal page extolling the virtues of the top-of-the-line solid-body. The crossbanding and quartersawn woods of the body are also mentioned.

LES PAUL PERSONAL—Low Impedance

Gibson engineers and "Mr. Guitar"… Les Paul, spent endless hours of research and experimentation in producing this exceptional instrument. A revolutionary new design with low impedance pickups. The Les Paul Personal is truly a giant step forward in musical electronics and tone reproduction.

FEATURES: Low impedance electronics and pickups. Microphone input jack. Clear grain British honduras mahogany body with center crossband. Three-piece laminated British honduras mahogany neck construction. The laminations are quarter-sawn for maximum strength. Buffed and polished clear walnut finish reveals all the fine grain-lined features of the basic wood. Ebony fingerboard with "fretless wonder" frets, mother-of-pearl block inlays. Gold-plated deluxe design machine heads with sealed gears. Goldplated Tune-O-Matic bridge. 18¼" long, 14" wide, 2" deep; 24¾" scale, 22 frets, neck joins body at 16th fret.

bout, with a more rounded horn for the cutaway. This new size was to give guitarists more of a "box" to hold onto, since many felt that the Les Paul guitar was small overall. The added mass from this extra size gave it more tone, but the often-heavy mahogany and added pickup weight (nearly two pounds) could be problematic. These larger guitars would range anywhere from 8.5 pounds up to 12 pounds, even with the large control routing. The denser wood gives this guitar a richer tone with lots of sustain, albeit with an added weight that made it better for sitting down in a studio than for long performances standing on a stage. With a two-conductor output from the external microphone jack, an unbalanced line out is sent via the stereo output jack to use for addressing the engineer or audience. Only 146 examples of this classy beauty were shipped between 1969 and 1971.

Set the Controls

All combinations of settings and pickups are controlled with the master volume. Treble frequencies are evenly rolled off in a linear fashion with the treble control, while the bass control affects the reduction of lower frequencies from 10 to 0. A quick look at the schematic can give the electronic wiz a good idea of how to sample the controls methodically and what to expect with the nearly overwhelming myriad of sonic possibilities.

The decade control has 11 incremental positions that add more resistance or capacitance and inductance into the system (or combinations thereof) that, in effect, add to the sound permanently. Fringing curve magnetic improvement (efficiency) increases the cap resistance ten times—plus off position. It changes the amounts of R (resistance), C (capacitance), and L (inductance). When the decade and resistance are used together, it uses notch filters between 2,000–3,000 Hz, etc., and changes the impedance at 7,000 Hz.

A straight-ahead 1969 Les Paul Personal model. *Courtesy David and Caroline Brass, 2004*

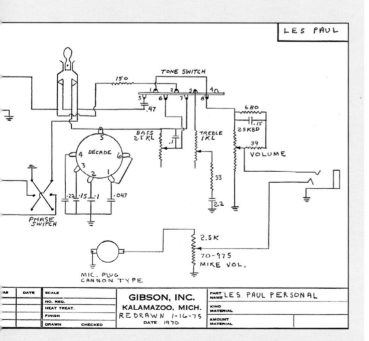

Gibson schematic for the Les Paul Personal.

1969 Les Paul Personal showing the Cannon XLR input for the handy talkback microphone and the separate volume control. This set-up was a novel idea for singing or communicating with the audience between songs. This guitar has a black selector surround combined with the rubber piece and black switch tip. *Courtesy David and Caroline Brass, 2004*

The lower settings can approximate an acoustic guitar tonality while using the front pickup (especially with the bass and treble controls backed off). Highest settings tend to fatten it up to a humbucking fullness, while in-between settings blend the two in varying increments. This effect is hardly noticeable unless you're using it properly into a board, without the line transformer in use for high-impedance amplification.

Original Gibson brochures state, "The 11-position decade control 'tunes' or alters the treble harmonics. Position 0 will peak the highest frequency and graduates accordingly down the spectrum in steps through position 10. This control is most effective when the tone selector is in position 2 and the bass response has been reduced. You will experience innumerous tonalities when used with the phase, treble and pickup selector toggle switch.

"Interesting tonal blends can be achieved when using treble and bass controls simultaneously. You can preset the desired amount of treble and increase (decrease) bass without affecting treble frequencies. The same goes for presetting the desired amount of bass. You will not affect the bass frequencies if you add (subtract) treble. (Treble and bass controls may be used with the tone selector, phase and toggle switch.)"

The large, three-way Tone Selector control (à la Tele-style) is effectively used for preset switching. Setting 1 (forward position or "down" on the recording) activates the volume, and decade control bypasses the bass and treble controls. Extra caps and resistors in this setting add

Les Paul Personal model #913542. *Courtesy Del (Casher) Kacher, 2007*

a different flavored tonality. Position 2 (middle) turns everything on, including phase switch activation (with both pickups engaged). Position 3 (up/back) gives the same as 1, but without the extra filtering.

Depicted are a protype Gibson low-Z guitar pickup (wax potted) and a production bass pickup tapped with eight leads.

(Right) Deep routed cavity for a big low impedance pickup on a Professional body. Note the slightly exposed thin sandwiched attaching layer on the lower laminated section.

Low-Impedance Pickups... Gibson's Effort

The task of recreating Les's pickups was done at Gibson's in-house electronics laboratory. Pickup-wise, the electronics we are speaking about produced one-tenth the output, more similar to that of the modern microphone. The wider coil and large Alnico magnet created a more even field around the strings. This enabled the outside strings to produce the same response as the inside four. Around this time, Les and Wally Kamin persuaded Mr. Berlin to buy a special magnetic calibrator (price tag: $20,000) for making these special low-impedance pick-ups. What may have happened to this machine in later years is still a mystery.

Two long Alnico V magnets were used in these units, with one in each coil and both oriented with north on top. The lower coil was magnetically separated from the other by a Mumetal plate that serves as the magnetic load. Guitar pickups were wound with 24-gauge wire, while the larger bass coils were 32-gauge wire. Guitar coils were reverse wound to each other and received 300 turns from approximately 160 feet of wire. Coils were protectively sealed in an epoxy that held the coils in place and reduced microphonics (which was slightly less effective than the more permeating wax procedure). All this resin, copper, and magnet material gave each pickup a weight of nearly one pound. The output was {11.5–12.5} 4.7–5K D/C wire resistance with an impedance of 50 ohms. (They can vary by several ohms because the 24-gauge [32-gauge] wire varies in thickness and resistance per meter.) The guitar pickups measured 1¼" by 1¼" by 3⅞", making these large cavities nearly 1⅞" deep. The pickups, which are adjustable with three screws for accurate height adjustments, have an outside black casing that features an embossed "Gibson" logo.

The Professional

The Les Paul Professional was the low-impedance economy model that incorporated a Standard-style, rosewood fingerboard, neck and front body binding, and chrome parts (although the catalog listed nickel), *sans* the nifty mic input setup—all for $480. Price-wise, this put it between the Custom and Deluxe models, prompting Gibson to claim "...perhaps the feature you'll enjoy the most is the modest price tag that accompanies this 'professional' guitar."

The larger 13⅞" body continued to utilize the customary ⅟₁₆" mahogany cross-band strip. Grain direction is optimally set at 90 degrees for bonding strength and can easily be viewed under the front pickup. The pickup switch's function was more accurately described with "Rear/Front" instead of normal "Rhythm/Lead" assumption. As on the other low-impedance solids, electronic function lettering was upside down to read easily while playing the instrument. Terry Kath of the popular eight-piece brass/rock group Chicago (CTA) was one discerning artist who used this versatile model in concert. It was also pictured on the front cover of *Guitar Player* magazine's August 1971 issue. Jimmy Page was another guitarist who realized their expanded tonal recording potential. He posed with one for his solo album cover.

Terry Kath performs with Chicago in 1971, playing his Les Paul Professional. He was one of Hendrix's favorite guitarists and used this guitar with a Bogen PA preamp through an Acoustic Amp. *Photo courtesy* Guitar Player *magazine.* Many thanks to Jim Crockett.

LES PAUL PROFESSIONAL—Low Impedance

The Les Paul Professional has many of the same exciting features found on the LP Personal: low impedance pickups; fast, low-action neck; and a 24¾" scale. But perhaps the feature you'll enjoy most is the modest price tag that accompanies this "professional" guitar.

FEATURES: Low impedance electronics and pickups. Clear grain British honduras mahogany neck construction. Buffed and polished clear walnut finish reveals the fine grain-lined features in the basic wood. Bound rosewood fingerboard with deluxe pearloid inlays. Nickel-plated shaller machine heads with sealed gears. Nickel-plated Tune-O-Matic bridge. 18¼" long, 14" wide, 2" deep; 24¾" scale, 22 frets, neck joins body at 16th fret.

1970 Professional Les Paul catalog description.

The Les Paul Professional gave the guitarist all the special hi-fi electronics without the frills at a modest price of $490. Same oversized cross-banded Honduras mahogany body but with a rosewood fingerboard with pearloid crown inlays. Large Gibson Schaller tuners completed the package. *Courtesy Buffalo Brothers, 2004*

Les Paul Bass

Next was the first official Les Paul Bass—with high-fidelity electronics. "The frequency response, range of harmonics, and crisp, clear tones of the LP Bass will exceed that of any electric bass on the market to date," claimed the instrument's ads. Many studios adopted these bass guitars once they heard what they could achieve sonically.

This model finally brought the single-cutaway design to the electric solid-body bass guitar for Gibson (unless there exists a special-ordered, 1950s, single-cutaway bass somewhere). The Les Paul Bass used the customary 30½" scale length with 24 frets and chromed Schaller enclosed machine heads. A fairly narrow neck design (1¹⁵⁄₁₆" nut width) was specified, with a large, unbound headstock, and pearl-inlaid "Gibson" logo and crown motif. The large Tune-O-Matic adjustable bass bridge was generally shipped with a sliding mute attachment, as on the EB series of the day. Its laminated (center cross-banded), enlarged body size (13⅞" by 18¼" by 2" without the arch) still gave it a big, round acoustic tone despite the multiple layers.

Electronically, the two low-impedance pickups used a selector switch (suspended with a rubber grommet surround, as on the ES-175), a three-way "tone selector" switch (created by the unique tap-coil wired circuit), and a phase switch (for the funky odd tones) on a small oval plate. Compared to the low-Z guitar pickups, they measure 1⅜" x 4¼" and use 32-gauge wire. Individual volume, bass, and treble controls adjusted all this. The bass control actually adds some volume as you bring it up, while the treble response is not affected. The attenuating decade control was absent on the bass models. As on the other guitars, small Estacion pins near the knobs marked the level.

Very distinctive tonal variations could be achieved by the tone-switch setup. Position 1 gives the extra deep bass, while 2 is normal bass frequencies, and 3 has the high pitch response. The pickups on these early models had extra taps for each coil. List price in zone 2 was $470, plus $80 for the 542 Faultless purple-plush black case.

Distinctive tonal variations could be achieved by the tone-switch setup, utilizing internal standoffs and extra taps on each pickup coil. Position one gives the high pitch response (26.7K), while two is normal bass frequencies (66.2K), and three has the extra deep bass (127.9K). Coupled with the right amplifier and some pre-amp gain, these basses can handle any musical style from jazz smoothness to a funky growl with vibrato. The Les Paul Bass is unique in the world of basses—built like a tank to take punishment, it sounds rich and full. It's also capable of throwing in a funky, out-of-phase twist. List price in zone 2 was $470, plus $80 for the 542 Faultless purple or golden-plush black case.

LES PAUL BASS—Low Impedance

The frequency response, range of harmonics and crisp, clear tones of the LP Bass will exceed that of any electric bass on the market to date. This instrument is the only bass equipped with two low-impedance, humbucking pickups. And the slim, single cutaway design is especially popular with today's groups.

FEATURES: Low impedance electronics and pickups. Clear grain British honduras mahogany with center crossband body construction. Three-piece laminated British honduras mahogany neck construction. Buffed and polished clear walnut finish reveals all the fine grain-lined features of the basic wood. Brazilian rosewood fingerboard. Chrome-plated Schaller machine heads with sealed gears. Nickel-plated Tune-O-Matic bridge. 18¼" long, 14" wide, 2" deep; 30½" scale, 24 frets.

The Les Paul Bass catalog description praising its extended tonal range beyond other basses.

The revolutionary Les Paul Bass features described in more detail.

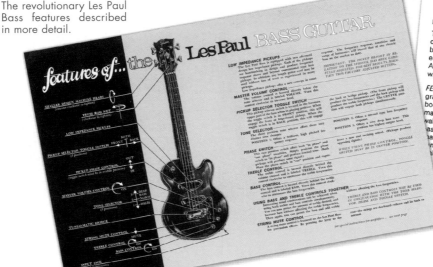

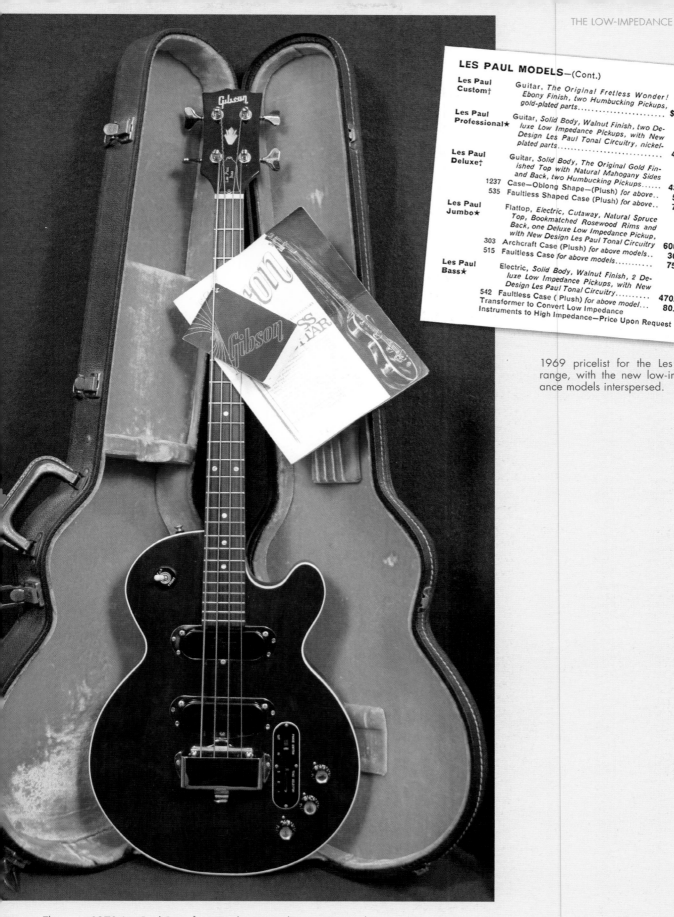

LES PAUL MODELS—(Cont.)

Les Paul Custom†	Guitar, The Original Fretless Wonder! Ebony Finish, two Humbucking Pickups, gold-plated parts	$580.00
Les Paul Professional★	Guitar, Solid Body, Walnut Finish, two Deluxe Low Impedance Pickups, with New Design Les Paul Tonal Circuitry, nickel-plated parts	490.00
Les Paul Deluxe†	Guitar, Solid Body, The Original Gold Finished Top with Natural Mahogany Sides and Back, two Humbucking Pickups	430.00
1237	Case—Oblong Shape—(Plush) for above	50.00
535	Faultless Shaped Case (Plush) for above	73.00
Les Paul Jumbo★	Flattop, Electric, Cutaway, Natural Spruce Top, Bookmatched Rosewood Rims and Back, one Deluxe Low Impedance Pickup, with New Design Les Paul Tonal Circuitry	600.00
303	Archcraft Case (Plush) for above models	30.00
515	Faultless Case for above models	75.00
Les Paul Bass★	Electric, Solid Body, Walnut Finish, 2 Deluxe Low Impedance Pickups, with New Design Les Paul Tonal Circuitry	470.00
542	Faultless Case (Plush) for above model	80.00

Transformer to Convert Low Impedance Instruments to High Impedance—Price Upon Request

1969 pricelist for the Les Paul range, with the new low-impedance models interspersed.

This mint 1970 Les Paul Bass features the original case, tag, and accompanying instruction brochure. *Photography by Sid Green, courtesy Rumble Seat Music, 2005*

Where Do I Plug In?

To hook up to the recording console board, you plug into (or follow your engineer to) a balanced line input. Many different types of extra preamps can further enhance the instruments' tones. For live performance through an amplifier, a special cord with an in-line impedance-matching transformer was supplied. It enabled the musician to either go direct into the console, or into a normal high-impedance (high-Z) amplifier. Many have been lost over the years, so the current A95U Shure mic transformer has the exact same specs for a replacement. Having the in-line setup near the amp was advantageous when using longer cords. These step-up transformers naturally created a loss of fidelity going through a standard amp, so the real answer was low impedance all the way. Low impedance actually requires more expensive tube preamp stages. Radio and studio console inputs were more costly to build than guitar amplifiers, which want to see higher voltages.

These are two prototypes from Les Paul's collection, with unique thin flat body styling and low-impedance electronics. They are lightweight and play great, but never quite made production. Note the Custom-styled guitar neck and long-scale bass neck. Two more of these low-Z prototypes somehow ended up at Strings & Things in Memphis, Tennessee.

The Les Paul LP-12 amp comes alive. "Be careful. This thing is mean!"

LP-12 AMPLIFIER

Gibson's new Les Paul Amplifier is specially designed to accommodate low impedance instruments. The preamp has two channels with a total of 5 inputs; high and low impedance inputs in each channel. And the powered speaker-cabinet delivers 190 watts of the cleanest, clearest RMS power you've ever heard. Those who have heard the LP-12 call it the "Monster"... and with good reason. This amplifier not only grabs you... it shakes you! If that's not enough, there are output jacks on the back of each cabinet to allow you to drive as many as ten amplifier speaker cabinets with one preamp.

FEATURES: NORMAL CHANNEL—volume control, presence control, bass control, treble control, crossover switch, two input jacks—one high and one low impedance. EFFECTS CHANNEL—volume control, presence control, bass control, tremolo depth control, vibrato depth control, vibrato & tremolo rate control, treble control, reverb control, cross-over switch, three input jacks—one high and one low impedance plus an auxiliary input for organ, rhythm, etc., three position tremolo, vibrato and vibrola switch. GENERAL FEATURES—three position power switch— off, on and on with reverse polarity, three position power, panel light and standby switch, output jack, foot switch socket, and AC cord retaining brackets.

The LP-12 Amplifier

Gibson produced a low-impedance, hi-fi "monster" amp to go with its new guitars and bass. Stated the ads:

"New Les Paul models give the player full control of the tonal spectrum right at the guitar with his never having to adjust his amp controls, once set. To enhance the new sounds of the Les Paul line, we added the versatile Les Paul low-impedance amp, 190 RMS with four 12-inch speakers, and two high-frequency horns. New Special Effects make this the hottest amp on the market today at only $995.

"Gibson's new Les Paul Amplifier is specially designed to accommodate low-impedance instruments. The preamp has two channels with a total of 5 inputs; high and low impedance inputs in each channel. And the powered speaker-cabinet delivers 190 watts of the cleanest, clearest RMS power you've ever heard. Those who have heard the LP-12 call it the 'Monster,' and with good reason. This amplifier not only grabs you—it shakes you. If that's not enough, there are output jacks on the back of each cabinet to allow you to drive as many as ten amplifier speaker-cabinets with one preamp."

This 111-pound behemoth amp setup really shook the room. With its nearly 200 watts of power, even the new bass could easily be handled. The LP-1 head is basically a sophisticated preamp with volume, presence, and bass and treble controls for both normal and effects channels. Effects included reverb, tremolo, and vibrato, with a vibrola switch beneath. Whether it did both volume and pitch shifting is another story. The whole panel lit up in multi-colors, which was great in a dark playing environment. The LP-2 power cabinet used four CTS 12" speakers and two high-frequency University Sound horns with a simple pull-off grill.

(Left Top) The ground-shaking "Monster" Les Paul LP-12 low-impedance behemoth cabinet and amplifier system. With nearly 200 watts of RMS power, this could nearly wake the dead with full power chords. Unfortunately, it didn't catch on during the heyday of big walls of amplification.

(Left Bottom) Les Paul's personal LP-12 "Monster" low-impedance amp and "Paulverizer" remote unit. I used to play through this amp while jamming with Bobby and Les in Mahweh. *Courtesy Cleveland Rock and Roll Hall of Fame & Museum, 2008*

Les Paul Jumbo

The Gibson Les Paul Jumbo brought Les's new electronics to a specially-braced, "jumbo" 16" acoustic cutaway model. Who ever thought that there would be an acoustic flattop Les Paul? Remarkably, it used the long 25½" scale length found on their best jazz boxes, J-200, and Dove models. The solid spruce natural top had a round hole and four controls (including decade) with a bypass switch. A height-adjustable wooden bridge with pins was standard. The modern, deep-curved cutaway was somewhat reminiscent of a "Macaferri Django"-style and unique to this model and the Bossa Nova. Its beautiful figured book-matched Indian rosewood body depth went from 3¹⁴⁄₁₆" to 5". With the added electronics, the top vibrations were a bit dampened. (The pickup alone weighs in at nearly two pounds.) For good response, you must use non-brass type strings as well. The West Coast list price in September 1969 was $600, and $75 for the Faultless 515 hard-shell case.

(Right) Catalog description of the LP Jumbo acoustic. Based on the Gibson Bossa Nova flattop model, this innovative electrified acoustic had clarity unlike any other model.

LES PAUL JUMBO FLATTOP—Low Impedance

The most revolutionary flattop ever made! The Les Paul Jumbo has a low impedance pickup; a volume control; decade control; and an independent bass and treble control. Natural select spruce top in a modern cutaway design.

FEATURES: Low impedance electronics. Beautiful book-matched rosewood back and rims, natural select spruce top. Deluxe ivoroid binding. Bypass switch to engage or disengage bass and treble controls. Rosewood fingerboard. Chrome-plated metal parts. 21¼" long, 16¼" wide, 4⅞" deep; scale length 25½".

303—Archcraft case
515—Faultless case

Beautiful book-matched rosewood back with multi-colored center strip. Quite a hip electrified acoustic, decades before the current trend.

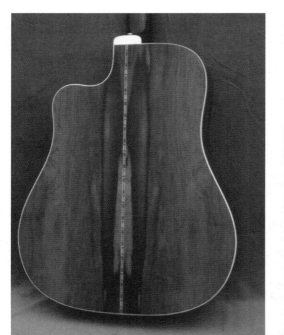

Jumbo electronics exposed, showing the potentiometers, Switchcraft toggle, and rotary decade control. Modern rubber-coated color-coded wiring began during this era. *Guitar courtesy David Swartz, 2003*

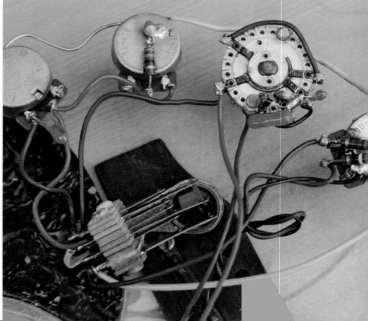

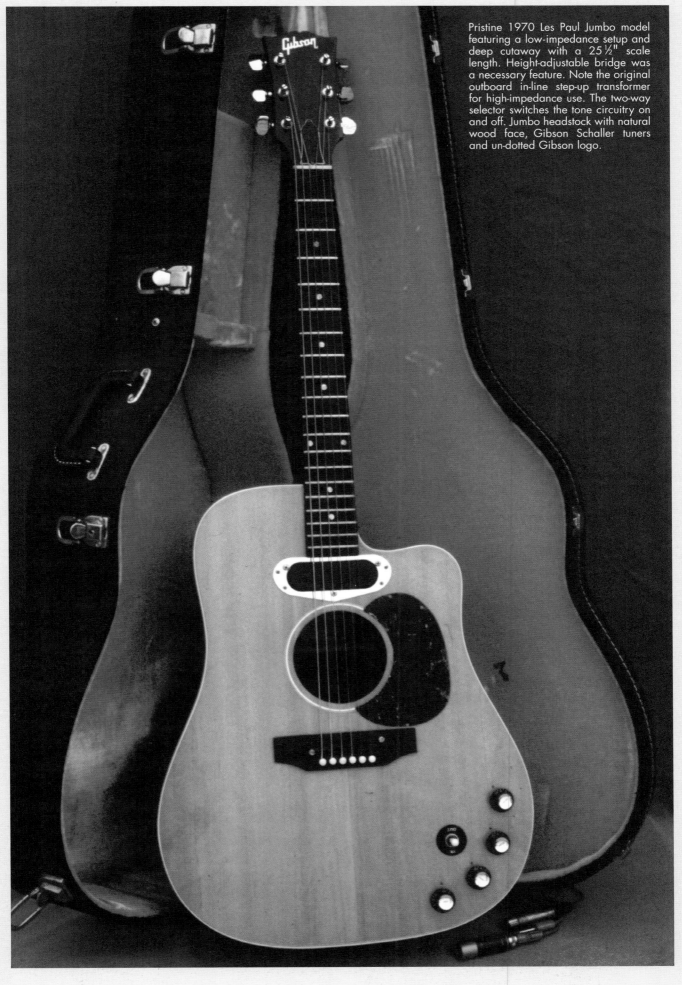

Pristine 1970 Les Paul Jumbo model featuring a low-impedance setup and deep cutaway with a 25½" scale length. Height-adjustable bridge was a necessary feature. Note the original outboard in-line step-up transformer for high-impedance use. The two-way selector switches the tone circuitry on and off. Jumbo headstock with natural wood face, Gibson Schaller tuners and un-dotted Gibson logo.

Recording and Triumph Models, 1971–'79

Within two years, the low-impedance guitar and bass models had their first makeover. First, they were trimmed down from 13⅞" to 13½". A wide, comfortable, rear chest contour was also incorporated. With such heavy woods and pickups, there wasn't too much change in overall weight, unless it was built with very light mahogany. A new black, four-ply binding was added on both the Recording guitar and the Triumph bass models. Headstocks had the undotted, pearl-inlaid "Gibson" logo and split-diamond inlay set straight into a black plastic veneer with no finish applied. The black body binding contrasted with the new lighter, natural-finished mahogany. (Some still retained the dark mahogany stain.) A swept-wing laminated pickguard with exposed white edge was used on the guitar with the new control platform.

Gibson still touted these models' remarkable qualities, saying, "With sensitive control panels full of revolutionary sounds, the artist can actually 'mix' his own sound the way a recording studio engineer does." All the electronics were now consolidated onto a large laminated plate with an added onboard lo/hi transformer output with slide switch control, Switchcraft 12013 pickup selector, and output jack. A front-routed 1¹¹⁄₁₆" by 8¼" by 3½" cavity received the guitar and bass console works. Gone was the need to use a bulky inline transformer, yet this defeated its capability to reduce capacitance (loss of highs) with long cables for high-impedance settings. Volume, treble, bass, and decade (on the guitar) remained, but with a short-lived, 2.2-value, "orange drop" capacitor that replaced the previous 4.7, and a 3300 (silver/black/ orange/orange) resistor added on the treble control CTS potentiometer. The stacked coil bass pickups (¼" x ½" larger) were constructed with multiple taps with expanded tonal variations connected to a long internal standoff for the tone switch. The output jack was conveniently put on the control plate, just as Les had done for years; unfortunately, many have cracked over the years from the plug pressure. All the knobs and switches were still complex for some individuals, but a plethora of great sounds was available for the learned tone devotee.

Dramatic studio photography graced the 1975 catalogs for Gibson, and the recording guitar close-up was no exception.

A more detailed explanation of the low-impedance Les Paul Recording works is given in this brochure.

(Opposite Page) 1975 Les Paul Recording guitar in white (missing its wedge pickguard), near Boney Ridge, Malibu. This guitar sounds amazingly quiet with a full spectrum of tones. It's very edgy when turned up cascading through a vintage Bassman and Bluesbreaker. *Courtesy Bruce Malm*

The normal Tune-O-Matic was used on the Recording model for a short while, before the new Schaller-built Tune-O-Matic bridge with its extended intonation "wide travel" capabilities was utilized. This also compensated for the occasional misplaced bridge that repairmen had to deal with. Its substantial ⁵⁄₁₆" by 1" studs finally gave the bridge a solid coupling for increased sustain, but lost the traditional ABR-1 look in the process. Grover machine heads with tulip grips were used. By 1975, both the LP Recording and Bass were available in the natural

The Les Paul Triumph bass now featured a bound neck with block inlays, split-diamond headstock, and continued the 24-fret rosewood fingerboard. A few original fretless versions were also shipped. *Courtesy True Tone Music, 2005*

Triumph bass brochure extolling the myriad features for this exceptional instrument. Recording and Triumph brochures courtesy of Joe Diamond, long-time low-Z LP player.

mahogany finish, a shaded sunburst, and a new white finish. A 0538 Faultless plush-lined case came with the guitar, and a 0542 with the bass instrument.

Gone was the top-of-the-line fancy Personal version with its handy microphone input and the Custom ebony/gold appointments. The Recording and Triumph models soon superseded all three original models and were brought into production during '71, while at the same time, the Personal, Professional, and LP Bass models overlapped into '73. A few of each were made during the last year, however. The

behemoth LP-12 low-impedance amp was soon discontinued, leaving enthusiasts to either build custom LI amps or use sophisticated preamps (and go "direct inject," per studio jargon). Until the amp manufactures wake up to sophisticated LI circuitry, these now-classic guitars (dinosaurs) are still way ahead of their time.

The new Les Paul Recording guitar and Triumph bass catalog from 1971. The cover shot was done with a cross-grain star filter. These brochures contained the floppy Evantone "soundsheets" clear insert with recorded sounds of Bruce Bolen demonstrating the Recording guitar and Les Paul narrating. The flip side is the original Bolen tune "Tomorrow, Today" song done with the "hi-fi" instruments. A diagram is included to give the potential buyer an understanding of the multitude of features available at a flick of the switch.

Late Recorder and Triumph Models

By 1976, a switch to the normal 12¾" by 17⅜"- sized Les Paul guitar was instituted. This time around, it featured a maple top and maple neck. Basically, it had the same appointed neck with a rosewood fingerboard and pearl block inlays, but with three-piece maple construction, including the volute. Some were triple-bound with ebony fingerboards and gold hardware. New colors included ebony black and cherry sunburst, along with the light walnut and white finishes. Now the back was bound and the comfortable contour was deleted.

The control plate was now consolidated with the four controls on top for easier access. Notation was reversed to ascertain the functions looking down at the controls. Some were shipped with gold low-impedance pickup covers as used on the early L-5s. The treble control was returned to earlier specs with a 4.7 capacitor and no resistor. Two separate output jacks were built into the lower edge, either to run individually or run stereo high-and-low setups. The LP Recorder listed at $849 in January 1979, and came with a $99.50 Pro-1 Protector Faultless case. Shipping totals during the seventies for Recording models: 1971, 236; 1972, 1,314; 1973, 1,759; 1974, 915; 1975, 204; 1976, 352; 1977, 362; 1978, 180; 1979, 78.

The last Triumph bass models retained their all-mahogany construction and came in either natural mahogany or white finishes. Scale length was specified at 30⅜" with 24 frets on its rosewood, block-inlaid neck. LP Triumph models listed for $839, with another $119 for the 542 hardshell case. Shipping totals during the seventies for Triumph basses: 1971, 321; 1972, 768; 1973, 959; 1974, 526; 1975, 208; 1976, 171; 1977, 101; 1978, 80; 1979, 44. These wonderful LP bass guitars gave the world a true fidelity that resounded on hit records. Steve Miller and Eddie Money's bassist Lonnie Turner has used one on many great recordings.

The last of the Recording models sported a maple top, closer control knobs in a straight line and dual-Z outputs (wisely mounted on the side since the control plates kept breaking). This fine 1977 dual-Z sunburst is from the Mike Slubowski collection. Photographed by Steve Pitkin.

Les and Wally's "Hi-Fi" Pickups

Les Paul's collaboration with Gibson on the low-impedance pickups resulted in a very close approximation of what he was actually doing. As with most of his inventions—the remarkable LP 70 acoustic cylinder pickup, for example—the full details are somewhat private. The exact specifications are still a secret between Les and Wally Kamin, who wound the original pickups. There were many variations in their experimentations throughout the years. Les Paul's modern Custom version had taps with six wires for more sound sends to the decade switch and extra switches. The big, full tone Les gets live—with sparkling highs, rich and warm lows—is still his signature sound on his personal Recording guitars, pure and simple. Gibson's standardized setup is very similar indeed, and certainly a breath of fresh air in comparison to the muffled high-impedance world.

A late-model Les Paul Recording in black from the Les Paul collection. *Photo courtesy Neil Zlozower, 1981*

What's Next?

With this distinctive voice of wider frequency response, the guitarist's "New Sound" was finally available. But was the solid-body, rock-guitar world ready for such full ambience and clarity of tone? This versatile new guitar was packed full of features that greatly increased the sounds available for jazz, blues, country, pop, and R&B—and without a doubt, put it in a class of its own.

Although high impedance is still very much in vogue, some pickup manufacturers start the signal with low impedance, since electronics have greatly improved. Most of us are used to the limited, muffled sounds compared to Les's personal electronics with expanded tonal frequencies. Guitarists in rock and blues naturally lean toward distorted, high-volume sustained tones. Those who use these guitars thoroughly enjoy the clean, articulate, and extraordinary sensitivity that these models make available to them. These instruments' versatility with other effects is virtually endless in many types of music. With high-volume amplification, compared to normal Gibson and Fender pickups, the low-Z pickups are unmatchable for smoothness and full tone. To make these amazingly sophisticated Les Paul low-impedance instruments match properly, more advanced pre-amplification circuitry is needed than is generally available in inexpensively built guitar amplification inputs. When set up properly, the difference between the two impedances is like night and day—a truly breathtaking sonic experience.

The last Recording version was the final culmination of Gibson's Les Paul low-impedance series solid-body guitar. Unfortunately, this series met its demise due to the lack of both industry amplifier support and major pop artist endorsements. Someday, these pioneering efforts will be incorporated into advanced guitar design, coupled with highly sophisticated amplification of the future.

As obscure an instrument as it is, some regional artists have discovered and utilized the remarkable sonic capabilities of this type of guitar outside of the studio. Mike Loce, guitarist in the Boston Rock Opera and the instrumental group Analog, does many types of gigs. He finds the Recording model to be the most versatile instrument for live performances. These are some of Mike's thoughts about the revolutionary Les Paul Recording guitar:

Mike: *It's an intuitive guitar for me, maybe not for others. It's hard to think about it as a guitar full of pre-sets. It always seems to be in a state of flux. For example, the tone seems to be constantly changing every time I pick it up and plug it in, based on a few little changes of the switch and turns of the dial. After a while you can hear things that fit into contexts of music. A jazzy sound might be the neck pickup on, position two on the tone with the treble rolled all the way off, but the bass all the way up. That's a pretty good jazz tone.*

I have a mental list of all the different types of tones that I've liked based on the settings. Plus, I think a good clean sound creates a good distorted sound. There is no guitar that can have a better clean sound, in my opinion, than the Recordings or the low impedance models. If you are looking at it like that's the start of your sonic foundation, then you are doing the right thing—like you said, cascading down and building your sound toward infinite sustain. The tone coming out of the guitar affects how you play. Whether it's distortion or clean, there's an infinite set of variables. I think low impedance guitars are the best foundation for almost any kind of guitar sound. It's all good stuff.

Robb: *Like the computer, people who learn the ropes easily can move quickly through it. I think once you get into the sheer dynamics of the Recording model, it's a more tonally expressive instrument.*

ML: *I think it takes a certain type of personality and disposition, though, to be drawn to the guitar. It's a unique type of club. I think they are extremely versatile instruments and they deserve more respect in terms of the types of sounds that could be achieved. A lot of guitar players are pretty impatient. I don't think they have the patience to play these things. Guitar players who just like to plug in and blast usually won't like low impedance. They are fairly complex instruments.*

RL: *It's not built for a simpleton. It's built for someone who has some overall prowess on the guitar, with an understanding of what tonalities you want and need to achieve.*

ML: *I think the low impedance guitars appeal to the experimenters, for lack of a better term. It's probably one of the best guitars that has ever been invented.*

Mike Loce enjoying playing his Les Paul Recording model with its multitude of tonalities.

Del Kacher

I bought the Les Paul professional guitar from West L.A. Music in 1971. Because it had features that no other guitar before could offer, I jumped at the chance to have this instrument. I remembered Les saying that he wound his pickups low impedance. From those conversations, I was aware of the importance of the low-Z guitar pickup. Having used low-impedance mics for many years, I could appreciate the value of clarity—with no loss of high frequencies. The problem with all high impedance guitar pickups is that high-end frequency loss occurs if the cable is longer than ten feet.

The low-impedance pickup was designed like an RCA DX-77 ribbon mic with an impedance of 150 ohms. These LP pickups were similar (but with lower ohms) and had no high-frequency loss. This allowed me to overdub a complete guitar orchestra with total clarity. Also, the circuitry made it possible to select and peak the various frequencies of the guitar. Therefore, I could get the clear harmonics of a rhythm guitar, all the way to a biting brassy sound for leads, all with total clarity.

While I was arranging and producing music for the TV show The New Zoo Revue and themes for IBM and Coca-Cola, I used this guitar exclusively because of the clarity in sound. During the Coca-Cola sessions I was asked to recreate their famous "It's the Real Thing" theme in several different styles. I recorded it with the guitar that I considered "the real thing." This LP guitar was so clean and clear in sound that the producers thought Les Paul had recorded these tracks! The guitar sparkled and allowed me to overdub with full frequency and clarity. I also did a lot of "sound-alikes" using this guitar, because it literally could sound like anything I needed. It was the "guitar of all guitars" because the low-impedance pickups were so versatile.

Les's long-time friend Del "Casher" Kacher (co-creator of the Wah-wah pedal) has been playing Gibson guitars for many years (including a prototype ES-5 from Julius Bellson and numerous modified Epi Zephyrs). Here's Del with a Personal model playing all those great Les Paul riffs with crystal-clear tones.

Al Di Meola

Hailing from Alpine, New Jersey, this versatile guitarist took the world by storm during the mid-seventies. It was the exciting jazz/rock fusion era as this 19-year-old guitarist joined up with one of the most popular groups of that genre, Chick Corea's Return to Forever. Di Meola played his Les Paul guitars high volume with a tonal edge unknown in jazz circles. He also did some superlative solo albums with a Spanish flair, including *Elegant Gypsy*, *Casino*, and *Land of the Midnight Sun*. Teaming up with greats Paco De Lucia and John McLaughlin for the "Super Guitar Trio" during the early eighties and mid-nineties was a guitarist's dream gig. Their lightning-fast runs and highly passionate styles on *Friday Night in San Francisco* inspired many guitarists.

When we first met, Al was using an unusual sunburst Les Paul Recording model with gold pickups and asked about getting hotter pickups. At the time, neither of us realized the full potential of the low-Z pickups with the right preamp. I put him in touch with pickup maker Larry DiMarzio and they both enjoyed a good endorsement relationship that helped kick-start his company. Larry installed Al's signature pickups on his Les Paul Custom and sold him a 1958 Standard, too. Di Meola successfully endorsed Gibson guitars and was pictured in their catalogs for many years. In 2003, we caught up during an acoustic Return to Forever gig at the Musicians Institute in Hollywood.

Robb: What attracted you to the guitar?

Al: Like anyone else, the sound, the feel, and the look. I listened to the Ventures. I liked all those instrumental songs. Elvis Presley, the whole aura of a person and a guitarist doing his thing. After that, the Beatles, the Invasion and the whole British sound. It was a phenomenal period.

RL: Who were your favorite guitar players when you were young?

AD: John Cipollina, Jerry Garcia, Carlos Santana, Jeff Beck… all those guys. I had their records. I liked some of Eric Clapton's stuff; I liked Cream. I got to play with Jack Bruce. That was an exciting period too.

RL: What was your first Gibson guitar?

AD: A '71 Les Paul. That's the guitar I used when I joined Chick Corea. I bought it brand new at Manny's Music. The Les Paul is the best guitar for achieving the type of sustain that was popular at that time. The combination of the Les Paul and the Marshall gave you a certain kind of overdrive and sustain capability that, for playing that jazz/rock stuff, was better than any kind of hollow-body or semi-hollow-body guitar. It had that kind of edge with a long sustain capability that was a popular thing, and still is. Even nowadays, to get the best sound, you've got to turn up to those high volumes.

RL: Tell me about your new Les Paul guitar.

AD: The one with the f-holes, the purple tiger stripe should be a museum piece. And at the time, many of the guys at Gibson were all lobbying to put out an Al Di Meola model guitar. It was kind of a hybrid Les Paul, with a jazz body. The center block of the body is all solid. It's more cosmetic than anything. It sounds as good or better than a vintage Les Paul. And when they made it, it was the most amazing thing I'd ever seen in my life.

A young Al Di Meola playing his recent model Les Paul Recording guitar in San Diego (circa 1977) with Chick Corea's Return to Forever group. He was getting some great sounds out of his Marshall rig and effects with this guitar. Al soon was endorsing Gibson and playing Les Paul Custom models for his successful solo career.

Al Di Meola still uses his Les Paul guitars for much of his recorded work, including his 2003 *Flesh on Flesh* and 2006 *Consequence of Chaos* CDs. The 2008 *Return to Forever* tour saw more of his blazing fretwork on the Gibson Les Paul.

Barry Cleveland and I attended this truly amazing 2008 *Return to Forever* concert in Montreal. Al is using his trusty '50s Les Paul Standard here as he winds up the grand finale of the concert. Much thanks to Andy Brauer and Stanley Clarke for their friendship and support.

The Signature Series

In 1973, Gibson introduced another style of guitar with low-impedance circuitry. Dubbed the "Signature series," this semi-solid (or semi-acoustic) model resembled the famed 335 series, yet with asymmetrical cutaway horns and a gold-topped finish. The 335 models had been very popular since their inception, and had the potential to generate a new interest in Les's hi-fi guitar circuitry. These Signature models had an attractive offset look and a substantial body to hold with far less weight. In essence, they were created to combine the sound and look of a LI Les Paul with a 335, giving guitarists the best of both worlds. In June 1973, the new Signature guitar listed for $595 (zone 1) with its $90 #519 faultless plush-lined case. The L.P. Signature Bass listed for $695 and $90 for the large #0521 faultless case.

As with the thin-line, *f*-hole, 335 series, body woods were comprised of thin laminated maple heat-pressed to an arch and glued to the neck block, which extended into the cutaway and a centralized center block of maple. This maple insert was not full-length and basically sat under the bridge and stop tailpiece. The customary 335 spruce longitudinal inserts were glued to the front and back full-length, however. This structurally strengthened the laminated portions and made them easily adhere to the blocks. Since they didn't retool, and basically used 335 forms, the offset cutaway was built with a special extended maple insert from the neck block. Les Paul worked with Gibson's new employee, Bill Lawrence (German guitarist/pickup specialist), to develop this new instrument.

Bill Lawrence recalls:

> *When Les wanted that guitar with a cutaway, they didn't want to spend the money to make a form. So I sent Hutch in the wood shop to cut that lower cutaway off and glue a solid piece of wood in. And then we cut the cutaway and used the stamp—the pressing die from the 335—and made that guitar. The sunburst ones had to be dark because the cutaway on the plywood box was cut off and a solid piece of wood was glued in. They didn't have a form to make this. This is also my design. Les Paul wanted them; Les Paul designed the form, and I designed the way how to make it.*

Body dimensions were a whopping 19" by 16" by 2⁷⁄₁₆". The necks were originally three-piece laminated mahogany of the period with the volute design. This

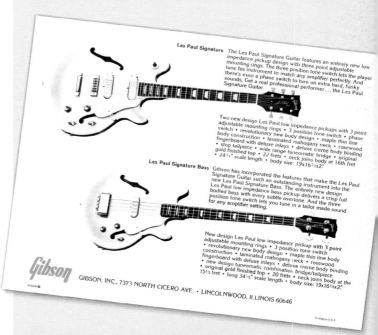

This flier page shows the early model with stacked humbucking low impedance pickups.

1975 Gibson catalog with both Signature Les Paul models. They were available in sunburst tops with custom necks on special order.

(Opposite Page) A gold Les Paul Signature model in nice shape with the low-impedance "Super Humbucking" pickups by in-house designer Bill Lawrence. The normal oversized square bridge has been replaced. This semi-solid-body design (nearly identical to the ES-335) was marketed from 1973 to 1979.

changed to the three-piece laminated maple style in 1975. Bound rosewood fingerboards with Deluxe crown inlays were standard on the guitar. The few Custom sunburst models built featured ebony, pearl blocks, bound headstocks and gold hardware. Basses were unbound rosewood. The guitar kept the standard 24¾" (24⁹⁄₁₆") scale length with 22 frets and 1¹¹⁄₁₆" nut width. It featured Gibson's new wide travel Tune-O-Matic extended-range bridge (#80040). This was coupled to a stop/stud tailpiece distanced 2½" down the body—unique to this model.

The exciting new Signature bass graduated to the professional 34½" scale with 20 frets—hallelujah! This long scale set a new sonic standard with its hi-fi electronics. "The entirely new design Les Paul low-impedance bass pickup delivers a crisp full bodied bass with every subtle overtone," touted Gibson literature. The pickup was strategically placed in the "sweet spot" to obtain the best tones. A bass Tune-O-Matic combination bridge/tailpiece with three stud bolts and a chromed cover was used.

Early versions of the Signature series utilized the original-style full-sized, low-impedance stacked pickups, yet with attractive cream covers to complement the cream body binding and pickguards. Soon afterwards Gibson unveiled their new "super humbucking," low-impedance cream pickup (standardized with the coils side-by-side) mounted in matching thin bezels. This smaller unit

(Above and Below) The Signature guitar's bass counterpart with the long 34½" scale length and a big tone. Sunburst was an option for both Signature models. *Courtesy Gary Hernandez, 2004*

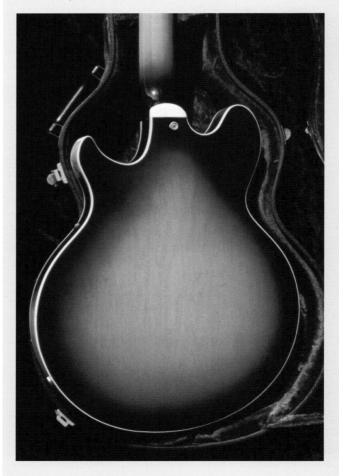

measures 3" by 1⁵⁄₁₆" and was fully adjustable with four slotted, semi-round screws. The entire pickup was encapsulated in the black antistatic resin epoxy material to protect the coils and reduce microphonics. Bill Lawrence developed this new trim, low-impedance pickup. He had the following to say:

Robb: What was the gauge of wire used on your Signature pickup?

Bill Lawrence: *I used fewer low-impedance turns, what you call 42-gauge wire.*

RL: So you went back to 42?

BL: *That's what Gibson had in stock.*

RL: And your coil forms—you had two coils.

BL: *Yes, the normal humbucker with two bars in.*

RL: But you under-wound those coils.

BL: *I wound them to low impedance—on that pickup, about 2,200. I don't know precisely. I mentioned, due to the particular transformer, I had to change the number of turns instead of using it with a low-impedance amp.*

Electronically, the Signature used a master volume and single tone control (two 2.5M audio taper pots) with a level rotary switch and phase "in-out" switch. The guitar's pickup selector was located way up on the top horn, unlike a 335. Gone was the individual tone mixing and decade control. The new impedance "level control" (a tapped step-up transformer) had three settings of 50, 200, and 500 to adjust to the amplifier or studio settings. Early catalog versions in '73 had two "chicken head" pointer knobs (the kind Les likes) with both low and high outputs on the side. The typical Signatures used gold speed knobs and cream surrounds (like an old Epi) with gold writing for the rotary controls. Its low-Z output jack was moved onto the face, while the high-Z out was still on the side. These dual outputs are a good way to record a live concert. Bill adds, "Plug that guitar into a low-impedance amp and it sounds great!"

Most Signatures have a lustrous, gold-finished top complemented with a light walnut-finished maple and "deluxe crème" body binding. The guitar's pointed cutaway had a uniquely curved plastic portion on the rim. Darker walnut shading was added to the heel and volute areas. Both instruments were available with a brown sunburst finish. Production totals from 1973 into 1978 count 1,400 gold, 380 sunburst, and 2 walnut brown examples.

Gleaming gold Les Paul Signature model #80682 with brown shaded maple back and neck. *Courtesy Freedom Guitar San Diego, 2008*

3

The Late Seventies and Eighties:
Anniversary Models, Specials, and Reissues

The Late Seventies and Eighties: Anniversary Models, Specials, and Reissues

During the seventies, Gibson began marketing special commemorative models to celebrate the upcoming anniversaries of the noteworthy Les Paul guitars of the past. They also had special models that featured themes with fancy woods such as the "Spotlight Special" and "The Les Paul." With the growing demand for the original Les Paul Sunburst Standard of the late fifties, Gibson issued their own Heritage Series in an attempt to recapture that old magic again with fancy figured woods and some extra elite features. Numerous dealers around the country also wanted to get their own recreations of the "holy grail" Sunburst model. Strings & Things, Jimmy Wallace, Leo's Music and Guitar Trader all had their own specially-ordered Les Paul replicas that earnestly tried to accurately recreate the all-hallowed '58–'60 Sunburst Standards.

Enter Norlin

In December 1969, ECL (Ecuadorian Company Limited) acquired Gibson's parent company, CMI. Founded by American E. Hope Norton in London in 1913, it was first set up to make use of the Panama Canal by running a cement business and railroad. By the sixties, they were exporting carnation flowers to America and operating quality beer breweries in Ecuador. Their first American enterprise, previous to buying into CMI, was called Aiken, an electronic and metallurgy company. Norton's grandson Norton Stevens became chairman and president in the late fifties. Unfortunately, the elderly Maurice Berlin was put out to pasture while his son Arnold, along with Norton, formed the new Norlin Company (an abbreviation of their two names). Although things looked good at first, rough times were ahead.

Norlin had considered manufacturing guitars in nearby states with easier labor laws. After a few labor strikes and loss of revenue, Gibson president Stan Rendell felt Nashville, Tennessee was less union-mandated, and

would meet the increased demand in guitars. Due to the different set-up procedures in the production of an electric guitar, the Nashville plant was originally planned for Les Paul guitars, but that soon changed in order to accommodate the new acoustic Mark series production. When that didn't pan out, solid-body construction began soon thereafter. They sent some key supervising personnel to guide the new facility and began hiring workers to begin production. Kalamazoo maintained their soft-tooling approach that was quite versatile for variations of models and easy modifications, while Nashville was set up with hard tooling, using their big machinery for set production designs. For the Kalamazoo plant, this simplified small production runs of special models—early Sunburst knockoffs, limited editions, and anniversary models.

Meanwhile, Norlin switched the incentives from profit to cost programs that soon undermined the Kalamazoo workers' initiatives for bonuses, raises, etc. Corporate red tape ensued, creating much frustration within the staff. Eventually, president Stan Rendell, who had been doing an excellent job, was now riding a fine line between maintaining his previous momentum and having to answer to someone else. He left in 1976 to start up a private-label producing string company called Sterlingworth, later bought up by Dean Markley. Consequently, Gibson was merely a brand name from 1979 to 1985. Things were slowly downsized and long-time employee Jim Duerloo was put in charge as plant manager in 1978, along with Marty Locke (from Lowrey Organs), who came onboard as president in 1980. Toward the end, they didn't know if either the new Nashville operation or Kalamazoo would be closing. With waning allegiance to fine Kalamazoo "Rembrandt" traditions, Norlin decided to close the plant's hallowed doors in July 1983. It took until June 1984 to move the big machinery south and let off the many employees. Jim Deurloo and many others decided to stay on by renting the grand old 1917 Gibson building. He bravely continued as Heritage Guitars with his trusted employees and devoted player following.

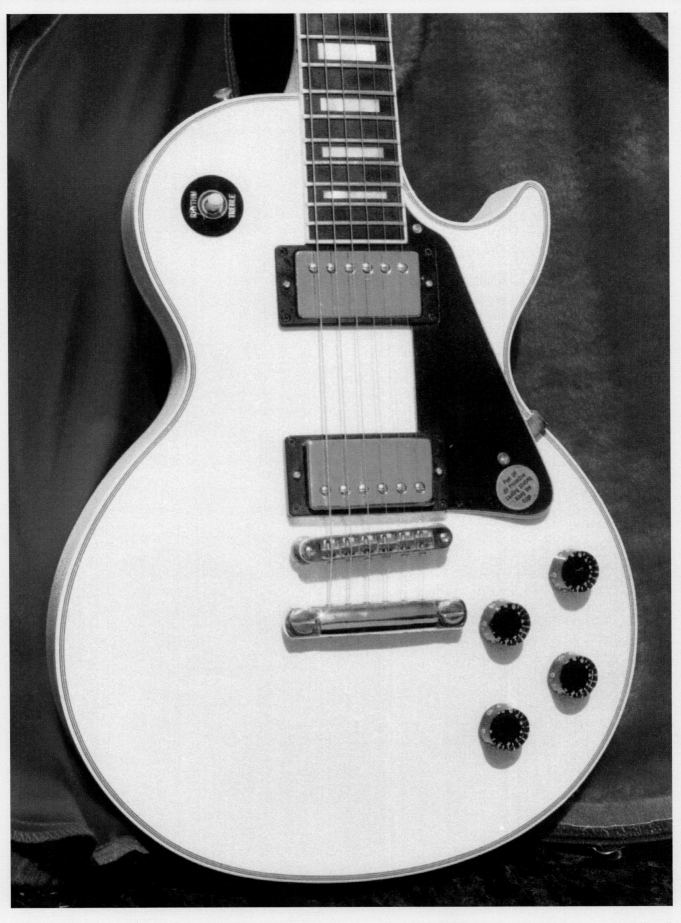

A virtually pristine white 1979 Custom Les Paul #298134 with original pickguard plastic still intact.Six-digit serial numbers were still used in Kalamazoo into the late '70s. *Courtesy Rich Stillwell, 2005*

Anniversary Editions (Les Paul Birthday Models)

20th Anniversary Les Paul

Although Gibson missed celebrating the original Les Paul model's 10th and 20th anniversaries, they realized the upcoming 1974 20th anniversary release of their classy 1954 Custom model was an opportune time to make a simple special edition. Although it didn't have the jazz-oriented, one-piece mahogany body and single-coil pickups, it was a modernized (and safely-marketed) version with twin humbuckings and a maple top. The only notation of the event was the "Twentieth Anniversary" words etched into the 15th fret pearl block inlay. It retained the current pancake body construction, three-piece maple neck, volute and the six-digit serial number with the customary "Made in USA" stamp of the period. Both black ebony and an off-white cream were offered, yet sunburst, natural, and other custom-ordered versions were available, such as this Rosewood edition. 20th Anniversary Les Paul Customs were quite successful and laid the groundwork for future birthday celebration models.

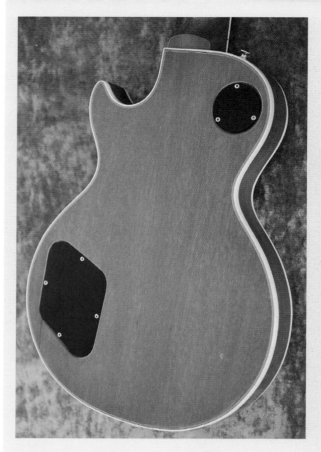

(Below) The 20th Anniversary Les Paul Custom was Gibson's first true birthday model that became a very popular seller. This extremely rare custom-ordered rosewood version (#100071) is quite striking. Mainly shipped in black ebony and ivory white, others were sunburst and wine red. *Courtesy Hollywood Guitar Center and Justin "the Killer" Slater*

(Above) Cross-banded bodies and three-piece necks were the norm for this period of construction.

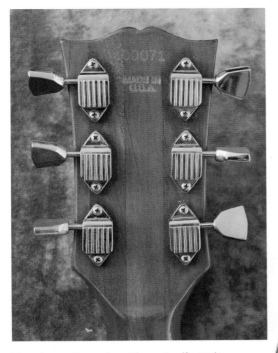

Note the medium volute, Kluson Sealfast Tulip tuners and low number. *Courtesy Hollywood Guitar Center, 2004*

25th Anniversary

The obscure 25th Anniversary model was a special edition commissioned by Hollywood's Guitar Center store in 1977. Oddly, the instrument was a Les Paul Custom model instead of the first 1952 model. This very classy guitar boldly featured a fine silver finish to commemorate the Les Paul guitar's silver anniversary and had the event nicely etched onto the stop tailpiece. The laminated black pickguards were also engraved into the white layer with the Les Paul logo. Most had chrome hardware, while some were gold. They had period Nashville bridges, tulip-styled Gibson Schaller heads, the attractive insert "top hat" control knobs, and the eight-digit serial number scheme. Nice job, Guitar Center!

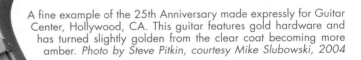

A fine example of the 25th Anniversary made expressly for Guitar Center, Hollywood, CA. This guitar features gold hardware and has turned slightly golden from the clear coat becoming more amber. *Photo by Steve Pitkin, courtesy Mike Slubowski, 2004*

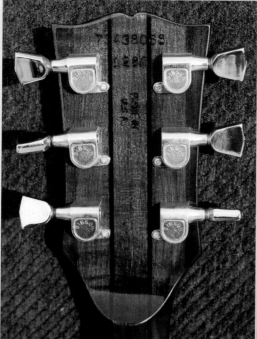

The five-piece stained maple neck with a large neck volute and stained imprinted numbers complete this double anniversary 1978 Les Paul guitar.

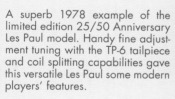

A superb 1978 example of the limited edition 25/50 Anniversary Les Paul model. Handy fine adjustment tuning with the TP-6 tailpiece and coil splitting capabilities gave this versatile Les Paul some modern players' features.

The 25/50 Anniversary Model

This magnificent celebration of both the Les Paul guitar and the start of Les Paul's professional career in 1929 was a true marketing success, showing the powers-that-be that you can market a high-end guitar with a valid theme. In-house designer/luthier Chuck Burge and mandolin expert Roger Seminoff contributed to this model by adding mixed hardware colors and the gorgeous F-5 mandolin antique Cremona styled sunburst finish.

Tasteful use of pearl and abalone make up the artistic 25th and 50th celebration logos designed by R & D's Chuck Burge.

Chuck gives us a heads-up on his input:

Robb: The 25/50 model was basically a silver anniversary and a golden anniversary. A golden opportunity.

Chuck: Well, nobody seemed to grab that idea. They said, "Let's call it a 25/50 anniversary," and kind of set me loose on it. I don't remember anybody ever making anything of the fact that the 25th anniversary was a silver anniversary and the 50th is the gold. I thought, "Here's a great opportunity to mix the hardware," because they never mixed silver and gold.

RL: Like a fine watch.

CB: We'll mix the hardware so that wear parts last like on the tuners. The buttons on the tuners would be chrome and the bodies would be gold. On the original prototype that I built, I had the tuners that were gold bodies. I pried the grease caps off them and put on nickel grease caps. Then I had nickel buttons with the gold screw. And of course with the gold body, then it was the silver screw to hold it down in place right in the nub. Same thing when we got back to the bridge. I did the gold bridge with nickel saddles because that was the wear part. You don't want to make that in gold, you'll wear it off. So I had everything completely mixed and matched.

Then the "divers flags" on the original prototype fingerboard were pearl on the outside and the center stripe was abalone. They ended up not doing that, but they did do the inlay on the peghead. I personally laid out and cut with a little handsaw the first ten 25/50 peghead inlays. I inlaid them by hand, which was the 25, the 50, and the banner with pearl. Then I took them out in the shop and set up a machine to post engrave them after they were inlaid in the head, which they had never done before. Then I did the vine part all in abalone, which is green because it's a plant. That's obvious. By the time I was done with all this mixing and matching with all this abalone and the silver and the gold, then marketing was saying, "We're going to put it out as a collectors' model. We're going to build only 3,500." Then of course, it went up later. Boy, them babies sold like hotcakes. Those were good.

The 25/50 Anniversary Les Paul model was a super guitar. The concept of honoring two events with both gold and silver appointments was a brilliant idea. The introduction of the original 1952 Les Paul guitar and the start of Les Paul's professional career in 1929 were jointly celebrated with this new model. The 25/50 finally hit the market in 1978. It was one year off, yet close enough to celebrate both anniversaries. Curiously, it was not included in the January 1979 Norlin price list catalog. "The Most Les" ads showed the exclusive belt buckle available to original owners after mailing in the detachable card. It also stated that the guitar had to be ordered by December 31, 1978, since it was a limited edition—properly noted with the extra four-digit serial numbers.

This instrument was accented by fancy Super 400 style split-block pearl fingerboard inlays coupled with an attractive pearl headstock pattern of both numbers, a banner and abalone vine. The creative use of gold and silver (actually chrome) on all the hardware parts is unique to these guitars.

Mail-in warranty card gave the original owner a special Symbolic 25/50 belt buckle. Guitar courtesy Albert Molinara, 2004

The back view shows its Custom-appointed bindings and refined details. Sturdy fiberglass and polypropylene compound Protector cases were standard equipment during the late seventies. This 10-lb. 4-oz. case sported red velour plush; its solid construction made it practically indestructible. The specially-designed contoured handle allowed it to be carried in both vertical and horizontal positions.

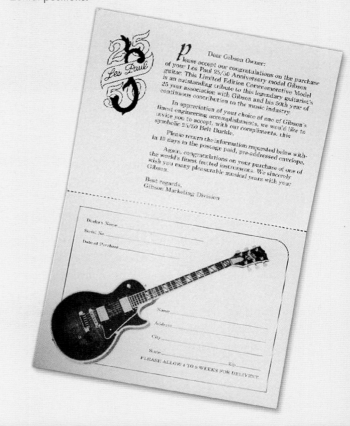

Concurrent to this era, it used a five- or seven-piece maple neck with two thin walnut pieces, a pronounced volute, wide cutaway binding, Nashville bridge, and the new TP-6 fine-tuning stop tailpiece. Other appointments included the engraved gold truss adjustment cover, Gibson's Schaller gears (with mixed parts), a lacquered brass nut, which was a popular addition at the time, and multiple-ply body and headstock bindings. Most of the metal on production models was gold, except for the polepieces and surround screws, bridge stud bases, tuner buttons, and lock-down nuts. The available finishes included antique sunburst, natural, wine red, black, and white. Roger Seminoff personally hand-shaded #0001 25/50 guitar, as on the new F-5 mandolin he helped create for a special presentation to Les Paul. Figured maple was the norm for all 25/50s models. Some were outstanding.

Electronically, this Anniversary model used two unique high-output Series VII humbuckings that were specially potted with a black rubbery compound that was difficult, if not impossible, to pull apart. Gibson used the normal wiring layout, but with a coil splitter two-way switch. In the down position, it disengages the non-adjustable coil in either pickup position for a brighter, less-muffled sonority, a bonus in the studio or with a large ensemble to cut through. Serial numbers followed the normal eight-digit designation, with the "Made in USA" stamped longitudinally and the four-digit limited-edition number. This popular Kalamazoo-built production run totaled 1,106 guitars in 1978 and 2,305 in 1979—just shy of 3,500. Evidently, their classy ads paid off and proved to Norlin that there was a market for more expensive models, even if times were tight. More of Les worked!

30th Anniversary

Gibson got back to basics with their 30th Anniversary Les Paul produced in Kalamazoo in 1982–83. It was a fairly accurate fifties Goldtop model reissue, but with the popular humbucking pickups and Tune-O-Matic bridge. Les Paul participated in this ad campaign with a warm, gleeful pose. Their "Vintage Voltage" ad, which exhibited a reflecting silhouette of the gold guitar, was quite eye-catching. This limited-edition guitar was also available with an optional all-gold finish (as on the original vintage Anniversary), one-piece mahogany neck (most were three), twin Tim Shaw covered humbuckings, chrome (sometimes nickel) hardware, speed knobs, and double collar Kluson machines to complete the instrument. This time, the anniversary inscription was on the 19th fret inlay. An unusual A, B, or C preceded the large inked four-digit serial number sequence with "Made in USA" stamped in wood beneath. The B variation was more common. This revival of the late-fifties Goldtop spawned the actual '57 reissue model the following year (1984).

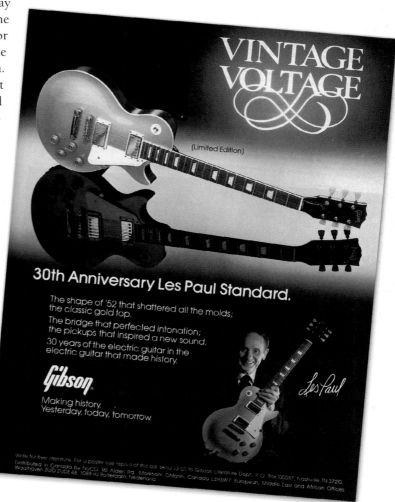

71

The Les Paul

First shown at the 1975 NAMM show, The Les Paul made its debut and totally surprised CMI's new president, Les Propp. It was the brainchild of president Stan Rendell and local talents of Kalamazoo luthier Richard Schneider. While traveling in Europe, Stan had bought a private reserve of well-seasoned top-grade Austrian flame maple that was intended for fine violins. The violinmaker had recently died, and the estate sold his specially aged maple to Stan. His initial idea was to use this amazing wood for 50 Bicentennial Gibson instruments for each state in the Union. This instrument was certainly the fanciest Les Paul at the time, and featured the finest combinations of woods. Carved rosewood was used in place of the customary plastic components. It was fashioned for the binding, pickup bezels, pickguard, switch surround and tip, truss cover, backplates, and knobs. Both Richard's brother Donnie and Gibson's Abe Wechter assisted in the project. With a basic lightweight mahogany core, they added the special maple across the back and sides, and used multi-colored strips of dark, light, and red-dyed maple for the border trim around the body and neck. Much of this trim was from the innovative Mark series acoustics.

Chuck Burge adds:

CB: Richard Schneider, who had already designed the Mark Series, was in process on The Les Paul when he did a lot of the work. Parts were made in the factory and whatever was appropriate to be handmade, instead, was all handmade and put together in Richard's studio six blocks away in the Saniwax Building where we all had studios. Richard was on the second floor and I was on the third.

RL: It had wooden knobs and a wooden pickguard.

CB: Not just wood, but rosewood.

RL: And rosewood pickup surrounds with an extra screw for pitch control, and this wide Schaller bridge?

CB: These are laminated wood and engraved into the wood, underneath which was red.

RL: As was this pickup selector switch ring.

Just looking at the spectacular backside could make a guitarist awestruck. Rosewood cavity panels contrasting on the book-matched Austrian maple with a dramatic flamed neck topped off these tour-de-force masterpieces. A special stitched-leather hardshell case with classy black velour and a gold Gibson banner complements The Les Paul guitars. Kudos, Gibson! *Courtesy David Brass of Fretted Americana, 2004*

CB: This was all Richard Schneider stuff, The Les Paul. So it ended up in R & D about '77, '78. Eventually, Richard Schneider kind of faded away because The Les Paul series was done.

RL: What was Dick's idea behind The Les Paul? All this rosewood everywhere?

CB: Just to come up with a really exotic Les Paul. Those guitars were $3,000 at the time.

No expense was spared. Such labor-intensive construction made this model so time-consuming and so costly that the 50 guitars planned for 1976 proved to be an impossibility. Manufacturing continued into 1979, with the guitars selling for $3,199—according to the January list price—a reflection of current high market values. The last versions used less red binding and plastic parts, since all the pre-done rosewood had run out after Schneider left town. Natural was deemed the premium finish, while others were a translucent ruddy red over the exquisite maple. Some sunburst versions exist, too. The final touch was the completion date engraved with the serial number on its pearl plaque above the tuners. The Les Paul, with its natural-wood highlights and fine Schneider finesse, became the most gorgeous of Gibson solidbody models.

The headstock was another exercise in laminations pearl and binding extravagance. The split diamond inlay is in abalone while the Gibson logo is mother-of-pearl. Its ebony and red maple truss cover was engraved for the guitar's scripted title. Note the laminated nut finely carved down between the strings. Somehow they forgot the dot on the "i."

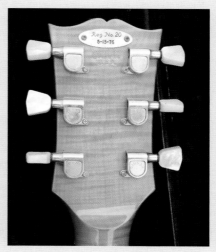

Gibson pulled out all the stops on this special-themed instrument, originally planned for the U.S. Bicentennial celebration. Independent luthier Richard Schneider was instrumental in creating this Gibson masterpiece with handcrafted rosewood and special red binding throughout. A third pickup height screw gave the humbuckings the extra angle adjustment for better coil-to-string placement. Schaller's flat bridge featured a wide movement for intonation.

Pearlized buttons adorned the Gibson Schaller gold keys. Its pronounced violin volute was visually appropriate on this inspired maple instrument. The date appeared only on these particular themed models.

This side view gives you an idea of the work involved with laminated rosewood and dyed red maple accents. The wooden flip switch knob tops it off! Also note the rosewood center strip down the ebony fingerboard and inset double red inlays within the black binding.

A heel view shows the cutaway with a full treatment of multi-colored trim alongside the rosewood contrasting binding. Such high-quality maple had never been used on a solid-body guitar before.

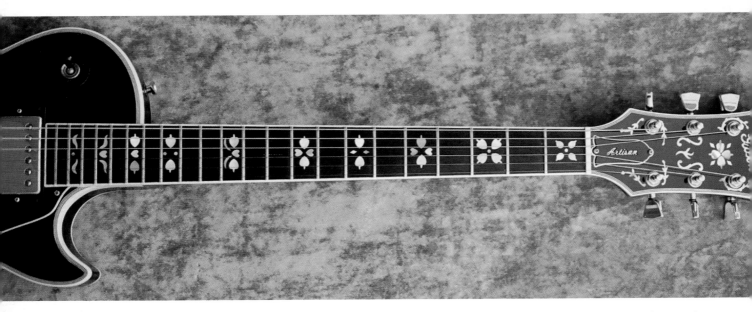

Fanciful Granada Banjo inlays graced this high-end Les Paul model. Traditional hearts and flowers with a thirties Gibson script logo set this distinctive Custom model apart from the rest of the pack. Earl Scruggs banjos also adopted these ornate patterns. Three gold pickups were on the first models and an option in later years. *Walnut-finished version courtesy Norm Harris, 2003*

Les Paul Artisan

Frills, bells and whistles…… loads of extra fingerboard trim, reminiscent of the early banjo days, was added to this fancy Les Paul Custom variation. Gibson's original Granada banjo design with the "exquisite hearts and flowers" patterns was artistically inlaid on the ebony fingerboard, along with the old-style Gibson script logo on the headstock.

Originally available in walnut in 1976, they were soon finished in black ebony, tobacco sunburst, or white. This model was first available with three pickups and then in 1978 with two Series VII humbuckings. The center pickup on triple versions used a "Super-Humbucking" pickup. Series VII pickups were a "special design that achieved increased output without sacrificing the effect of high and mid-range frequencies."

A new TP-6 fine-tuning tailpiece was also standard by 1978. Both the Les Paul and Artisan models introduced the TP-6 adjustable tailpiece. The 1978 catalog notes, "The new exclusive Gibson gold-plated instant adjustment fine tuning TP-6 tailpiece." It was a great idea, similar to the locking vibratos that were becoming popular, but it didn't cut up your hand as easily.

Says Chuck Burge:

> "The TP was Rendell Wall's. They found that they couldn't patent it because they had something that was too similar on a violin. But I loved it and I still have one on my Les Paul. I thought it was a neat thing. It had a nice look about it. It worked well. You could tune down without the string slipping out of tune then, unlike when you're tuning down with a tuner."

The Les Paul Artisan's overall fancy package included a one-piece mahogany body with a three-piece maple top, three-piece maple neck, no volute, multiple Custom style binding, built-in string winder tuners, diamond-shaped strap holders, and gold trim. Production began with two in 1976, and ended in 1982; the peak year was 1977, totaling 1,469. Prices were $1,039 for the LP Art and $1,139 for the extra pickup LP ART 3-PU. Guitarist Dave Davies of the Kinks used an Artisan with three pickups.

Les Paul Pro Deluxe

Essentially, the Pro Deluxe was a hybrid version of the Deluxe Les Paul, which had been retrofitted with cream P-90 pickups and an ebony fingerboard. Although earlier Deluxes were occasionally shipped with P-90s, this Pro version gave guitarists the smooth feel of ebony. Many still enjoyed the direct-sounding P-90 that came with the arched maple Les Paul guitar. Aluminum plates were still used for the pickup attachment. Laminated bodies were basically gone, but the three-piece maple neck was used with a large headstock and crown inlays. Tune-O-Matic and stop-setup was standard, with M-6 Schaller machine heads. Soapbar pickups blended nicely with the cream binding and speed knobs. Pros came in various colors, including black, cherry, and tobacco sunburst (all over), and sometimes in gold. The mid-priced Pro was produced from 1976 into 1982, and retailed for $839 in 1979, plus $99.50 for the sturdy Protector case. Many still felt the P-90 ruled the earth!

This hybrid Pro model was a desirable guitar for those in the know who appreciated the open sound of the single-coil P-90 and the smooth feel of ebony on your fingers. *Guitar courtesy Todd Stemmerman, 2003*

Les got into the act with a simple ad for a new walnut "The Paul" model in 1979.

The Paul

Here's an economy model made entirely of walnut with a dot inlaid ebony (c grade) fingerboard. The lack of binding enabled the body to be comfortably beveled or contoured on the front and back where your arm and chest meet the body. They were generally four-piece bodies and three-piece necks with laminated headstock wings, done in a smooth satin-type natural furniture finish. Headstocks were without any veneer, used a gold Gibson decal, and had "The Paul" on the truss cover. Necks had the volute, nickel tulip Grover tuners, and were imprinted with eight-digit serial numbers and "Made in USA." Electronically, they came stocked with dual exposed T-top humbuckings and four normal controls with the toggle switch right above, eliminating the long body channel. A laminated black/white pickguard and chrome standard Tune-O-Matic and stop/stud tailpiece arrangement completed the $529 budget Gibson solid-body. Introduced in late 1978, The Paul gave a lot of bang for the buck.

The Paul model with its walnut multi-laminate body, ebony fingerboard, and Standard components. Exposed humbucking were black coils, while this one sports a pair of Seymour Duncans. *Guitar and photo courtesy original owner Steve Kinkel, 2005*

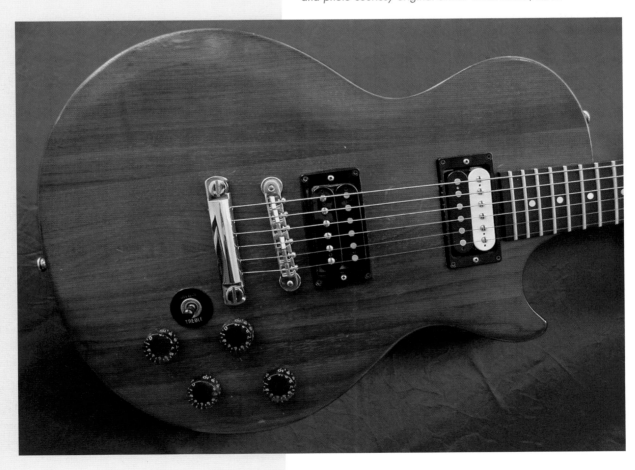

Les Paul KM

During 1979 in Michigan, Gibson released their current approximation of the Sunburst Standard—a Les Paul Kalamazoo model. The name alone was a strong statement that these guitars were, without a doubt, a Michigan product. Still built with Deluxe attributes, the Les Paul KM had a wide headstock, volute, three-piece neck, wide cutaway binding, and Nashville bridge. However, it did have full or half-cream exposed T-top humbuckings and a few sunburst finishes to choose from. Finishes included the antique sunburst, bright or deep cherry sunbursts, and natural. Shaded backs were also available. Their maple tops were generally two-piece and non-figured, yet some were nicely flamed. The truss cover simply said "Les Paul KM." Early versions had a "Custom Made" plaque that was placed either below the tailpiece or separately in the case, for mounting wherever you pleased. It was considered a limited edition, with 1,052 LP Kalamazoos sold.

This 1979 bright cherry sunburst Les Paul received the KM model designation as one of Kalamazoo's efforts to recreate the original late-fifties Standard. Some came with leftover "Custom Made" plaques (placed here on the side of the body). Its three-piece neck with volute, wide cutaway binding, and flameless tops prompted vintage aficionados to order a more accurate Les Paul Sunburst for their stores. *Courtesy David and Caroline Brass, 2004*

The Les Paul Artist

As keyboard synthesizers came into widespread prominence, active electronics also became popular with guitars. Gibson forged forward into this new field with their 1977 RD Artist series. Gibson's new R & D guys, Chuck Burge and Tim Shaw, came up with design ideas that incorporated some of Dr. Robert Moog's new electronics (since Norlin had acquired the concern). A non-traditional take-off on the Firebird idea was the first series to be released, but was met with little public support. Its unusual Gumby-esque shape and excessive maple-bodied weight hastened its demise. RD prototypes were first built with detachable necks that were quickly modified just before the show.

Continuing with the new active electronics idea from the RD Artist series into the ES-335 and Les Paul range, the Les Paul Artist model was born. "New Gibson active electronics featuring expansion and compression circuitry, a bright mode and two specially designed gold-plated Series VI active Gibson Humbucking pickups." The original RD Artist used one large three-way switch for the "selection of the expansion/compression standard active electronics or bright mode," and the dual volumes with bass and treble control knobs, which "act as expansion and compression intensifiers (front pickup compression, back pickup expansion)." All this actually used quite a large circuit board that wouldn't easily fit within the confines of a 13-inch Les Paul model. Tim Shaw redesigned the whole set-up to fit within the confines of two large routed areas of the back of the guitar. The two green circuit boards filled this enormous cavity with "state of their art" electronics. A convenient nine-volt battery compartment door was added just above. You always had to remember to unplug the guitar or the battery would expire.

Chuck Burge adds:

CB: The three switches were compressor, expander, and an active bright switch. It was Dr. Moog stuff. It was like the Entwistle spider bass stuff (which was never completed). That's where they finally got people going with having the onboard active stuff.

RL: You had to push to get the active electronics on the Les Paul guitar?!

CB: I had to fight for that. It was like pulling teeth, telling Bruce and everybody, "Why don't you have some onboard active stuff?" There were people with Les Paul copies already that have this. Come on! We should be the leaders here! It was 1978, for crying out loud.

Exquisite 1979 "Custom Shop Original" version of the Les Paul Artist (#10), built by Chuck Burge, with extra electronics, special contouring, and a beautiful flamed maple neck. *Photographed by owner Nick Ffrench, 2007*

Gibson's foray into active electronics led to this Les Paul Artist model based on the LP Custom. Created with modified RD circuit boards, the instrument utilized a master volume and bass and treble notched tone caps with + and - 0 to 5 control knobs. Brighter, compressed and expanded tonal settings were achieved with three mini-toggle switches.

The Les Paul Artist was released in 1979 on the Custom model platform with master volume, bass, and treble controls. The tone controls were center-notched neutral for adding (boost) or subtracting (cut) the active circuit. Three mini-toggle switches added brightness, compression, and expansion for the various enhancements. For a high-impedance instrument, it had myriad tonal variations, from glassy Fender tones to dark and woody jazz box sounds. For the Average Joe guitarist accustomed to simple electronics, it was a little more complex than they wanted to deal with. For the more advanced and savvy musician/engineer type, it was a versatile and sonically-expressive instrument.

Cosmetically, Chuck Burge came up with an attractive LP headstock design:

> *This was the active Les Paul (Artist). I designed a peghead inlay that had a lightening bolt weaving through it. In fact, my wife was telling my little son at the time, "Don't get too active or your father will put a lightning bolt on your forehead." (Laughs) We ended up calling it the flying f-hole inlay. That is all mine and I'm very proud of the flying f-hole. I talked them into doing the lightening bolt as a designation for anything with onboard active stuff. In fact, I started that with the RD Series. The active one that was an f-hole with wings had lightning going through it.*

Besides the new electronics, the LP Artist model featured a "scarfed" contoured back for more comfort against the chest, the new TP-6 fine-tuning tailpiece and two "Sustain Sisters," $5/8"$ brass submerged studs, and bridge attachments for added sustain (and more weight). Also helpful was the new "Posi-lok" strap buttons that helped insure that the guitar would not fall. Easily dropping a Les Paul guitar has been a problem all along, with the typically small front button. LP Artist models were available in black ebony (shown here), antique sunburst, and an attractive three-color antique Fireburst. They were produced through 1981 and cost $1,299, just above the Custom and Artisan models.

This 1980 ebony Artist model headstock has Chuck Burge's fanciful flying lightning bolt LP inlay and brass nut. *Courtesy David and Caroline Brass, 2004*

The Spotlight Special

One of the visually-unique Les Paul models of the early eighties was the Spotlight Special. What set it apart was its 2" walnut center strip, three-piece top with fancy curly maple sidepieces. Some feel that, with this dramatic-looking guitar, Gibson was proving they could build one of the most beautiful wooden instruments in the world. Although they sport the Custom Shop rear decals, many Spotlight Specials were built on Nashville's production line from various surplus woods (narrow maple pieces and leftover walnut from The Paul). Only 211 of these beauties were built in 1983; hence, the 83 XXX numbering scheme. Two basic models were constructed, both with gold parts and Standard style necks, with pearloid crown inlaid rosewood fingerboards.

The Antique Sunburst "ASB" version had quilted maple sides with cream binding, ebony head veneer, and definite variations in shading and book matching of the maple. The Antique Natural (ANT) versions utilized multiple brown and cream bindings on the body and fingerboard (from the Chet Atkins surplus). Headstocks used a stained walnut head veneer and Gibson Schaller pegs with pearlized buttons. Following the early reissue era cues, they lacked volutes, had mostly one piece necks, uniform cutaway binding, cream pickup surrounds, deep gold bell knobs, SP-1 tm. 17° head pitches, and light 9+ pound weight. Close your eyes and you'd think you were playing an '83 reissue Standard. Due to their rarity and distinctive good looks, these "Spotlighted Specialty" Les Paul models command premium prices today.

This beautiful Spotlight Special in antique sunburst is unusual, with its brown and cream binding and the walnut headstock veneer usually found on the natural ANT model. *Guitar courtesy Mike Slubowski, photo by Steve Pitkin, 2004*

Chuck Burge tells an interesting story of Les and the cross-banded tone:

Chuck: *Okay, you got $1\,7/16"$ of mahogany back on the body. Let's start out with $9/16"$ for the top. Between those two, lengthwise with the body, there's a veneer that went cross grain the other way.*

Robb: Like a sandwich.

CB: *There was a veneer a little less than $1/16"$ I think it was holly, because I remember seeing it. The grain ran the other way to hold things together better. The other thing was, as a lot of things go, it was an ease of manufacturing thing to put that cross-band in there. Because you throw the veneer through a roller just like on an old washing machine. Now this roller would roll glue onto both sides of the veneer. When it comes out the other end of the roller, it falls right on the mahogany body, somebody slaps the maple top on it, and they put it in the stack that's sitting in the press. The next one falls out and they throw the top on it and they put it in the stack. So you didn't touch anything that was glued. They glued both sides of the veneer, the cross-band and stuck it in there.*

RL: And that made it easier to put together.

CB: *Glue it together, stack it up, and press it. They would stack up bodies four or five or six feet tall when they were pressing them. Maybe a half-dozen stacks like that with the cross-band in-between them. It was just fast and easy to glue them up.*

We were wondering, "Wow, is there really any difference in the sound or anything with that cross-band?" One of the things with the reissue, and with the later models before the reissue, is that in the cutaway, the binding got wider and covered up that area where the top was glued on the back. So you wouldn't know by looking at it if it had a cross-band or not, because the binding got wider there. Well, the old ones in the fifties still had a 1/4" binding that just came up over that hill in the cutaway. If you looked in the cutaway, you could see where the maple meets the mahogany straight across there.

So Bruce said, "Make us two guitars that are both Les Pauls and they're exactly the same. Do one with a cross-band and one without a cross-band and let's see if they sound different. Then when Les comes in, we'll give them to him and see if he can tell the difference." I doubt it, is what the poop was on it. I built two bodies. The very next piece of maple in the board was the next guitar, so it was the same piece of wood. One-half of it went to this guitar and one-half went to the other. I did the same thing with the bodies and with the necks, all out of the same pieces of wood. We just basically cut it in half and made two guitars. One had a cross-band and one didn't. That's the only difference. Maybe there are some slight differences in pickups, but basically acoustically they were built to be identical except the cross-band. On both guitars I put a little piece of masking tape in the cutaway. They had the old-style binding now because it's a reissue. So you couldn't look in the cutaway and see the veneer or no veneer.

Les Paul came in and sat down in the lab and I told him what I had. I plugged him into an amp and I handed him the first one. It was already tuned up and ready to go, right? So he sat down and played the first one. And then he said, "Okay." I took that and handed him the second one. He sat down and played that. Without any hesitation he pointed and said, "This is the one with the cross-band in it." I peeled off the masking tape. That was the one with the cross-band! I couldn't hear the difference, but Les claimed to hear the difference without any hesitation. He was in his sixties at the time. There wasn't any hesitation. He picked it... he told me right out which one had the cross-band in it and which one didn't. So we ran the reissues without a cross-band and with the binding that goes up in the cutaway so you look right at it and see there's no veneer between the top and the back.

RL: *And the vintage nuts got what they wanted.*

CB: *Yes. Then production had to run everything with just one roller. You've got to split the roller apart so you can roll a thick, thick piece of wood in there. For one thing, I think you're going to tend to roll and glue on the back—on the face of the back of the guitar, the mahogany part, which is usually about 1 1/2" thick. You've got a two-piece top that's glued together in the middle of it. You're not necessarily going to want to run this glued-together thing through a bunch of pinch rollers, just to try and break it apart before you glue it down. So production had to take a minute longer to glue the damn things up and that was fine.*

RL: *So you solved that. What year did that happen?*

CB: *I'm remembering '78. I was designing and proto-typing and everything at least six months in advance to get everything done, because they didn't only want to get done with the prototypes and prove out wher-ever we had to prove out to have an appearance sample. In the case of the Les Paul, have Les look at it. But you also want to have a set of blueprints, all the changes, templates, and patterns I made up to go to the pattern shop, so they have something right off to work with, rather than just leaving them clueless. I don't think we ever did that before. They just said, "Here's the guitar!" and gave it to the pattern makers. I tended to figure this out in advance, because I was worried about them screwing it up in production. So it was probably '78 when I worked on it and '79 when it came out.*

Jim Durloo and Chuck Burge posing at the 2004 summer NAMM show in Nashville.

Heritage Series
Standard and Elite 80

Gibson's beautiful Heritage series was a valiant effort to get back to the original charm and depth of the Les Paul Sunburst Standard. Two choices were first available in the 1979 catalog for 1980. The Standard 80 came in vintage cherry sunburst, honey sunburst, or antique sunburst with rosewood fingerboard and nickel hardware. The maple was specified figured and some actually had exceptionally nice flame maple tops. The Heritage Standard–80 Elite, on the other hand, had a top grade smooth ebony fingerboard, nicely quilted maple top and came in all three finishes. A third model, the Heritage Award 80, was available in 1981 with much-figured maple tops (generally) and gold fittings. Supposedly only 50 of this exclusive model were built for dealers who sold the most of this series, but some think 300 is a more accurate count. All three models were considered a Limited Edition series, made into 1982.

The Heritage model's most notable visual difference from other Les Paul guitars was its slightly shorter body and wider radius cutaway with its more pointed tip. Binding in the cutaway was once again uniform as the originals and current Custom models. The carving of the top was purposely improved, "with highly figured traditionally sculptured carved maple top – .040 cream colored fingerboard binding." The standard model used a three-piece neck while the other two with ebony fingerboards had one-piece necks. Some Standard 80s had Elite necks, too. A return to the original headstock pitch, "Vintage SP-1 17-degree peghead" was reinstated. The neck volute was deleted from these early reissue models. Tapered "Top Hat" gold knobs with dial pointers were also specified (not all had the pointers, however). Standard 80 models had nickel plating, while 80 Elites had chrome fittings, although the catalog says nickel and showed gold on the guitar.

All models used the classy Grover Rotomatics with kidney-shaped buttons. Each of the three models had their particular designation on the truss rod covers in gold ("Heritage Series – Elite 80," etc.). Serial numbers were only four digits on the Standard 80 and Elite, while

Behold! The new Les Paul Heritage in all its quilted GLORY! The 1979 NAMM show guitar certainly turned many guitarists' heads.

Les Paul's Heritage Standard–80 Elite with beautiful bubble blister maple, a dark antique sunburst finish and ebony fingerboard. *Photo courtesy Neil Zlozower, 1981*

1980 Les Paul Heritage Series Standard-80 (#83050578 1089) in honey sunburst.

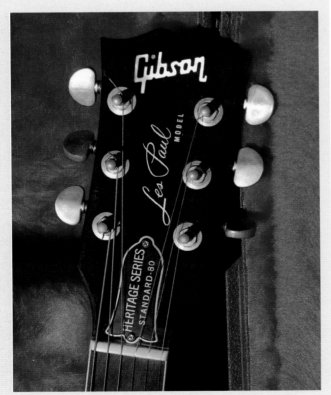

the Award serial numbers were on an oval pearl or white medallion on the back of the head. Dimensions stated in the catalog were 12 31/32" wide, 17 3/8" long and 1 15/16" deep. Scale was still their compensated 24 3/4" (24 9/16") and a comfortable 1 11/16" wide at the nut.

A new "Pat. Appl. For" humbucking reissue series was instigated for these guitars as well. New in-house pickup specialist Tim Shaw set out to recreate the original PAF humbuckings so sought after by the new crowd of player/aficionados. Tim really made an honest effort to recreate the best of the old pickup design and did a terrific job, considering the materials available. The most difficult thing was getting the wire coating correct. Many of these new modern PAFs came in full cream and half cream colored coils. The base plates were metal stamped with the old erroneous patent number (for Les's tailpiece) 2,737,842, a black three-digit number (or two three-digit codes) and soon had new "Patent Applied For" stickers affixed.

This beautiful early reissue series guitar was played by the late Steve Clark of Def Leppard fame. *Courtesy Lorelei Shellist, 2009*

Both Tim Shaw and Bruce Bolen had made a strong effort to persuade Norlin to release the new Heritage series. It was their quest to get back to basics with the finest production effort of yesteryear everyone was clamoring about. It did quite well and they were finally "On the road to 1959!"

This series evolved from the multitude of guitarists who wanted a more accurate representation of the original Sunburst Standard. In-house R & D luthier Chuck Burge made up some prototypes (from the old carving template) that were taken to the NAMM show.

Tim Shaw and Bruce Bolen deservedly resting on their laurels and preparing to play darts in the office. *Photo courtesy Mitch Holder, 1983*

Robb: What was involved with creating the Heritage Series '59 model. It was your first response to come up with an old-style Sunburst.

Chuck: *I remember the Heritage was a reissue. The tops are carved more concavely. Basically, there was no design work to do about it, but what I did was the tops. I went out in the mill room and found the old fifties sample [1954 carving template]. I brought them back down into the model shop and started carving new tops that were more concave, more violin-like. I made heavily-contour tops, sanded them by hand. They went to the show like that.*

One of the problems with that situation was that when we actually started production, they put it on the machine that carved the top and it didn't matter how much they would contour that top. I would make a new sample to put up, (the piece the machine would run on to carve the tops) and we would carve them more deeply. The problem was, they would go on the stroke sander. Now this is a sander where you put the body on the table and it rolls up underneath the sandpaper going by, with a 30-foot roll. They would put a block of wood or a paddle on the top of this. This started hitting off the high parts, missing low parts and bringing it back to the stupid old dumb thing. It was good for Gibson Kalamazoo, but for quite a while then you could tell the difference between a Kalamazoo Les Paul and a Nashville one because they killed the top with sanding. The Nashville tops were kind of a gentle dome and the Kalamazoo was more dished.

It took people with long years' of experience, and every time I built a model, I made the templates and blueprints or I would instruct Dale how I wanted to do the prints. I went out to every section of the shop, out in Gibson where it was important for somebody doing a certain job, and talked to the people at the bench doing that job. I said, "Here's what's important!" With that Les Paul reissue I said, "What's important is that you give a gentle once-over and don't kill that top. Don't take off too much, because we're looking for this deeper dish kind of thing." It worked there for a while.

An attractive catalog page depicting the 1980 Heritage Standard-80 Elite model in cherry sunburst.

LES PAUL STANDARD-80 ELITE

BODY SPECIFICATIONS
Solid mahogany body with exquisitely figured traditionally sculptured carved quilted maple top • Single cutaway • Cream colored body binding • Adjustable nickel-plated Tune-O-Matic bridge with nickel-plated stop-bar tailpiece • Cream colored fingerrest • Original specification "Pat. Appl. For"™* nickel-plated Gibson Humbucking pickups with cream colored mounting rings • Individual volume and tone controls • Tapered "Top Hat" gold knobs with dial pointers • 3-position toggle switch for pickup selection (individual or both pickups simultaneously) • Body size: Length 17-3/8", width 12-31/32", depth 1-15/16"

NECK SPECIFICATIONS
Traditional 1-piece solid mahogany design • Width at fingerboard nut 1-11/16" • Vintage SP-1 seventeen degree peghead • Ebony shaded head veneer with Les Paul model script and Pearl Gibson inlay • Highest quality ebony fingerboard with Pearl inlays and corresponding side dots • .040 cream colored fingerboard binding • Nickel-plated kidney shaped individual machine head buttons • Gibson truss rod with distinctive Heritage Series truss rod cover • 22 frets • 24-3/4" scale length **LES PAUL STANDARD-80 ELITE** • Vintage Cherry Sunburst, Honey Sunburst or Antique Sunburst Finish Complete with the "Classic" Faultless plush lined case

*Trademark of Norlin Industries
Not notice of patent application

(Left Guitar) The Heritage Award #039 in vintage cherry sunburst with a nice maple top. *Photo by Steve Pitkin, courtesy Mike Slubowski, 2004*

(Right Guitar) The Heritage 80-Elite in honey sunburst with a quilted maple top. *Photo by Steve Pitkin, courtesy Mike Slubowski, 2004*

(Left) The Heritage Award serial number plaque with Grover tuning pegs.

In early 1982, Los Angeles ace session player and Gibson enthusiast Mitch Holder visited Kalamazoo to pick out a body for a Les Paul 12-string. He took these great pictures on his tour of the factory with Gibson A&R man Pat Aldworth. The following photos show some of the processes involved in how a Les Paul guitar was produced.

Here's enough maple and mahogany to make 100 Les Paul flametops!

This happy worker proudly holds some fine bubble maple.

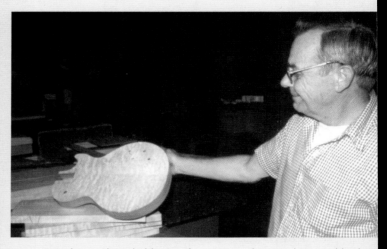

James "Hutch" Hutchins, holds up a fantastic maple-topped Les Paul body.

A bevy of leftover bodies marked accordingly, with some old necks on top.

A mill room master body marked "deep dish carving form, LP Elite Standard '81, 2-17-82."

The hand-held jig set-up is used for rough shaping necks. It takes a steady hand and even pressure to operate this procedure successfully.

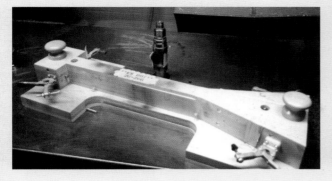

Moose trims off the rough edges from shaping with the spindle carver.

Routing internal cavities on SG models.

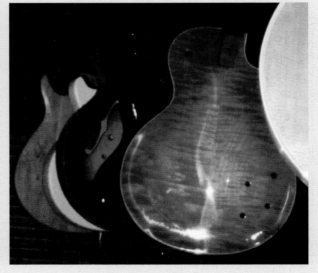

The worker is fine prepping the neck tenon for a good fit.

And in goes the neck!

A rack of curing bodies with a great flametop LP standing out.

This lady is fine trimming around the Gibson logo.

Bassist Dave Kiswinew is holding up a bursted guitar in process.

This worker is holding a freshly-painted Artisan.

Six humbucking coil forms are being prepared for winding.

The coils are fully wound with their copper wire.

Rows of finished gold humbucking pickups.

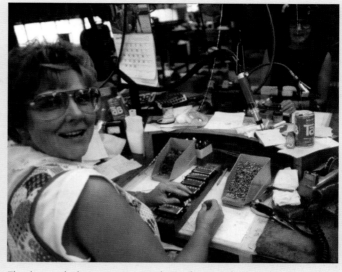

This happy lady spring-mounts the pickups to the bezels.

A very nice flametop at the final setup table.

Pat Aldworth holding a great body reserved for Mitch Holder's 12-string.

A 1983 side shot of the 1917 Parsons Street Gibson factory across from the railroad tracks.

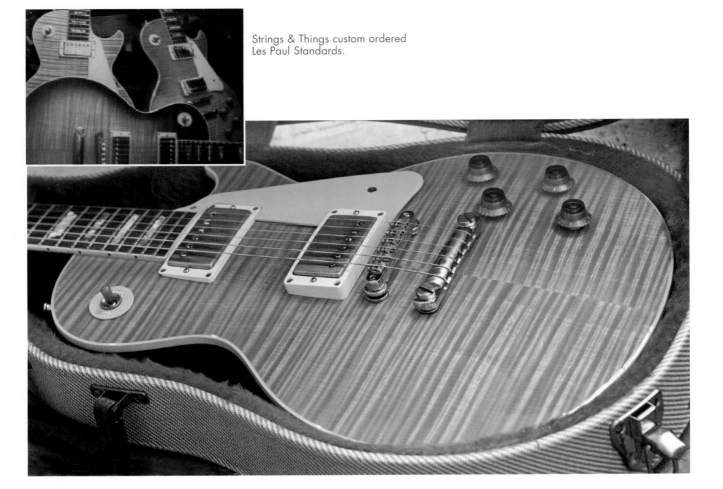

Strings & Things custom ordered
Les Paul Standards.

Dealer Specials

With such a growing interest in vintage guitars and with various stores wanting a more real-looking Les Paul Standard built to vintage specifications, Gibson began receiving custom orders to accurately recreate the original 1959 model. Different parts of the country each had their own store models from the mid-seventies into the eighties. Most of the early ones were production models completed as custom-built specials. Kalamazoo's Jim Deurloo first coordinated these "Sunburst specials" as close approximations of the original top carvings, neck profiles, and cream binding attributes. For these times, many guitarists were elated to have a very select replica of the ultimate Les Paul model.

Strings & Things Les Paul Models

During the early seventies, Strings & Things vintage guitar store in Memphis, Tennessee began customizing new and old Les Paul guitars into various forms. They soon became known worldwide as one of the best musicians' stores in America. Stax and Sun recording studios attracted many great players to visit, too. Custom work featured inlays like "My Gibson" in old script on Les Paul heads, double-neck Juniors (glued together). They also added original humbuckings to redone Goldtops (hence, Jeff Beck buying the famous Oxblood Les Paul that he used on *Blow by Blow*).

In 1974, many local customers—along with others around the country—were wondering how to get an original-style Les Paul Standard. Owners Chris Lovell and Greg Lawing contacted Gibson. They discussed the originals with the shop foreman and ordered a couple of prototypes. With great anticipation they arrived a few months later, apparently with unusually-shaped cutaways. Gibson tried again, but this time with the proper jigs. When they arrived, Chris exclaimed, "They're right as rain!" Over the next four years, four batches of six were built with various types of flame maple. Most were shipped with a thin natural finished top so they could have the resident experts do their specialized vintage sunbursts.

Chris Lovell tells what was happening back in the day:

Chris: *We did a lot of finish work. No one really finished guitars much to speak of in our area and Gibson certainly couldn't get any colors right. We were good at restoration or coming up with making a new guitar look old with vintage finishes by Tommy Stinson and Tom Keckler's help. We were also cutting Les Paul Juniors—the top off of one and bottom off another— and making double-necks out of them. Back then we didn't know any better. It was like Frankenstein.*

Robb: *Then you started ordering Gibson vintage-style Les Paul 'Bursts fairly early on.*

CL: *Ours were the first. I'll tell you the story behind it. All anybody ever wanted was a flametop reissue of late-fifties Les Pauls. Some wanted a sixties neck and maybe others wanted the '58, '59. All in all, they wanted the same guitar—maybe with a little different neck—but the guitar wasn't available. You had all these guys playing them—Clapton, Page, Walsh— everybody and his dog playing a guitar that wasn't available. So we just decided to get Gibson to build them right. Gibson reissued the wrong everything. They reissued a black Custom with Fretless Wonder Frets, which was useless to a rocker anyway, because it's impossible to bend notes. Then they reissued a guitar that was never made, which was the Les Paul Deluxe with baby humbuckers. I thought, "My God, all anybody wanted was a Goldtop or Sunburst Standard, and the two things they reissued were anything but that." All in all, they missed the one guitar.*

We drew up the specs for what we wanted and figured we didn't need to draw the thing for them; they already knew how to make a Les Paul. So we got the first two and they were wrong! The cutaways looked like a can opener. You could look and say, "That's not right!" So that's when I got the guy at Gibson in Kalamazoo on the phone and said, "These cutaways are just wrong. I think somebody just hand-sketched these or something. They are not right." He said, "Oh, yeah, they're right." I said, "Nah, I bet you if you had the blueprints and put them up..." He said, "I'll send you the blueprints." So he sent me the original blueprints and sure enough, we laid the guitar down on it and, just as we

suspected, the cutaway was wrong. So we sent the guitars back to them and said, "Your blueprints are right. These guitars are wrong. Can you build them to your blueprints." So they did another run of six. At this time they were charging us $750 apiece for these guitars, if you can believe that. We sold them for 15 and we didn't discount them a penny to anybody. We sold everything we could get them to build. I think we built 24 total and we may have lost four of those when our store burned down in 1978.

We then started ordering them in lots of six. When the next ones came in, they were cool except that the cherry sunburst was so cherry it was terrible. They were way too red and yellow, so we stripped the tops and then reburst them to a faded burst. Stinson was the main guy doing that. So we called them back for the next run and said, "Okay, here's what we want. Just finish the back and the sides and neck. Don't finish the top." He said "Okay." Then he called back and said, "Can't do this. We don't send guitars out unfinished." I said, "Okay, tell you what, just put clear on the top." So that's what he did. They would clear the tops and that was easier for us to remove. I think maybe five or six got sold without us doing them. They did one in viceroy brown that looked awesome. It was cool with gold parts. So that's kind of how we did it from there on out.

RL: *Did you have a chance to choose the wood?*

CL: *No, they did it. That guy in the shop was picking out some great stuff. Not much of it was the same. They all looked pretty different, so he was using all kinds of different woods. Some of them were fiddle back maple. Some of them were like crazy looking maple, like more of a burl to them than just a tiger strip.*

RL: *Nowadays, because of their obscurity, it's often hard to properly identify them without documentation.*

CL: *None of the vintage collector guitar gurus knew what those guitars were. We never advertised them nationally. They were all sold to local people because we couldn't get enough of them, anyway.*

These first custom-built String & Things Les Paul Standards were made fairly close to vintage specs for this early reissue period. They featured narrower headstocks, mahogany necks without volutes, fairly accurate top carving, and the uniform cutaway binding. Some later ones, however, were made with three-piece necks for stability. Altogether, Kalamazoo produced four runs of six, totaling 24 vintage-style Standards for them from 1974 into 1978. The first two were later given to Kiss! "Strangs & Thangs" (the local drawl) 'Bursts retailed for $1,500 during the mid-seventies. This might have been a bit steep then, yet they were indeed special instruments and well worth the investment.

When visiting Memphis in 1972, along with seeing the new Strings & Things store, we went to Mike Ladd's Music City, directly across the street from Elvis Presley's Graceland. He specialized in vintage instruments and made special visits to Gibson's secret backroom during the late sixties. Along with scoring a unique fifties korina Flying V without parts, he unearthed the original Epiphone Les Paul double-cutaway prototype guitar. This all-mahogany "Rarebird" features a slightly thinner body, identical Standard cutaways, Custom-front binding, a contoured back, and the typical Epiphone wider headstock. It is now owned by guitarist/collector Robert "RJ" Johnson, a talented Memphis musician who played with many local stars with his many vintage Gibsons.

"It's amazing how much a cranked Les Paul sounds like a violin."
—Chris Lovell

One of the last Strings & Things true reissue highly chatoyant flame-top Standards, built in 1978. Tommy Stinson first lightly bursted the guitar, which is now faded to "lemon-drop" and with old PAFs added in '79 and a three-piece mahogany neck. *Photo courtesy original owner William Correro, 2006*

A vivid green burst graces this 1993 Jimmy Wallace reissue #3-9019. It weighs in at 8.033 lbs. Gazing at it is like being in a deep-quilted maple jungle! *Courtesy Barney Roach, 2003*

Jimmy Wallace Les Paul Models

Texan guitarist/dealer Jimmy Wallace has been playing and selling vintage guitars for many years. While working at Arnold & Morgan music, he took off for Kalamazoo with his '59 Standard and ES-335 in tow with vintage reissues in mind. Jimmy began ordering fine vintage-style Les Paul Sunbursts for his dedicated customers in 1980 and was honored to have them entitled under his own name.

Naturally, they have many of the same vintage attributes of the other Sunburst knockoffs, yet with their own subtle differences. Jimmy first ordered guitars from Kalamazoo (with Tim Shaw's PAF pickups) and continues getting models from Nashville today. Wallace LPs also came in many other interesting colors, as seen here in green. Early versions had his name in block letters on the truss cap and then went to a cursive script logo. Later models had a small Wallace sticker inside the control cavity. Jimmy's Les Paul models also came with distinctive figured tops in varied quilt and flame patterns. Some early models were built with korina wood (African Limba) in place of mahogany; they change hands for considerably

more. His models generally had a fuller-shaped '59-type neck, while later versions were slightly thinner. Serial numbers began with the eight '58 prefix and also used nine and zeroes. Jimmy and Mark Pollack founded the original Texas guitar shows during the mid-seventies. They always have a great guitar booth and musicians from all over the world congregate to buy the best vintage guitars on the market.

Here's Jimmy's story:

That's the first one (shows picture in layout). As a surprise, we did 50 335s with J.P. Moats—with real union orange labels, not copies. At the time, I was a Gibson endorsee and on the Gibson advisory board. The district and national sales manager came in. I said, "I understand why you made these changes to the Les Paul from a sales standpoint, and you're constantly selling these things. Why don't you make anything in the traditional sense?" He pointed down at his Rolex watch and said, "This is why." I was 20 years old at the time. I said, "I don't get it. Because of this?" And he said, "What you want won't keep buying me these Rolexes." I asked him, "Can you do it?" He replied,

"Do what?" I asked, "Can you reproduce what was done in the fifties?" He said, "Absolutely."

So, long story short, I flew to Kalamazoo. I already had a Gibson endorsement as a musician. I took an original '59 Les Paul of mine that was my player, along with my '60 Dot ES-335. We started dissecting the guitars. There were no records of the initial instruments to speak of, regarding how to reproduce them. They didn't care. It was all just going to work. The first order was 100. They sent them to us ten at a time. There were 50 335s, 40 blondes, and ten sunbursts. The wood was out of their woodbin, which was a couple of stories high. We would climb up these old ladders and someone would pull them down to me and I would say, "Yes, no, yes, no." With those first 100 guitars, they sent me Polaroids of the tops and I would say yes or no. So, every one of the first 100 was hand-picked. We started the whole thing in 1977 and I received the first one in 1978. It was a great guitar. When they came in, much to my surprise, they had my name on the bell piece! There had been no mention of it, and I hadn't asked for that. Here's the cool thing... When you ordered these, you couldn't piggyback anybody else's order at all, flat out. You couldn't say, "I heard so-and-so is getting this, so I want to do it." What you had to do was go in and instruct your order screw by screw—every aspect, in other words. That was a fair way to do it.

All our guitars on the first run were done in Kalamazoo, as were many subsequent runs. We stayed with Kalamazoo till the last minute they would let us build something there. On the first batch, Seymour Duncan bought one. He got one for Jeff Beck. Tons of people came out of the woodwork. And the Japanese swooped up many of the first ones. It has been a fun project and went way into the nineties. We recently started doing them here again. [The Custom Shop continues to builds the Wallace LPR-9.]

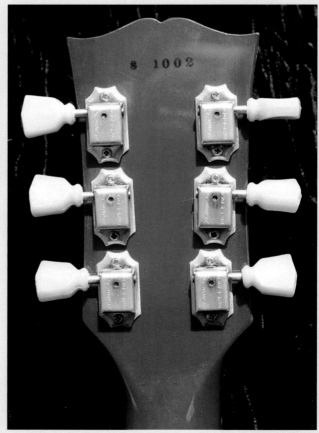

(Top) Attractive cursive script truss cap writing on this Jimmy Wallace model. It has a normal period Gibson logo. The Wallace models were reissues with the model logos properly placed in the center.

(Bottom) 1958 through 1960 style serial numbers were used on Jimmy's reissues, this one being #8 1002.

(Opposite Page) This early 1981 Jimmy Wallace reissue #8 1002 has shading similar to a 1960 Standard and very evenly-striped medium-curl maple. Pots are stamped "137 8010" and "137 8011" (March 1980). *Courtesy Fretted Americana, 2005*

Leo's Les Paul Reissues

Leo's Music of Oakland, California also jumped on the true reissue bandwagon. During late 1981, Rich Bandoni headed up the effort to oversee this quite collectable and accurate Les Paul Sunburst. In conjunction with collector/dealer Norman Harris (who showcased them in Southern California), they sold around 500 Sunburst Standards between 1981 and 1985. Leo's Music had a contract with Gibson for a series of refinements to create a their exclusive Les Paul Sunburst. They coordinated their efforts with Jim Deurloo and Pete Markovich at the factory to create a remarkable '59 reissue for that period. Bill Stapleton and Glenn Quan both worked at Leo's Music over the years and championed vintage Gibsons, sparking the local zeal for these great new guitars.

Leo's Music sales flyer showing their three Les Paul reissue models available. *Courtesy Rich Bandoni*

Shown here is an early Leo's Reissue Burst # L1 0035 with tight fiddle-back maple and bright cherry sunburst. This 1982 instrument weighs 10.5 lbs with pickup outputs of 7.52k and 7.33k. *Courtesy Fretted Americana, 2006*

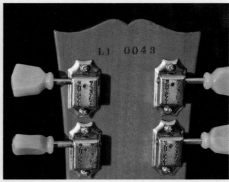

Gibson Deluxe Kluson tuners with single-collar opal grips accompany this low serial number sister guitar.

This early Leo's Reissue 1982 Les Paul Standard #L1 0043 (80892011) has tight fiddle-back maple and bright cherry coloration (shot during sunset) used in their ad. Real Pat. Pending pickups were added by owner. *Guitar courtesy Chuck Kavooris, 2003*

Single-collar Klusons with their distinctive L1 number.

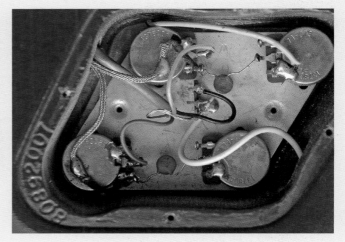

Typical period cavity with plate-mounted electronics (protective can removed) showing production stamp for #L1 0035.

Rich Bandoni tells us how it happened:

I was hoping to buy a great fifties LP reissue. I originally had high hopes for the Gibson Heritage series Les Paul, but after finally seeing them, I was disappointed as the body shape and numerous other features were way off from a fifties Les Paul guitar. My next hope was a Les Paul that Jimmy Wallace was having Gibson build for his store, Arnold and Morgan Music in Texas. I ordered one, got it, and again was disappointed. The shape and binding in the cutaway were wrong, as well as other issues. At the time, I owned a real '59 Sunburst, '54 and '57 Goldtops, and had sold quite a few fifties Les Pauls while working at Leo's Music in Oakland, California. Leo's was a mecca for famous musicians and known for always having a great selection of vintage instruments.

Next, I was at a friend's place and saw a Japanese guitar magazine called Young Guitar and saw a great-looking Les Paul Sunburst in a nice fifties type brown case that looked like a really good copy of my '59. The friend I was visiting said that he could get me one if I was interested. I was interested! The guitar was a Tokai. Once I got it and compared it to the current Gibson Les Paul Standard and the Wallace, then to my '59—the Tokai was the closest to the '59! Next, I talked with Leo Malliares (Leo's owner) about doing our own LP reissue. He thought it was a great idea. I gave the then-rep Pete Markovich a call. He talked with the appropriate people at Gibson—Jim Deurloo, head of production; Lane Zastrow, VP; Tim Shaw, electronics; Rene Brezniak, marketing—and the project was a go.

I sent the Tokai to Jim Deurloo with a letter listing 14 changes that needed to be made for the Leo's reissue on August 10, 1981. By the middle of September, I got the first prototype. It was a great first attempt. I called Jim and suggested some minor changes and decided to order 100 units initially—a gamble. Leo's received 100 at the end of October 1981. Fifty went right to Japan through the Hikari Trading Co., as well as Okada International. The remaining 50 sold by year's end. Our cost for the guitar was $850. They were sold to Japan at $1,650 wholesale and the average American sale price was from $1,600 to $2,200, depending on the flame. Gibson had a problem with production and

initially would commit to building only 250 instruments for 1982, but that number was later increased to 400-plus, again, with almost half going to Japan.

At some point, I decided to get validation on the guitar from Norm Harris, a well-known collector. He thought the guitar was great and became Leo's only US seller, much to my happiness.

The bad news came when I was told that the Kalamazoo plant was closing and the guitars were now going to be made in Nashville. I really wanted all the guitars to be made in Kalamazoo, for the obvious reason. I went to the Nashville factory and was shown a prototype. It was good, but not quite right. I brought one of my '59s to Nashville and left it there to be analyzed and copied. I was sent another prototype from Nashville that was great, so production went ahead. Around this time, Leo's one-year exclusivity was winding down and I heard that Guitar Trader in New Jersey wanted to make a reissue. Knowing this in Nashville, I asked to see all the flame maple the plant had. All the wood was good, but I cherry-picked my favorite flamed pieces. The rest went to the Guitar Trader. There was plenty of great wood left, but first I got what I liked best.

The quirks that set the Leo's LP apart are as follows:

The serial numbers started at L1 0001–L1 for Leo's and the production year 1981. The regular Gibson production number is etched around the lip in the control cavity. Also, I purposely had the Les Paul silkscreen and Gibson logo set higher on the headstock. My motivation was that I didn't want forgeries made out of the Leo's guitar without a hassle. The pickups were Tim Shaw designed PAFs done in both solid black coils and zebra colors. We didn't do full cream because of the DiMarzio color issue. The headstock eventually had a holly laminate rather than the plastic overlay Gibson was using at the time. The Kalamazoo guitars had the correct large sidemarkers, while Nashville's had smaller versions, much to my dismay. The cases were the vintage brown cases that Gibson was making at the time. I think the overall production was between 400 to 600. Also, two other prototypes were built, a '57 Goldtop brown back and a '56 all-gold P-90 LP.

Another bright cherry sunburst Leo's RI Standard #L1 0205 with tiger flamed maple. *Courtesy Norm Harris, 2003*

Leo's L1 0205 regulation headstock with high logo (with the G on fire!).

Norman Harris recalls their efforts to get Gibson in gear for these early reissues:

They had contacted me and said, "We know you have had a lot of original ones and we want to figure out what Gibson is doing wrong and what can we do to improve it." We made some corrections to the guitar, and at the time, it was it was a lot closer to what a real one was than what they were doing with the Heritage series. They did some for Guitar Trader and some others like Strings & Things and Jimmy Wallace that were very nice, too. What we did was look at some old ones and point out what needed to be done to try and correct them. I think they did very well with them. That led up to today with the Historic ones that are fairly close. Whenever you're dealing with a big corporation, things go in little steps.

Cutaway view of Norm's Leo RI showing vintage-style construction.

Kalamazoo-built Leo's models had the eight-digit control cavity numbers while the later Nashville production models had written initials and a date. Although they were built for a few years, serial numbers retained the L1 before the four inked numbers. Most are medium in weight and have nicely-figured tops with various flame patterns. These reissues were sprayed with either a bright cherry sunburst or a special honeyburst finish. Bay Area luthier Ken Fidkin helped Gibson dial-in the subtle honey color sunburst finishes. Leo's also had a few goldtop reissues made up, one of which was shown in their flier. Cases were fair representations of the fifties 535 versions but with furrier plush and an insert to keep the guitar from bouncing around. Between 1982 and 1985 they sold around 600 Sunburst Standards to many eager West Coast and Japanese customers.

Honey faded February 1983 Sunburst Leo's RI Standard #L1 0377 with nice figuring. *Courtesy Bernardis, 2006*

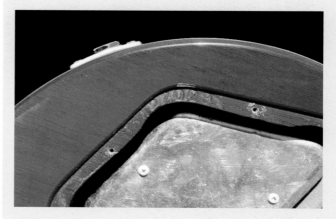

Telltale 1982 Kalamazoo stamping sign showing its authenticity.

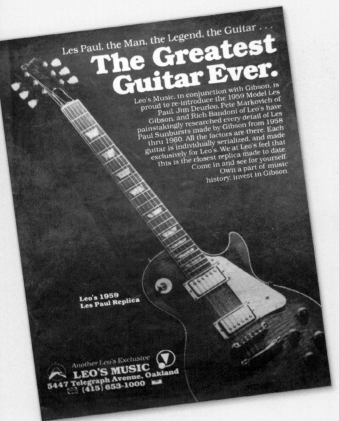

Advert in BAM magazine for the Leo's '59 sunburst replica showing #L1 0043. *Courtesy Chuck Kavooris, 2003*

(Above) Close-up of this '82 reissue's "Patent Applied For" humbucking pickup. Note the deep neck tenon and "Made in USA" stamp within the pickup cavity.

Serial number stamp L1 0264 and later Gibson Klusons with diagonal stamping. Note the evidence of the trimmed rings.

Nicely-flamed 1982 cherry sunburst Leo's RI Standard #L1 0264. *Courtesy Jim Mead, 2003*

Norm's Rare Guitar NRG Models

After helping Leo's Music do their sunburst creations, during the late eighties Norm Harris began ordering some very fine reissue models under the NRG title to satisfy his numerous customers. These fancy versions led to the introduction of the Historic Collection series (that actually featured a NRG on the first catalog cover).

Norm recounts the story:

> *We did another one, which was not the Leo's model, but one with the NRG on the back of the headstock (for my store). That was in the late eighties, early nineties. Those were even closer. A lot of it had to do with top contours and headstock details, lightweight, things like that. There were a number of things we asked them to do for us to try and make them a little more authentic. Some had monster tops on them and heavy chevron with wide flame, since I was paying them $500 extra per instrument. I was trying to do it on a low key, since everyone else would be trying to do it. It's something I had worked out with Gibson and didn't really advertise it, just sold it to my players like Mick Mars and other celebrity clients. They are very collectable today. A lot of them are in Japan. We were doing a number of them (40 or 50) and eventually Gibson brought one to the NAMM show. They had it next to a regular '59 guitar and everyone wanted one of mine. Everyone said, "I don't want that. I want this one." It caused so much of an upheaval that they stopped making them for me. It became a problem for them because buyers wanted the lightweight and special fancy woods.*

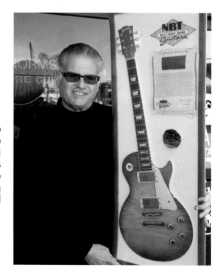

Norm also made up some novel, life-size NBT (Next Best Thing) cardboard prop guitars for people to embrace as if they were holding the real 1959 Les Paul in the picture.

Guitar Traders had quite a realistic headstock with the correct Gibson logo, custom truss covers, and authentic nut materials.

Modified old-style Gibson Deluxe Klusons and smaller font numbers were used on these Guitar Trader models.

Dramatic figured maple with deep brown chocolate shading give this 1982 Guitar Trader reissue Standard #9 0913 a distinct character all its own. This one was shipped with 50s "PAF" pickups. *Courtesy Nigel Taylor, 2004*

Modern Gibson wiring with a raised plate was standard with these early reissue models. Serial numbers (#82232037) stamped along the ridge further identify the instrument.

Guitar Trader '59 Flametop

After seeing fairly inaccurate Gibson Les Paul Sunburst models on the recent market (KM and Heritage series), Dave DeForrest and Tim Kummers of Guitar Trader in Red Bank, New Jersey decided to pursue a far more accurate 1959 Standard representation with great figured tops. They made a concerted effort to coordinate the building of these rare reissues including picking out very nice quarter-sawn maple tops and overseeing various details. Their first newsletter announcing the collaboration with Gibson to recreate the '59 Flametop touted an extra bonus: "If you order it by December, you can have real vintage parts, subject to availability."

Their true obsession to '59 details resulted in owner Dave DeForrest visiting Gibson in May 1982 to pick out 25 book-matched flame maple tops from 200 sets. Small details were addressed, including a square channel routing, the proper "rhythm-treble" switch font, neck pickup, output jack position, and accurate top contour specs. Besides adding real PAF pickups to the first 15 orders, such things as bridges, knobs, and truss caps that didn't quite meet their vintage reissue requirements were supplanted with custom vintage parts. Even double-collar Klusons were trimmed to single specs.

Particulars on the headstock included accurate Gibson logos with the open "b" and "o" with the dotted "i" and very similar, but smaller, inked-on fifties type numbers, e.g., 9 0923. Inked numbers varied starting from eight to zero. To set them apart from the other reissues, the vintage style silk-screened Les Paul logos were distinctively closer to the truss cover than other Standards. The additional eight-digit number coded scheme is stamped into the control cavity on the upper ledge corner to properly identify them. Codes seen have a 172, 223 or 225 day stamp between the split '82 year with the last three sequenced lot numbers, e.g., 82252052 (80892007). Some other Gibson Standard productions coincided during this period with similar eight-digit codes, making Guitar Trader paperwork essential evidence besides the telltale 900 number.

The vintage arching, correct cutaway shape with small binding, larger side dots of translucent red celluloid, and headstock specs round out this very accurate reissue model from Kalamazoo. The color, however, was definitely a ruddier brownish red in the sunburst and a deeper cherry red, filler-stained mahogany back. They took a unique 1959 Standard to Kalamazoo with a darker burst to develop this color. Early models sold had actual PAF humbucking pickups (which today make them more collectable) and retrofitted vintage hardware (if so desired). Rhythm pickups were properly placed, slightly away from the fingerboard. Correctly-sized pickup rings were supplied by Larry DiMarzio. They were first available with Tune-O-Matic bridges with C-clips inserted and later with Allparts bridges. Most Guitar Trader Sunbursts featured Tim Shaw's fine PAF replicas. Guitarist and vintage connoisseur Brad Whitford of Aerosmith graciously did some advertising for the '59 Flametop Guitar Trader Reissue. He even traded a re-necked '59 flametop for his double-white PAF pickups installed on his own GT 'Burst. This older LP was later used as a template for the very last models.

Brad Whitford of Aerosmith proudly holding his new flametop Les Paul model with real full cream PAF pickups.

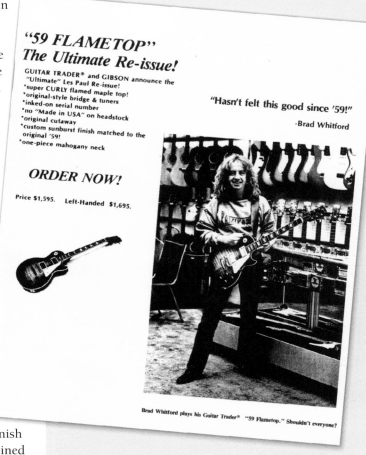

Guitar Trader's hip monthly newsletters featured a vintage instrument article and ran an advert for their '59 "Ultimate Re-issue" Les Paul model. This issue introduced their reissue '59 Flametop.

Tim Kummers elaborates on their '59 reissue endeavor:

Robb: *How did Guitar Trader's '59 reissue idea start?*

Tim: *I was on the sales floor and every guy who came in to buy a Standard 80 complained that the body was ¹/4" short. Now they didn't at first. Guys came in to buy them for the tops. Eventually, because we did that little magazine, I decided maybe we should do a comparison between a real '59 and one of these reissues like we did with the Flying V. When I compared the two, the measurements looked like they were off. It looked like the tailpiece was in the wrong place. They also had a severe belly on the top of the Standard 80s that was maybe a little too pronounced, but that didn't bother anyone. It was kind of like a refreshing thing. At least it didn't look like the plank that they'd been doing. But the body was a full ¹/4" short, setting the tailpiece practically level with the neck volume knob. It should be set much further north. The KM model was actually more fifties accurate looking than the Heritage Standard 80s. These were small things that could be refined. I said to Dave, "Do you think they would do this thing right?" Basically it was customer pressure that made me request that he at least ask them.*

Dave got in touch with Deurloo and started arranging to go out there. First they said, "Let's make you a prototype," which is how we got the first one. They sent it out. The body was correct as far as the length, but the color was a little off. We didn't want quilt. We really wanted tiger stripes. The biggest thing was the length of the body, the one-piece neck with a rosewood board, and an open "b" open "o" logo. Now all of those small little things in my comparison came up. They said we could do this and do that. The only thing that we requested was that they fell short on was the neck joint. Dave, in his infinite wisdom said, "Let's not fight them." It's not apparent to the end user—until they plug it in and play it. (Laughs) In those days, appearance was everything.

Dave went out there and took pictures of maple blanks. They weren't even shaped like guitars, just blanks of wood. He numbered them all before he flew back. And then I picked through them in Red Bank. We would just call and tell them which ones were acceptable and which ones weren't.

RL: *You added various parts for the first versions.*

TK: *We mounted the PAFs. I personally hand-soldered them in. There were no original rings or truss covers, so we made truss rod covers that were accurate. Gibson used only the double-ring Klusons. We had to saw off, individually, one of the two rings on every one of the tuners. I did it with a little saw, cutting on one side and then turning them over to the other side. We did them on the guitars! We used a little one-sided saw. If you look at any original tuner from that period, you'll see that it's pretty primitive.*

RL: *The ruddy sunburst colors were unusual.*

TK: *There's a footnote to that. We had a real '59 that we used as a color sample. It was a little more translucent. There was a subtlety to it that's hard to describe. It was a guitar that we had that was almost on the verge of a darker tea kind of color. This is a little browner than that, but it was definitely in that same vein. Not in the tobacco vein but kind of in that iced tea vein. Dave took it to Kalamazoo and they looked at it. We didn't give or send anything to Gibson in those days! (Laughs)*

RL: *Did you put any bridges or old knobs on them?*

TK: *In those days, those parts were available. If the customer wanted to buy knobs, he could have bought a set of four for about $50. Tune-O-Matics we didn't do. There were two variations on them we did do. Gibson wouldn't ship it without the wire retainer, so we wound up having to fit each individual saddle with really small clips so they wouldn't fall out during normal string changing. By the eighties they just didn't fit very snuggly. Without the wire retainer, they were falling out every time you tried to change a string. The stainless steel C-clips we put on all the screws and the saddles. We also used some Allparts bridges that didn't have a wire string retainer. That was toward the end of the run. Maybe a dozen guitars got those. We also used different volume and tone knobs. Gibson used those really dark amber things, so we used Allparts versions that were more authentic-looking. They made better-looking vintage parts than you could buy back in those days.*

RL: What about the decreasing work force in Kalamazoo affecting the delivery?

TK: That's what we were getting from them on their side. I think it was more about whether the factory was running up to their expectations. I can only guess why they weren't delivering to us on time. Actually, all of the 47 were pre-sold. We never hung one on the wall. They were ordered before they ever showed up at the shop.

RL: The first ones must have sounded great with those original humbuckings.

TK: They did. Even the ones with the Shaw pickups sound amazing. Now these guitars are over 20 years old. When you find one that's been played a bunch, it's a good guitar!

According to their September 1983 bulletin, apparent delays were announced due to the decreasing workforce in Kalamazoo. They had to notify the anxiously awaiting customers (with pending $750 deposits towards the $1,495 list) that delivery was slowed down. Orders before July '83 were delivered later that year, while early '84 orders were finally filled that following summer. During January 1984, Jim Deurloo sent quite a few letters. One stated the relevant facts behind their combined efforts and authenticity of this reissue (included in their newsletter). Another note announced the eminent closing of Kalamazoo in June and emphasized the need to get any last orders in soon. This newsletter flash about the situation "insured the lasting value of our Kalamazoo production '59 Flametops as collectors items." After the increased $795 deposit, another $800 was due upon completion of these last instruments, for a total of $1,595. At the time, vintage Sunburst Standards listed in their newsletters were well over five times this price.

Along with the quilted-top cherry sunburst prototype #B1 0001, 47 were originally built during two spread-out completion runs of these special guitars. Date codes show the two runs were begun in 1982 and finished over that two-year period. One lefty was built and only three were designated as 1960 models starting with a zero serial number. According to Tim, all these had "wicked" tops. One of the sixties has an amazing "shattered glass" figuring. All still had the ruddy coloring, however.

After their Kalamazoo production fizzled, a handful of finely-crafted, real-looking cherry Les Paul Sunburst copies were built by their ex-repairman/local luthier Michael Dresdner and a friend from Pennsylvania. Their tops were shaped from Whitford's '59 and featured the tonally-desired longneck tenons. They were to have the new Guitar Trader logo in place of Gibson on the headstock and '59 Flametop silk-screened. Nine of those ten said Gibson, so a cease-and-desist order was issued by Gibson. Definitely a Gibson and Lester Bozo no-no!

For the time, exceptionally-accurate details, finely-shaped necks and outstanding tonality with the traditional Kalamazoo craftsmanship vibe marked the Guitar Trader '59 Standards. Many agree these particularly rare models are quite collectable due to their higher build standards and the fact that they are one of the first historic Sunburst reissues.

This beautifully-quilted Guitar Trader reissue #8 0831 was originally stamped 82252052 on Friday the 13th, 1982 weighing in at 9.4 lbs. Quilted maple, electronics dated 1979, pickups read 7.25 and 7.21k. *Courtesy Fretted Americana*

Les Paul Standards & Flametop Reissues

By overwhelmingly popular demand, the humbucking-equipped Standard was officially reintroduced in late 1975. It retained the previous lightly-domed arched top, wide cutaway binding, and cross-banded body. They were available in gold, natural, wine red, ebony, and cherry and dark sunbursts. Production was slow at first, but by1977 the pace picked up and sales were brisk. The original two-piece body was reinstated during 1978 while three-piece maple necks with volutes, wide headstocks, and eight-digit stamped serial numbers continued through the late seventies.

In the early eighties, they finally took on some of the Heritage models' current updates with the Standard 80 and 82 models in Kalamazoo. Four-digit ink-stamped serial numbers (e.g., 0001, etc.) were used between 1980 and 1982, with inside production stamped sequence numbers below 500. Limited editions in new vivid colors also were released (some with gold parts, ebony finger-boards, and stamped eight-digit numbers). Solid metallic red, Ferrari red, blues and a dark green complemented the cherry, honey sunbursts, and gold finishes. Goldtop Standards became Heritage Standards into 1983. Even a handful of custom-ordered 12-string Les Paul guitars were produced in Standard and Custom versions.

Continuing the Les Paul Sunburst Standard guitar in Kalamazoo took on a new light as the workforce thinned out and morale weakened by 1983. Fancy maples were oftentimes featured in those last years, some with spectacular one-piece tops as the torch sadly passed from Kalamazoo.

A unique Bahama blue model shipped in 1981 from Kalamazoo. Gibson's West Coast competitor also had an international color scheme that ran concurrently. *Courtesy Larry Meiners, 1997*

This rare Ivory 1984 Standard is cream-colored, matching the binding perfectly and contrasting with the black plastic and rosewood fingerboard. *Courtesy Gary Hernandez, Del Mar, 2005*

A stunning natural Standard 82 in its amber-flamed glory. *Photo by Steve Pitkin, courtesy Mike Slubowski, 2004*

LES PAUL STANDARD

BODY SPECIFICATIONS
Solid mahogany body with carved maple top • Single cutaway • Cream colored body binding • Adjustable chrome-plated Tune-O-Matic bridge with chrome-plated stop-bar tailpiece • Cream colored fingerrest • Two large chrome-plated Gibson Humbucking pickups with cream colored mounting rings • Individual volume and tone controls • 3-position toggle switch for pickup selection (individual or both pickups simultaneously) • The new ultra-safe Gibson "Posi-Lok"™ strap button • Body size: Length 17-3/8", width 12-31/32", depth 1-15/16".
NECK SPECIFICATIONS
3-piece solid maple construction • Width at fingerboard nut 1-11/16" • Rosewood fingerboard with deluxe inlays and corresponding side dots • Cream colored fingerboard binding • Chrome-plated individual machine heads • Gibson truss rod with distinctive truss rod cover • 22 frets • 24-3/4" scale length

LES PAUL STANDARD • Cherry Sunburst, Ebony, Natural, Wine Red or Tobacco Sunburst finish
535 Faultless plush lined case

1980 catalog page showing a wine-red example with the new Standard attributes.

Very nice 1985 Les Paul Standard (#5 0305) considered a pre-Historic model with added Seymour Duncan rhythm pickup. *Courtesy Sean Cummings*

(Right) Bruce Bolan and Pat Aldworth contemplating how to customize the Les Paul Standard with new complex circuitry. This 1983 catalog page reminds everyone Gibson made—and continues to make—custom instruments.

The Custom Shop

Gibson has always been more than simply a source of outstanding instruments. For professional players whose music is a living passion as well as a livelihood, Gibson is a Mecca of ideas, expertise, technology and know-how. It's a place well-marked on the map of stardom.

Musicians come to Gibson to locate that most elusive of musical qualities — a "sound." Not just a fresh sound or a new sound, but a voice all their own, so unique and magnetic in its appeal that it becomes a virtual signature in sound — a personal trademark.

And they come to Gibson to be "fitted" with instruments unlike any they could buy in a music store, even from the Gibson line. They may want a slightly different neck or a particular body configuration — one or more of a hundred variations and alterations that personalize an instrument and make it "feel right" in their hands.

The Custom Shop is, in every sense of the word, Gibson's "tailor." Here concepts are transformed into finished instruments, one-of-a-kind guitars created under strict quality specifications by a highly specialized team of luthiers and craftsmen.

The instruments are beautiful. The materials and workmanship incomparable. Each bears the indelible stamp of individual achievement.

If you would like more information about the capabilities and services available in the Gibson Custom Shop, contact your local Gibson music dealer. He or she can put you on the path toward designing the instrument of your dreams.

26

1983 catalog depiction of the Les Paul Standard, extolling its long-standing virtues. Straight-ahead Standards were generally plain maple examples, as shown here. They utilized the new version of "Pat. Appl. For" humbucking pickups.

Brilliant 1983 catalog spread with a true exploded view of the Standard and its construction techniques.

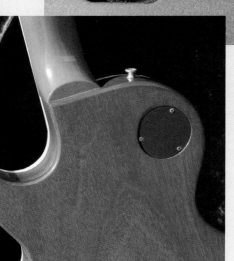

Beautiful 1988 Showcase Edition Goldtop Pro from a series of exclusive Custom Shop monthly models. Silverbursts, Standards, and ruby red Customs with EMG pickups were also made. Note the unique P-100 stacked-coil pickup construction. *Courtesy Ian Cohen, Malibu, 2007*

The Heritage series faded during 1983, but these special models were soon revamped into the new Les Paul Reissue Flametop (now known as '59 pre-Historics). It became their own flagship reissue with highly flamed maple and many of the vintage 1959 attributes that eventually led up to the real Historic models of the early nineties. Vintage refinements took a firmer hold, virtually coincid-ing with low production dealer reissue specials. They were constructed with one-piece necks without volutes and uni-form cutaway binding. The LP Reissue Flametop and Standard were on a course of constant but slow refinement. For the next ten years (1983 to early 1993), the large inked-on serial numbers adopted the old style (gapped), with the first digit for the last digit of the decade's year (e.g., 3 xxxx), as they moved into the nineties Premium Plus models.

By 1983, Gibson was promoting their new Reissue Model with flame maple, which was becoming much like the special dealer-ordered reissue '59 Standards. Also depicted are two Customs and Standards, all with 1959 Reissue humbucking pickups.

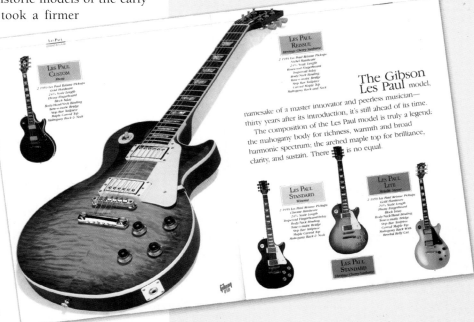

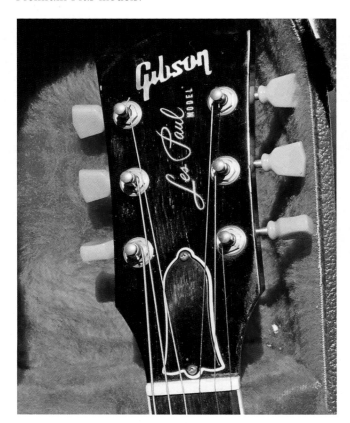

Michael's '88 LP reissue's headstock in the furry pink plush. Details include Gibson logo with open lettering and single collar Klusons. Note the extra top padding for neck protection.

1988 RI serial number reflected in the large eight-number sequence. Gibson Deluxe Kluson style tuners round off this fine instrument.

Beautiful 1988 (pre-Historic) Les Paul Reissue HCSB (Standard flametop) with paperwork that replaced an early 1960 flametop Standard #0 0608 featured in Volume One. *Courtesy Michael DeTemple, 2003*

As Nashville continued the Les Paul guitar with their own hard-tooled production, the Standard and Reissue remained two of Gibson's most popular models. It retained the popular maple/mahogany construction, sunburst or colored finishes, and chrome or nickel parts on through the eighties. The somewhat subdued red, but more authentic-looking, Heritage Cherry Sunburst was added to the line in late 1987 and is still a favorite today. By mid-1988, other colors were added—Alpine white, vintage sunburst, and even a short run of silver bursts. P-100 equipped Goldtop Standards were a limited run in 1989.

Picking up where the other dealers left off, New York's Sam Ash stores sold a limited run of Les Paul Standard CMT (curly maple top) models beginning in 1986 until mid-1989. Thick cutaway binding, metal input jacks, and stamped eight-digit numbers were used, however. These curly top versions soon became a popular East Coast "Les Paul Reissue" series with the Heritage cherry sunburst. The 1987 catalog featured a large representation of the flamey reissue Sunburst in all its resplendent beauty, all the time getting closer to capturing the original 1959 essence. The 1988 Gibson USA catalog was booklet-sized, with captions written by in-house expert Tim Shaw. Les Paul Standard models included the Heritage Cherry Sunburst Les Paul Reissue (flametop), Reissue Gold Top (both with nickel parts), and a plain Sunburst Standard with chrome hardware. These humbucking models used the 1959 Les Paul Reissue pickups.

LP Reissue Gold Top
Antique Gold

Les Paul Standard**
Heritage Cherry Sunburst

Available in left-handed styles at additional charge

Standard catalog description for 1988 showing their mainstay in plain trim—chrome parts, '59 LP RI pickups, solid Nashville TOM, and a plain-to-lightly-figured maple top.

(Left) Considered the "Goldtop Reissue," this antique-gold-finished '57 model had the same basic specs as the Les Paul Reissue.

This Les Paul Reissue depiction starts off the 1988 catalog, featuring a "perfectly flame maple top" and nickel parts.

Les Paul Reissue
Heritage Cherry
Sunburst

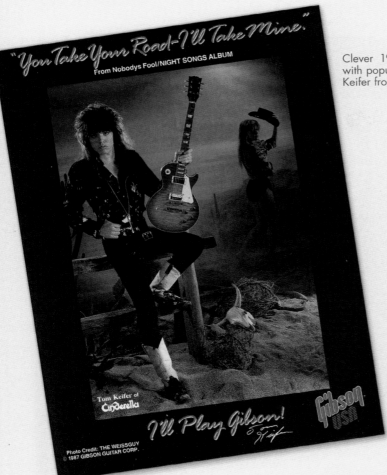

Clever 1987 Gibson ad with popular guitarist Tom Keifer from Cinderella.

Pat Traver's original custom-ordered, double-cutaway Sunburst Standard with Floyd Rose vibrato system. *Guitar courtesy Barney Roach and photo courtesy Rick Gould*

(Left) Brilliant guitarist Mick Ronson with David Bowie played Les Paul Standards and favored this natural one. One of the nicest guitarists I ever met in the business. *Photo by Neil Zlozower*

115

Les Paul Custom Models 1975–1989

Custom Les Paul models continued through the seventies with a big following, thanks to Peter Frampton, Mick Ronson, and new young players like Randy Rhodes—plus various metal and country guitarists. White became a popular finish, while wine red, natural, and sunburst models sometimes had two-piece flame maple tops. The early-sixties style reflector bonnet knobs were reinstated, thankfully. Unusual lacquered maple fingerboard versions were available from '75 through '81 on black and natural finished Customs. Jumbo frets finally arrived by 1975, thanks to popular demand. The sandwich-constructed body gave way to a solid mahogany piece with maple in 1977, and the volute disappeared in 1980.

The triple-pickup versions (considered a Special Edition in 1977) and Customs with nickel-plated parts were also available in natural, ebony, and wine red (as a limited edition '79 catalog model and from '85 to '87). Silver Burst became a new color option from '79 to '82 that went from a deep grey black into a light silver. It was a popular limited edition and was complemented by a spectacular golden burst Custom model made during 1981 in very limited quantities. With the gold hardware and contrasting black parts, the burnt copper to gold burst was one of the most attractive of all custom-colored Les Paul Customs. Fancy Gibson Schallers, with a novel swing-out windup apparatus for quicker string changing, were used in the early eighties.

During 1984, a sunburst "Super Custom" model was produced, first in Kalamazoo, then in Nashville. Maple veneers on the back and sides complemented the curly maple top. Super 400 slash-block neck inlays, LE on the truss, and one exposed humbucking also set this Limited

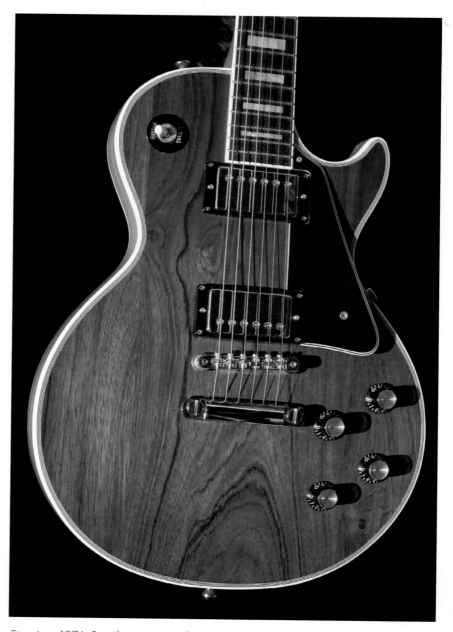

Stunning 1976 Brazilian rosewood-topped Les Paul Custom #377182. Owner Rick Norman received a 1979 letter from service manager Ken Kilman at Gibson estimating they built between 50 to 100 of these special editions.

Edition model apart from the normal Custom. A run of 250 Ruby red finished "Showcase Edition" Customs were also released in March of '88 with active EMG electronics.

Refinements took place as the reissue fervor continued with improved arching and removing the unpopular volutes and laminated body construction. The fancy Les Paul Custom models seemed to maintain a quality standard many other models didn't always possess.

A nicely faded 1976 white Les Paul Custom.
Courtesy Shane Gudlow, Timewarp Music

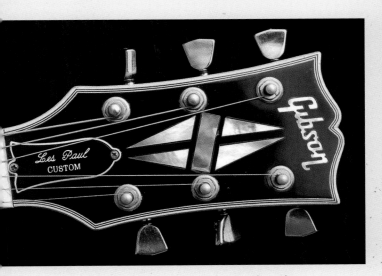

The 1976 LP Custom head, clearly showing the etching marks outside of the inlays.

The model's name was used on their headstock decals for a few years in the mid-seventies, along with a 00 designation for 1976.

Gibson's newsletter featuring the LP Custom during 1978.

(Below) 1980 catalog depiction of tobacco Sunburst Custom mentioning the 3-piece maple neck, ultra-safe "Posi-Lok" strap button, and exclusive Gibson "crank" button.

Randy Rhodes poses with his cream Les Paul Custom. *Photo by Neil Zlozower, 1983*

The famous 1978 Les Paul Custom that Randy Rhodes performed with over the years. *Photo by Neil Zlozower, 1982*

Adam Thomas Jones, guitarist and visual artist with the band Tool, and one of his three silver burst Les Paul Customs. *Photo courtesy of his talented wife, Camella Jones*

The striking "Gold Burst" LP Custom #81701503. *Photo courtesy Paul Moskwa, PM Blues*

1983 catalog page with the Silver Burst Custom parts.

1980 LP Custom in Silver Burst shading. *Courtesy Don Breeze, 2005*

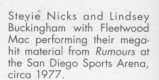

(Below) Influential guitarist Steve Clark of Def Leppard playing one of his many Les Paul Custom models on the 1987 *Hysteria* tour. Photographed by his ex-fiancée Lorelei Shellist. Steve "The Riffmaster" enthusiastically showed this author some of his favorite Les Paul guitars at the L.A. Coliseum during the 1983 *Pyromania* tour.

Steve Clark's 35th Anniversary 1989 Les Paul Custom #9 0179 triple-pickup Black Beauty. This '54 reissue used the traditional all-mahogany body construction, yet featured the more popular three-humbucking setup. Serial numbers started with a 9 for 1989 and were inked on cream numbers in larger size 2 font. *Guitar courtesy Lorelei Shellist, 2009*

Stevie Nicks and Lindsey Buckingham with Fleetwood Mac performing their mega-hit material from *Rumours* at the San Diego Sports Arena, circa 1977.

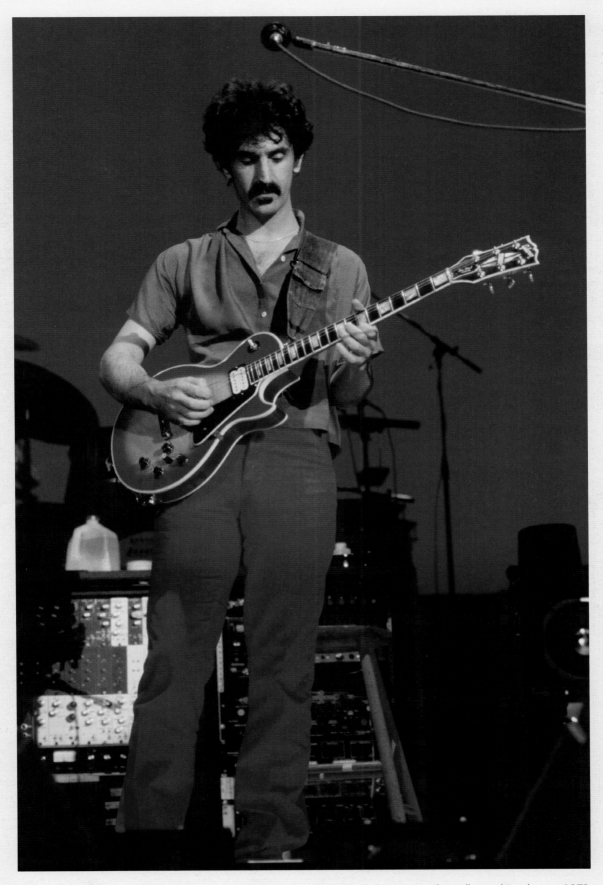

Frank Zappa performing live, awash in red with his cherry sunburst Les Paul Custom at the Hollywood Bowl, circa 1973.
Photo by Neil Zlozower

Custom Lite

By 1987, weight watchers caught up with Gibson and the Custom Lite arrived. It was $5/8"$ less deep, measuring $1\,3/8"$ and knocking a few pounds off for the shoulder-weary. The back was also relieved with a "Beveled Belly Cut" for comfort concerns. Controls consisted of two volumes, a master tone, and a coil-splitting switch. It featured twin 1959 LP reissue PAF pickups and all the attributes of the Custom model, but with an extra $79 added on for tooling costs.

During August 1988, another 250 "Showcase Edition" Lite models were produced, featuring active black EMG pickups and a gold finish. Black chrome hardware with Sidewinder SW-5 and L8 humbuckings without poles were also done in 1989 prior to the model's 1990 demise. With its new pink and metallic sunset colors, this "lite-weight" was a perfect guitar for the female guitarist. Les Paul also presented Carly Simon with a sunset (burgundy) Custom Lite at a special tribute concert.

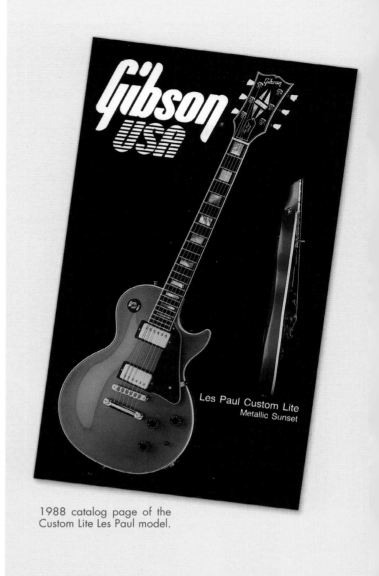

1988 catalog page of the Custom Lite Les Paul model.

The pink 1988 Les Paul Custom Lite. *Courtesy Norm's Guitars, 2004*

Note the extra-thin body and nice contoured back.

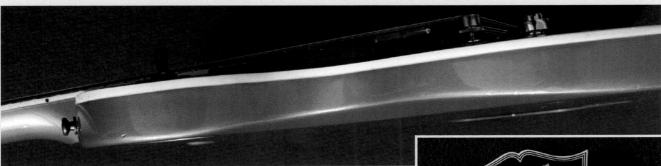

A 1988 Les Paul Custom Lite model in Metallic Sunset. *Courtesy Cal Vintage, 2004*

Les Paul Studio Models

The Les Paul Studio evolved from the need for an inexpensive instrument that retained the basics—the arched top, bridge components and electronics of the Standard model—but without binding. Gibson figured they could save the customer hundreds of dollars by mass-producing a simple, straightforward model that could do it all. The model name came to Bruce Bolen after visiting a recording studio. Putting the two together, the new "Les Paul Studio" was born.

Actually, the previously-released LP XR-1 of 1981 had similar appointments. When the Studio was first introduced in early 1983, it was $300 less than the rest of the arched line. Early models featured alder bodies with maple tops, rosewood fingerboards with dot inlay, twin '59 LP Reissue pickups and single-ply black pickguards. Soon the mainstay of mahogany with maple was reinstated with ⅛" less depth. By 1986, leftover C-grade ebony was being substituted for rosewood fingerboards, according to what was available. The 1988 catalog still stated rosewood. Problems arose with some of that ebony, however. Mitch Holder remembers the dealer reactions in the next chapter.

A Studio Standard with crown inlays and a Studio Custom (with gold hardware) became available during the nineties. Humbucking pickups switched to a 490-R Alnico rhythm and a 498-T Alnico (with wider pole spacing and the Gibson logo stamped on the bottom) for the lead position. The concurrent weight-conscious Les Paul models also included a Studio Lite, first with thinner beveled bodies, then to something entirely new—ultra lightweight Chromite™ (balsa wood) inserts in the mahogany. The Lite was available in "hot new translucent colors" and equipped with black chrome hardware. With its exposed higher output 496-R and 500-T ceramic pickups, the catalog boasted, "This guitar really screams."

Substantial and precision-built Schaller Tune-O-Matic bridges from Germany with body stud inserts were standard. Truss covers said Studio or the full name. Colors were generally wine red, white, ebony, sunburst, and natural. The Les Paul Studio is still a popular model for Gibson solid-body enthusiasts with a need for the big tone at a moderate cost.

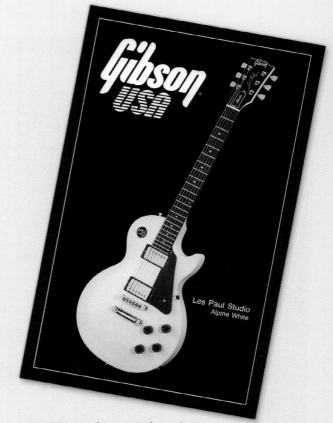

A 1988 catalog page for Gibson's popular in-between entry model with no-frills (lack of binding), based on the Standard's basic attributes.

1981 saw the limited release of the XR-I with coil taps and the XR-II, a flametop version with Deluxe pickups.

Les Paul Special '55, Junior and Double Cut '58 Reissues

Both fifties Les Paul Specials and Juniors were resurrected during the seventies. First the '55 single cutaway version was begun in 1974 and continued into 1975 with just a few built in 1976. They weren't included in the normal color 1975 catalogs, but were certainly being built when this author did a factory tour. Wrap-around stop tailpiece, one-piece bodies and bound pearl dot inlaid rosewood fingerboards were all in keeping with the fifties version. They did, however, have a three-piece neck, but without a volute or "Made in USA" stamp. The parts were now chrome and they upgraded to Kluson Deluxe double-ring

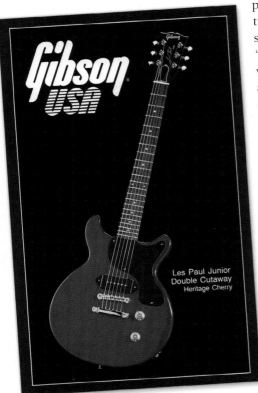

plastic Keystone tuners and black speed knobs. A "dark sunburst" was standard and some wine red models were made. To make the grain stand out, a cream filler paste was used to enhance the overall effect. By 1977, they had a Tune-O-Matic bridge addition and were available in Limed mahogany, wine red, and two sunbursts into 1979. A new SSC-1 adjustable single coil pickup was then instigated on the '55/78 versions. List price was $659 for the guitar and $99.50 for the protector case.

The Special had returned and was well-constructed for those players who enjoyed the old-style flat-top Les Paul with P-90 pickups. In 1988, production resumed to date with the Reissue Special (shortly named the Junior II), including the Tune-O-Matic bridge and P-100 stacked humbucking pickups for noise reduction. Black was added to the list of colors.

The popular late-fifties double cutaway '58 version was next to see production in 1976. Now with a Tune-O-

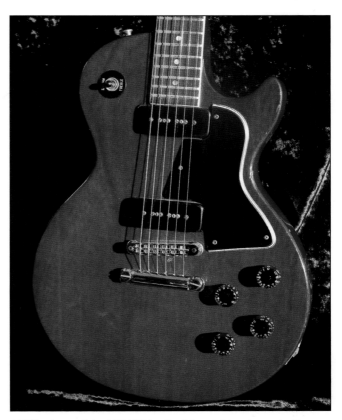

1977 edition of the '55/77 Les Paul Special in wine red. *Courtesy Shane Gudlow, Timewarp Music, 2008*

Matic bridge in addition to the stop bar, various colors included limed mahogany, ebony, wine red, cherry, and sunbursts. Construction differed with 20 frets clear of the body, which gave the neck better support and placed the pickup back in the normal Les Paul position, giving the guitarist a bit more of a stretch for those last two frets! By the late seventies, both models used metal-grip tuners. Gibson kept the Les Paul Junior alive in 1975–76 and 1977 with dark sunburst or wine red versions (which was a rare custom color during the fifties) and updated Tune-O-Matic bridge.

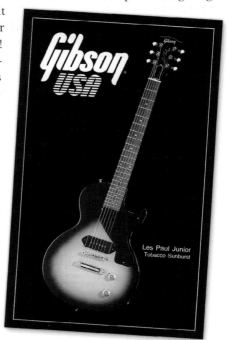

Gibson Changes Hands Again

Over the many years Gibson has existed, they have had their share of near-disasters. The torch first changed hands in 1902 as Orville signed his agreement with Lewis Williams to start the company. Maurice Berlin of CMI took the helm in 1944. Norlin acquired the concern in 1969, but by 1980 had decided to put it up for sale during the rough financial times experienced by many American manufacturers. They had lost focus and interest and were going in a different direction. With a recent yearly loss of $12.6 million, and just three months before liquidation, three MBA Harvard boys stepped in to the rescue—Henry Juszkiewicz, Dave Berryman and Gary Zebrowski.

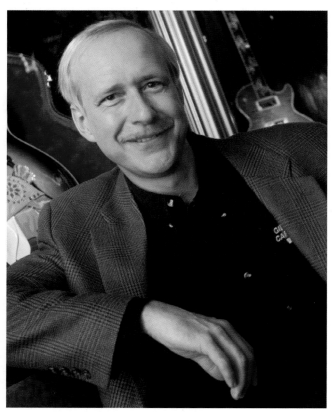

Henry Juszkiewicz. *Courtesy Gibson archives*

Henry Juszkiewicz, an Argentinian-American, grew up in Rochester, New York, playing guitar and working in the automotive industry. Dave Berryman, a part-time guitarist, was an accountant with Price-Waterhouse. Gary Zebrowski was a Harvard MBA guy who roomed with Henry. The three negotiated for seven long months to wrestle the ailing concern from Norlin. On January 15, 1986, they officially bought Gibson for five million dollars and set out to turn things around for the once-prestigious company. After 17 years of ups and downs with Norlin, Henry, with his aggressive business manage-

ment style, affected an immediate turnaround and soon started to show a profit. Henry became chairman and CEO while Dave was president. Gary soon took off for Phi-Tech.

Meanwhile, guitar-wise, their competitor's 1954-contoured thoroughbred reigned supreme—but then rock 'n' roll grabbed for the Gibson Les Paul guitar. None other than guitarist Slash from the hit group Guns N' Roses championed the all-hallowed Sunburst Standard—and the rest became history! The Les Paul was resurrected as the other true sonic wonderhorse and the Gibson solid-body returned as the major force it was originally designed to do: mean business. It successfully relaunched Gibson and the Les Paul guitar into the nineties.

Les Paul Photon/Hyperspeed MIDI Guitar

During the era of keyboard/MIDI electronics and Roland's synthesizer guitars' rise to popularity, Gibson teamed up with Phi Technologies in Oklahoma to produce their pitch-to-MIDI converter interface system called the Photon guitar. It utilized a built-in or retrofitted pickup system (either infra-red or magnetic) to scan strings for fast and accurate tracking. Custom software cartridges fit into the midi converters with many parameters for adapting to the various styles of playing techniques.

Gibson showed a Hyperspeed Les Paul Custom in their '88 catalog; other models were available with these onboard electronics. The dedicated controller guitars were devoid of normal audio pickups, while retrofitted versions used an output adaptor box. The standard guitar program was compatible with their special audio pickups, while the Hyperspeed system worked best for tracking with a full set of .013 strings. This could be difficult for some guitarists to adapt to, since all the strings were tuned to the same pitch (to B with 13s or 10s to E). This wasn't quite as bothersome with headphones on, however.

Mitch Holder used a Hyperspeed prior to Gibson's involvement and remembers, "Roland's system didn't set the world on fire, but it was a great way to program if you're not a keyboard player." The idea was ahead of its time, as were many other brilliant electronic ideas that the staid public ignores. The guitar audiophiles in the studio found a plethora of sounds available to them at a flick of the controls.

Hyperspeed
Les Paul Custom
Ebony

Gibson's first entry into the MIDI world, the Photon Les Paul.

Gibson West

With such a large artist base in Southern California, Gibson set up a new West Coast Custom Shop in North Hollywood in 1988. After eventually designing a headless guitar that became a Steinberger "M" guitar (under Gibson's umbrella of products at the time), popular British luthier Roger Giffen was asked to head a new Custom Shop for Gibson in Los Angeles, along with fellow guitar builder Gene Baker.

They made a multitude of great specially-ordered one-offs for many popular artists, including Joe Walsh, Peter Frampton, Jimmy Page, and Malcolm Young. The more unique ones included a few acoustic versions, such as a black, oval hole with a Filtertron pickup and gold Bigsby (like an electrified Orville Style 0-3), a non-cutaway with cat's eye holes for Malcolm Young of AC/DC, and an *f*-hole semi-solid version with P-90s and a Bigsby that became the basis for the later Bantam/Florentine series.

A handful of great Les Paul long-scale basses were built, including a double-cut junior and a "Black Beauty" Custom. Others built included Hawaiian koa-topped Customs, a double-cut silver sparkle Standard, a few half-sized 'Bursts and a nice Sunburst Standard for Jimmy Page. Unfortunately, Gibson closed the shop in late 1994 due to the consolidation of the Nashville Custom facility. Many happy customers treasure their West Coast Gibson specials.

Roger Giffen's cute half-size Gibson Sunburst Les Paul. *Courtesy David Swartz, 2008*

The Nineties into 2008: Gibson USA,
Epiphone, and Custom Shop Models

The Modern Les Paul Guitar

As the Gibson company moved into the nineties, further refinements continued with the Les Paul guitar line. With high-quality competition from the makers in Japan, top guitar builders in the States strived to enhance their lines, bringing a virtual renaissance to the American efforts. Gibson answered the challenge with a number of finely crafted instruments and accurate reissues. They upped the ante with their exquisite Custom Art guitars.

In this extensive chapter, we will see how the soon-to-be-popular Classic, Plus, and Premium Plus Standard models emerged to satisfy guitarists with comfortable necks, hot pickups, and fancy flame maple tops. Deluxe and Studios continued, along with the ever-present Special and Junior range—in addition to some bizarre off-shoots. Eventually, numerous artists and themed instruments evolved and a fully realized Custom Shop arrived to deliver a quality of craftsmanship rivaling the best refinements Gibson ever produced.

Les Paul Classic 1960, Standard, and Custom Plus

With the growing demand for 1960 slender profile necks at the Gibson Custom Shop, J.T. Riboloff showed some samples at the tradeshow that were met with great interest. A 1990 Gibson USA production version was given the go-ahead by Henry Juszkiewicz and a new approximated reissue began. It evolved with some popular vintage attributes: a normal (smaller) headstock, single collar Kluson-style machine heads, gold bell knobs, ABR-1 bridges, nickel parts, and cream plastic. Exposed ceramic 496R/500T humbuckings gave the guitarist a hot tone right out of the gate. Narrow cutaway binding was used for the first few years. This effort gave players a chance to have an affordable reissue model. Thus, the notations "Classic" and "1960" were scripted in gold on the truss cover and on the pickguard, respectively. By 1993, "CLASSIC" was on the Les Paul silkscreen in place of "MODEL." Colors were basically intended to be a faded sunburst (as on early faded '60 models) and the maple had little, if any, figuring. Bullion gold became an option in 1991.

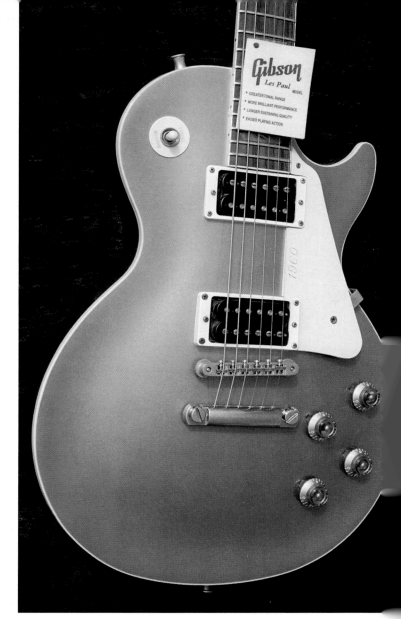

This 1991 Les Paul Classic (#1 1390) is entirely finished in their Bullion gold paint and shipped with a Standard truss cover, gold 1960 scripted pickguard, and no pickup covers—for those hot tones.

Flame maple and new sunburst colors entered the picture in 1992 with the new Classic Plus model. The wood wasn't particularly dramatic until the Classic Premium Plus (CPP), with AAA figured tops introduced in 1993. Since wood quality is subjective between AA and AAA, there wasn't always a definite demarcation between the two. Either a factory serial number check or looking under a pickup will reveal the difference. Premium Plus "LPCPP" models most often came without pickguards attached.

A beautiful 1994 Les Paul Classic (#4 2093) in sunburst, showing very nice figuring on the top and neck woods. *Courtesy Howard Lubin, 2004*

A few variations of the Classics were built through the ninties. A Celebrity Series Classic model in black, with gold hardware and white pickguards, was done in July 1991. Some Classics were fitted with M-III electronics (triple pickup combinations) from late '91 into '93. Classic Birdseye maple models were also produced around 1993. In February 1994, marking Gibson's first hundred years, 101 Les Paul Classic Centennial models were released for their "guitar of the month" edition. They were goldtops with gold hardware, had a gold medallion on the back of the peghead, and sported diamonds inlaid for the dotted "i" of Gibson and first digit of the 1894 to 1994 sequential serial numbers on the gold tailpiece.

Gibson USA LP Classic colors of the early nineties ranged from the Heritage cherry sunburst, honey burst, and translucent amber. As Custom Shop labeled CPP versions began during 1995–97, great translucent colors emerged, including deep purple, emerald green, ruby red and royal blue. Special stains brought out the curl, even though the chatoyant effect was mild. The rear decal stated Custom Shop instead of Classic on the neck because they were finished there. Half-cream (Zebra) '57 reissue humbuckings were installed, too. [Some '57 classic alnico pickups were covered, while others were naked to the world.]

This amazing Deep Purple Classic Premium Plus (#5 9275) sports zebra '57 pickups and the Custom Shop sticker. *Courtesy Greg Golden of Bizarre Guitars and owner Shen Schultz, 1996*

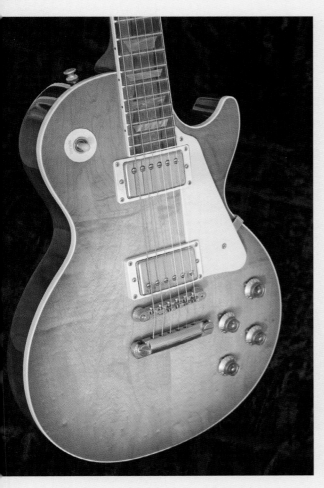

This 2000 Les Paul Classic Plus (#000734) has the faded honey sunburst and faded (greenish) pearloid neck inlays with nickel covers added. The 1960 script is virtually worn off. *Courtesy Robby Mohr, 2006*

Classic Plus models continued with bullion gold and flame maple for the translucent amber and red finishes, hot output ceramic 496R and 500T humbuckers and slim-tapered 1960 necks. These Plus versions, also considered Premium Plus models with high grade maples, were discontinued in 2002. In 2003, Classic sunbursts included honey, light, vintage and heritage cherry complemented by ebony, wine red, and an unusual copper natural. The copper, light and heritage cherry bursts were discontinued in 2005. By 2006, LP Classics came in vintage and honey sunburst, wine red, and the ebony finish available with gold hardware. The Les Paul Classic is still a 21st century favorite with many players due to its "screaming fast" slim-taper neck and "supercharged powerful" ceramic pickups. Burn on, Classic brothers and sisters!

The same 2003 flier showing the Classics in a variety of colors.

Gibson's large foldout 1993 catalog showing the Classic Premium Plus and Plus models.

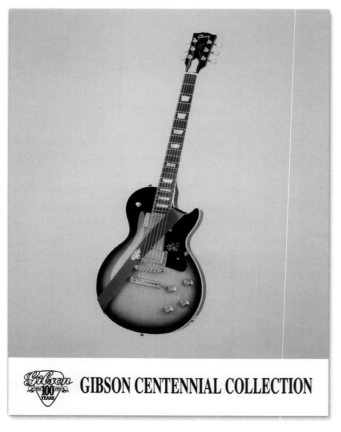

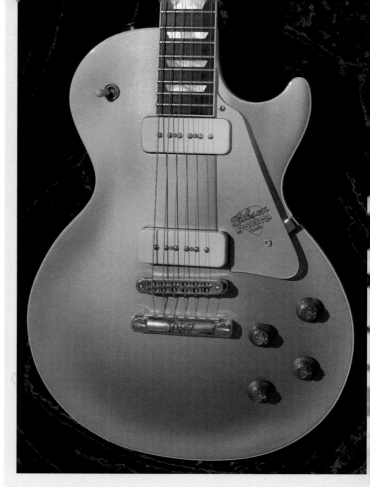

GIBSON CENTENNIAL COLLECTION

Glossy Gibson dealer promo for the Centennial Les Paul Standard. *Courtesy Mitch Holder*

Wonderful Centennial Classic Goldtop (#1987 4) with its serial number on both the headstock and the tailpiece. *Courtesy Bob Rudolfo, Seattle, 2008*

The Les Paul Custom and Standard also joined the "Plus" figured maple bandwagon—in 1993 and 1995–97, respectively. They maintained the 1959 or fifties rounded-neck profile with respective gold and chrome parts. Both Classic and Standard models were available with generally plain tops while the Custom and Standard Plus were complemented with a Premium Plus top version. Alnico magnet 490-R and 498-T pickups were installed on all versions. Straight-ahead Customs were available primarily in alpine white and wine red.

A limited run of Custom/400 models was released in 1985 and from late '91 into '92 with Super 400 split-block fingerboard inlays. Then a super-fancy, ebony-finished Centennial Custom was the guitar of the month during November 1994 with dual or triple-pickups, similar diamonds (serial numbers on the pickguard) and gold accoutrements—plus the 16" x 20" framed photo and signet ring. A similar Centennial Standard in vintage sunburst was presented in October 1994 while a P-100 equipped 100th Anniversary Goldtop was produced in April. Serial numbers went from 1894 to 1994 for each model. These fine instruments also feature an inset gold medallion of Orville on the back of the headstock and various inlayed diamonds.

Gibson's 1991 LP Collection page of Custom Les Paul models.

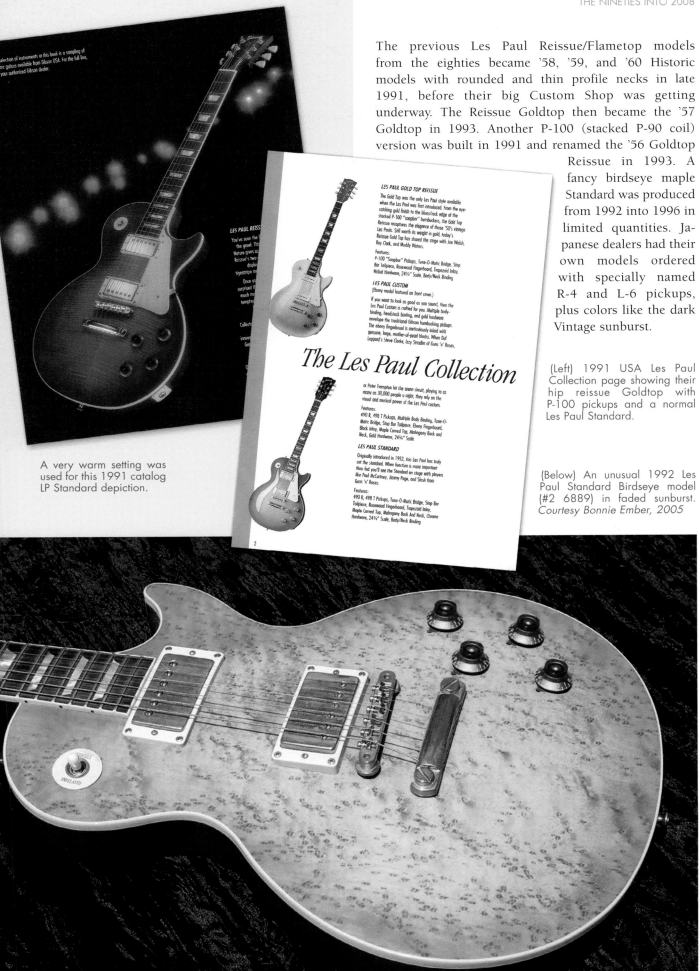

The previous Les Paul Reissue/Flametop models from the eighties became '58, '59, and '60 Historic models with rounded and thin profile necks in late 1991, before their big Custom Shop was getting underway. The Reissue Goldtop then became the '57 Goldtop in 1993. Another P-100 (stacked P-90 coil) version was built in 1991 and renamed the '56 Goldtop Reissue in 1993. A fancy birdseye maple Standard was produced from 1992 into 1996 in limited quantities. Japanese dealers had their own models ordered with specially named R-4 and L-6 pickups, plus colors like the dark Vintage sunburst.

(Left) 1991 USA Les Paul Collection page showing their hip reissue Goldtop with P-100 pickups and a normal Les Paul Standard.

(Below) An unusual 1992 Les Paul Standard Birdseye model (#2 6889) in faded sunburst. *Courtesy Bonnie Ember, 2005*

A very warm setting was used for this 1991 catalog LP Standard depiction.

LES PAUL GOLD TOP REISSUE

The Gold Top was the only Les Paul style available when the Les Paul was first introduced. From the eye-catching gold finish to the blues/rock edge of the stacked P-100 "soapbar" humbuckers, the Gold Top Reissue recaptures the elegance of those '50's vintage Les Pauls. Still worth its weight in gold, today's Reissue Gold Top has shared the stage with Joe Walsh, Roy Clark, and Muddy Waters.

Features,
P-100 "Soapbar" Pickups, Tune-O-Matic Bridge, Stop Bar Tailpiece, Rosewood Fingerboard, Trapezoid Inlay, Nickel Hardware, 24¾" Scale, Body/Neck Binding

LES PAUL CUSTOM
(Ebony model featured on front cover.)

If you want to look as good as you sound, then the Les Paul Custom is crafted for you. Multiple body-binding, headstock binding, and gold hardware envelope the traditional Gibson humbucking pickups. The ebony fingerboard is meticulously inlaid with genuine, large, mother-of-pearl blocks. When Def Leppard's Steve Clarke, Izzy Stradlin of Guns 'n' Roses,

The Les Paul Collection

or Peter Frampton hit the arena circuit, playing to as many as 30,000 people a night, they rely on the visual and musical power of the Les Paul custom.

Features:
490 R, 498 T Pickups, Multiple Body Binding, Tune-O-Matic Bridge, Stop Bar Tailpiece, Ebony Fingerboard, Black Inlay, Maple Carved Top, Mahogany Back and Neck, Gold Hardware, 24¾" Scale

LES PAUL STANDARD

Originally introduced in 1952, this Les Paul has truly set the standard. When function is more important than fad you'll see the Standard on stage with players like Paul McCartney, Jimmy Page, and Slash from Guns 'n' Roses.

Features:
490 R, 498 T Pickups, Tune-O-Matic Bridge, Stop Bar Tailpiece, Rosewood Fingerboard, Trapezoid Inlay, Maple Carved Top, Mahogany Back And Neck, Chrome Hardware, 24¾" Scale, Body/Neck Binding

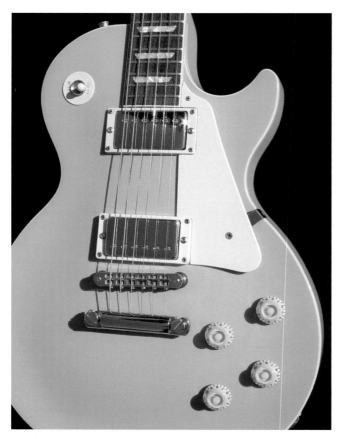

A unique 1990 yellow Les Paul Standard (#91000522) with nifty ivory knobs. *Courtesy Buffalo Brothers, 2005*

Approximately 300 special 40th Anniversary Les Paul Standards were produced from '92 into '93. An engraved 12th fret inlay marks the celebration of 40 years since the Les Paul guitar's introduction. P-100 stacked humbucking pickups and gold hardware complemented the black-and-cream-highlighted instrument.

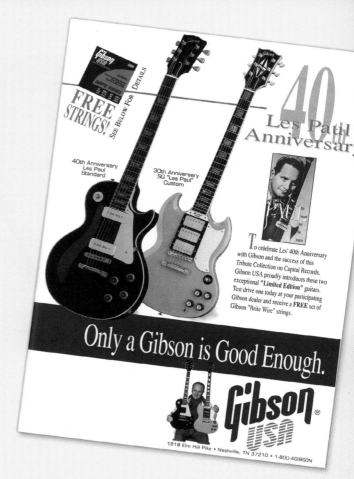

(Above) Gibson's 1992 ad for the 40th Anniversary Les Paul Standard, combined with the 30th for the SG LP Custom, and both in conjunction with a Capitol Master's Les Paul compilation release.

(Below) Curiously done in black and sporting P-100s, the 40th Anniversary Les Paul Standard is an attractive instrument with its own color scheme. *Courtesy Todd Stemmerman, 2003*

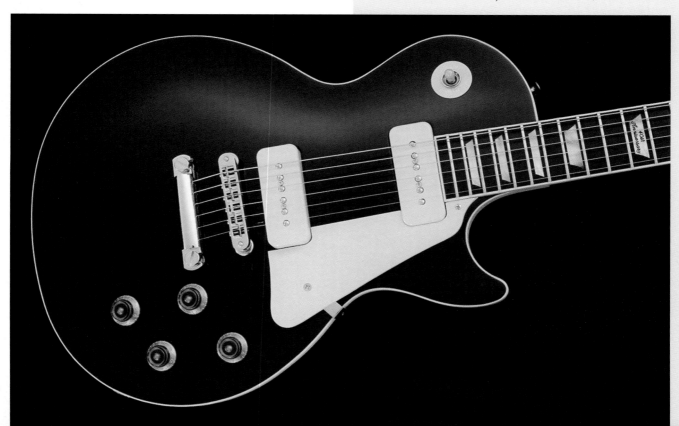

A beautiful 1998 LP Standard Plus flametop in Heritage Cherry Sunburst. *Courtesy owner Waddy Wachtel and Kim Shaheen, 2005*

Here are a few notable guitarists playing Gibson USA models:

(Left) Waddy Wachtel on-stage at Joe's Joint in L.A. playing his weekly Big Monday show, 2006.

(Right) Ultimate slide maestro Sonny Landreth plays this Les Paul Standard in many tunings with the "Performer" servo-driven tuners from the Transperformer Company to instantly keep tuned.

(Below) Neil Young is playing Waddy Wachtel's ebony Standard with Bigsby at the Joint, 2005. It's similar to his black finished '56, but without the P-90 and Firebird pickups. Gibson did a limited reissue of Neil's customized '56 for Japan.

(Left) Kim Simmonds performing at the Texas Guitar show in 2008. He was a founding member of the early British blues band Savoy Brown, and is also known for playing the Flying.

Just before a 2004 John Hiatt show, Sonny shows his unique playing style.

Mitch Holder Interview
September 4, 2003

Mitch Holder is truly one of the "main cats," as they say. Being Howard Roberts's true protégé for years and becoming a veteran studio musician par excellence, Mitch also shared the responsibilities (switch-hitting with the great Bob Bain) as staff guitarist with the Doc Severinson Orchestra on *The Tonight Show with Johnny Carson*. He also performed with Sergio Mendez and Peggy Lee, and did hit recording dates with Barbra Streisand, Frank Sinatra, Leonard Cohen, Herb Alpert, Smokey Robinson, Johnny Mathis, Dionne Warwick, and Joe Cocker.

Mitch is a true-blue Gibson player who takes great pride not only in owning and playing Gibson guitars exclusively, but also in making a difference in the field as a product specialist for Gibson's vast range of instruments. After a stint during the early nineties, he also became a Gibson rep during the early 2000s, setting up many special dealers. We visit regularly and this time we thought we'd look through catalogs from his tenure—while sitting amongst his vintage Gibson array.

Robb: *Here we are at Mitch Holder's humble abode, talking about his quality years with Gibson while looking at a top USA model from early nineties, the Les Paul Custom Premium Plus.*

Mitch: *It was a Custom with a flame top that didn't last very long on the market. It came and went very quickly, as did the Custom Plus that just didn't have as much flame. There was a grading system we had. There was the C, the AA, and the AAA. The AAA was the real flame.*

Those were from the beginning of '94 to the beginning of '96, just a couple of years there. They had graded tops, and the AAA was the best one. The AA, you could see the flame was not as intense on that one.

RL: *Here's the straight-ahead Les Paul Custom in white!*

MH: *That's funny, because when I got there, all they made was alpine white and wine red. I couldn't figure out why they didn't make the black. Why don't they make the black beauty again? What's going on? The thing was, the Custom Shop was just starting and they were making the Les Paul Custom and they wanted the exclusive on black. So that's how it was for a while. Eventually, they started making these black again while I was there.*

RL: *Then they have the Classic Premium Plus.*

MH: *The difference between the Standard and the Classic was that the neck had what was called a '60. There were two necks they were making at the time. The '59 was a little thicker then and the '60 was a*

thinner taper, slender. It had the hotter ceramic pickups; it had the 496s and the 500.

RL: *This one has pretty nice wood on it. The Heritage cherry sunburst—and the Premium Plus of that was their extra model.*

MH: *The tops got even better than this. This would have been a Plus top later on. In the beginning of the program, this was a Premium Plus.*

RL: *And the Les Paul Premium.*

MH: *They didn't make this for very long. By the time I got there, they'd already pretty much built them and were in the stores. They quit making them because they didn't have a whole lot of birds-eye. They made as many as they could.*

RL: *Premium birds-eye. That's like a faded version. And here we have the Classic…*

MH: *…in bullion gold, which was different than the gold they eventually used in the Custom Shop. They called it a different shade. The Custom Shop was calling it antique gold. They went back and got the original formula from the people who first made it. This not quite as gold; it is a little more tan, kind of lighter. Here's the Standard you could get at the time, a '93 Standard birds-eye.*

RL: *It had the '59-type neck?*

MH: *Yes, the Standard had the '59-type neck. They would spell it out. The '59 was rounded and the Classic had the '60 slim tapered neck. That's what they called it.*

RL: *And that's a plain old Les Paul Standard with the bigger Tune-O-Matic.*

MH: *Right. It has The Nashville Tune-O-Matic and speed knobs. Over the years, the colors would change. They would add colors and delete colors. They're usually heritage cherry. That was always a stock color. They still make those, of course. This is one that didn't survive. This was the Studio Lite.*

RL: *Les Paul Studio Light in translucent blue. What colors did the Standard come in?*

MH: *At the time, 1992, ebony, honey burst, heritage cherry sunburst, and vintage sunburst. Ebony came back to the Standard a couple of years ago. Colors would come and go. I don't know if they mention the sculpted back in the literature. Here's the Studio. They still make the Studio. It's a no-frills Les Paul.*

RL: *That's basically a Standard without binding. Gold parts?*

MH: *Gold parts were put on certain colors. Let's see, wine red and ebony. Sometimes with alpine white it had gold parts only. Hardware was chrome or gold. The dealer could order whatever hardware they wanted, the wine red with chrome or gold or the black with chrome or gold.*

MH: *The Special evolved with P-90s… then the Special became the low-end humbucking model. A few years ago, they did the Special again… the real Special. With the double-neck 1275, the plant and the marketing guys hated these because they count for only one guitar. They wanted them to count for two guitars because they had two necks on them.*

RL: *How did you get involved with the Gibson company?*

MH: *Toward the end of 1993, I went to see Mike McQuire, who had just been hired. He was moving from here and I went over to his house right before he left. He said they were looking for some people and asked if I was interested. I said, "Yeah, sure." Eventually, I got a phone call to come to the NAMM show, where I ended up playing for them. Right after the NAMM show I was hired as a product specialist position by Richard Head, who was in charge of marketing. He had started with nobody and eventually hired a lot of people. He expanded the marketing department to include 12 employees.*

Mitch Holder at the 1995 NAMM show, during his product specialist days. Yo, Mitch!

This flier shows the heart of the Sunburst Standard's electric tone.

Catalog depiction of the '57 Classic humbucking pickups.

'57 Classic Vintage Humbucker

Modern Pickups

Gibson renamed the eighties Tim Shaw PAF pickups as the new '57 Classic in 1990 and released some fliers and guides later in the decade. This was to inform guitarists how to select the right humbucking pickups by discussing magnets, comparative output (scale of 10), and tonal characteristics. '57 Classic/Plus pickups used Alnico II magnets with 6 and 7.5 output. They produced creamy, warm tones with smooth distortion and still had the old-style PAF stickers. 490T/R Alnico II pickups output are 6 on their scale, and have four-conductor wiring. They are similar to the '57 Classic, but give slight increase in the upper mid-range. 498T Alnico V output is 8 with hotter and brighter vintage tones. 500Ts use ceramic magnets and rate the highest output at 10, with maximum sustain for the bridge position.

With Japanese interest in the PAF sound, another replica was made in 1996 that became known as the BurstBucker pickup. By summer 2000, these new BurstBucker pickups arrived on the American line for the Gary Moore Signature model and various Custom Shop models. Their harmonic complexity and design are similar to the unmatched coils of yesteryear, with their popular Alnico II "singing magnets." As on the originals, the magnets were unpolished. A slight sonic edge with more highs and lows was obtained by the inherent different coil windings. Three distinct variations were copied to replicate their differences. With output strengths of 1, 2, and (eventually) 3, they were mixed on the guitars through the years in various combinations (1 and 2, then 2 and 3) for two-pickup guitars. By 2002, a BurstBucker V hit the market with the extra kick of Alnico V magnets, expressly for the 50th anniversary of the Les Paul guitars. By May 2003, it was renamed the BurstBucker Pro and came with a wax-potted coil to cut back on microphonics through high-gain amplifiers. These come in calibrated pairs with output similar to the original I and II models.

The ceramic magnet 496R pickup gave guitarists great sustain, cutting power with definition, and highs without too much muddiness. The screaming 500T "Super Ceramic" pickup has multiple-magnet structure for rich lows and clear highs with lots of growl when turned up. Both are available in full black and Zebra half-cream open coils. Factory-installed versions have two conductor wirings, while Gibson aftermarket versions come with four, for split/series and parallel settings.

Amazing 2008 one-piece flame maple top sunburst Les Paul Custom # CS82533. Exquisite curly maple also graced the back and neck of this unique Custom Shop Les Paul. *Courtesy Centre City Music, 2008*

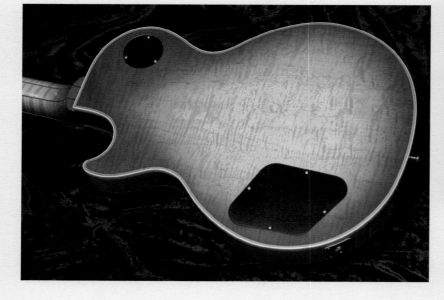

Striking Ice Blue Les Paul Standard featuring ebony fingerboard and P-94 pickups with pearloid plastic trim. NAMM 2004.

2004 quilted Les Paul Custom with Bigsby tailpiece. *Courtesy Centre City, 2006*

2007 natural Les Paul Custom flametop. *Courtesy La Mesa Guitar Center, 2008*

A stunning 1995 LP Standard Premium Plus (#5 5395) with wild flame maple in Root Beer with gold hardware. *Courtesy La Mesa Guitar Center, 2005*

The ever-popular, tried-and-true P-90 pickups carried on as a "super vintage," while the P-100 stacked humbucking "vertical vintage" version slowly caught on for quieter use, despite the somewhat-compressed mid-range tonality. An unusual-looking, large-sized P-94R/T single coil pickup with metal sides was made for installing in humbucking sized holes for various models.

By 2000, the forever-elegant Custom was still available in ebony, wine red, and alpine white, while the plain top Standard came in heritage cherry sunburst, honey burst, and vintage sunburst. 2001–2003 Standard Plus models maintained the fancier grades of AA maple, stamped in numbers, both neck shapes, and either nickel or chrome parts. Some even came in a deep cherry and the darker desert burst with black backs. Pickups were specified Alnico 490R and 498T humbucking.

And for the shredders, a natural, satin-finished Les Paul Raw Power model surfaced in 2000 with EMG 81/85 pickups. A flashy LP Standard Sparkle finish was re-introduced in 2001 in three radiant colors, including a blue frost, silver sterling, and red crimson with gold hardware. They came with 490R/498T Alnicos and were discontinued in 2005. The Les Paul Standard Mahogany model was available 2003 in heritage cherry over the reddish-brown mahogany top with nickel parts and three Duncan Distortion humbucking pickups.

This alpine white Les Paul Custom was strategically singed with a cigarette by Alice in Chains guitarist Jerry Cantrell. It is on display with his '63 split-window Corvette at the Peterson Automotive Museum's "Cars & Guitars of Rock 'n' Roll II" exhibit, 2006.

Sparkle LP Standards really light up in the sunlight. This crimson version has Zebra pickups and a see-through pickguard. *Courtesy Norm Harris, 2003*

Above) This LP Standard Faded in heritage cherry (#01455307) uses a special satin finish over its hand-done shading. *Courtesy Instrumental Music, 2006*

In January 2005, a new Les Paul Standard Faded series began, with a hand-stained satin finish for the weathered look—without the wear and tear. Gibson states this lacquer process "allows the wood to resonate and gives the neck a natural feel." Some believe the unique finish contributes to the tone and is less to worry about compared to gloss. AA figured maple tops were available with their faded "worn" tobacco, honey or cherry sunburst finish. Pickups are the "zebra coil" uncovered BurstBucker Pro variety with Alnico V magnets for that authentic vintage tone. Care must be taken since they are exposed and have short bezels. Their combination creates more bite and seductive "airy" tones, according to their promo. Both size necks are available, along with left-handed versions.

(Below) The Standard faded mahogany grainy-textured back shows the partially-filled wood pores.

The normal glossy LP Standard then had mild AA tops, BurstBucker Pro pickups (but nickel covered), and a bevy of colors including ebony, gold, ice tea, root beer, light/honey/desert and heritage cherry sunbursts. There were also some wild versions in cayenne, gecko, and latte creme.

(Above) The latte creme (aka mocha burst) LP Standard. *Courtesy Saul Frank, Centre City Music, 2006*

(Left) A unique green gecko burst Standard displayed at 2004 NAMM.

To complete the 2004–06 Standard family, a Limited Edition was added that features exotic colors, ebony fingerboards with bright pearloid crown inlays, bound headstocks with classic double-crown inlay, metal button Klusons, black/silver insert top-hat knobs, and white plastic parts. Cool colors include Manhattan Midnight (top to bottom shaded), Pacific Reef Blue (blue with green shading), Santa Fe Sunset, and black cherry with cream binding.

Today's fancy Les Paul Standard Premium continues the tradition of AAA flamed maple tops that shimmer with lustrous nitro-cellulose lacquer sunbursts. Gibson states that these improved translucent shaded colors show the flame maple out to the edges. Finishes include the above Standard bursts, wine red and trans amber, 17-degree headstocks, nickel parts, BurstBuckers, gold top-hat knobs, and green-keyed Gibson Klusons. All in all, with their Standard model, Gibson USA has continued to refine the modern return of the original Les Paul tradition that so many purists have desired.

The 2004 NAMM Les Paul Standard Limited Edition LP5 lineup. Right to left, *Pacific Reef blue, Santa Fe Sunset, Manhattan Midnight and a LP6 slim-neck Goldtop, all with nickel parts.*

An attractive Standard Limited Edition bound headstock with double crown inlay.

(Below) This '05 Les Paul Standard Premium in "Ice Tea" sunburst has a nine-digit serial number and the '60s Style Neck sticker on the truss cover.

Les Paul Standard Limited Edition (#01123661) in Black Cherry and cream binding. *Courtesy Instrumental Music, 2006*

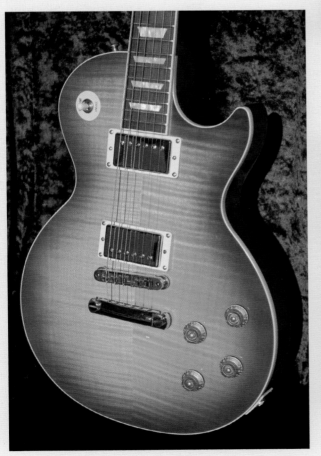

Beautiful lefty Limited Edition '03 Les Paul Standard in Manhattan Midnight. *Courtesy DeForest Thornburgh Blue Guitar, 2008*

Les Paul Deluxe

1969–85 marked the temporary end of the first Les Paul Deluxe run. In 1991, a Deluxe "Hall of Fame" edition premiered the first reissue Deluxe models with an all-over gold finish. The beginning of the first "Re-issue" Les Paul Deluxe that was faithful to the original came in 1992. This continued into 1997.

"The 1969 Deluxe is back!" With a 30th anniversary model, Gibson reintroduced the new Deluxe Les Paul in 1999. The now-famous "mini" humbucking pickup replaced the P-90 on the 1968/69 Standard. It now delivers the "crunch and sweet bite" of the original models—with the capability of enabling the player to switch from single-coil guitars to mini-equipped Gibsons without a significant change in EQ. The limited-edition

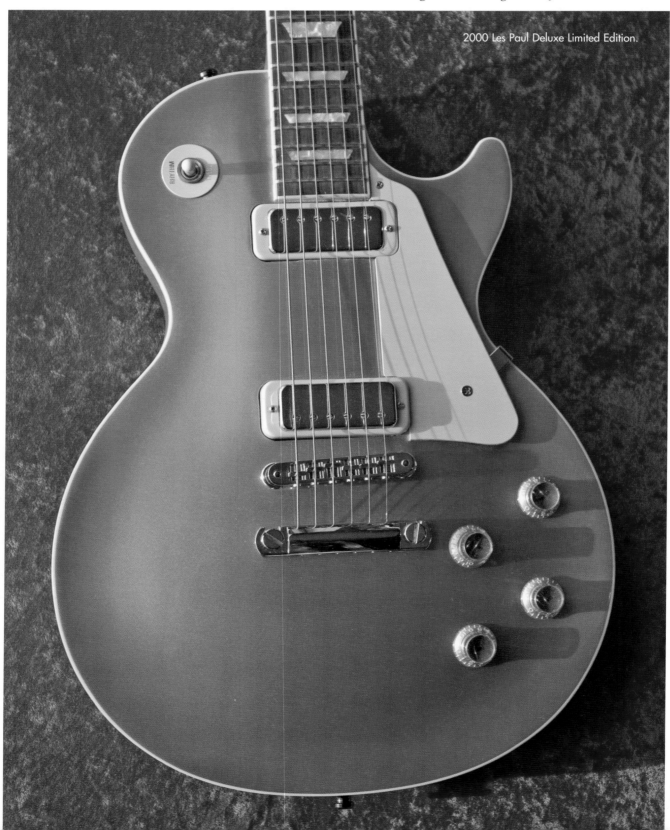

2000 Les Paul Deluxe Limited Edition.

The Gibson Les Paul 30th Anniversary Deluxe

Gibson USA commemorates the 30th anniversary of the original Les Paul Deluxe with a new limited production model. Originally released in 1969 to replace the P-90 Les Paul, the Deluxe featured the now famous "mini-humbucker" pickup. Gibson has faithfully recreated this pickup including it in a contemporary Les Paul Standard to accurately reproduce the look and better yet, the crunch and bite of the original. Today's Deluxe features a one-piece mahogany back and neck, bookmatched maple top, and vintage style tuners. The Les Paul 30th Anniversary Deluxe is available for a limited time in nitro-cellulose lacquered Ebony and Wine Red finishes.

Body Construction
Mahogany back, carved maple top

Pickups
Dual mini humbuckers

Controls
Two volume and two tone, three-way toggle switch

Hardware/Tuners
Chrome/Vintage Kluson style tuners

Scale/Nut width
24.75"/1.6875"

Fingerboard
Rosewood, 22 frets

Inlay
Pearloid trapezoid

Neck
Mahogany/1959 rounded Les Paul

Binding
Body and fingerboard

Bridge/Tailpiece
Tune-o-matic/Stopbar

Finishes
Ebony, Wine Red

Limited Edition

Ebony

Wine Red

Call 1-800-4-GIBSON for more information on the Les Paul 30th Anniversary Deluxe or visit us at http://www.gibson.com

© 1999 Gibson Guitar Corp.

Gibson USA

Only a **Gibson** Is Good Enough™

Les Paul Deluxe models shown in ebony and wine red.

30th Anniversary Deluxe was set up on a Les Paul Standard's one-piece mahogany body and book-matched figured maple top. These models featured a slender 1960 neck, yet the literature mentions a 1959 rounded neck, vintage-style Kluson tuners and nitro-cellulose lacquered ebony, bullion gold, and wine red finishes. All in all, it was quite a deluxe version of the original Deluxe.

By 2000, the Deluxe became a regular item (many had Limited Edition stickers) and was also available in bullion gold, similar to the originals. The guitars still retained the current one-piece body and book-matched top with the '59 neck. Mini Hum perfection! [69 neck a bit squarish up top]

Detail views of the 2000 Les Paul Deluxe Limited Edition (#01400763) in bullion gold. *Courtesy California Vintage Guitar, 2006*

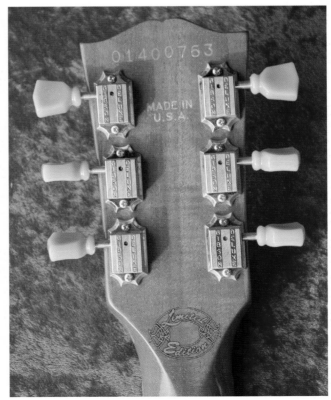

The 2005 Les Paul Standard Bass guitar in Heritage Cherry sunburst. *Courtesy True Tone Music, Santa Monica, CA 2006*

Les Paul Basses—Special, Deluxe, and Standard

After a hiatus of 14 years, Gibson Les Paul models jumped back into the bass world with three new "retro-vibed" bass guitars introduced in late 1991 (replacing the long-horned Q-80/90 series). In-house designer Phil Jones had a major hand in developing this traditional single cutaway style bass guitar (with the same dimensions as the guitar body). The instrument utilizes the extended harmonic professional scale length of 34" neck ($1\frac{11}{16}$" or $1\frac{5}{8}$" at the nut) and two newly designed bass pickups. Together, they produce deep bass tones with warm sustain and sweet highs. Its strong mid-range response can easily cut through the mix in many situations, while the back pickup can even achieve that growl tone of the old Thunderbird bass. Now-popular slap-popping funk style works well from the inherent rich tone and powerful pickups. With loud fellow musicians (two guitars and drums), these basses can certainly show their muscle and solo well with added mid-EQ. Plus, many players especially enjoy its sleek fingerboard and the neck's comfortable rounded profile.

This new bass range consisted of three models—the Special, Deluxe, and Standard. The Special had an unbound flat body and two pickups and a dot-inlaid neck. The similar flat-style Deluxe generally had body binding, while the upscale Standard model features the

This angle shot shows the Schaller bridge and twin Dual TB Plus humbucking pickups.

arched design. All had 20 frets on their unbound ebony fingerboard; the Standard and Deluxe used the trapezoid crown inlays. Headstocks were reminiscent of the original 20's L-5 shape with the decorative flowerpot headstock inlay (for the first year and for '93 five-string models). Grover and Gibson/Schaller bass tuners were used for precision tuning. Gibson's Thunder Plus .045-.100-SS strings came stock.

Deluxe and Special versions (based on the original LP Special with dot neck inlays) have black-chrome hardware and a Schaller-designed Warwick-style three-way mounted, four-saddle bridge. By 1993, two Bartolini TB Plus humbuckers with the matching TCT active 9-volt electronics were added, with volume, bass, treble, and blend controls in the shielded cavity. These bass guitars were finely finished in nitro high-gloss lacquers. Specials came in classic white, ebony, heritage cherry, and translucent amber, while Deluxes were available in clear, heritage cherry sunburst, transparent amber/black/blue/green and red, vintage sunburst and a hand-rubbed oil finish (like the popular boutique basses).

The top model took on the radiance of the arched Les Paul Standard attributes (especially the heritage cherry sunburst nitro finish version) with chrome hardware, cream plastic pickup bezels (with chrome covered pickups), and a separate bridge with a stop/anchor tailpiece. Its carved and bound flame maple top, mahogany neck, and chambered body with an ebony fingerboard and crown pearloid inlays and four gold bell knobs completed the effect. Prices in '93 were $1,047 for the Special, $1,599 for the Deluxe, and $1,649 for the Standard. Five-string versions of the Deluxe were available in '93, while the Standard arrived in '95. The Smartwood series also included a similar exotic bass version in 1998 that came in emerald and earthburst colors.

The flat Deluxe and Special (and Premium Plus) versions were eventually discontinued in 1998, while the Standards continued. By 1998, product manager Max Ruckman stated, "We want bassists to think Les Paul and try this exceptional instrument." There was a contest to win an NOS Q bass just for trying it out at a store, plus an offer for a free denim shirt if you bought one before May 31st.

Slightly redesigned '99 LPB-3 Standard basses continued the classic styling. The Bartolini set-up was abandoned by 1998 in favor of the new high-output expanded-range TB-plus ceramic pickups (passive), with four normal volume/tone controls. Engineers have remarked how quiet the instrument is, while having such potent pickups.

The popular Korean-built Epiphone versions of the LPB premiered in 1999. When the five-string (ELPBCS) version came on the market, it garnished rave reviews from Guitar World during 2000. These Epi models have remarkable quality and are set up in the U.S. Their use of the 34" scale rosewood fingerboard on a maple neck, Dual Rail pickups using a five-way rotary switch, and the five-string Tune-O-Matic/stop set-up is exceptional. Their LP Standard Plus had flame maple with the "Limited

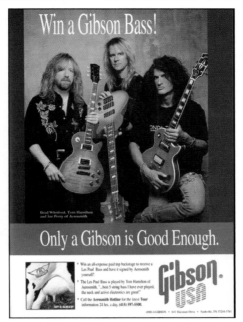

Tom Hamilton and band mates promote the new Gibson bass.

(Right) Flip side of the 1999 LP Standard bass advert showing available colors.

Edition" label, while the Special economy version had a detachable neck. An artist signature model, "The Vinnie" Hornsby model (of Sevendust), sported a bound maple fingerboard with star inlays, EMG active pickups, and a flame maple top.

By 2001, only the Standard was in the lineup, available in the HCS, honey burst, and vintage sunburst. These basses give rock-solid bottom performances—from the guitar that means business.

Various pop, blues, and rock artists enjoy these unique basses. It's a wonder they didn't build a few in the fifties! Woody performing with the Allman Brothers and Government Mule championed the LP bass live in concert. Les, Rusty, and I certainly heard Woody get a big, full tone with the Allmans one night. Tom Hamilton of Aerosmith plays a five-string version live, too.

In 2005, an attractive Les Paul "Double Cut" bass with "a new level of playability and styling to the Gibson bass family" was introduced. It features a bound AA maple top (arm contoured!) on the mahogany body, a 34" scale with 24 frets on the rosewood fingerboard, dual TB plus ceramic pickups and asymmetrical dual cutaway horn design (not unlike that of the LP Signature bass, but similar to the DC Series). It is available in root beer brown or black cherry red with either chrome or gold hardware.

Les Paul SG Models

The Les Paul version of the sharp-horned, sculpted SG series was virtually a forgotten animal from the mid-sixties to mid-eighties. Les didn't particularly care for the silhouette model back in its original heyday, due to a lack of maple and thin body tonality. Multitudes of SG models were made (even a 25 ½" scale SG 90) and not until 1988 did the three-pickup "SG Les Paul" Custom in antique ivory (finally with a stop tailpiece) share the LP moniker once again. Even the SG '61 and '62 vintage reissue Standards in heritage cherry still didn't use the name. Many still love these guitars, however, simply because of how well they play and their comfort-contoured styling. They also feel these "dialed-in" SG necks are super-smooth and endless. The sculpted double-cutaway design, with total access, makes other Gibson guitars seem hard to play in comparison.

To coincide with Capitol's '92 release of Les Paul's box set and Les's 40th anniversary with Gibson, a similarly-named 40th Anniversary SG Les Paul Custom was sold (with the black p-100 Standard) as an "exceptional Limited Edition" in TV yellow with gold hardware. Both wine red and white LP SG Customs were built during the early nineties alongside their heritage cherry-finished Standards. Frets on the modern Custom were naturally larger by popular demand. Rare korina versions were

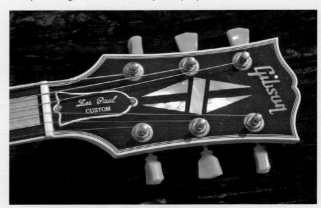

A gleaming ivory NOS Les Paul SG Custom (#040201) with triple '57 Classic PAF pickups and the long Maestro Lyre Vibrola. The color is reminincent of the old "Polaris" white. Note the high-quality Gibson Deluxe machine heads by Grover. You can just imagine how smoothly this plays!

(Left) A special-ordered 2001 Les Paul SG Standard (#031192) in TV yellow finish. *Courtesy Chuck Kavooris, 2004*

Elliot Easton playing live in Malibu, 2006, with his signature model two-pickup Les Paul SG Custom, part of the "Inspired By" series, available in Pelham Blue and Classic White, with extended upper horn and Tiki tailpiece engraving.

An ivory 2005 Custom Shop Les Paul SG Standard with Lyre vibrola.

built and also featured in the new Epiphone line. In 1994, the Historic Collection catalog depicted it as a 1960 Les Paul SG Custom model in classic white, with its slender neck, triple '57 Classic pickups, and identifying logos between the neck and pickup and on the truss cover. A soulful Carlos Santana is shown playing one in the catalog.

Late 1995 into 1997 saw a novel '63 Corvette hybrid SG Les Paul model available in silver, black, or Riverside red, with the center raised like the fastback split-window feature. Angus Young of AC/DC played SGs and had his own signature model. Black Sabbath's guitarist Tony Iommi endorsed a black-finished SG in 1998 (sometimes referred to as a Les Paul in ads) with his special pickups, 24 frets on an ebony fingerboard, and sterling silver-cross inlays.

This lightweight breakthrough design of the early sixties has endured from popular appeal and sheer basic ergonomics, not to mention a novel, eye-pleasing, distinctive, and stylized shape. Today's thinner finish work gives the instrument an aura of fine furniture to the touch. After years of longer, bulkier-yet-sturdier neck heel construction, Gibson reverted more closely to the

old-style neck joints for these modern faithful renditions. Gibson's Custom Shop made some fine guitars in the aged versions and custom colors. As with other fragile mahogany Gibson guitars, carefully keep these Les Paul SG models from falling—by all means!

The sculpted back of the LP SG Standard. *Courtesy Cal Vintage, 2005*

2006 Custom Authentic Les Paul Custom SG #067473 in vintage cherry. *Courtesy Norm Harris*

Les Paul Studio

Although the affordable Les Paul Studio went through a few upgraded variations during the eighties, the bound-bodied Standard and Customs fell by the wayside— in '88 and '85, respectively. Both Studio and Lite versions added trapezoid crown inlays on their unbound ebony fingerboard and gold hardware became optional in 1990. TV yellow was available for that first year. Gibson even produced 20 Miller Genuine Beer promotional versions with the MGD logo in 1992 (and a few Coors Specials).

The back-contoured Studio Lite of 1987 maintained its 1⅜" depth with composite chromyte/mahogany tone chamber construction and uncovered 496R/500T pickups into the nineties. Translucent red, blue, and blacks were complemented with vintage and heritage cherry sunbursts during '92. A limited number of figured two- and three-piece maple top Lites were available during late 1991. M-111 electronics arrived in '91 through '94, with its Strat-like single coil center pickup and five-way slider switch. By 1998, all the Lite models faded.

Exotic-colored Studio Gem models with cream P-90s were available from '96 into '97. Colors included sapphire blue, ruby red, topaz yellow, amethyst purple, and emerald green. Ninety were built with P-90s, in white with gold parts, for Guitar Center in 1997. Rosewood fingerboards came back in 1994 for the LP Studio, and ebony was reinstated for the white models in 1996. Rosewood received ¾ size pearloid crown inlays in 1999. Colors were trimmed down to ebony, emerald, and ruby, available with either chrome or gold parts, which is still a mystery on an inexpensive instrument.

A beautiful Blue Teal Flip-Flop finished variety was available from 2000 to 2005. It was developed with BASF automotive division using Vairocrom effect pigments to change spectrum colors when viewed from different angles. A beautiful AAA maple topped Studio Premium Plus model with full-sized crowns on rosewood was introduced in 2006. Colors include natural, root beer, and translucent amber, black, and red. The Studio PP lack of binding brings the construction price down, while the fancy wood and gold balance it out for economy-minded who want figured maple with flash appeal. Ultimately, the economy-priced Les Paul Studio has been Gibson's best seller for many years, delivering the goods to the guitar masses.

Darth Vader and Vincent Price meet Orville Gibson and Les Paul… and the Studio Gothic series arrived in 2000 for all those pale-skinned, black-haired death/metal/grunge rockers! Finished in satin black, it sported black chrome parts and the earliest Gibson symbols—a 12th fret star and crescent moon on the fingerboard and Orville's portrait behind the headstock. It has simple appointments and is right-to-the-point with its versatile 490R/498T alnico pickups, 14:1 ratio Grover machines, and '59 profile neck. Basically, it has the Standard's full-bodied rich rhythm tones. With distortion, it gets an even and brutal tone. With more gain, it can create a barrage of paint-peeling metal-ness (could be in the finish!). It goes without saying that most players used Marshalls and Strap-locks to let this animal loose onstage. And it looked soooooo bad! It was discontinued in 2003, to the dismay of many a Goth/metal fan. Somewhat similar 2002 Voodoo models came out with ash bodies, a blackish/red JuJu textured satin finish, novel black/red

This 1991 wine red and gold Les Paul Studio (#92531469) is a comfortable workhorse for owner Kim Shaheen, 2004.

A Les Paul Studio in action at Hollywood's Mint Club, with Jason Pilalas from Spokane's popular Holfiller group.

coil humbucking, and a red skull on the fifth fret. They were discontinued in 2005. Today's scary version is the flat black Les Paul Menace for those "take-no-prisoners look and face-melting tone" metal guitarists. They are done with only a brass fist inlay on the fifth fret, tattoo-style Gibson logo, carved "tribal" bodyrouting (fluted) on the sides, and smoky-coil 490R/498T brassstud humbuckings. Look out!

With the arrival of the Les Paul Studio Baritone guitar, there was finally an instrument that filled the in-between registers with Gibson bottom-end gusto and Les Paul business. The cool colors included blue mist, black, sunrise orange, and pewter metallic. The hardware was pewter as well. Its 28" scale length allowed the opportunity to tune either to C♯ or low B with whatever string gauges that worked. It came with a 12 to 52 Powerline strings. Perfect for playing those reverberated movie theme lines or profundo killer chords.

El bosso Studio Baritone six-string bass guitar in ebony finish with pewter parts. Dig the silver surrounds and painted knobs.

A Les Paul Gothic version of the Studio model with blackness everywhere! *Courtesy Mike Grossi, 2004*

Orville may be a little spooked on this one!

The elongated head of the Les Paul Baritone is evident with the more massive Grovers. *Courtesy Instrumental Music, 2005*

155

Les Paul Junior, Special, and TV

The single cutaway Les Paul Special (shortly known as the Junior II in 1989, Gibson's original code name) It was produced into the nineties with an added Tune-O-Matic bridge. It was available in heritage cherry, tobacco sunburst, and TV yellow. It was on its way to becoming a fairly accurate version during the nineties. A limited edition of 300 Specials (LE prefix #) was also done with P-100 pickups in 1990. An unbound Special "SL" version (signifying "sans lacquer" instead of a Mercedes) was produced in 1998 and designated with a poly finish, yet some had nitro-cellulose lacquer.

A Centennial Special single-cutaway was duly announced in 1994. Some prototypes in gold and TV yellow were used for promotion with Aerosmith and Six Flags, but never put into production. Instead, the Centennial Special double-cutaway model was produced as guitar of the month during January 1994, with all the accoutrements.

Rick Vito playing slide with John Mayall on David Swartz's Les Paul Special. Malibu, December 2007.

The single cutaway Special model was renamed the Junior Special in 1999 with an unbound neck with half-size crowns, contoured back, added Tune-O-Matic, and dual P-100 equipped. Colors included natural, ebony, and cinnamon. The double cutaway had the same neck appointments, but now joined the body near the 22nd fret, for better access than the 20th. Its rhythm pickup was set farther away for a more solid neck joint. Colors were the same on both models.

A 1998 Historic 1957 Les Paul Junior in TV yellow.

Single-pickup-wise, the original distinction between the old-style Junior and yellow TV models went by the wayside, and both became officially known as the Les Paul Junior in 1990. To the rest of us, it assumed both titles, according to coloration. The Junior/TV also saw the addition of a P-100 pickup under the dog-eared cover and was finished in heritage cherry, TV yellow, and traditional tobacco sunburst before being discontinued in 1992. In 2006, a black Les Paul Junior version was available with a tortoise-type pickguard as a Billie Joe Armstrong (Green Day) model.

More recent USA Special models did away with P-90/stop set-up in favor of humbuckings plus a TOM/stop combination. One of the two models included their shortlived LP Special with Humbuckings (actual title) in three worn finishes of ebony, yellow, and cherry. The worn spots are where the player's hands would most likely wear the finish. The second is a glam flash Special New Century in black with a full mirror face plate pickguard à la Bootsy. Both have the '60 taper neck and unbound rosewood fingerboards with 490R/498T Alnico pickups.

The Custom Shop started their original double cutaway version in 1998 as the 1960 LP Special with dual P-90s

and the customary stop bridge in Vintage sunburst, faded cherry, and TV yellow. By 2004, the 1960 moniker was applied to a faithful reproduction of the single cutaway and included a bright TV white finish.

The modern Custom Shop upped the ante in 1998 with their accurate P-90 equipped '57 Les Paul Junior Single Cutaway in vintage sunburst, faded cherry, TV yellow, and a brighter TV white version. By 2001, a flat maple top LP Junior Special Plus was marketed with gold hardware, 490/498 Alnicos and Trans amber and red. Today's Custom shop VOS nails the vintage past directly (including the aluminum stop, CTS pots and bumble bee caps) with a sunburst '57 or TV yellow Junior '58, TV yellow double cutaway Junior model, and both single and double cutaway Specials in the TV yellow. Hats off for these "VOS" vintage original spec versions. The rock 'n' roll raucous tones of the Specials, Juniors, and TV models keep the 50-year tradition proudly moving into the new century.

A rare Custom Shop 1960 Les Paul Special Double-cut (c2005) in faded cherry. *Courtesy the Custom Shop traveling showroom*

This 2004 Custom Shop 1960 Les Paul Special (# 0 4172) in TV white looks much like a wheatstraw vintage version.

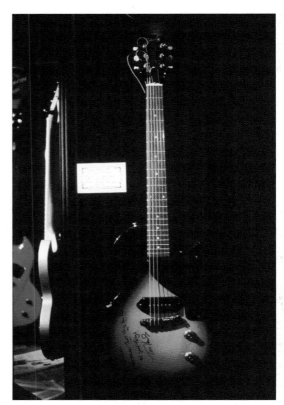

(Above) The signed 2000 Les Paul Jr. guitar used in the Tom Hanks rock band movie, *That Thing You Do!*

(Left) 2005 Les Paul Junior in TV white. *Courtesy Cal Vintage, 2005*

Les Paul Smartwood and Exotics

South America supplies some of the most important oxygen-giving plants for the planet. With ongoing awareness of the unfortunate deforestation crisis, many today are concerned with ecological issues and how to manage them. We have assumed our wood resources to be fairly unlimited, but that is now being reconsidered. It finally hit home with the total embargo of Brazilian rosewood in 1992. When supplies became scarce, opportunistic harvesters started carving reckless tractor paths into pristine forests to cut down the magnificent 125-foot-tall trees, leaving the local ecology a mess. Major guitar manufacturers tightened their belts and used similar Indian rosewoods for fingerboards and acoustic bodies, while slowly using up old reserves sold at premium prices.

In comparison to the large guitar firms, small volume luthiers have lesser demands and a harder time locating rare and prized tone woods, relying on a network of hardwood suppliers with past inventories. It also became difficult to ship vintage guitars overseas if they used Brazilian rosewood. To state their commitment for environmental protection, Gibson, Martin, Yamaha, and Drum Solo quickly jumped on the eco-friendly wood program with "certified" hardwoods. Others—including Fender, Taylor, and Santa Cruz—also followed suit. Gibson's chairman and CEO, Henry Juszkiewicz, has been a long-time supporter of the Rainforest Alliance by donating his time and financial support for their ongoing programs.

Enter "Smartwoods," a term coined by the new Rainforest Alliance organization (a non-profit conservation group) endorsed by the Forest Stewardship Counsel (FSC). Scientific Certification Systems have put their stamp of approval on eight million acres of forests worldwide, from which a very small percentage of certified land trees is used in making musical instruments. Hence, Gibson produced the first certified wood guitar (harvested from renewable forests) in 1996, a Les Paul Smartwood Standard that retailed for $3,390. A portion of the sales was donated to the Rainforest Alliance. Initially using maple from a Wisconsin-based Native American reservation, and chechen wood from a cooperative in Mexico, appointments were like the improved mahogany Standard, but with the addition of gold hardware and a satin finish—sans the pickguard. In place of the customary rosewood fingerboard was Chechen, a very hard but lighter-colored wood with a pronounced grain pattern (which further darkens with lemon oil). A gold "Smartwood Series" crest decal is present on the back of the necks, signifying the efforts of Gibson to protect and preserve the rainforests.

In catalogs and on the website, the new guitar looked somewhat bland, without a fancy-colored finish or chatoyant maple effect. Some reluctantly ordered them, then discovered that they sounded great. With a slightly thicker, well book-matched, straight-ahead maple top, vintage Standard construction, and a fast SG type neck, many owners soon appreciated the idea behind the instrument and its inherent build qualities.

Gibson then came out with their Smartwood Exotic guitar models in 1998. They featured six different types of rare and beautiful South American hardwoods harvested in an environmentally friendly manner. These prized tropical exotics (mostly from Paraguay) included ambay guasu, banara, taperyva, curupay, and peroba. They were constructed with thinner bodies (and a rear contour) that were chambered for weight reasons with the heavier exotic wood tops. A Smartwood (Standard) bass appeared at the 1998 Summer NAMM tradeshow with maple, mahogany, and chechen construction. It featured Gibson TB plus pickups and Bartolini active electronics.

The various hardwoods differed tonally and each had their particular way to be machined. For example, curupay (or curupau) is from the family mimosaceae; it reaches 80 feet with a trunk diameter of two or three feet and is found in provinces of Bolivia, Argentina, Brazil, and Paraguay. Its sapwood is pale pink with an abrupt transition to dark reddish brown heartwood and is used for outdoor furniture, beams, and truck beds. The dark-colored peroba rosa (its Spanish name is jichituriqui) from the apocinaceae family, can reach a height of up to 125 feet and a diameter of six feet. Rose red when cut, it is often streaked with yellow, orange, and purple. As with many woods, it needs to be milled wet, due to the difficulties with processing it mechanically when dry. Peroba is slightly heavier than hard rock maple and costs 50 percent more. The reddish-brown wood is used for furniture, flooring, cabinetry, and hand tools.

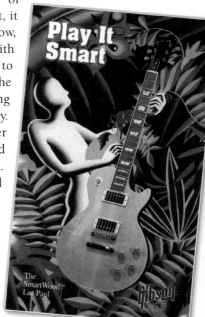

Tropical handbill for the Smartwood Les Paul.

Great ad for the Smartwood Les Paul series, with the exotic woods displayed.

Concerned musician Jackson Browne headed up a series of Rainforest Alliance benefit concerts in 1997 and duly received one of the first "forest friendly" prototype Smartwood models. Songster/bassist Sting also received a Smartwood Standard in 2000 with his Les Paul Award for the 15th annual Technical Excellence and Creativity event. Sting also did a tour in support of the Rainforest Alliance. The challenge was to clue guitarists into its being the right choice for both traditional "more noble" tone woods, as well as the exotic substitutes. The different companies involved are audited on an annual basis by Smartwood to maintain their certified status. FSC-stamped woods are stored in separate areas to ensure the customer's confidence.

Les Paul Smartwood flier pages showing the muiracatiara Muir top.

Construction-wise, Exotics were more like an unbound Studio model with a thinner and chambered mahogany or poplar body with a small back contour (like The Paul), yet still retained the gold hardware. To complement the nuances of the natural woods, a durable UV-cured matte finish was applied. They were lighter and more affordable at $1,299. 490R and 498T Alnico pickups with cream (sometimes black) surrounds were used with the typical control layout. Cases were very attractive, light-colored hemp (burlap) covered with the black plush (plus a shroud) interiors. Les Paul Smartwood Exotics were discontinued in 2002, supplanted by the Smartwood Studio models officially introduced in 2003. They are now built with a carved muiracatiara (muir wood) top, mahogany

or poplar back and neck with a preciosa or curupay fingerboard. A 1959 rounded neck profile with the 17-degree headstock pitch, gold parts, no rear contour, and a metallic green leaf on the truss rod cover completed the current model. Recently, the great Hubert Sumlin has been performing with a Smartwood Les Paul model.

Apart from environmental issues that make those concerned quite proud to own them, having a rather unique "Smartwood" guitar from renewable resources makes it that much more special.

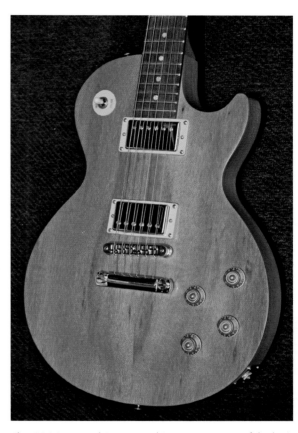

This 2004 Les Paul Smartwood (#02644336) is of the later variety, featuring a muiracatiara top on mahogany and a preciosa fingerboard. *Courtesy Instrumental Music, 2005*

Smartwood headstock with the iridescent leaf truss cover.

Orville and Epiphone Les Paul Models

As might be expected, Japanese copies of the popular Les Paul were built and sold worldwide from the sixties into the eighties, with a number of Ibanez, Greco, Tokai (Love Rock), Burny, and Yamaha models in various degrees of quality. Some of these faithfully represent the fancy maple tops and rich tones. Everyone wants a quality Les Paul guitar, but not everyone can put out big bucks for one. During the late eighties, Gibson authorized their own Japanese replicas to be marketed in Japan. Therefore these overseas models, with good-to-fine quality, had become an introductory guitar for multitudes of young guitarists and many others in Asia.

During the seventies, Gibson had successfully imported various acoustic models from Japan under the Epiphone moniker. They even built a limited edition "Epiphone USA" Spirit model as a double cutaway Special. As the new management team acquired Gibson from Norlin, the line expanded with archtops and the solid-body range. With the influx of copies hitting American shores, in 1977 Gibson put its team of lawyers to work to stop their import into the United States. This soon created the nick-named "lawsuit" models, often advertised privately.

The Orville Les Paul Guitar

Gibson awarded the Fuji Gen Gakki Corporation, who built Ibanez and Greco guitars, the licensing agreement. A high-quality Les Paul version was developed and available by 1988. Since Gibson was already trademarked in Asia, it was named Orville—after Gibson's founder. They became Gibson's original Japanese division from 1988 into 1995 and were intended for released only in Japan. Later Orville versions were produced in South Korea.

High-quality, well-detailed Orville Les Paul models were built during these years. Their logo font was Gibson's late-forties block-style logo, still used today. They featured normal vintage Gibson Standard and Custom head-stocks. Some productions added a smaller "by Gibson" next to the Orville pearl inlay. Standard models came with exquisite figured tops featuring cherry sunburst, faded honeyburst, and translucent finishes, authentic-looking pickups, nickel parts, old-style serial numbers, and rosewood and ebony fingerboards. Set necks with old-style long tenons and one-piece mahogany backs were standard features. Darkly dyed rosewood and ebony, medium frets and white pearloid were used on Custom

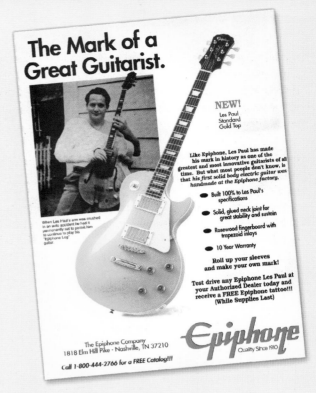

Les Paul endorses the new 1994 Epiphone Les Paul Standard Gold Top. This old photo shows Les playing his Epiphone, wearing a cast while recovering from his car accident.

(Right and Below) Orville (by Gibson) Les Paul Standard #G206115 in cherry sunburst finely crafted in Japan. *Courtesy Paul Love, 2008*

model fingerboards. Many were quite accurate '59 models with stickered PAF style pickups, long tenon construction, great coloration, and solid flametops. Nitro finishes in tobacco burst and deep (burnt) amber/orange translucent tops and backs graced quite a few. "Gibson" was engraved onto the truss covers, while the back of the headstocks sometimes said "Made in Japan." Although solid flame maple tops were used, sometimes other versions had a thin veneer or "foto-flame" over the maple. Orville (by Gibson) Junior and Custom models were also available in various color schemes and pickup configurations. They also produced some fine SG models. The fit, binding, and finish on these original Orville instruments were very nice.

Dating wise, the first digit of the serial number signifies the last digit of the year during the eighties into the nineties Japanese production numbers also included a prefix: A, F, J (Japan), K and G (Orville by Gibson) that were followed by six digits. K prefixes or no number signify Korean construction. The first digit of the numbers being the last digit of the year (e.g., G88xxxx=88 and 50xxxx=95). By 1990, Orville models were also being manufactured in South Korea (MIK)—to be sold in Japan and other nearby regions. For many, the well-crafted Orville guitar has a special place in the history of Gibson's legacy of the Les Paul guitar.

The Epiphone Les Paul Emerges

By 1992, Jim "Epi" Rosenberg headed up the new Epiphone line with expansion and advertising. Now the United States and abroad had an official Gibson-sanctioned Epiphone Les Paul model on the market. Dave Berryman made numerous visits to South Korea to organize the new operation. Les Paul did an ad for the new instruments with the 1947 picture of him playing his old Epiphone Zephyr. In 1995, the 80th celebration of Epi Stathopoulo's reign of Epiphone products was observed. Gibson eventually looked to China to complement manufacturing. The Qin Dao Gibson Les Paul models have taken up the newer productions.

Instead of the traditional Gibson headstock, the new Epiphone models adopted the classic "clipped edges" of the 1939 Emperor. Veneered "foto-flame" tops were common on the less-expensive versions, for an instant visual impact. Radically large birds-eye type veneer tops were incorporated on the Les Paul Classic Birdseye. Blue and black bursts joined the normal sunburst finishes; Epiphone "VibroTone" Bigsby tailpieces were available. Left-handed versions were constructed, too. Les Paul Classic 12-string sunburst models were made in 1998 and use conventional trapeze tailpieces. A 1998 Les Paul Signature VS model (asymmetric semi-solid) low-impedance guitar was built in limited quantities in Korea with the narrow 1960s headstock.

In the nineties, upgrading took place with full-sized potentiometers for better throw and longer life. Their Humbucking pickups utilized a double vacuum waxing process that insured squeal-free, high-volume capabilities. The one Achilles heel is the flimsy toggle switches that can drop out and eventually fail. Many change them out to the quality Switchcraft versions.

Epiphone Les Paul brochure from 2003, showing Ace Frehley, the Customs, and a '56 Gold Top.

Special and Limited Editions

Many promotional and store specials were created over the years, including a Heineken GRAMMY® Special and Alabama Farewell Junior. A nifty 50th Anniversary 2002 Epiphone all-black Custom Les Paul with an engraved gold truss cover was sold with a depiction of Les's Log on the back, two vintage Gibson ads, and a Goldtop, plus a paragraph of Les's involvement with Epiphone instruments. A Les Paul "Chrome" Black Beauty featuring all chromed parts (pickup rings and pickguard), and a Studio Deluxe with gold hardware and covered pickups were two "Guitar of the Month" Epiphone models in 2005.

The unique 7-string Les Paul models were almost piano-like instruments. Consistently even plucking with the fingernails helps facilitate the expertise on this instrument, much like George Van Eps's style on his 7-string wonders. Some find using a .064 for the low B string removes some of floppiness found with the standard .056 gauge. This sweet, harmonically rich LP 7 fills a gap other guitars can't. It's definitely a little more Les for the discerning musician—also available in '06 as the Studio Gothic version for Music123. On another low note, a 27 ¾" scale baritone Les Paul model was produced for the deeper-voiced tones in natural and a variety of custom graphic color schemes. The beefy bottom-end sounds prompted the ad literature to state, "Order yours today and play more manly."

Special edition VLOS University Les Paul models were produced in different school colors with one humbucking and a dot fingerboard. Epiphone Les Paul Studio and 100 models are constructed of mahogany/alder body woods in sunburst without binding and two uncovered humbucking. A half-sized "Epi Roadie" Les Paul in red was produced for the traveling fellows who handle the road gear. These morphed into the current Rave Rig sunburst Pee Wee model and travel amp.

The elegant Custom Les Paul recreates the traditional fancy multiple bound and gold appointments and is available with two and three humbucking pickup versions in ebony and white. Custom "Flame Top" Plus models featured fancier flamed maple tops in Heritage cherry sunburst, while limited editions included translucent white or cherry showing the flame maple. All had white pearloid blocks and, curiously, used rosewood fingerboards instead of ebony. Serial numbers sometimes started with EE and eight or nine digits starting with 06 for 2006. They are handcrafted in China with stickers

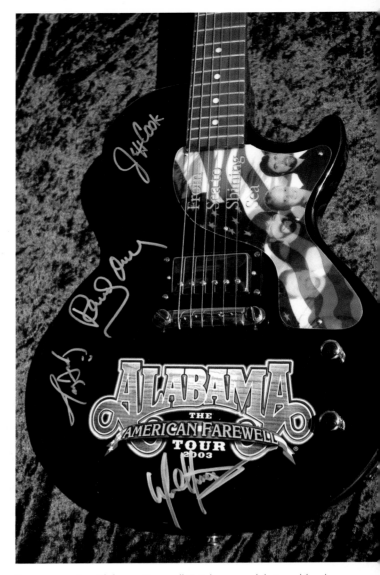

Commemorative Alabama Farewell Epiphone model signed by the artists. *Courtesy Centre City Music, 2007*

stating they are "100 percent inspected and setup in USA by setup #xx." Ebony Les Paul Elite Hollow-body models were built like the Florentine Gibson series. By 2005, Qin Dao even produced the new Supreme arched back replica.

Recent Limited Edition Custom Shop Standard Plus models are handcrafted in China. Rear stickers state these special facts just below the Grover tuners. Cream plastic, ABR-1 bridges, nickel hardware, sunbursts and deep cherry burst finishes grace these beautiful flamed and quilted Les Paul models. The faithful reproduction of the 1956 Goldtop with P-90 pickups and a Tune-O-Matic bridge gives the vintage guitar fan a great blues axe to wield onstage. Many players who collect and enjoy these Epi Les Paul guitars say, "They're the closest you can get to the real thing."

Player/endorsers of the Epiphone Les Paul line include Nancy Wilson of Heart, who plays the Ultra model. Other artist-endorsed signature instruments include Les Paul models for Ace Frehley, Slash (Snakepit Classic), Bob Marley, Joe Perry (Aged Tiger flame maple Bonehead model), Zakk Wylde (Bullseye, Camo, and Buzzsaw) Custom, a Lynyrd Skynyrd 30th Anniversary Goldtop, and John Connolly and Vince Hornsby of Sevendust models.

Korean-built Epiphone Les Paul 7-string model (#U00052070) in black burst over veneered flame maple. Its extended voicing is popular with jazz/fusion, world music, and metal fans. *Courtesy Dave Waterbury, 2006*

Epiphone Elite Les Paul models built in the year 2000 took up where the Orville models left off. They too were built where the Orville models were made and used long neck tenons and other '59 appointments. Fancy book-matched chatoyant African mahogany often complemented the curly maple tops that graced these special Japanese versions. A red and gold Epiphone Elite sticker was affixed below the Grover tuners that signified the model (e.g., 2002 #F201138). Many feel the Elite Les Paul models are similar to an accurate USA version, and a big step up from a regular Epiphone.

The 2006 Elitist series replaced the Elite models and further upped the ante with a number of Japanese Epiphone models. Among the Les Paul range included a Standard Plus with fancy maple and USA 50SR(490)/60ST (498) humbuckers, a Custom (2PU) in sunbursts/ebony/ Alpine white/wine red, and the '57 Goldtop with a hard maple top in metallic antique gold. The Elitist Standard Plus artist model for Tak Matsumoto features quilted maple with a faded Tak burst, black binding, abalone crown inlays, and half cream Burstbuckers. Another Elitist model was built for Twisted Sister's guitarist Jay Jay French. It features a book-matched maple top and contoured mahogany back in a striking Twisted Sister Pink burst.

A 2005 Ultra Les Paul was introduced with "strategically placed hollow cavities" for weight considerations (weighing around 5.5 lbs) and for a more acoustic sound. The Epiphone Les Paul Standard comes with a veneered flamed maple top in honey burst, Heritage Cherry and vintage sunburst, translucent blue or amber, and wine red. Bodies are mahogany/alder with set mahogany necks. The normal Standard is in sunbursts and ebony finishes. The Standard Plus replaces the series, maintaining the fancy maple veneers. A 1998 Les Paul Deluxe with small humbuckings came in ebony finish.

A Limited Edition run of sparkle-top Les Paul Standard Flake models was built in silver, green, red, purple, and blue from 1996 into 1998. Champagne gold versions were produced for Mars Music Company as well. Attractive Les Paul Standard Translucent models came in trans blue, amber, and red over foto-flame top. Gothic Les Paul models were based on the same successful Gibson line, with its satin black finish and black hardware for that wicked look—ready to wake the dead.

Les Paul Special and Special II were entry-level guitars featuring the flat body and dot-inlaid neck (bolt-on II), twin open-coil humbuckings with the Tune-O-Matic/ Stop setup, and single volume and tone controls with a toggle switch in the middle. Epiphone Les Paul Juniors featured either a P-90 or one exposed humbucking. Limited Edition '57 Junior single cuts came in vintage-style sunburst, TV yellow, and cherry sunburst with a P-100, while the double cut versions included the cherry and TV finish.

Epiphone Les Paul Basses from South Korea included the maple/alder Special (bolt-on neck), 5-string Standards with Dual Rail pickups and 1 $^{21}\!/_{32}$" nut set necks, a Limited Edition 2001 Standard Plus 4-string with twin humbuckings, flame maple top, flowerpot inlay and set neck construction, and a Vince Hornsby (Sevendust) signature edition with a maple fingerboard. The hip Jack Casady Signature low-Z bass models round out the series.

The recent Korean and Chinese production virtually reinvents the Epiphone Les Paul, with well-crafted models that sell worldwide. Instruments from all three overseas factories serve their function very well to supply the ever-increasing demand. Les Paul feels the new line from the Asia must be absolutely top quality if his name is going to be on it. The Gibson/Epiphone overseers of the line make a point to keep that quality top notch for the public and for Les.

2006 Epiphone Les Paul Ultra with chambered body, deep rear contouring, quilted maple top, and faded cherry sunburst finish. *Courtesy John Bertolet, Ventura*

Colorful catalog page showing various Limited Edition Les Pauls including the translucent, metal flake, Slash, and Custom models.

1996 Epiphone Limited Edition Les Paul Standard Flake in green sparkle. *Courtesy Alan Foust, 2007*

(Opposite Page Bottom) 1999 Epiphone Les Paul Standard (#90010191) in deep cherry sunburst with set neck, alder body, Gotoh tulip tuners, white serial number label, and Gibson-shaped export headstock. *Courtesy Nick Brokaw, 2005*

165

(Right) Clean white Epiphone Les Paul Custom. Photo *courtesy Donny Sarian, 2006*

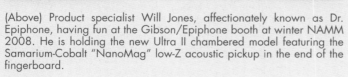

(Above) Product specialist Will Jones, affectionately known as Dr. Epiphone, having fun at the Gibson/Epiphone booth at winter NAMM 2008. He is holding the new Ultra II chambered model featuring the Samarium-Cobalt "NanoMag" low-Z acoustic pickup in the end of the fingerboard.

(Right) A great Heart performance with Nancy Wilson playing her Les Paul Ultra model at the NAMM Epiphone concert in 2008.

High-end Epiphone Les Paul GX Prophesy model in Deep Cherry finish with USA Dirty Fingers pickups. EX version comes in Midnight Ebony with EMG pickups. Winter NAMM 2008.

Signature Players

Jack Casady has played the Les Paul Signature Bass guitar for many years. He provided the solid bass backing behind the innovative Jefferson Airplane, one of San Francisco's seminal 1960s psychedelic rock bands, known for classics like "Somebody to Love" and "White Rabbit." Jack also lent his talents to a few incredible Jimi Hendrix live studio tunes for *Electric Ladyland*. He later collaborated with Airplane guitarist Jorma Kaukonen in 1971 to form Hot Tuna, a popular blues-oriented side group, resulting in 22 albums to date. Known for his unique improvisational solos, his eclectic first solo effort, *Dream Factor*, was released in 2004, showcasing his talents with many notable players.

After playing various modified Guild bass guitars, Jack discovered the merits of the Gibson Signature Bass and went on to have his own signature Epiphone version released in 2003. He enjoys the full-sized, long-scale, semi-acoustical instrument's resonating properties, which generate a natural tone with sustain. He feels the lower bass range is quite smooth and round with this particular model. It looks cool, too! These unique Signature models are certainly head-turners to those who've never seen them before.

I caught up with Jack Casady at the Gibson/Epiphone booth during NAMM 2006.

Robb: Jack, how did the new JC-B1 Epiphone Bass come about?

Jack: Jorma Kaukonen and I were doing some Hot Tuna shows on the East Coast and living in New York City, at 7th Avenue and 19th Street. There was a guitar shop on West 23rd Street, right next to the Chelsea Hotel. In the window I saw Gibson Goldtop Double Cutaway that appeared to have a long-scale neck with a single pickup. I was very intrigued by it, so I went in and played it. I loved it. I had played the Guild Starfire, an f-hole guitar, back in part of the Airplane years and the early part of Hot Tuna years. The problem with the Guild was that it was a little shy on the low end because of the short scale. But in any case, I played it for a number of years and experimented with electronics. Stanley Owsley and Ron Wickersham did the first conversion. Later on, I had the first Alembic made by Rick Turner with Ron, but I liked the sounds of the acoustic guitar and the f-hole bass. I played those for a number of years in the mid-seventies, along with a solid-body bass.

It was in the mid-eighties when I saw this guitar and I loved it. I thought, "Gee, I didn't even know about it." What I loved about it was not only the fact it had the 34-inch, full scale, but it had all the acoustic properties I liked. It had something else. It had bracing in the back that only came up about 5/8 inch. And it wasn't like putting a solid block down the center like quite a few of them have. It was also a low-impedance bass designed with a single pickup. I hadn't heard that. The Signature pickup was designed and the whole number was put out in 1972, according to Walter Carter, the historian of Gibson. Walter said they made a run of about 400 and sold them through 1979.

Epiphone models arrive…

I approached Henry at Gibson about reissuing this, but I told him I would like to design my own pickup. He put me in touch with Jim Rosenberg at Epiphone, because Epiphone is within the Gibson companies. Jim thought it was a great idea, so we started the process of having the instrument rebuilt by the craftsmen in Korea who make the Epiphone instruments. We hunted up the original pressing plates for the laminated tops and bottoms and duplicated them. The next issue was for me to work on the pickup. The top Gibson man at that time was J.T. Riboloff. J.T. and I went down to Nashville with the old pickups and the old bass and we duplicated them. I said that the problem with these old pickups is that they get lost in modern tracks, with the wide expansion of the tonal spectrum that you hear in the music today, especially if you have to battle with keyboards and synthesizers. What I wanted to do was increase the power of the

Jack Casady happily playing his new Epiphone Signature Bass model, developed with J.T. Riboloff and released in 1998.

pickup, the Alnico pickups, the magnets, so we did that by about one-third. That's what I used to do with my old Starfires. I would set the pickups out [Hagstrom/Guild "Bi-sonic" versions] and epoxy another Alnico magnet on the other side to raise the level of the pickup, the output. That's because we had flipped the system over to low impedance, which did not have a high output. That was part of the reason why my Starfires sounded so good—because they were low impedance as well, allowing you to have the full spectrum.

We kept that whole issue alive with this new version, which was going to be called the Jack Casady Epiphone Bass. So the instrument itself is duplicated, with double cutaways and a hollow body. This is a hollow body, but it has a fluted piece attached to the back just enough to keep the resonance down so that there's no feedback. But you still get hollow-body qualities that come out through the pickup. That helps the tone, giving it an acoustic-like quality. At the same time, you have real control over the tone. There's a block to mount the three-point bridge, but otherwise there's plenty of hollowness left (taps top). You can hear right here (plays some Hot Tuna notes). You get a good deal of sound out of it.

The next issue was to continue using a transformer for selecting low-impedance to mid- to high-impedance. I kept that at 50, 250, and 500, although I personally never use the 250 and 500 settings; I keep it in what I call the pure setting, 50. But others liked it like that. It sort of compresses the sound down and bumps up the volume, but it makes it kind of box-like, which is not exactly the kind of tone I like. But then the issue was the pickup itself. I told J.T. I wanted to keep the windings 28-gauge thick, like those used on a lot of the old lap steel guitars.

We had to deal with some new issues along the way. It used to be that the center pole was wrapped in masking tape and you just wound the wire around it, so we had to experiment with the definitions on that. That actually took about the longest; I think we must have made 20 prototypes. When I finally got the resonance and the full sonic spectrum that I wanted, I said, "OK, let's put it into production." So it's out on the market and I've no ringers. Every year there's a new manufacturing run and I have them send me two. I string them up, set them up, and take them out on the road. Those are the ones I use for that year. This way,

I can make sure that the production quality is up on it; it keeps it current. It isn't like I've put any other pickups in here. The pickup I wanted is the pickup they're making, so I have no issues there. This pickup is called the Jack Cassidy bass pickup, the JC-B1. It's made with the Epiphone moniker on it, but the model is my pickup.

RL: *Thank you so much for sharing the history of the Epiphone Jack Casady Signature Model.*

Well-stocked Epiphone Les Paul wall at Guitar Trader, San Diego, 2005.

Les Paul Supreme

Gibson USA had been considering making a truly new design Les Paul guitar in the high-end market spectrum. Between general manager Jeff Allen, engineer Keith Medley, and plant manager Tom Montgomery, they came up with an plan to pull out all the stops. After some brainstorming, the magnificent idea of incorporating the classic L-5 flame maple back took hold to create this "Supreme" version of the Les Paul.

The challenge was to devise a way to get the electronics installed in production without compromising the front and back. Maple is naturally heavy, so the instrument was to be chambered for weight considerations. That also added a fuller hollow-body tonality. The widened rectangular input jack area and wiring channels were necessary for easy installation. They used longer pickup leads to solder outside, plus stiffer wires for stabilizing the assembly to help slide the electronics inside the inner mahogany chambers.

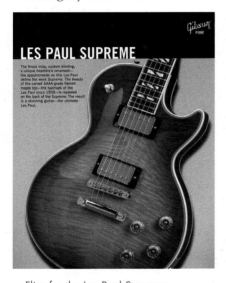

Flier for the Les Paul Supreme.

After the top and middle are glued together, the chambers are routed and the top is carved, then maple back is fitted on last. Complementing the book-matched AAAA figured maple construction is the fancy Custom binding and gold hardware. Even special nickel-free gold fret wire is used that is 20 percent harder than normal wire. Super 400 split-pearl block neck inlays on the ebony fingerboard are naturally fitting for an instrument of this caliber. Jeff designed and Keith created the prototype of the attractive pearl banner/abalone globe design for the headstock veneer. 490R/498T Alnico humbuckings were used for great dynamics, coupled with the normal four-control electronics. Grover Tulip button machine heads and a gold-plated truss cover completed the instrument. First year finishes included trans amber, root beer, and heritage cherry, and desert bursts. Soon afterward, wine red, trans black, and alpine white finishes were added. TKL black cases with a green or white interior were supplied with all the case candy.

(Left) The highly touted Les Paul Supreme maple back, unique to the Les Paul range.

(Below) 2003 Les Paul Supreme model (#01853487) in all its grandeur. *Courtesy Don Breeze, 2004*

(Above Left) The Supreme headstock with a very attractive worldly banner announcing its supremacy.

The guitar first debuted at NAMM in January 2003. It then took some time to fill the many orders for that year's limited edition, so there were many impatient guitarists writing about it on the Les Paul Forum. CEO Henry Juszkiewicz said the Supreme was the perfect guitar to "kick off the next 50 years of the Les Paul." This unique jewel of an instrument, with its sheer maple grandeur, is considered by many to be the true top-of-the-line for Les Paul guitars. With its remarkable looks, it will reign Truly Supreme in the Gibson range.

2003 Nashville NAMM show Les Paul Supreme maple back in root beer finish.

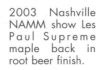

The Music Rising Les Paul guitar, signed at the 48th GRAMMY Awards® (2006) by numerous celebrities. Starting at the top left, signatures include; Sting, Bono (across the toggle), Joss Stone, Paul McCartney, Joe Perry, Beyonce, Edge (on the edge), Adam Clayton, Ray Benson, Kanye West, Allen Toussaint, Matt Dillon, Jamie Fox, Randy Johnson, John Fogerty, John Legend, Tom Hanks (on the pickguard), and Ryan and Jamie (from Maroon 5).

The back is profusely signed, too. Celebrities include Tony Bennett, Stevie Wonder (both on the neck), Kelly Clarkson, Elvis Costello, Nicole Kidman, Steve Vai, Jeff Watson, Faith Hill, James Taylor, Bonnie Raitt, Ivan Neville, Dr. John, and others. Everyone legibly signed a map of the guitar, too.

This Music Rising Les Paul #033950617 was 299th of 300 built for this musicians' fund raiser. Special thanks to David Weiderman at GC and Donna Lynn.

Music Rising Les Paul Katrina

After the devastation of Hurricane Katrina in 2005, U2 guitarist The Edge helped coordinate an effort to raise funds to help musicians who were affected in the Gulf Coast region. The November 21st unveiling of Music Rising was partnered by Gibson guitars, producer Bob Ezrin, and the Guitar Center Music Foundation (Larry Thomas). The goal was to collaborate on designing, building, and selling an exclusive Gibson Les Paul guitar, with proceeds going to the Music Rising program. Rolling Stone, MTV, VH-1, Musician's Friend, Spin Co, and Ticketmaster also helped the relief program. The Edge visited the damaged areas in New Orleans, meeting musicians who told him about what had happened. Much of today's popular music originated in this area and evolved to the jazz, blues, and R&B we enjoy today. The area has a rich history of American music and talented musicians.

The instrument features specially painted Mardi Gras artwork that is done individually with varying wild color schemes. Most of the plastic parts are made of wood from the states affected. The Music Rising logo was etched into the wooden pickguard. Music Cares, a non-profit organization, handles the qualification process and has already contributed $1.5 million for 1,800 musicians. One of the guitars, shown here, was signed at the 48th GRAMMY Awards® show by many artists. Edge signed 31 of the Les Paul Hurricane Motif guitars at Guitar Center unveiling, 14 of which sold for $10,000 each. The list price was $4,899, discounted to $3,334 at Guitar Center. President Clinton also gave guitarist August Williams a very colorful one at the Baton Rouge airport.

Edge Music Rising Les Paul display at the 2006 NAMM show.

The Bantam and Florentine Arrive

Bringing the concept of the *f*-hole archtop and solid-body technology together with the Les Paul guitar finally entered onto the Gibson Custom Shop lineup. The 1995 limited edition Bantam Elite series first premiered semi-solid Les Paul 13" models with their specially routed one-piece mahogany backs and 1/2"- to 1/4"-thick carved maple tops with both diamond and *f*-shaped sound holes. Gibson's West Coast Custom shop built an experimental *f*-hole Les Paul model in 1992 that set the stage. The Nashville production models were called the Bantam Elite series when first released. They were available in heritage cherry sunburst, antique natural, emberglow, faded blue, emerald green, rosa red, concord purple, midnight blue, root beer, peacock, and translucent black. The Plus models featured two-piece flame maple tops, while the Elite Sparkle models had gold, red, or silver sparkle (metal flake) finishes. They soon discovered the new Washburn Company was already using the name, so it became the new Florentine and Diamond Elite series in 1996. By that time, diamond sparkle versions had switched to diamond shaped holes (à la Trini Lopez models).

These beautiful new instruments are basically a hybrid of the Les Paul Custom (gold hardware, multiple bindings, and fancy split-diamond neck appointments), with a comfortable 1959 neck profile and a thin-line ES series type construction (sans the maple centerpiece). The design is almost a throwback to the hollow lightweight Guild and Gretsch models of the fifties. Gibson's novel combination (which was expensive to build) can generate true Les Paul grind and sustain, along with the warmer tones approximating that of an ES-335. Since the body size is considerably smaller and the top is nearly twice as thick, it is not as resonant with the complexities of the 335 rhythm tones. Some feel the guitar is like getting three guitars in one, with a vast variety of tones and easily controlled feedback qualities. Compared to full solids equipped with '57 Classic pickups, the treble position's brighter tone (with a slight twang) give it a new presence and versatility, "producing an edged sound that cuts like a knife," as Gibson puts it. Guitarist Noel Gallagher from Oasis played a silver sparkle Diamond model and, according to one fan, got a "big honking snarl" from his bridge pickup sustaining through his Marshall amp.

The Custom Shop's build quality on this series was excellent, with good fret finishing (without chatter marks or sharp edges) and refined binding details. Gold Grovers were standard tuners with the Tune-O-Matic and

stop/stud combinations in gold to complete the instrument. Serial numbers follow the large stamped Classic scheme, with the last digit of the year followed by a space, then the decade number and actual production number (e.g., 7 9328). The striking Diamond Elites were continued into 1997, while the Florentines were temporarily suspended in 1998—only to resurface by popular demand in 2004. Plus models are now complemented with a Standard neck model and even with exotic tops of bubinga. The Florentine Plus finishes soon expanded further to a total of 16 colors, with ebony and faded blue, plus eight metallics that included black, Brunswick blue, copper, gold, ice blue, lavender, silver, and pink champagne… and that faded denim blue jean special.

Flier for the Les Paul Bantam semi-solid-body series, showing the Elite model.

Les Paul Florentine series flier showing the sunburst model.

A special-ordered purple Les Paul Florentine for Al DiMeola held by Ron Marinelli at the NAMM show.

NAMM show Les Paul Florentine Plus in antique natural with nice maple figuring.

Very green Les Paul Florentine f-hole model. *Courtesy Todd Stemmerman, 2003*

The Catalina Series

Another short-lived version loosely based on the Standard was the Catalina model, built from 1996 into 1999. Available in opaque Riverside red, canary yellow, and cascade green (a great 1956 Corvette color), its stand-out bright colors were offset with a white marine pearloid pickguard, truss cover, and input jack plates along with white bindings and pickup surrounds. These "nice to look at" custom-colored Les Paul guitars were a complete departure from the customary sunburst shades and translucent color schemes.

Catalinas were built with dynamic sound chambers (similar to the Florentine), compound radius ebony fingerboards, and "Custom Shop" imprinted around a pearl circle on the headstock. They came standard with nickel hardware, '57 Classic pickups, and real mother-of-pearl crown neck inlays. Although the flier stated they utilized an expanded neck tenon, some were made with the shorter rounded versions just under the fingerboard. Some lacquer cracking and peeling took place around the necks and edges that were due to inadvertent finish problems.

The semi-hollow chambered body actually enhances the acoustic tone while bringing the weight down, a welcome relief from the normal back-breaker syndrome. Nice jazz sounds that can be warmed with sustain are obtained from the front pickup. Pickup combinations are often more pleasant for some players. Like its sister, the Florentine, versatile sounds for many musical styles can easily take you from rock, to blues, into light jazz.

Custom Shop canary yellow Les Paul Catalina (#6 9762) with pearloid pickguard and bound headstock.

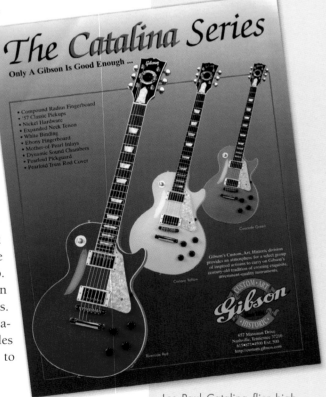

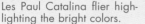

Les Paul Catalina flier highlighting the bright colors.

The Elegant Series

Following in the footsteps of the Catalina series were the 1999 Elegant models. Their construction, playability, and tone mirrored the previous model, with dynamic sound chambers, player-friendly compound radius ebony fingerboards, '57 Classic pickups, and the round Custom Shop pearl headstock inlays. What differed was the cream-colored binding and pickup bezels, colorful abalone trapezoid inlays, and beautiful AAA grade curly maple under the three translucent finishes. Two subtle sunbursts consisted of butterscotch and firemist, while an antique natural filled out the color options. In more recent times, peacock and heritage cherry sunburst were added. With all these modern attributes, the Custom Shop felt this Elegant model lives up to its name and "is perhaps the best-looking and -sounding Les Paul offered in the Custom Collection."

Gibson's Les Paul Elegant in Firemist Red at the 1999 Anaheim NAMM show.

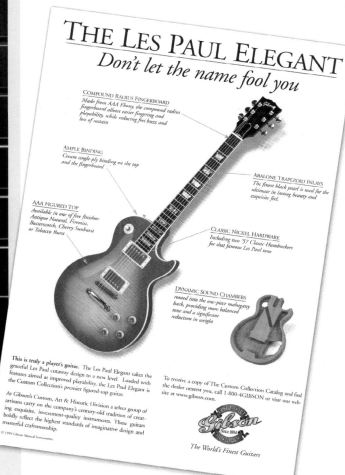

2000 Les Paul Elegant advertisement showing chambered body.

2003 Custom Shop Les Paul Ultima with quilted maple in heritage cherry sunburst. *Courtesy La Mesa Guitar Center, 2004*

The Les Paul Ultima's exquisite tree-of-life inlays.

LES PAUL ULTIMA

The Ultima marries the craftsmanship of the Custom Division with the structural features of the Les Paul. A highly figured maple top and abalone binding are but two of the many features of this incredible instrument.

The selection of hand inlaid fingerboards are among the most beautiful created by Gibson, including the Butterfly, the Tree of Life, the Harp and Flames. Set off by the original Heritage Cherry Sunburst finish, this line of guitars is the Ultimate.

Construction:	One-piece mahogany back with carved figured maple top and one-piece mahogany neck
Binding:	Abalone binding on top, white binding on fingerboard and peghead
Hardware:	Gold-plated with pearl or gold Grover Imperial keys
Bridge:	Tune-o-matic bridge with stopbar
Pickups:	Two '57 Classic humbuckers
Controls:	Two volume / two tone / 3-way selector switch
Fingerboard:	Ebony with choice of four custom inlays
Other Features:	Abalone side dots, dynamic sound chambers, engraved pearl Custom Shop headstock inlay

Butterfly   *Harp*   *Flame*

Tree of Life

Available Finishes:

Heritage Cherry Sunburst

2000 Les Paul Ultima catalog depiction showing the flame neck and all four neck patterns.

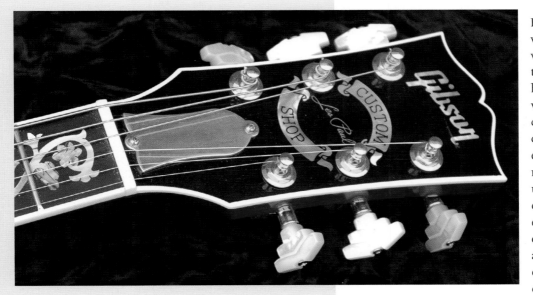

The Les Paul Ultima takes the cake for ornamentation—right on out to the headstock.

The Les Paul Ultima

The Custom Shop presented their Ultimate Les Paul production model in 1996, bringing the fanciest appointments of woods, pearl-inlaid border trim (à la Martin's 42/45 decor), and four of the most elabo-rate fingerboard inlays ever to grace a Les Paul guitar—certainly a contender for the discerning player/collector. It takes a particular type of person to invest in such an extravagant instrument.

Some of the most beautiful inlaid fingerboard designs grace this special model. Exacting and painstaking effort is done to inlay the mixed abalone and mother-of-pearl pieces into the ebony. Unlike the days of yesteryear, laser-cut pearl and CNC fingerboard routs greatly speed up the time involved. The traditional tree-of-life and harp patterns are quite intricate, inspired by Orville's dancing girl and vases done on his special reverse scroll harp guitar. Butterfly and flame patterns complete the four fingerboard options. Even the side dots were abalone.

A special edition Winter NAMM 1996 model #WN96 with the harp pattern may have helped generate this Ultima model to fruition later in the year. The neck base was specially carved, as on a vintage banjo. The ivoroid heel was engraved "Winter NAMM '96." Even the truss says "One of a Kind."

Exquisite figured maple with striking patterns were hand-picked for the Ultima. The popular heritage cherry sunburst was the chosen finish color. Dynamic sound chambers lighten the expensive leaden instrument. Gold hardware was used, while the tuners consisted of Grover Imperials with gold or pearl deco grips. Headstock appointments consisted of the Custom Shop pearl circle, while the pickup selector ring and pickguard are left off. '57 Classic humbuckings were fitted, and either a stop bar or special Ultima Loop tailpiece was available. As the 2000 catalog says of such eye candy, "This line of guitars is the ultimate."

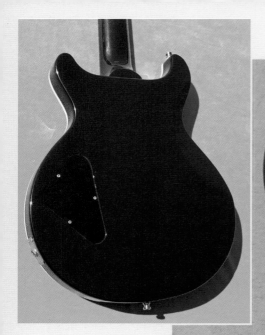

(Above) Les Paul DC Pro contoured back with indigo filler stain.

(Right) This 1998 Les Paul DC Pro (#8 9451) in indigo features the optional 25 ½" scale length, P-90s with the stopbar set-up. The blue teal finish covers the entire instrument. *From the author's collection*

(Below) 1998 flier for the new Les Paul DC Pro series, showing the evolution of the Les Paul double cutaway.

Les Paul DC Models

The DC double cutaway model began as an arched maple top version of the revamped 1958 Special, with complete access to the entire neck. Generated by the new PRS competition of a 24-fret, double-cutaway design, Gibson wanted to give that new market niche a dose of modern Les Paul reality. The previously-released double-cut XLP from the mid-eighties didn't fare too well, due to its Explorer headstock, big heel, whammy bar, and bizarre electronics. Now with AAA maple tops and various player-oriented options (professional-friendly), Gibson's new 1997 DC Pro entered the marketplace with clout and pedigree.

Custom Shop designer Matthew Klein was behind the innovative ideas incorporated into the DC Pro model (the original version released). Using a similar arched maple top of the single cutaway models, they came up with a partially hollowed-out mahogany body construction (1 ⅛" thick) and featured a comfortable rear chest contour. This chambering added to the resonant acoustical quality and kept the weight well below eight pounds. Sustain from the maple top was still noticeably strong. Single decorative cream binding graced the top of the body only. A modern compound radius on the smooth ebony fingerboard (decreasing the curvature as you play up the neck) enabled easy chording in the first positions and buzz-free bending in the upper registers. The neck width was unusually wide, measuring 2 ¹⁄₁₆" at the 12th fret and 2 ¼" at the 24th, while maintaining the 1 ¹¹⁄₁₆" at the nut. Its medium slender profile was quite comfortable compared to the large '59 or thin '60 shapes. Simple pearl dots and medium-sized tall frets complete the fingerboard.

The simple nearby control configuration (practical proximity) of volume, tone, and three-way toggle switch gave the performing guitarist easy electronic composure. Many enjoy the master volume within easy reach of pinky finger while in the playing position, which is unique to these DCs. Available pickup and bridge options were either (495R and 500T) humbuckings with the Tune-O-Matic/stop bar combination or Special style with cream P-90 "soapbar" pickups and the stop/stud combo bridge. The steep five-degree neck pitch was also used on both versions, leaving the bridge and stopbar tailpiece quite high.

Most important was the optional professional scale length of 25 ½" (actually 25 ¼"), giving tall, long-fingered guitarists comfortable playability with ample room between the upper frets—the norm in the Fender and full-sized Epiphone and Gibson archtop lines. With the extended scale length came the expanded full harmonic tonalities of a crisper and richer sound, similar to the contrast between a Steinway concert grand piano and other pianos. The naturally-smooth ebony texture allowed for greater ease in bending notes with the slightly increased string tension. Unfortunately, this option wasn't widely promoted and only a few runs of these advanced instruments were made into 1998.

Rivaling its market counterpart, the DC Pro also had 24 frets that filled in the essential neck joint tenon area for neck stability. However, having the pickup moved back compromised the rhythm pickup's full string response, as it did in 1959. The need for straight string-pull across the nut for smooth tension release during bent notes gave rise to the narrow "snakehead" style design. Though even smaller than the twenties versions, the slightly odd but highly functional design was pioneered on the prior ES-336 model. They squeezed the pearl logo onto the top and put Les Paul DC Pro on the truss cover. Gibson brand mini Schallers tuners fit well on the small headstock.

Upon close inspection, one can see a fine maple cross-banding glued under both the ebony and maple cap, attaching it to the mahogany neck and body. DC Pro finish colors included faded cherry, butterscotch (burst), translucent black, indigo (with a deep turquoise blue top) and cool custom colors like indigo/blue-burst and a dark tri-burst. Listed at a pricey $3,200, this exclusive Custom Shop DC wonder was discounted down to around $2,600 in most stores. Altogether, they created an

Another beautiful indigo '98 DC Pro (#8 9452) from the same long-scale production, but with humbuckings and the Tune-O-Matic set-up. *Courtesy William Olvis, 2005*

all-around professional player's guitar on which Gibson, Fender, and PRS lovers could find their expressive needs met. Kudos to the forward-thinking Mr. Klein! "This cross pollination of traditional and modern features breathes new life into the fabled Les Paul family tree," stated the 1997 flier. Considered evolutionary in their literature, the DC Pro model design literally introduced new functionality to a Gibson.

Soon afterward, in 1997, the DC Studio model was developed in the USA plant as an economy version retailing at $1,400. It had the same body construction, sans the binding but with plain maple, and available only in the short-scale neck. Twin humbuckings with only a stop/stud bridge were standard. By early 1998, an up-scaled DC Standard (sunburst) was shown at the NAMM show, with fancier AAA maple and Les Paul Standard neck appointments and truss logo. Deemed an instant collectors' item, this limited run of 600 featured "lush tangerine burst and the elegant lemonburst" nitro-cellulose lacquer finishes (as used on most of their models), fast-action '59 slim-tapered necks, and Grover tuners. They became available in September and listed for $2,409. When released, this Standard DC Sunburst set a sales record for a new model.

The Custom Shop temporarily discontinued the DC Pro in 1998 (the only model with ebony and a compound radius), while the Standard DC Plus (AAA top, gold parts and Grovers) and Lite (plain and unbound) replaced the existing Standard and Studio. 1999 Les Paul Standard Lite models (actually without the DC title in catalogs) featured gold parts, 492R Alnico and

'57 Classic Plus Humbuckings, ¾-sized crown inlays. They came in translucent black, amber, and blue. Black was dropped the following year. 2001 Les Paul Standard double cutaway models were available in translucent black, amber, red, and even emerald green sunburst.

A Les Paul "Classic" DC was built from 2003 into 2005, bringing the best attributes of both models together. It featured a bullion goldtop finish, dark back, slim-tapered 60 neck, medium-sized frets, nickel parts, aged binding on the neck and front of the body, greenish cast trapezoid inlays, and classic (14:1 ratio) "Green Keys" Gotoh (Kluson Keystone style) tuners. It came equipped with 490R and 498T model humbuckers that emphasized the mid ranges but didn't quite capture the liveliness of the instrument for some players. P-90s were also an option for the gold DC Classic. As on the P-90 equipped DC Pro, the pickups lay flat, parallel to the back of the body, instead of perpendicular with the strings as with top mounted humbuckings. The DC Pro guitar was reintroduced in 2006, sporting a 22-fret rosewood fingerboard, faded crown inlays, and BurstBucker Pro pickups. It was available in root beer, black cherry, trans amber, and red. The LP Standard Plus was also released then with AAA tops, gold hardware, Grovers and finished in root beer, amber, black, and red transparent colors. Both versions have slender '60-styled necks.

Guitarists like its brighter SG-like tones combined with the chunkier rhythm tones. The well-defined bass and sweet midrange with singing trebles conveys complex voicings with ease. Many feel the versatile DC series sounds much like a cross between the Les Paul, SG, and a Telecaster. Double cutaways are also easy instruments for left-handed players to convert. For many, the DC series fills an important niche for Gibson solids and easily takes players into newfound directions.

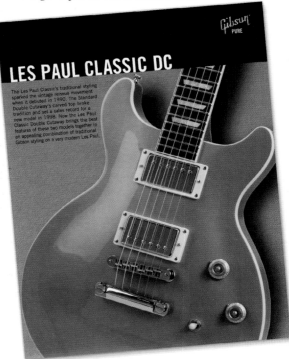

2003 flier for the Les Paul Classic DC in gold with body binding.

Pretty Les Paul DC Pro in blue burst. *Courtesy Warwick Rose, 2005*

Fine example of a 1997 natural Les Paul Standard (#791301) with korina wood construction and a quilted maple top; manufactured by Gibson USA with the Custom Shop decal. *Courtesy David Robinson 2006*

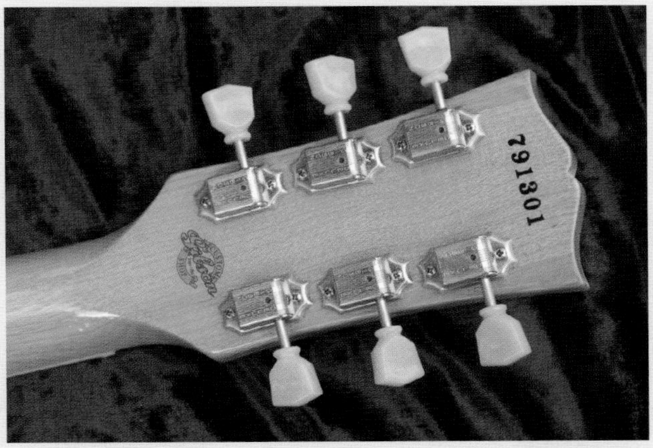

Les Paul Korina Models

Gibson used African limba wood (more popularly known in guitar circles as korina) for their twin-neck Consolette steel guitars during the early 1950s. Later in the decade, it was famously used with futuristic solids and Skylark steels. Korina (Terminalia superba) is a type of Swietenia mahogany displaying distinct light yellow-green coloration. It is often seen in period furniture, even in the original Gibson offices. Like its cousin mahogany, korina is easy to work with, but has some purportedly poisonous qualities. It is recognized as a worthy tone wood with good highs and sustain.

Gibson Les Paul Korina models were produced during the 1980s in very small quantities and generally with beautiful figured natural maple tops. Because of the high premium on the original Flying V and Explorer models, they are quite collectible. The small quantities of quilted maple guitars built since then also show the natural amber coloration throughout the instrument. Some versions used all-korina (except the fingerboard) construction often showing the inherent ribbon-like chatoyant effect. Now considered to be an ultimate tone wood, these exquisite Les Paul Korinas hold a special place among modern Gibson enthusiasts.

Les Paul Tie-Dye Guitars

Colorful tie-dye clothing has been in and out of fashion over the years, displaying an image of the creative side of hippiedom. The term itself conjures up the renaissance of late 1960s music—with Chet Helms concerts in Golden Gate Park, lightshows at the Fillmore West, or listening to *Disraeli Gears* at a dosed party. With this new music, art forms, and fashion, tie-dye clothes were in during the "Summer of Love." They are still with us today as a statement of freedom, worn in remembrance of that exploding youth movement. They're also in vogue as a fashion statement with today's Dead Head and Allman Brothers music. Thanks to George St. Pierre, a line of Gibson guitars is also deeply imbued with psychedelic, colorful patterns.

George's background was in woodworking and furniture; he was also a DJ and concert promoter. Having a lifelong love affair with vivid colors, George mastered the art of tie-dying cloth, running a tie-dye business with his wife, Dorothy. Later, George was working at a furniture shop in Nashville when he put in an application at Gibson and visited regularly until they hired him. While working at Gibson, his tie-dye endeavors carried over onto a discarded Les Paul guitar body.

After two years of experimenting, George perfected his technique and showed his colorful creation to Henry Juszkiewicz in October 1995. He was given the go-ahead to build 103 of these amazing beauties. Based on the Les Paul Standard with Humbuckings (#1 had P-90s), cream binding, no pickguard or switch ring, the intricate artwork surrounded the entire guitar. Samples were made in late 1995, then 103 officially signed versions were constructed during 1996. Each was entirely unique.

A creatively painted 1996 green Tie Dye Les Paul Standard #85 (91516602) by artisan George St. Pierre. *Courtesy GC Hollywood, 2005*

I spoke with George in May 2006 about how the Les Paul Tie Dye came about.

Robb: How did you hook up with Gibson?

George: A guy came by our furniture shop and had this Gibson shirt on. I said, "You play Gibsons?" He said, "Yeah, I also work for Gibson." I put in an application and I got excited, going there every two days for two weeks until they finally hired me, because they got tired of me coming out there. (We laugh.)

RL: Did you start in the paint department?

GSP: Yes, in the color department. I was always messing with colors and stuff on breaks. I started experimenting with guitars that were supposed to be scrap and came up with some crazy painting techniques. A few of them were proposed to Henry Juszkiewicz, the CEO. He said, "Do 103, one for every year Gibson has been in business."

RL: How did you get into the tie-dye shirt business?

GSP: The colors of the '60s, I guess. I just always loved colors. My mother was in the beauty shop boutique business. For the most part, I spent my summer vacations remodeling and painting her beauty shop and just getting creative. I made a few mistakes and splattered a little paint here and there. So pretty much, it's like how the Reese's cup started. (Laughs.) I sort of goofed up with the paint and did something with it and said, "Whoa, I can do that again!" And just went on and on and on. Peter Max was fabulous with what he did and I really didn't want to be like anyone else. I wanted to be totally unique.

Four weeks into this, I had done 50. We had a long weekend and had pretty much shut down except for the buffers. Production had a lot of guitars to get ready for final assembly the following Tuesday. Two of the guys—as far as we could tell, it was a jealous thing—squirted Super Glue over all 50 I had done, totally destroying them. So they *were hidden in a room for later repair. I duplicated those except for number one. Luckily, I hung it in my gold booth just to keep everyone from touching it, so it didn't get glue on it. Somehow, a few years after I left, these made it out onto the market. Every single one I did has my signature on it—except for the 50.*

RL: You used a fine cloth mesh?

GSP: I did my designs over cheesecloth with pheno-acelate and hot shot and then stretched it over the guitar and sprayed through that. Once I get my viscosity right, without it pulling the paint or dragging or bleeding, everything was fine. I could easily do 15 or 20 of them in ten hours.

RL: Did you affect the colors with a sponge or anything like that?

GSP: I used a few things. There are a lot of things I used in my closed booth that I pretty much kept to myself.

RL: It seems the darker highlights were over the first part.

GSP: Really, I don't have a rule of thumb. Pretty much how I feel that day is how I'm going to paint. I don't follow any rules.

RL: I saw a real psychedelic one with vivid turquoise and green and silver over it. That was striking.

GSP: Some of them were. It all depends upon what your base is and how you get an effect of something else. I also did a floral one for President Clinton with an abstract flag in the background. Today, I've got many more designs that blow those out of the water.

George's Les Paul Tie Dye instruments first had a fine cloth mesh laid onto the base-coated wood surface and various colors applied. Then the stencil cloth was removed and more colors were artistically applied during this whole process. The entire treated guitar was sealed and lacquered over, then sanded smooth and buffed. Each of the authorized ones was personally signed by George in gold or a matching color near the fingerboard, while the individual sequenced number was written on the heel.

Themes included traditional bright-colored tie-dyed effects, paisley and floral patterns, webbed patterns with bright dabs in various vibrant colors. Many were with shaded pastels and darker highlights or vice versa, plus the contrasting bright colors integrated. Some are truly psychedelic, with vivid colors and metallics. The guitars show well onstage and in displays. Overall, George did a myriad of trippy color schemes. The guitars have become quite collectable today.

Les Paul Tie-Dye Standard guitars had maple/mahogany construction and used chrome parts with gold knobs. Some of the first unsigned 50 had nickel parts and exposed pickup coils with black bell knobs and toggle switch to match the black highlights. These unique Les Paul models listed for $4,999; all 103 signed versions were sold. George left Gibson in 1999 after they moved him out of painting to final assembly. He has a website and continues to do special guitar finishes, with even more mind-blowing designs.

Guitar Center's display of two authentic 1996 Tie-Dye Les Paul models and one 2001 rainbow Standard.

The Digital Les Paul

To boldly go where no guitar has gone before.

From the sublime and eloquent to totally ripping explosive tonalities, the HD.6X-Pro digital Les Paul will take you there, opening up a new world of guitar sounds. The unbelievable 21st century digital guitar has arrived!

This new instrument features modern, cutting-edge guitar electronics to confront the digital frontier ahead. Early test models were initially shown in 2002 as Gibson unveiled their new media delivery system innovation, MaGIC—Media-accelerated Global Information Carrier. It is a proprietary protocol that transfers 32 channels of digital audio bi-directionally with a standard Cat-5 Ethernet cable.

Upon hearing of such an instrument, most players shrug off the idea, thinking it's another modeling guitar or synthesizer setup. Not so. This "high definition" wonder grew out of ten years of research and was first collaborated with 3Com, AMD, and Xilinx, utilizing Sonar Producer Edition software. It was demonstrated at Microsoft's Windows Hardware Engineering Conference in Seattle in 2002, and *Time* magazine named it one of the Coolest Inventions of 2003. Las Vegas saw an early version demonstrated with Les Paul and Neal Schon. The DLP guitar's release date was delayed until 2006, when a production model was finally ready for the public.

Here's how it works: The new hexaphonic pickup reads each individual string that is fed into the built-in analog/digital converter, using Gibson's patented MaGIC digital transport to send the signal digitally (up to 100 meters with no signal loss) into their Breakout Box (BoB). This input/output hub converts the signals back to analog for multiplex use in your amplification or recording machine. The BoB unit uses three ways to connect: 1) The Sum output puts all the strings together mono. 2) The Stereo output mode routes various dual combinations of the six strings via 1e (1-2-3 L) and 2b (3-4-5 R) outputs. 3) The Hex configuration uses six individual outputs for a mixer, six amps, or a PC audio card—for innumerable application complexities.

The normal electronic mode is the real deal, too, with pure ear-bending Les Paul guitar tones that can be mixed in with the digital. In their Classic Mode, the analog signal from the twin humbuckings are converted into digital information (the darker sound usually associated with Gibson hi-Z pickups) and is sent through the RD-45 jack to the hub box. Adding the digital domain brightens the original guitar's spectrum to new sonic heights.

The hex pickup has 90dB of dynamic range with relatively good separation from string crosstalk—a minimal amount of bleeding, considering the natural harmonic resonance interplay of the guitar—and has to be set in careful approximation to the strings. Special rare earth magnets are used to accurately focus around the full range of circular string motion. The pickups are set in careful approximation to the strings to capture this three-dimensional focused field. The gauge and tension coefficients of the string set are also balanced for a uniform output level. With the added mic jack capabilities mixed into the output, the headphone jack gives the guitarist an advantage hitherto unheard of for headset mixes while performing and singing.

2006 production HD.6X-Pro Digital Les Paul model courtesy of Richard Barone, Gibson artist consultant who regularly uses this high-definition instrument for his recordings, New York, 2008.

Close-up of Sean Fields' 2003 prototype Digital Les Paul guitar #0235357x showing an early hex pickup with vertical instead of 45-degree poles.

DLP prototype showing the Cat-5, analog, microphone, and headphone jacks with knurled volume control. Earliest prototypes (sunburst) had only the normal analog and Ethernet jacks, while the production models are similar to this black guitar. *Prototype photos courtesy William Odell, 2008*

The Breakout Box (BoB) for the digital Les Paul, showing input and outputs. Six colored patch cords also come with the unit for total interfacing.

Though it uses Ethernet Cat-5 patch connections, the protocol is uniquely different for the MaGIC network than for the Internet. Guitarist Sean Fields, founder of Audio Video Entertainment, was brought in to create a new protocol for the HD.6X-PRO. His assistant and amp specialist William Odell elaborates on Sean's involvement. "Sean was part of the team and helped choose the protocol based on what is being used in the whole-house automation equipment that we work with. It's the way the devices communicate with each other…They shake hands, talk, and share digital information."

Songwriting with the DLP is a process that evokes dynamic responses to new interactions with expanded sound. With symphonic chord structure possibilities, the sheer freedom to use orchestral ideas combined with the drums/percussion input easily creates a big "wall of music." And with the 5.1 surround-sound capabilities of a modern studio setup, the composing musician can be creative, with a spacious grandeur for big soundscapes.

The digital guitarist can now employ layering, sequencing effects, and splitting signals similar to what keyboardists have been capable of for many years. Using octave dividers, distortion, chorusing, and echo effects can create shimmering high-string lead sounds, while simultaneously creating full-bodied rhythmic tones on the lower strings for distinctive powerhouse (three-piece) work. Stereo multi-channel string spreads with various effects can give simulated movement across the field, while plug-ins like AmpliTube add more tonal options.

Engineer Craig Devin helped with the initial development of the technology behind the instrument. He feels that it will someday have the capability to set up preferences for automating the tones per changing room acoustics. With creative ingenuity, limitless possibilities will unfold. Its sonic uniqueness is already starting to break into modern pop music.

The final leap into the total digital realm for computer hookup is the next step with the MaGIC signal path. The current setup is for live use, analog recording input mixers, and conceptually is a brilliant new studio tool. Gibson is working on a USB interface to bring it to the next level for DAW audio editors for Pro Tools input. Simply put, the HD.6X-Pro opens up a whole new world of guitar sounds. It is a giant leap forward from the first electric guitar pickup. Its time has come, and will be further enhanced as we enter the sonic frontiers of the future… aboard the digital Les Paul guitar.

Gibson's First Edition Les Paul Robot Studio in Blue silverburst set against a promo display showing the lit MCK control knob. *Courtesy Instrumental Music, Thousand Oaks, CA. 2007*

The Les Paul Robot Guitar

Everyone tries to stay in tune while playing, and keeping a guitar that way takes a good ear and constant vigilance, with little adjustments after each song. Strings are sensitive to temperature and lighting conditions, so there are many variables while going from backstage to onstage performances. Now, with the revolutionary Robot self-tuning guitar, all you have to do is use the optical lens/LED Master Control Knob (MCK), strum the instrument, and you're perfectly in tune in seconds. Any desired tuning or pitch can be attained easily and accurately.

Teaming up with German guitarist/engineer Chris Adams, Gibson first produced their innovative Les Paul Robot models in 2007. After ten years of perfecting the system, Chris also devised a way to utilize multiple tunings, string up, and even intonate a guitar. Once you learn how to use the system efficiently, it's easy to adjust to while performing, and eases the typical burden of keeping the guitar tuned well between songs—ensuring good show continuity. Guitarists Billy Corgan and Uli Jon Roth and a host of others have integrated the new guitar into their sets and love it.

I spoke to Chris Adams during the 2007 NAMM show in Anaheim.

Robb: How is the new Robot guitar doing?

Chris: Very well! We sold everything within two days, a limited edition of 4,000 guitars, so it's crazy. We have very many people calling, even from Pakistan. It's a big success. Just last week we won the Best Picks award from the CES consumer electronics show in Las Vegas. So, yes, we are very happy.

RL: Good. How did it come about?

CA: I've been a guitar player for 20 years, so I was always annoyed by the tuning problem and felt I had to change something about it. I started ten years ago to develop something. Of course it took me some time. To integrate it into the guitar without changing it in any destructive manner took some serious engineering.

RL: Did you utilize servo machines?

CA: Yes, we use some DC models. We have some very sophisticated designs with different parts of a gear that is very efficient and lightweight. The Powerhead is actually 46.5 grams. That means it's less weight than the regular Gotohs. It can move torque-wise up to 50 kilograms. That's 1,200 times its own weight.

RL: That's amazing. So the electronics go from the LED knob up to the neck?

CA: Actually, it goes through the guitar strings. They are like two microphones and are communicating through the strings above the audible frequency range. The MIDI control knob has a color module display on it that gives you the different options, different tunings. We have six different presets plus regular tunings. You can preset your own open tunings. You can go to micro tunings. It can go reference tuning. That means you tune just one string.

To get started, you simply pull up on the lower tone knob MCK (which mutes the guitar), lightly strum the strings, and the servos take over. The various strings go green as you brush them, then the display turns blue. You then push the knob back in and you're ready to play. Zero is used to select regular tuning while E & G is used for open E and G chord tunings, and D for DADGAD. Your own alternative and open tuning can easily be programmed, too. Intonation is addressed and made simple. By turning the MCK control to I, holding down three seconds and plucking a string, it first tunes that string. Then hit the note at the 12th fret and either the red or green LED lights will let you know which direction to adjust in half-turn increments. Automatic string-down and string-up

mode winding and unwinding for string changes also help out. Multiple exotic tunings and classic blues slide work is far simpler. It's a definite advantage to be able to bring fewer guitars on the road, too. Exploring alternate tunings can expand your musical horizons and are made easier when using this guitar.

The Tronical Powerhead servo tuners and CPU unit that operate the Robot Les Paul.

The tuning operation technically begins with the Tune-Control bridge's individual piezo pickups to measure the string's pitch. A microprocessor in the rear cavity relays tuning data and electricity through the strings to a central processing unit (CPU) on the headstock, which, in turn, activates the servo pegs within the Powerhead tuners.

A certain amount of hoopla preceded this new innovation. After considerable advertising, banners, and distribution to participating dealers, the show hit the road on December 7, 2007. This first Limited Edition, based on a chambered Les Paul Studio model, came in a Blue silverburst nitrocellulose lacquer with bound neck and headstocks. Special silver-lined and silver tolex covered (robotic colors) cases were featured items with the certificate. The power adapter for the rechargeable AA lithium battery system charges through the guitar jack to full power within 90 minutes for 250 tunings. A performance safeguard Neutrik locking output jack was another featured item. It came standard with 490R Alnico II and 498R Alnico V humbucking pickups for warmth and some upper mid-range boost, respectively. To avoid damage while creating manual custom tunings, the Powerhead tuner buttons must be pulled out to disengage them. Standard A=440 can be adjusted to between 435 to 446Hz.

Dealers estimated one-per-minute sold in certain parts of the world from the wave of anticipation. Some reported quicker sell-outs of their allotted ten guitars than any other instrument before. This first edition of 4,000 self-tuning Gibson guitars sold remarkably well. The second production of Robot Studio LTD instruments in 2008 included metallic red, green, black silverburst, purple, and wine red, plus SG models.

A smoked see-through panel shows the electronics of the Robot guitar.

Artist Models

USA and Custom Shop Artist Models

Jimmy Page

Considering the enormous popularity of the Led Zeppelin group, Jimmy Page is probably the one rock guitarist who is most closely associated with the Gibson Les Paul guitar. Even though Clapton, Beck, Bloomfield, and Green played Sunburst Standards prior, Page possibly helped Gibson sell more Les Paul guitars in their heyday than anyone before the Slash era. It is fitting for this axemaster to finally have his own signature model released. In his early studio days, his use of the LP Custom can be heard on various sessions. Through the Zeppelin days, Jimmy acquired and played two late-fifties Standards that were soon modified to his requirements. His #1 guitar was the 1959 with a shaved neck, while his second was a '58 he acquired from Joe Walsh. Both eventually had push-pull pots installed for coil-tapping the pickups. The '58 also had two little mysterious buttons installed under the pickguard that are believed to be for phasing and series/parallel wiring. Page and his tech haven't publicly admitted exactly what they do, if anything. At any rate, the wiring is unique and can be heard listening to early Zep tracks and live recordings.

Moving up to 1996, in fitting tribute to one of rock music's leading songwriter/lead players, Gibson collaborated to release a close approximation of the Les Paul guitar Jimmy enjoys playing the most. First, to recreate his famous customized '59 tonalities, they devised a novel push-pull set-up to ingeniously arrive at combinations of series-parallel wiring and split-coil tapping. This widened sonic palette goes from full-on humbucking tones to the searing single-coil bright sound, à la his Tele lead work. When both individual single coils are used in parallel, a glassy Strat-like sound emanates. Therefore, the various combinations of four, three, and two coils in series and parallel give this guitar a modern approach to tone modification within small physical parameters. Some even flip the rhythm pickup around to have the single-coil option under the main harmonics.

When the player learns all the various setting and nuances, many of the real Zeppelin tones are there. Even Jimmy's violin-type tonality can be obtained with the right control settings. A lower-register growl with mid-hollowness can be found with both pickups out of phase and the bridge pickup backed off (with a suitable overdrive). Small increments on the volume control alter the tones considerably. The 496R neck and 500T bridge exposed ceramic pickups give the guitar a full tone and

Original early-1995 issue of the Jimmy Page Les Paul Standard Signature model with nice maple and light honey brown shading. *Courtesy Don Breeze, 2004*

The plastic push-pull control layout instructions for the Jimmy Page model. Volume controls split coils in the up position, while the lead tone controls the phase according to the series/parallel setting on the rhythm tone control.

(Above) The Custom Authentic Jimmy Page Signature Les Paul Standard (#JPP 008) in all its flame maple and sunburst glory. Instrumental Music, 2005.

(Right) Jimmy Page Signature model head with Grovers over the simulated Kluson imprints.

JPP 008

JIMMY PAGE LES PAUL
Body
Top wood: Carved figured maple
Back wood: Solid mahogany
Binding: Single-ply cream on top
Colors: Custom Authentic Page Burst

Neck
Neck construction: 1-piece mahogany w/long neck tenon
Fingerboard: 22 fret rosewood
Inlays: Vintage trapezoid
Binding: Single-ply cream
Profile: Jimmy Page custom
Scale length/nut width: 24 3/4"; 1 11/16"

Electronics & Hardware
Pickups: Custom Burstbuckers
Controls: 2 volume, 2 tone, 3-way switch, push/pull pot
Hardware color: Aged Gold/nickel
Bridge/Tailpiece: ABR-1/Aluminum stopbar
Other: Aluminum jackplate, Schaller strap buttons

Jimmy Page Signature Les Paul 2004 catalog shot.

some extra bite. Some lower these high output pickups and utilize the controls carefully with more amp volume. Use of a lightweight stop tailpiece can help to get a more authentic Pagey tone, too.

Secondly, the shape of the neck is addressed by creating a version that is more slender than most Standards. Shaped somewhat between the sometimes "blocky" '59 and a thin '60, the neck has a smooth feeling that suits a number of musical styles—and Jimmy. Some still consider these necks quite thin. The compounded radius fingerboard makes bending notes up top an easier experience, especially with the .050 specified fret height. During 1996, the frets were reduced to .038" for faster playability, but it takes a little more push for bending notes. Contrary to popular belief, a set of .09 strings can work quite well with the thin neck and low action. This allows a lighter touch and more speed, like Jimmy's set-up. Thus the guitar was shipped with Les Paul Signature 9-46 hybrid set.

Woods conform to Standard Plus AA specs on top and one-piece mahogany construction. Some tops are closer to AAA figuring and were certainly fancier than Jimmy's guitars. Coloration of the top is a lightly-faded sunburst with a honey brownish hue that's fairly authentic. Cherry-stained back woods nicely contrast the cream binding and bursted top. Bursts varied in later years, some getting more brownish, some more reddish.

All this is complemented with gold hardware and Grover Roto-matics with the old-style "kidney bean" grips. Tulip button Grovers soon replaced the round ones and Keystone versions were used in later years. Standard is still embossed on the truss cover. The black HS case comes with either green or maroon plush and a satin cover with Jimmy's stylized symbolic signature, which is also imprinted on the cream pickguard. A locking nut was later added to secure the bridge height. By spring 1997, list price was $4,899. Around 500 were manufactured into 1999, with excellent build quality. Due to the model's overall popularity, resale values are strong. Many enthusiasts feel it's the most versatile and professional of all USA Les Paul models, with a seemingly infinite personality.

When Gibson renewed their contract with Mr. Page, they really honed in on the whole guitar, creating a new aura around the Les Paul Sunburst. The Custom Shop version followed in late 2004 with three editions of the #1 Les Paul. This time around, an exhaustive study of Jimmy Page's favorite guitar was done to faithfully duplicate the many unique attributes. This includes 25 signed guitars and 150 limited "Page Burst" finish versions, all carefully aged by Tom Murphy. An unlimited Custom Authentic "Page" burst edition is offered for the normal version. Even the hardware used aged gold and nickel. Pickups are Custom BurstBuckers, set to Jimmy's specifications. Also, a very exacting elliptical neck profile that tapers down in the middle complements the compound-radius fingerboard and long-neck tenon. An ABR-1 Tune-O-Matic bridge set-up with aluminum stopbar and jackplate is used. Schaller strap buttons are attached for safe playing. The bridge pickup cover is off, as on Jimmy's personal '59. A slight finish fade where the player's arm rests is done on the Custom Authentics, too. Tom Murphy models are aged (slightly indented, etc.), much like Jimmy's stage guitar. The gold Grovers are reinstated with kidney bean buttons and the Kluson imprints are still there. CA serial numbers begin with JPP. Electronics are simplified with just one push/pull potentiometer working the special magic tones. This reworked version is built lighter than before and still plays like butter with .010 sets. I still prefer .095s.

Classic Jimmy Page Led Zeppelin shot, playing his #1 with a violin bow. He would then invoke spirits into the concert hall by waving the bow in the four directions, along with the guitar's echo effect.

List price is a whopping $9,811 for the Authentic models, generally discounted down to the mid-6K range. All 25 signed by Jimmy, Murphy aged guitars retailed for over $23,000 and came with a wall display, violin bow, and a portrait him with the prototype. Two of the first few Murphy finished guitars changed hands for over $50,000! Jimmy received the new #1, and the rest were numbered 2 through 26. The 150 unsigned versions by Tom were instantly spoken for by Custom Shop dealers. All this unmatched enthusiasm is predicated on the celebrity aura of Jimmy Page's music and Gibson's masterpiece Les Paul Sunburst Standard. The magic lives on… with rock 'n' roll, well-crafted woods, and electronics coming together.

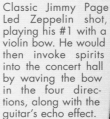

(Above) Gibson's certificate for the original first 25 Jimmy Page models dated May of 2004.

(Right) This is #4 of the first 25 signed by Jimmy Page and aged by Tom Murphy in its display case. *Instrument and photo courtesy Mike Slubowski, 2006*

Jimmy Page's unique signature.

Before Jimmy Page used Les Paul Standards, he had a 1960 Custom #0 6130 for his early session work and touring with Led Zeppelin. His Black Beauty was electronically modified with three upper toggle switches and two of its three pickup covers removed. Unfortunately, it was stolen at an airport in 1970. Page's dearly departed Les Paul Custom now makes a modern comeback, this time sporting a novel electronic switching setup. The new multi-toggle switch has six settings to obtain various pickup combinations with a unique forward position. Its normal three-way movement works as a triple pickup guitar with the outside pickups individually on, or the rear and middle together. Push into the back settings (à la Euro six-speed shifting) and you get the neck and middle, all three together, and the bridge and neck on. Thus far, this six-way set-up is a Page exclusive. You can also activate the push-pull treble tone control for switching to bridge pickup split-coil sounds—and up the stairway to heaven!

Since it's an approximation of a 1960 Les Paul Custom, it has a slender neck profile with the long neck tenon, and an ebony fingerboard with the comfortable rolled-over edges. The all-mahogany body construction also lends the jazzy warm tone of the originals. The cosmetic Vintage Original Spec treatment gives it a gently-aged dulled patina over the nitro-cellulose finish and slightly worn gold hardware parts. Only the reflector knobs and zebra coil pickup were left off. Of the 500 JPC models available, most were available with Bigsby vibrola tailpieces, while others used the optional stop/stud setup. Several of the 25 signed and played editions came with waffle-back Klusons instead of the Grover tuners. Jimmy's insignia signature is on the truss cover and silk-screened onto the Custom Shop case shroud.

Signed 2008 Limited Edition Jimmy Page Les Paul Custom #17 VOS with Bigsby vibrola tailpiece and novel six-way switching. *Courtesy Centre City Music, 2008*

Joe Perry

Guitarist Joe Perry came to prominence playing guitar with the popular Boston rock band Aerosmith. Les Paul guitars came into his reality in 1967: after seeing Jeff Beck play the Tea Party, he soon found an old Junior. Shortly thereafter, he acquired an old Goldtop and did like many others—stripped the finish off to see nice maple underneath. Getting used to playing a Les Paul then felt like home. Once the band took off, he started collecting lots of great guitars, including some vintage sunbursts. Joe feels a Les Paul is "as close to a perfect guitar as you can get," and has enjoyed their tones throughout his career. After so many years of keeping Aerosmith vibrant with fellow shining guitarist Brad Whitford, who also truly cherishes his Les Paul guitars, Joe started his new affiliation with Gibson for a special signature model with his favorite attributes.

Being quite familiar with the instruments from playing and recording with older Les Paul guitars, Joe used his personal vintage Standards as a starting point for the designs. Basically, he picked out the best attributes of the ones he's played to put into his new signature model. The neck shape of his very early 1960 Standard, much like a normal '59, was the profile he wanted. The comfortable rolled edges of the fingerboard were also important, along with the extra step of finishing the frets well, which he felt meant a lot to guitarists.

Electronically, some new fancy sounds could be achieved with a tone-shaping circuit (an internal wah-wah modification previously installed by his local guitar guy) for accentuated mid-range. It's an active mid-boost attached to the bass pickup's tone control as a push-pull pot. This enabled the player either to do left-hand hammer-ons using the wah effect with the right hand or pop up the control for a fixed setting, like a Vox MRB amp control. A master tone control is another feature that Joe used on his guitars. All this gave a new spectrum of altered tones plus the trademark LP sounds. The rhythm position had a Burstbucker 1 pickup, while the lead BurstBucker 2 was specially wound to Joe's likings, too.

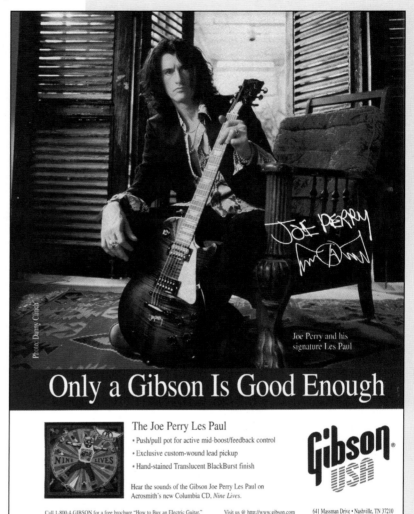

Ad with Joe Perry and his first Les Paul Signature model.

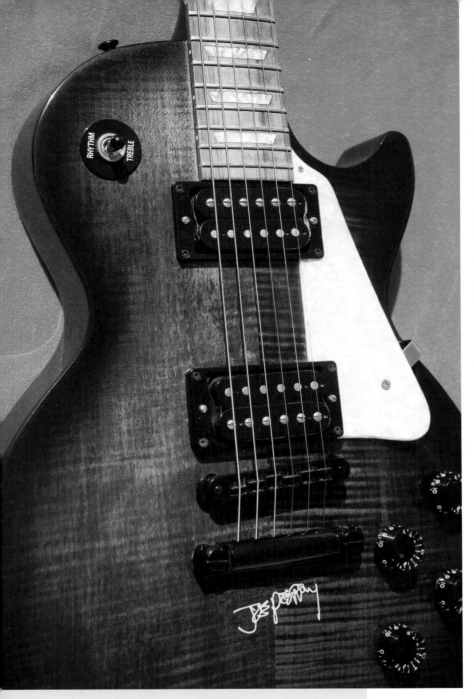

The cosmetic change from a normal bound Sunburst Standard to the unbound body and Translucent Blackburst was an artistic turning point. In good light, the hand-stained translucent black burst accentuates the figured fiddle-back maple as it shines through. Some have figured marbled maple tops as the literature says. A contrasting white pearloid pickguard and truss cover add to the overall appeal.

Initially, the Joe Perry model was begun in the Custom Shop with a typical JP117 number scheme and a gold CS shop decal on the bursted maple neck. Joe's signature in white was on the headstock and the scrimshawed winged Aerosmith inlay was on the ebony fingerboard. In 1997, production switched to the USA plant. Black chrome hardware was continued, along with the Nashville Tune-O-Matic. To complete the later model, Joe's signature was placed just below the tailpiece and on the case. This unique Les Paul, based on the Studio model, sold fairly well and was produced until 2001.

(Above) Clean example of the Gibson USA edition of the Joe Perry Les Paul model. *Courtesy Guitar Center Hollywood, 2006*

(Left) 1997 Joe Perry Les Paul Model headstock with black chromed Grovers.

While visiting Nashville's Custom Shop, Joe's wife Billie had a brilliant idea and disappeared for a while to chat with the paint boys about a special stained finish on some tiger-figured maple. Over the years, she's given Joe numerous instruments in his collection. So Billie secretly ordered a Les Paul guitar with a greenish/yellow stain on a fancy AAA maple top (it really looked like a big tiger's markings) to give him for a Christmas present. She soon surprised him with the wild guitar. Joe was stunned and thought it was quite beautiful. He started to enjoy playing it and kept it with his guitar army downstairs in the "Boneyard" studio (once a workout gym). With a few more inspired ideas, the new Joe Perry Boneyard Signature model was boned!

This new Custom shop version featured the AAA figured maple with an aged tiger green maple top and black back. (It seems the early ones were somewhat orange, like a real tiger.) An enhancer is added to the maple to bring out the contrast, yet it diffuses the depth of flame. This time, he had the neck done more like a big 1958-style profile and used the aged acrylic crown inlays on the rosewood board. The headstock featured the Boneyard skull logo piece and his signature was on the truss cover. For practical reasons, the mahogany backs were weight-relieved to manage shoulder pressure. Aged nickel hardware was specified with an ABR-1 and an optional Bigsby vibrato tailpiece in place of the stopbar. Joe enjoys the Bigsby sound with the extra mass and the slight waver movement it affords.

Electronics-wise, the BurstBuckers were back but with a reversed magnet 2 for the front, and a hot 3 for the back. They inherently have a strong tone with ample clarity when played clean. Joe likes the distinctive (vintage 3-pickup mixed LP Custom) tones from two together magnetically mismatched in the middle position. However, it can be very sensitive to amp and guitar controls plus picking dynamics. Add to that the mid-range boost electronics as before and it's time to rock!

Striking 2004 Custom Shop Joe Perry Boneyard Les Paul (#BONE118) in aged tiger green over tiger-striped maple and aged hardware. *Courtesy Don Breeze, 2003*

The original "Pilot Run" had those words written between the Kluson Keystone tulip tuners and the low two-digit number ink stamped, while normal serial numbers had the BONEXXX white stamp. Add the silk-screened bright green Boneyard on the CS black case with maroon plush and there you have it. One user commented, "If this is your primary axe, don't take your eyes off it, because it will WALK AWAY!"

The official launch party for the guitar took place in Cambridge on May 17th, 2003 at the House of Blues, with Mike McQuire and Rick Gembar from the Custom Shop on hand. Joe Perry unveiled the first production guitar, signed autographs, and had a great jam session. The new guitar also coincides with his Rock Your World Boneyard Brew Hot Sauce he markets. Today, Joe takes a few of them on the road with Aerosmith—and our boys from Boston are still Rocking the World with Gibson guitars.

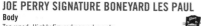

JOE PERRY SIGNATURE BONEYARD LES PAUL

Body
Top wood: Highly figured carved maple
Back wood: Solid mahogany
Binding: Single-ply cream on top
Colors: Custom Authentic Tiger Green

Neck
Neck construction: 1-piece mahogany w/long neck tenon
Fingerboard: 22 fret rosewood
Inlays: Aged acrylic trapezoid
Binding: Single-ply cream
Profile: Rounded
Scale length/nut width: 24 3/4"; 1 11/16"

Electronics & Hardware
Pickups: Burstbucker 2(R) and 3(T)
Controls: 2 volume, 2 tone, 3-way switch
Hardware color: Aged nickel
Bridge/Tailpiece: ABR-1/Stopbar or Bigsby

2004 Custom Shop catalog shot of the Joe Perry Boneyard Les Paul model.

Joe Perry plays his signature "Boneyard" Les Paul model live with the great Buddy Guy and veteran drummer Kenny Aronoff at Les Paul's 90th Birthday Salute concert held on February 7, 2006 at the Gibson Amphitheatre in Universal City, CA. Unfortunately, Les was not feeling well enough to attend this amazing show that featured Joe Satriani, Steve Lukather, Neal Schon, Robben Ford, Edgar Winters, Alison Krauss & Jerry Douglas, Vinnie Colaiuta, and many others.

Brad Whitford captured live in Southern California playing one of his favorite Les Paul guitars. *Courtesy Rick Gould*

Brad Whitford

The other half of Aerosmith's guitar duties is shored up by Brad Whitford, who joined the band shortly after its inception in 1971. After a few months of lessons in the mid-sixties, he honed his early band skills with songs by the Beatles and tuned into players like Steve Cropper, Eric Clapton, Jimmy Page, and—especially—early Jeff Beck. After a year at Boston's Berklee College of Music and playing with Justin Tyme, he developed his refined rhythm chops to complement his burgeoning lead work. Joe Perry and Tom Hamilton soon noticed the young local guitarist and the rest is rock history. Over the years, he and Joe have created one of America's most popular guitar duos.

Robb: What did you think when you first saw a Les Paul guitar?

Brad: Wow! The biggest Les Paul impression I had was when I saw Zeppelin in 1969 in Framingham, Massachusetts. Jimmy was playing a Sunburst Les Paul. I was blown away when I heard that thing. He was playing through two [Marshall] stacks. I didn't have a Les Paul then, but right after that I decided I had to have one. My first was a 1968 Goldtop P-90 that I used on the first Aerosmith album. I think it was the only electric guitar I had back then.

RL: Were you using Vox amps then?

BW: No, I was using a 100-watt Marshall. I had this really nice Super Lead. They're pretty hard to beat.

RL: What did you like about the sound you were getting?

BW: When I got the Marshall and that guitar together, it just had the sound! It was reminiscent of what I was hearing on those English records. Everybody who heard it wanted me to come to their jams because they wanted to hear that sound. (laughs) I was one of the few people who had a Marshall among the people I knew. I still have the angled cabinet with the 100 up in the corner. It's my favorite cabinet. It still has the original speakers and sounds incredible.

RL: Then you wanted to get a Les Paul with humbuckings?

BW: I don't remember if the one I got from you was the first one. That was a special guitar. I think I would give up almost everything to have that '57 Goldtop back. It was amazing!

RL: It had an original Bigsby tailpiece without the stop bar holes. That was a sweet guitar! What did you pay me for it?

BW: A thousand dollars! (We both laugh.) It was a thousand dollars. Ohhh!

RL: Those were the days. An old Guitar Trader booklet shows you holding a flametop guitar with a quote about their '59 reissue Les Paul. They even put old PAFs in some of them.

BW: I had one of them. I used to go down there a lot. I would be in New York and it was just a hop, skip, and a jump to Red Bank. It was a nice guitar, that's for sure. I think Gibson finally caught up to the quality with what they were doing.

RL: Did Gibson give you any guitars after that?

BW: Oh gosh, yeah. They've always been really good to me. I got one about two years ago. I went to the Custom Shop and they said, "Go ahead and find one. It's yours!" (laughs) Took me all day. I found a really nice tobacco burst with a big fat neck on it and they let me take that home. I also have one that Tom Murphy did his whole thing to, with finish cracks and all. I bought it in Japan. Somebody over there was bringing in fabulous guitars. I was in the store, saw that guitar and made the mistake of playing it. (laughs) It was like, "Oh man, I have to have this guitar." That guitar has a little #1 sticker on it because it's probably the best one of the vintage reissues that I have. It might be around eight or nine years old.

RL: Their quality has really come up a long way.

BW: Yes, it has. Especially with this last one I got from the Custom Shop. It's very well done.

RL: Did they ever talk to you about an endorsement?

BW: We talked a little bit about it. I was never a real big fan of that stuff. I thought it was silly to put a name on a guitar that already had a name on it. Unless I could come up with my own revolutionary design, I don't think that's going to happen. It's pretty hard to improve on the basic toolbox. Nothing really looks much better over your shoulder than a good Les Paul, a good Stratocaster, a good Tele. They've stood the test of time. I look at these pictures of me playing these hybrid guitars and [wince]… Jack Douglas said to me one night, "What are you playing that stupid thing for? Play one of your Les Pauls." I said, "Yeah, no kidding." Sounds good, looks great.

RL: Often nothing else will do. I love the tone.

BW: I know. You can't beat it.

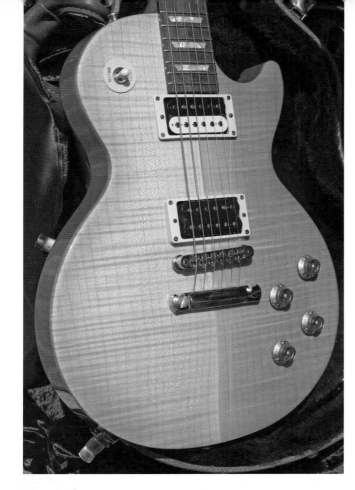

The Gary Moore Les Paul Signature model in lemonburst, with fine maple and the first BurstBucker pickups. *Courtesy Joe Barrese, 2006*

The Gary Moore fans had their wish come true with his special new model in 2000. He wanted his signature guitar to be versatile, yet striking in appearance. It was also intended to be along the lines of Green's 'Burst, but without binding—for a sleeker look and lower cost (below the normal Standard). Moore's featured a somewhat orange-tinted "lemonburst" (light honey flavored) on a particularly grained AA flamed maple top, with a large '59-sized neck profile (for big-handed players) and the slightly out-of-phase pickup configuration.

Since the original '59 had faded some over the years, the new Gibson version was a similar coloration. This model also sported the first Les Paul guitar pickups in America to use the new smooth and aggressive BurstBucker. It has a BB-1 reversed-mounted Zebra half-cream for the rhythm position and an uncovered black BB-2 for the treble spot. The middle setting creates interesting coloration as you adjust the tone and volume controls.

As with other Les Paul models, the weight and amount of flame can vary. It came with the popular big frets and acrylic pearloid crowns on the rosewood fingerboard, Grover Keystones, and his signature in gold on the truss cover and optionally mounted pickguard. The tan case has beautiful blue lining and a satin inner cover with Gary's signature. Some say that if you like Moore's blues tones, this model guitar can do it to a T. With its great Les Paul sound and terrific wood selection for a more-than-reasonable price, it sold quickly in stores through 2002. Hats off to Gary Moore and Gibson. It's a home run!

Gary Moore

Irish guitarist Gary Moore is one of the finest players to come out of the UK. He came to fame in 1970, first playing a Tele and SG with the Skid Row, then Colliseum II with Jon Hiseman, Greg Lake's solo projects, and the eclectic Thin Lizzy group with Phil Lynott (also in Skid Row). He has enjoyed a long, successful solo career, exhibiting finesse in many musical genres. Gary did some powerful hard rock albums and then his "Still Got the Blues" project with Albert Collins, BB and Albert King was very well received. His '92 video *Back to the Blues* was a big hit, too. Writing and playing some exciting gigs with BBM (Jack Bruce and Ginger Baker) expanded his musicianship. His friendship with Peter Green resulted in his acquiring the famous 1959 Les Paul Sunburst Standard (used on "A Hard Road" with Mayall and Fleetwood Mac) and 1961 Stratocaster. He has used this historic Les Paul guitar for many years with the reversed pickup still intact. Gary did a *Blues for Greeny* concert and album as a thank you tribute, too. This historic guitar, shown in chapter 7, is soon to be an "Inspired By" signature model.

Gary Moore signatures on the pickguard and violet shroud.

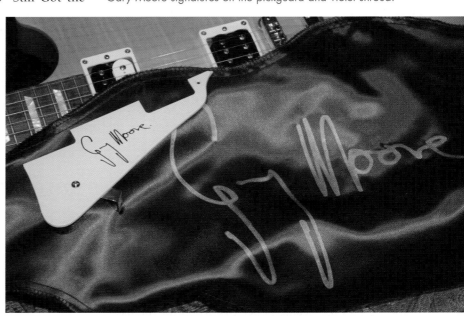

(Left) The Ace Frehley Les Paul Custom model from 1997, with full DiMarzio Distortion pickups. *Courtesy Music Ground, London, 2005*

(Below) Ace Frehley's makeup masked portrait inlaid headstock with his signature Intergalactic energy nickel plated steel 9-46 Gibson string set.

Ace Frehley

The word was out: Gibson was finally releasing an Ace Frehley Les Paul model in 1997 to coincide with the Kiss original-line-up reunion tour. Since they were one of the biggest rock acts since the seventies—and a lot of kids grew up with the whole Kiss thing (makeup and fireworks)—the Custom Shop announced the arrival of a new Ace Les Paul model for all the fans.

Ace had been playing various seventies Les Paul Sunburst Standards and a black '69 Custom (with a third D'Marzio pickup added) onstage with Kiss. He made an exclusive contract with Gibson for his three DiMarzio humbucking pickup, Les Paul Sunburst idea. A few prototypes built by Custom Shop luthier Phil Jones in the Custom (ACE 1) and Standard (ACE 2, invoice #EB5679) versions were shown at NAMM '96 to get dealer response. The guitars featured a multi-colored portrait from his solo album on the headstock, with an engraved ace-of-hearts playing card and horizontal Les Paul logo on the truss cover. Lighting bolt inlays (to shock you) graced the fingerboard. Both flametop sunbursts had cherry backs, normal binding, and chrome Grovers pegs. The Custom model won out and they decided to release 300 models during 1997 with AAA tops and '59 profile necks. At NAMM, all 300 pre-sold out in two days, with a suggested $6,400 list. Custom Shop manager Rick Gembar credits Ace for the success of the overall look of the instrument.

With the high demand continuing, the Gibson USA plant took over and put out the regular production of the model in 1997 with a AA figured maple top. The legions of guitar-playing Kiss fans were elated, to say the least. Production models used his pickup of choice, the full cream-coil DiMarzio Distortion pickups for the front and middle, and a high-octane Super Distortion for the back

position (by '98 they were all SDs). The outside two-toggle position activates the front and back, while the middle uses only the middle pickup, which was also changed in '98 to both the middle and back with a reversed magnet for that in-between sound. For some, the middle pickup gets in the way and must be lowered. Ace uses his bridge pickup, mostly; some say that sound is exactly the same on theirs.

Even though it's a Les Paul Custom with multiple binding and an ebony fingerboard, chrome parts were used with the Nashville bridge and stopbar, Grover kidney bean tuners, etc. Neck shape was specified as the rounded '59 shape as on the CS versions. Ace's signature was also inlaid in the 12th fret position and eight-digit stamped in serial numbers with "Made in USA" in back. Heritage sunburst was the only color available with the cherry-finished back. The case was black with the cool blue lining and Ace's signature on the satin cover piece. Buying the guitar new also included a life-size standup of Ace and the special bonus Ace power pack with a year's supply of strings. Production continued into 2001. Playing this souped-up Les Paul Custom Ace model will make you want to "Rock and Roll All Nite!"

Peter Frampton

After performing with a fifties Les Paul Custom during his touring days to support the #1 selling album Frampton Comes Alive (1976), Peter Frampton got back to his favorite model Gibson—but with some refinements to share with other like-minded guitarists. The Custom Shop collaborated with Peter to recreate and improve his mainstay instrument.

Though the original was solid mahogany, he specified a maple top for sustain and a chambered mahogany back—not only for weight reasons, but to open up its resonating properties for a fuller tone. The one-piece mahogany neck with silky-smooth ebony fingerboard and split-diamond headstock was in keeping with vintage specs. Since his original neck was modified to a slender profile, the Frampton Custom has a very thin '60 shape. He felt it best to keep the traditional "Black Beauty" ebony-finished theme and complement it with gold hardware, Grover machines, and their antiqued binding around the guitar's body and neck.

Electronically, Peter wanted to create a simple but effective way to utilize three pickups. Essentially, having the outside two pickups wired normally to three positions of the toggle switch enabled him to blend the "live" center pickup in to the mix. The magic in this wiring method is that it gives you front and back individually, all three together, or combinations of two with the two bottom controls to mix them. Meanwhile, the master top controls naturally work the outside pickups. Humbuckings consist of the '57 Classic at the neck, a '57 Classic Plus for the middle, and the hotter 500T ceramic for the bridge. These uncovered Classics provide a robust vintage tone for clean rhythm-playing, while the 500T gives the needed crunch for the burning solos. It's a versatile and well-thought-out set-up without too many controls to deal with during performance.

Frampton's signature is carved into the 12th fret pearl block neck inlay and included on the black case's velvet shroud. Dunlop strap locks insure this beauty stays put, too. Being a limited edition of 500 instruments, each guitar came with Peter's hand-signed certificate. Its debut was February 3rd during the 2000 NAMM convention.

Elegant, simple, unique and dynamic... it's ready for a stadium show or black tie event. It is certainly worthy of the Peter Frampton Signature. He uses it on tour and it's great to see him back in action with the real deal.

Peter Frampton, posing at home in 2003, with his new signature Les Paul Custom model and vintage AC-30 Vox amplifier. Photographer Neil Zlozower shot this with a special format Meyer camera and commented that Peter is one of the nicest people he's ever worked with.

Peter Frampton Les Paul Custom (#PF 389) with his signature on the pearl block inlay. *Courtesy La Mesa Guitar Center, 2004*

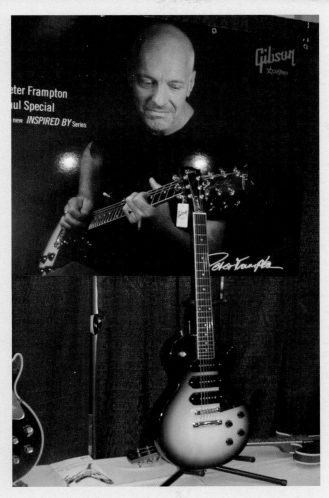

Peter Frampton Special display at the 2006 NAMM convention.

A 2005 prototype of the limited edition Peter Frampton Les Paul Special (Inspired By series) This sample (PF 40 08) has aged gold hardware. *Courtesy Gibson's mobile showroom, 2005*

Mr. Frampton also has a passion for his old 1958 Junior that, in turn, has evolved into another creation—the Peter Frampton Les Paul Special. Part of the "Inspired By" series, Gibson and Peter have created an expanded version of the original LP Junior, but with some of his personal electronic touches and attributes found on the previous Custom model.

This guitar features something unusual for a flat instrument: a two-piece mahogany body with the rear portion weight-relieved (honeycombed) for light and responsive results. Finish-wise, the tobacco with red burst is much like the last of the Juniors in 1958. Its back is walnut-filler stained with a light brown color. The raised tortoise-style pickguard is callback to the ES-125 models and attached with the pickup screws. A Nashville TOM and stopbar keep everything secured.

Gold hardware is new for this genre, along with three pickups—namely, dog-eared P-90s. This time around, they all have their own volume controls and are complemented with a master tone. The three-way toggle works the same as a two-pickup Gibson, so the middle pickup is once again blended in when needed. Magnetically, the center pickup is reversed for the humbucking effect with combined pickups, a novel and practical idea for quiet use whenever you want to blend them to perfection. Last but not least, the neck gets Peter's preference for the slim profile, ebony board, signed truss cover, and the those bean-gripped Grovers. Eat your heart out, Leslie West!

Duane Allman

For this most sacred of tribute models, Gibson's Custom Shop went to the Nth degree to duplicate the "Sky Dog" maestro's beloved "Hot 'Lanta" Les Paul Standard. Gibson's Historic Program manager Edwin Wilson basically dismantled and photographed the original Standard of Duane Allman's for an extensive documentation to faithfully recreate the guitar in a very limited edition. Tom Murphy came in on the project to give them the professional aged-finish treatment. From the unique seagull flame pattern maple top and dark tri-burst colors to the imbedded frets used across the back, they did a spectacular job of making a "Hot 'Lanta" reissue a reality.

There was some serious anticipation by those who ordered them (including those Les Paul Forum boys). It took Gibson almost two years of searching for the appropriate woods to get the DA edition to delivery. The original pilot run of ten went to Japan, and some have since returned to the states. Then the limited edition of 55 finally was constructed with those hand-selected matching gullwing tops. They didn't get dead ringers each time, but after the color and aging, they were close enough. The special "Duaneburst" finish is reserved for only this run of instruments. A reissue Lifton-style case is supplied with the instrument, along with the documentation. Most were shipped with the specially-designed wall-mounted display case. Some feel these reverent reproductions of Sunbursts are the most beautiful artist signature models ever produced.

(Above) While visiting the Custom Shop, the original prototype #01 of the Duane Allman Reissue was displayed in their showroom. Note the accurate coloration applied from the further-aged Standard of Duanes.

(Right) Duane Allman's name was pressed into the back of #01, as Twiggs did to the original guitar. Some were authentically worn across the area before installing the frets.

(Left) D ALLMAN accompanies the serial number of this historic recreation. Many thanks to Mike McGuire and Rick Gembar for the opportunity to play and photograph Hot 'Lanta #01.

(Left) 2001 NAMM show limited edition Duane Allman R9 Les Paul reissue. Shows some excellent simulated weather checking by Tom Murphy.

(Left) Dickey Betts live in San Diego at 4th & B with the his band and his cool reissue Goldtop Les Paul. *Photo courtesy Martin Miller, 2001*

(Below) Dickey Betts signature model (#DB 109) with Tom Murphy's specially-aged finish. Purposely shot with more reflection to show the simulated weathered patina. *Courtesy Music Ground London, 2005*

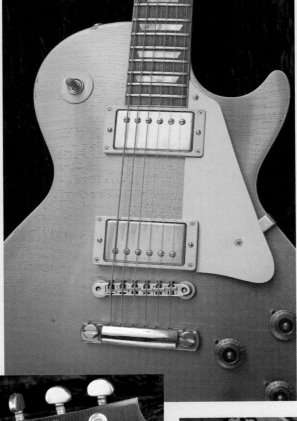

Dickey Betts

Fellow guitarist with the famous Allman Brothers Band was Dickey Betts, another true devotee of the Les Paul guitar. His lyrical and melodic style blended beautifully with Duane's while they played together. After Duane's untimely death, Dickey carried on for many years with the famous band (along with Warren Haynes and then Derek Trucks) until parting ways in 1999 to resume solo work. He's played beautiful '59 Standards (seen in chapter 8) and old Goldtops for many years.

In July 2000, Gibson created an Artist Authentic series and examined the years of wear-and-tear on his 1957 Goldtop to create the Dickey Betts Ultra Aged 1957 Goldtop. All 115 guitars were hand-done by Tom Murphy with appropriate weather checking, dings, and the lighter neck coloration. On some, the dark back finish borders on a very deep red. It came with Grover machines and '57 Classic pickups. Serial numbers started with a DB. They also put a "Dickey Betts Goldy" silkscreen on the dark brown faux alligator case (green plush) and included a replica of Dickey's fancy beaded and embroidered wide leather strap. An exclusive party at the Custom Shop was thrown in late July to celebrate the release of his new guitar and solo album, *Let's Get Together.*

After the successful run of '57 Goldtops, Gibson decided to release another of Dickey Betts's favorite playing guitars. It was based on an old funky goldtop whose back he contoured. He then stripped and hand-colored the top with red alcohol-based stain and covered it with nitro lacquer. The experts at the Historic division carefully matched the technique and color to produce 55 of the Dickey Betts Red-Top '57 Les Paul. Pickups are '57 Classics and serial numbers began with DB2, with his gold signature in between the Kluson Keystones. Charlie Daniels even sang about Dickey playing his old red Les Paul in "The South's Gonna Do It Again." Press releases in July 2002 announced the debut of this limited edition with its "scarfed" back, his special neck profile, and Native American silver concho-styled jack and switch plates.

(Right) A live shot of an Allman Brothers show at New Orleans Jazzfest 1999, with Dickey Betts playing his old Redtop Les Paul and tasty slide player Derek Trucks on his Gibson SG.

Gary Rossington

A popular band called Lynyrd Skynyrd made its debut in 1973, featuring three guitarists playing hard-driving Southern rock 'n' roll. With tunes like "Sweet Home Alabama" and "Free Bird" that have virtually become rock anthems, this group persevered through plane crashes and continues today. Songwriter/guitarist Gary Rossington was a great advocate of the original Les Paul guitars, performing with them on many concerts and on their famous recorded tunes through the years.

In 2002, Gibson's Custom Shop got in on the action by adding to the line a limited edition "aged" Gary Rossington 1959 Les Paul Standard and his sixties SG Standard model. The 1958 Explorer that belonged to Rossington's deceased Lynyrd Skynyrd band mate Allen Collins was also added. All were expertly hand-crafted by Tom Murphy. The '58 and '59 models sport aged gold hardware, which is unusual for this aged artist series. Gary's '59 "Bernice" is faithfully recreated with a special "Skynyrd 'Burst" that's true to the worn original—complete with his stage battle scars and serious belt buckle rash across the back. At first glance, it looks all beaten up, but after playing for a while, it's such a convincing player that you won't want to put it down. Even the neck binding rolled edges give it that great extra touch.

Rossington '59s come with screaming Burstbucker two and three pickups. Many of these models have exceptionally warm, rich neck tones for great high register soloing and responsive, articulate bridge tones. They came with a special wall-hanging display case with Gary's picture, plus a Skynyrd "Grease Monkey" short-sleeved mechanic's work shirt. This guitar truly looks as good as an oldie and is bargain-priced compared to other aged '59s.

The SG Les Paul replica is a brilliant copy of the guitar that he used regularly on "Free Bird" and with which he wrote many popular songs. Gibson evidently got this one right with the proper beveling, original '63 (almost slender) neck profile, Brazilian fingerboard, and wide (but not too tall) frets. The distinctive mahogany wood grain is a welcome sight for many. Some have quite attractive swirling patterns. Aging is mild-to-moderate overall, with the exception of the big wear spot on the back that some feel could've been left alone. Even the slightly-tarnished longtail Maestro Lyre vibrato tailpiece works fairly well.

Controls are versatile and can readily back off the amp's distortion without losing volume. The electric tone found with Burstbucker pickups compliments the guitar nicely and gives it a punchy personality. Lastly, Gibson seems to have strengthened the neck joint to get rid of the fragile and wavering pitch problems found on the originals. People who don't even know about Skynyrd will buy this accurate recreation for its inherent quality and vintage vibe. Both Rossington Signatures are built in a limited edition of 250 each. Gary was on hand at the 2004 Winter NAMM show with his lovely singing wife and bandmate Ricky Medlock to sign autographs and talk about their new signature models.

Gary Rossington Les Paul model with that built-in aged feeling. When you pick it up, it's remarkable how authentic it seems compared to a real one. *Courtesy Instrumental Music, 2003*

A nicely faded Les Paul SG Rossington model, with aging by Tom Murphy, quite reminiscent of the way early-sixties SGs would get. This is the #2 prototype of the series.

GARY ROSSINGTON

To Robert
Gary Rossington

Rossington LP back with quite the worn spot already.

Gary Rossington's Gibson promo picture with his new '59 Les Paul model.

Slash

Slash (Saul Hudson) came into the limelight as the guitarist with Guns N' Roses during the eighties. His influences were blues-based hard rock and heavy metal stuff like Deep Purple, Led Zeppelin, Jeff Beck, Aerosmith, UFO, Cheap Trick, Metallica, and the Sex Pistols. The latter punk stuff affected their Guns N' Roses group.

Guitar-wise, his preference has been Gibson Les Paul guitars. He owns a few old Sunburst Standards, a '56 Goldtop, and Flying V, besides newer Les Pauls for performing. The popularity of their band directly influenced the Les Paul guitar's market resurgence. He left the band and then formed Snakepit.

Slash got together with Gibson's Custom Shop to do a Signature Les Paul model in red, with a mother-of-pearl snake on the neck and painted snake logo across the body. Production totaled 75 between 1996 and 1998, including his two (one is pictured here). They retailed for $8,000 at the time. Epiphone made a version which he likes, without the pearl snake (a white marking instead), and sticker snake instead of the paint.

In 1994, Gibson released another Slash model, this time in Custom Authentic tobacco sunburst, nickel parts, two Seymour Duncan Alnico II pickups, and a Fishman Power bridge attachment for acoustical sounds. A mini-switch activates the Fishman set-up. A slender neck is his preference. Schaller tuners complete the guitar. The guitar lists for $6,035 and comes with the Custom Shop case and care kit.

(Above) Slash's personal Snake Pit Les Paul model. *Courtesy Dave Weiderman/ Guitar Center Hollywood*

(Right) NAMM 2004 Slash Les Paul in dark tobacco with Seymour Duncan and Fishman pickups. Note the mini toggle switch.

(Below) Slash with his vintage Les Paul collection. *Courtesy Rick Gould*

After striking the big-time twice with Guns N' Roses and Velvet Revolver (in 2002), rock icon Slash did a best-selling memoirs book with Anthony Bozza. A series of official Slash guitars hit the market in 2004 and soon evolved into four separate versions, including Epiphone, all featuring Seymour Duncan Alnico II pickups. As of this writing, another Gibson "Inspired By" recreation of his first recording guitar is taking shape under Pat Foley's special expertise. A billion dollar Guitar Hero III music video game in 2007 went hand in hand with clinching *Guitar World*'s "Best Rock Guitarist" of 2008.

While he was putting the final touches on his first solo album, begun in 2008, we had an enjoyable talk about growing up with guitars and his solid preference for the Les Paul:

Robb: When was the first time you saw a guitar and said, "Wow!" and had a feeling about it?

Saul (Slash): *I was raised around musicians because my parents were in the music business. There were a lot of rehearsals, shows, and recording studios. I recall having a distinct fascination with equipment, especially guitars. If a band wasn't playing, and they just had their gear set up, I would go, "Wow!" I was fascinated. Guitars always had an unspoken, deep-rooted kind of hold over me. An electric guitar was a showstopper for me, like a Ferrari that we all loved the looks of… naked girls, or whatever. (laughs) I had a twisted fascination with instruments. I liked music a lot and listened to the radio. I went to sleep with it on and woke up with it on. We were always surrounded by music. I never once thought I was going to be a musician until later.*

I started with an acoustic guitar. My grandmother had one buried in the closet. All of a sudden I decided I was going to play guitar. How do I do that? (laughs) So I started with a one-string acoustic guitar she gave me. I learned a lot of stuff on that one string, a low E string. I was always drawn to riffs more than anything else. So, one-string riffs are always a single-note thing. I eventually thought, "Well, okay, now I need to do something." So I decided to take some guitar lessons. The guitar teacher said, "First of all, you need an instrument. And secondly, what do you want to do?" He was playing Jimi Hendrix and Eric Clapton on the stereo, so I said, "That's what I want to do!" That turned out to be lead guitar, and I started taking guitar lessons. This guitar teacher, probably still to this day, is one of the most phenomenal guitar players

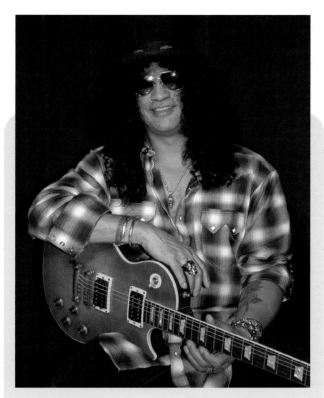

Guitarist Slash poses in the studio with the mainstay 1987 Les Paul Standard he bought in 1988. The finish near the tailpiece has a deep burned spot from a cigarette stuck on the sweaty surface while performing. This guitar is the basis for his first "Inspired By" reissue model.

I ever met. He would get me to do sort of rudimentary guitar scales and tried to teach me how to read music, just like piano lessons. This didn't excite me at all. At the end of every lesson he would teach me any song that I wanted to learn. He would pick it up off the record and teach it to me. That's how I started, watching people learn from records. Eventually I quit the music school and starting teaching myself that way.

RL: Those were fertile times when everyone wanted to be in a band.

SH: First I had to get an electric guitar, so I got a Memphis Les Paul copy. I was obviously drawn to Les Pauls from the get-go. Then I started with bands, and the last year of junior high and through high school I picked up the guitar in earnest. I was very serious about it, much more serious about it than anyone I went to school with. They all thought I was out of my mind. I was a workaholic. I tried to get the band to practice.

RL: So you would go to music stores and see a real Les Paul?

SH: At that point, you're sort of like a sponge. You've

got guitar stores all over the place, guitar magazines all over the place, and you're overloaded with information. Of course there are all the guitar players out there that you sort of try to figure out what they're playing. There is a lot of incoming data. I didn't necessarily know what I wanted, and was going with my gut on this whole thing.

I went through trial and error with different guitars for a few years. The Memphis Les Paul copy didn't last very long. I went to a BC Rich at one point, then I had a Strat and a copy Explorer. Eventually I got another Les Paul, a Black Beauty. At that point I had three guitars. (laughs) That's because I worked in a music store so it was easy to get stuff. Then when Guns N' Roses started I ended up with a Les Paul that previously belonged to Steve Hunter. That's really when I was a Les Paul guy. It wasn't something I decided consciously, I just always gravitated toward it. I felt the most comfortable with it and I thought they were the coolest looking. I guess that's the difference between Strat guys and Les Paul guys. (laughs)

I went through another trial and error period with guitars that were given to me by different companies. When we did the Appetite for Destruction record, I realized all those guitars sounded like crap. My manager gave me my Gibson Les Paul '59 replica, which was handmade by Kris Derrig, who is no longer with us. It came out of a store named Music Works in Redondo Beach. That guitar was a godsend at the time, because I was really tearing my hair out trying to figure out what instrument I was going to use to make this record. I did all the overdubs with that Les Paul, and it has been my main recording guitar ever since. I took that '59 copy on the road with me and beat the hell out of it. I realized I couldn't put this guitar that I loved so much through that.

RL: *There's another one you played that Pete "Max" Baranet made.*

SH: I had two that Max built. Over the years, I got the other ones. I think I bought the biggest bulk of guitars in the early nineties when I was doing Use Your Illusion with Guns N' Roses. I have a '58 and a '59 Sunburst now. I had another one, the guitar that used to belong to Joe Perry that I got a while back. A few years ago, I gave it back to Joe Perry for his 50th birthday.

RL: *That's so cool of you.*

SH: It was something he had when I was first into Aerosmith. I would see certain pictures and think, "That's the coolest Les Paul I've ever seen," because it was a tobacco sunburst and it was real faded. Years later, I managed to acquire it from a guy who had it and got in touch with me. I used it for a video, I recorded one song on it, and then it just sat around. After several years I thought, "Joe would love to have this," so I gave it to him.

Slash's well-worn 2003 Signature Model and 2008 Limited Edition Goldtop Les Paul guitar, together with his famous hat.

RL: *Then you hooked up with Gibson.*

SH: I've been hooked up with Gibson since the end of the eighties. I'd done a couple of guitars with them. I caught them selling these sunburst Les Paul Standards without a pickguard, which is pretty much what I was known for at that moment. I said, "When did you guys start doing these?" So then they started talking about Slash models. That was in the early nineties. We did a couple different color flametops like that which weren't really for commercial sale. And then in the millennium (since Velvet Revolver), I retired my '88 Les Paul Standard that was pretty beat up and vintage-like at that point. So they built me a Slash model Standard tobacco like Joe Perry's with my Duncan Alnico II humbuckers and a piezo pickup still trying to reinvent the acoustic-electric deal which actually works. That's really the first thing that I did with Gibson and they went for sale. Then just recently we did another few models. They've been going really well. They're out the door and gone.

RL: *What was the idea behind the Snakepit guitar? It's beautiful.*

SH: The Snakepit is a cool guitar. It's something I had Gibson make for me with the inlay and that sort of thing. It's basically a Standard guitar with a couple of different aesthetic bells and whistles. They decided to make a limited edition [of 75] and they all disappeared, so that was basically it. We didn't take it very seriously from a commercial standpoint. As far as the Epiphone version goes, they made a few. But as far as the Custom Shop one, only 50 of them were made.

RL: *In your tobacco sunburst version, you added a steely gray color to the dark brown.*

SH: The newer ones are tobacco as well, but they are a little steelier. I was never happy with just the plain stock tobacco, so I got into customizing that color on the newer guitar, which I was really happy with.

RL: *Then you had the Gibson USA Tobacco burst.*

SH: Right. It had a piezo pickup and a little toggle that you can switch it on with. That was 2004.

RL: *Now you've got the VOS "Inspired By" version.*

SH: The "Inspired By" is based on my 1988 guitar. It's an exact replica of that instrument, the neck specs. It has everything: cigarette burns, the crack in the neck, all that stuff. It looks amazing.

RL: *When you were growing up and playing these different guitars, what was it about the Les Paul that you really were attracted to?*

SH: It was an unsaid thing, an innate attraction. It was partially the way it looked. And a lot of the guitar players I liked played Les Pauls. I felt comfortable with the Les Paul from the visual point of view and from a tonal point of view, obviously. I remember my first Les Paul copy: it had two humbuckers. I had a Fender Princeton amp and an MXR distortion pedal. I recall the day I made a sound with it that I identified with.

Slash's Gibson personal USA 2008 signature model, with exceptional maple figuring and signature case. All guitars courtesy Slash Hudson

I think I was playing "Cat Scratch Fever" and that was it. I'd finally arrived.

Getting my own type of tone together was always very important. You read the interviews of a lot of guitar players and they really think about this stuff and work on certain particulars. They're always tinkering around with it. But I've never been like that. I just sort of know what it is that feels or sounds right and I go for that. Touch a knob here, treble should be here, I guess. (laughs) I think I always liked having the tone rolled. I always liked using the rhythm pickup, for obvious reasons. I started doing the tone rolled off thing in the nineties. It's just a really sweet, sustained, creamy sound, especially the high notes and melodic stuff.

RL: *And the way you hold the guitar up in the air… Did you do that when you were young?*

SH: I don't know exactly. (laughs) I think that came when I started doing the Use Your Illusion tour. I became aware of it because they had more pictures of us in magazines at that point. It's just sort of a natural thing.

RL: *When I'm in the studio, if I want the real big sound, nothing but the Les Paul will do.*

SH: Les Pauls are like Les Pauls. They have their limitations, but you just work with them. For me, it's a guitar of choice. There's nothing that can't be done on a Les Paul. It may be done easier on other guitars, but you can always find it with a Les Paul. And there are certain things that Les Pauls do that other guitars don't do, so I always felt very comfortable trying to do whatever it is, whatever sound I need to get with a Les Paul. I'm doing a session now. I own 90 guitars and I have only one guitar at the session! (laughs)

RL: *Getting the amp to work well makes the guitar sing. There's something magical about getting the resonance of the Les Paul guitar when it's on fire.*

SH: Definitely. I have those moments where everything works just fine. (laughs) I suppose you spend your whole life chasing it around.

Bob Marley Tribute

Considered to be the first superstar of the Third World and the greatest artist in reggae music's history, Jamaican Bob Marley's revolutionary music captured the hearts of the Western hemisphere. Robert Nesta Marley learned guitar from bandmate Peter Tosh. He married Alpharita "Rita" Anderson, their backup singer who introduced them to Rastafarianism. Their group, the Wailers, became popular worldwide from their Island LP releases *Catch a Fire* and *Burnin'*, with singles like "Get Up, Stand Up" and "I Shot the Sheriff," also covered by Eric Clapton to #1 success. After an unsuccessful attempt on his life in 1976 and exile to England, his next release, *Exodus*, was on the British charts for over a year (*Time* magazine recently chose it as the greatest album of the 20th century.) In 1978, he was awarded the International Peace Medal at the United Nations by the African delegation and was an official guest of Zimbabwe's independence celebrations. He was a lifelong vegetarian and drove a BMW simply because of the initials. After a mysterious toe infection became cancerous, he died in 1981 at age 36.

Marley's posthumous box-set anthology—with songs like "One Love" (used on Jamaican tourism commercials), "Waiting in Vain," "No Woman, No Cry," and "Is This Love"—made him one of the top-selling solo artists of all time. In 1994, he was inducted into the Rock and Roll Hall of Fame and in May 2001, BBC News online users voted Marley the third greatest lyricist of all time, following Dylan and Lennon. His music defined the sound for a genre that is still immensely popular.

Gibson paid their respects in 2002 by doing a limited edition of the Les Paul model Marley was famous for playing. The Custom Shop Tribute Les Paul Special is quite distinctive. Tom Murphy created a faithful replica of Bob's guitar finish right down to the wear marks and dings—making it look like it was played at countless concerts around the world. Marley's original fifties Special had been completely stripped and modified with an added Tune-O-Matic bridge, brass nut, extra binding around the complete sides of the headstock, and small-block fingerboard added. For years, his Special had its original pickguard, with an added large round switch plate (like a soccer ball). Toward the end of his career, aluminum was put in place of the plastic pickguard and switch plate (now shaped like a big football).

The Custom Shop's version replicated this guitar (on display in the Bob Marley Museum in Kingston) with the same wide head binding, Schaller tuners (with old screw holes), doweled stud holes, and a natural finish with sanding marks and open mahogany grain. The

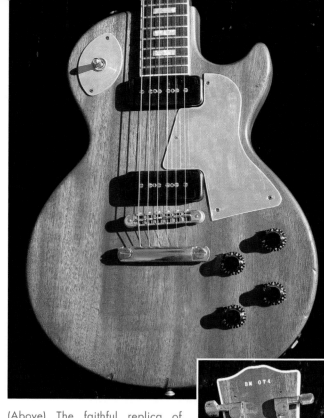

(Above) The faithful replica of famous reggae master Bob Marley's Les Paul Special. *Courtesy Buffalo Brothers, 2005*

(Right) Custom Shop Bob Marley Les Paul #074 with a copy of his signature and limited run in gold. Note the corroded Schaller tuners and make-believe strip tuner holes.

guitar has dual P-90s like the original, and the metal parts are aged to be authentic. Nearly 200 guitars were built and sold with a display cabinet (with a Lion of Judah emblem print) and a Bob Marley/Custom Shop tribute t-shirt. This iconic instrument pays homage to the musical spirit of a guitarist who was both a great man and a great human being.

To complement this tribute series, its cousin in the Epiphone line was a colorful commemorative Bob Marley Les Paul Special "dedicated to the memory of the legendary reggae pioneer." It featured solid mahogany construction with Bob's caricature on the body, Alnico Classic and Hot (zebra) HB pickups, red, green, and gold (yellow) Ethiopian flag (traditional rasta colors) fingerboard inlays. The similarly-colored "One Love" on the headstock, Grover tuners, and signature hemp gig bag completed this very popular model. Many loving fans have these guitars as a wall display. Son Ziggy Marley performed at Bob's 60th birthday anniversary at the Ethiopian Festival in 2005 with a cherry Les Paul Custom.

Pete Townshend Les Paul Deluxe model (#75), built as a recreation of the guitar he played with The Who during the late seventies. *Courtesy Dave Amato, 2005*

The Custom Shop's version of Townshend's Deluxe has Grovers and maintains the old style volute.

Pete Townshend

Pete Townshend is the mastermind behind The Who group from England. His brilliant songwriting and amazing rhythmic guitar-playing is rivaled only by Keith Richards, who is more blues-based. He's played (and destroyed) many a guitar in his day and has enjoyed numerous Gibson models. Today he endorses Gibson with a J-200 model and the Les Paul Deluxe, one of his favorite stage guitars, to which he added some electronics.

Gibson and Townshend used his modified quirky Deluxe platform to create the new model, with an added DiMarzio Dual Sound M pickup in the middle and another few toggle switches for tapping coils and throwing it out-of-phase. The other two are the mini-humbucking type as per the early seventies. The body is once again sandwiched, pancake-style, but with poplar added; the maple neck is also three pieces. A volute is added for good strength, even though it has fallen from favor in popular circles. Pearloid crowns on the rosewood fingerboard with Grover Kidney button tuners round out the neck (with his specially shaped profile).

To keep this machine from flying away, dual major thumbscrews are provided to lock on the strap too securely at best. "Number 1" is emblazoned on the guitar's face like his old ones. Townshend's signature is found between the tuning keys and on the case as well. This limited edition of only 75 also comes with vintage reissue strings.

Pete Townshend of The Who plays his modified 1970s Les Paul Deluxe Goldtop alongside Roger Daltry for a big show at the Anaheim Stadium, circa 1977. Thanks to guitar tech Alan Rogan for a great time!

Neal Schon

Teenage guitar prodigy Neal Schon did auditions in San Francisco, first with Carlos Santana and then with Eric Clapton. He won both auditions and had to choose between the two. Being a big fan of Eric's and living in the Bay Area near Carlos, the choice wasn't easy. He ultimately went with Carlos because Carlos had asked him first. They became a terrific tour de force dual lead guitar show and recorded the LP *Santana III* together. After a short stint with Azteca, he formed the mega-hit supergroup Journey, which still tours today. In the interim, Neal recorded some majestic instrumental discs with Higher Octave Music.

Neal and Les Paul performing in Las Vegas during the Consumer Electronics Show, 2005. *Courtesy Miles Kitchen*

Schon's association with the Gibson guitar goes back to his early career with an ES-335 and his '56 Goldtop. Eventually, he endorsed Gibson and started having numerous custom-built guitars made to his exacting specifications, including some 25.5" scale versions. A limited pilot run of 25 signed Neal Schon Signature models was made in 2005—with his preference for the Floyd Rose vibrato, a cleanly scarfed neck joint for easy upper access, a DiMarzio Fast Track with a Fernandes Sustainer, and Burstbucker Pro pickups, and two mini-toggles to activate the sustainer and octave device.

Our interview took place in the spring of 2008.

Robb: When did you first get a Les Paul guitar?

Neal: I bought a Goldtop a couple of years before playing with Santana. I had a Barney Kessel and was going for the bigger boxes. I had the 335 originally, which I really liked and I saw the small body. I'd never seen that before and I thought, "Man, this is an interesting looking guitar." I loved the way it sounded and played, and the size of it.

Neal Schon in live performance with his Signature Les Paul model. *Photo by Marty Moffett, courtesy Neal Schon, 2008*

Neal Schon's new Signature guitar being set up by Gary Brawer in San Francisco, 2008.

RL: *You experimented with different pickups on your Les Paul guitars, didn't you?*

NS: I've pretty much used '57 Classics forever. I like the old PAFs, but they're hard to come by. I had a lot of them. I was collecting them out of old guitars before they were so expensive. Working with Gibson now, I like the '57 Plus. I do a lot of live playing, so I like a little bit of the extra push and bottom end that they have over a regular '57. It's not a really high-output pickup. It seems to have more low-mids and low-lows. For live, I like having the speakers pushing a bit more. If I need a little more clarity out of the amp, I just roll some more top on there.

Neal with his recent edition signature Les Paul at the Plant in Sausalito, 2008

RL: *You did an ad for Gibson in the 1980s with a P-90 Les Paul.*

NS: I think that was the first Paul anyone ever put a Floyd Rose on. I was definitely the first guy. It was a P-90 Les Paul and I'd taken the treble pickup out [for a humbucking] and kept the P-90 in the bass position. I really like the way it sounded in the bass position. And the treble position, once I put the Floyd on the guitar, it didn't quite have the output or the warmth that I needed. You're adding so much metal to the guitar with what goes on with the nut and the whammy bar. The only thing that was wrong was the higher neck angle for a Floyd. It took some getting used to. I didn't really use the Floyd so much for dive bombing

and all that stuff that was going on in the 1980s. Playing live, I liked the fact that I could tie it down and block it from the back, so that if you busted a string, it would still stay in tune. Once it was pretty much locked down, it stayed in tune throughout the set.

RL: *How did the Fernandes harmonic sustainer happen?*

NS: I was working with the company back in the late 1980s and 1990s, and I had some friends who were also working with Hiwatt. I checked one out and thought it was pretty interesting. I liked the singing ability when playing a slow song. You can always get a lot of sustain out of a Les Paul. You don't really need a sustainer. It's a different type of sustain, though. It's a lot cleaner. So I got into them and started tweaking them a lot more and figuring out how to make them sound more natural… They vibrate like you have an Ebow on them and you adjust the knob. I have only one master volume on my guitar setup on the top. And the other volume is the sustain volume. You dial it in. You can turn it up or down.

RL: *Your guitar has a lot of things going on with it.*

NS: My Gibson guitar is very hard for them to build. The coolest thing I think that came out of it is the neck joint. Working on getting that neck joint right took years. We're talking right now about simplifying my guitar a little bit, so it's easier for them to make… just using the neck joint, my new knob configuration, the angle of the neck, with or without a Floyd.

RL: *What would you like to say about Les Paul?*

NS: He has to be one of the funniest, warmest, most incredible guys I've ever met. And of course an amazing guitar player and designer. God knows if anyone would have an electric guitar if it weren't for him. I've enjoyed every moment since I met Les in New York, when I went to the Iridium and started sitting in and playing. He's a great guy straight up. He's always been really cool to me. Treated me like he's known me for years when I just met him. I think Les is one of those genuine people that have been like that their whole life.

Zakk Wylde

Zakk Wylde (Jeff Wiedlandt) is the current lead guitarist with Ozzy Osbourne and has his own band, Black Label Society. Readers of *Guitar World* have voted him most valuable player for three years; he was also named best metal guitarist and best shredder. His use of unique pinched harmonics and chicken picking in the metal field is unusual. He is known to play in dropped very low tunings with heavier gauge strings.

Zakk's Les Paul series is based on an '80s Les Paul Custom—"The Grail"—his folks gave him, on which he had special work done. When sent to be painted, it was supposed to be a spiral design, but returned as a bullseye. He decided to leave it, and it has become his moniker. He also had a preference for stripped finished necks and EMG pickups which continue on his new guitars.

A few Gibson signature models were done for him in red and flame maple combination, an orange buzz saw version, then antique white and black circles, both with an ebony fingerboard. The green camoflage bullseye artwork is his design plan for the recent series. It has to do with his strong ties to the U.S. military and an old guitar's Confederate flag theme. This guitar brings together all his favorite aspects, with the unfinished neck and the maple fingerboard, EMG active electronics, and distinctive Camo Bullseye artwork.

Zakk Wylde with his arsenal of signature Les Paul models. Note the bottle-cap-laden Rebel Model. *Photo for Gibson by Neil Zlowzower*

Robb: Zakk, tell me about your association with the Les Paul guitar.

Zakk: Between the sound, the way it plays, the whole feel of it, and everything like that, it's the perfect guitar for me—without a doubt. You have Strat guys, you have Tele guys, and some guys love their Vs. I love Vs and the SGs. With a lot of Les Paul players, you either have Standard guys or Custom guys. They all have their own sound—even the Juniors do. It just depends upon what sound you want. So it's that and a Marshall. To me it's like beer and pretzels. They just go together. It's a perfect combination. After seeing my teacher Leroy playing one and then seeing Jimmy Page play it, I definitely wanted one. Randy Rhodes had one. All the great guys had Les Pauls.

RL: You got one for high school graduation.

ZW: Every lawn I mowed, I knew I was ten dollars closer to getting the damn fiddle. I had 500 dollars saved up. Then, when I graduated high school, I got home and they said, "There's something sitting for you on the kitchen table." I walked in and there was my first guitar, a Les Paul Custom in Alpine white. It

was like the one Randy Rhodes had that faded yellow. That thing is now at the Rock and Roll Hall of Fame in Cleveland.

RL: And you namd one the Grail?

ZW: That's another Les Paul I have, the one I recorded all my Ozzy records with. I name my Les Pauls. It depends upon the serial numbers, the Bullseye Les Pauls that Gibson makes for me, the Zakk Wylde model thing. I name them all after Yankee players. I had number 3, so obviously that's Babe. Number 4 is Lou and number 5 is Joe D.

RL: Did you scrape the lacquer off the back of the maple necks? Is that why you like the unfinished neck?

ZW: Yes. It feels great. It almost feels like a baseball bat. The reason it was maple is because that's what was on that neck. So that was like when I had the Grail. It was maple with an ebony fingerboard. I love the sound of that guitar, so I said, "Guys, make it just like this one." I found out it was a maple neck on the back because the paint came off it. You have to figure maple is a bright wood because it's super hard. That's why you get all the high end. You get the bottom end because of the body.

RL: I like that combination, too. So, for the first design, you had a spiral Hitchcock Vertigo kind of thing in mind?

ZW: That's what it was supposed to be, originally. Max (Peter Beranet) ended up painting the guitar. When I was at Max's, I opened it up and it was a bullseye. We were getting ready to go to Japan and I said, "The hell with it. This is fine the way it is. It still looks cool. Don't worry about it." So that's why we ended up sticking with the bullseye.

RL: How did the camouflage thing come about?

ZW: Originally, I bought a Camo '78 Les Paul Custom with a maple neck. It was a black one with a maple fretboard. I'd never seen that before. I said, "Dude, I've got to buy this damn thing." It had its own sound. It's got more top end because it's got a maple fretboard.

RL: *What's the story on the Union Jack guitar with the bottle caps on it?*

ZW: *That's the Rebel flag. I was listening to Skynrd and the Allman Brothers and put a Confederate flag on it. People think I'm from the South. I say, "No, South Jersey." Ozzy asked, "What the hell is that?" And I said, "Skynyrd and Allman Brothers." All I remember is we were coming out of a photo shoot and there was a ten-foot flame shooting off this thing. They wrapped it in newspapers and put gasoline on it and lit the guitar on fire. I said, "What the heck are you doing, man?" Then just hanging out at the house one night, it was already messed up enough, so I just started pounding beer bottle caps into it. The thing has had the headstock broken off of it twice already. It's been burnt and it's got bottle caps in it. I still record with that guitar all the time now. It's one of my best-sounding guitars. We call it the tetanus guitar. That's why I wear the leather wristband, because those things are all rusted. If you cut your arms on that thing, you're headed to the hospital for sure, bro. It's like stepping on a rusty nail.*

RL: *How did your Epiphone Buzzsaw Les Paul come together?*

ZW: *Gibson does the Buzzsaw as well. The Epiphone thing is cool, too, because not every kid can spend $4,000 on a guitar. Everybody over at the Gibson company are super cool people. They said, "Zakk, do you want to do an Epi?" I said, "Of course, man." This is great for a kid. I could go onstage with that and still sound slamming. They did a really good job.*

RL: *You were influenced by Al Dimeola and Randy Rhodes, weren't you?*

ZW: *Al Dimeola played a Les Paul, too… Al, Hendrix, Frank Marino, Robin Trower, Tony Iommi, Jimmy Page, all the usual suspects who destroyed my life. (Laughs.)*

RL: *What would you like to tell all these guitar players about playing Les Paul guitars?*

ZW: *It's like beer; you can't go wrong with any of them. (We laugh.) Whether you're a Standard guy, a Custom guy, or a Junior guy, they're all good!*

Zakk Wylde Camo Bullseye Les Paul Custom with EMG pickups and maple fingerboard. *Courtesy Centre City, 2005*

Original Zakk Wylde Les Paul signature model in antique white. *Courtesy Centre City Music, 2005*

Zakk's Les Paul model has the black stinger and the raw maple neck for the naturally clean feel.

217

John Lennon Tribute Les Paul

John Lennon was an enormously influential musician and poet, known worldwide for co-creating the music of the Beatles. Their impact on modern music and on Western culture will forever leave a lasting impression on many of us. After playing Gibson and Epiphone models with the Fab Four, he also played a 1950s sunburst Les Paul Junior guitar when he began his solo career. While living in New York City, Lennon met Ron DeMarino, a local guitar repairman/luthier, through an amplifier deal in 1971. Ron gained his confidence and was soon doing setups and giving him advice on various guitar deals.

One day John wanted an extra rhythm pickup added and asked about a "humberdincker!" Ron instead suggested installing a 1930s-style Gibson bar magnet pickup (today known as a "Charlie Christian" pickup) to complement the P-90. These had a robust and clear tone that was great for rhythm playing, and Lennon agreed to try it. Ron had to do some extensive modifications for the long deep magnets, and installed a toggle switch as well. When John and Yoko hosted the Mike Douglas show for a week in February 1972, John played the guitar for a few songs with Chuck Berry.

Lennon liked the way it sounded with the new setup, but wanted a different look, too. Both his Epiphone Casino and Ricky 325 were redone natural during his Beatles days, so he asked Ron to strip the bright yellow sunburst finish off (much to Ron's consternation), returning it to its raw natural reddish mahogany color. Lennon also complained about it not staying in tune, so Ron moved the stop tailpiece back and added the Tune-O-Matic bridge plus modern tuners.

Shortly thereafter, John played the instrument at the historic One-to-One Organization concert at Madison Square Garden in August 1972. This show was a benefit for the Willowbrook State Hospital for mentally challenged children. John later had the Les Paul guitar lacquered in a cherry finish and enjoyed it for the rest of his life. Some years after his untimely death, the guitar was put on display at the Rock and Roll Hall of Fame Museum in Cleveland before being sent to the John Lennon Museum in Tokyo, where it now resides.

Enter Gibson's new "Inspired By" series of famous musicians' well-played Gibson instruments. The Custom Shop's Historic program manager Edwin Wilson thoroughly examined the historically significant guitar and oversaw the building of the new instrument. He flew to Japan and, per Yoko's stipulations, carefully kept the original strings intact and used cotton gloves. He noticed that even though Lennon was an energetic musician, his guitar touch was quite light, reflecting in his minimal wear on the original frets, plus his use of .009 gauge strings. Edwin documented the various dents, scratches, and Ron's routing and wiring, for a truly accurate reproduction (sans the .009s). Included are the unusual circular scratches between the pickups and the reversed blade pole piece with the typical indentation below the 5th string instead of the 2nd (some flip it around afterward). With a variety of stains, along with special glazing and buffing, they replicated the aged look of John's historic Les Paul. Some players appreciate the fact that it can rock like a Junior and not worry about minor scratches.

Three-hundred production models of the Lennon Les Paul Junior were produced in 2007. These came with a special green cloth folder embroidered with John's autograph. The package includes Gibson's authenticity certificate, an article with DeMarino by *The Beatles Gear* book author Andy Babiuk, a sleeveless New York City T-shirt, and a signed print of John by Allison Lefcort. This tribute to one of the most influential of musicians reflects Lennon's creative spirit and rock 'n' roll flavor with a Gibson solid-body guitar.

2007 John Lennon "Inspired By" Les Paul Junior tribute model #029. *Courtesy Dave Weiderman GC and Donna Lynn*

Warren Haynes

Robb: I read that your brothers turned you onto some old blues records.

Warren: I had two older brothers who were record collectors, so I was fortunate to grow up with a music library that had thousands of records in different genres. My brothers were constantly pushing me toward stuff they thought I would like. The first music I was passionate about was soul music, before I ever heard rock 'n' roll. I started singing when I was seven, before I ever picked up a guitar. I was listening to Otis Redding, Sam & Dave, the Four Tops, the Temptations, Stevie Wonder, James Brown, Wilson Pickett. Years later, I heard Cream, Hendrix, and others and said to myself, "Wow! Maybe I should play guitar."

RL: What was your first guitar?

WH: When I was 11, my brother got an acoustic guitar and I played it more than he did. Then for my 12th birthday I got my first electric guitar, a Norma with a Norma amplifier from the local hardware store—$49 for one and $59 for the other. Then I graduated to a copy of a Gibson SG.

RL: What guitar players were playing a Les Paul back then, that you were aware of?

WH: So many people were playing Les Pauls at that time. Most of the people I was listening to went through a Les Paul phase or played them quite a lot. Clapton. Most people don't realize that even Hendrix played a Les Paul for a minute or that Johnny Winter played one for a while. Jeff Beck played one, as did Peter Green. I always loved the big meaty sound, the thick tone.

RL: When did you get your first Les Paul?

WH: I didn't get my first Les Paul until I was with the Allman Brothers, in 1989. I played other people's Les Pauls. I joined Dickey Betts's band around '86 and was playing a Paul Reed Smith guitar at that time. The sound of Dickey's Goldtop was so huge I started thinking it might be nice to start playing a Les Paul after all these years. When in Rome… I was a huge Duane Allman fan and loved his tone on the Les Paul, but was also trying not to copy that tone, always looking for something different. When I joined the Allman Brothers in '89 I decided it was time to make that switch. That was 20 years ago, and it just made so

much sense from that point forward. I don't know why it took me so long to actually get one.

All of a sudden, I was able to get much closer to the sound in my head that I'd been chasing. A Les Paul lets you relax and not fight your sound as much. Most people who improvise for a living are constantly chasing a sound they're never 100% satisfied with. We get satisfied for a moment, and then we're looking for something different. A lot of the people that I really admire are constantly adjusting the pickup selector and the volume, the tone, whatever. On a Les Paul, when I'm playing, I'm changing moment by moment just to accommodate what I'm looking for at that moment. But you learn how to coax different sounds out of it. It definitely widens your palette, your vocabulary, and makes it much easier to express yourself and have your own voice.

RL: It must be a bit of a challenge filling the shoes of Duane Allman and getting in that ballpark to create such an effusive, beautiful sound.

WH: Yes, it is a challenge, but it's a necessary challenge, just like in your formative years of playing when you're learning or copying what someone else played. And then at some point you abandon that and play whatever pops into your head. That's really early on in the life of any musician. It's a similar thing with tone when you're starting out. How did so-and-so get this tone? You chase that for a while, but eventually you start pursuing the sound you hear in your head, the one that makes it easier for you to sing through your instrument.

RL: I feel the same way. So then you finally had your Les Paul.

WH: The first one I got was a Standard. Then I went to the Custom Shop and picked out one. I tended not to stray too far from my original, the Standard. A lot of my Les Pauls, especially early on, were like tobacco sunburst. I got hooked and started thinking, "Well, let's see what the difference between this one and that one is." The second one I got had a fatter neck and, consequently, a richer sound. Some of the compromise is how thick a neck you can manage to play your best on, so you're weighing the sound against the playability. I never liked the real skinny necks; I don't think they sound as good. It might be easier to play them, but if what you're hearing is not satisfying, then it's more important to fight the guitar a little if it sounds better.

The Warren Haynes Signature model,
backstage at a Grateful Dead concert.

Warren Haynes playing a soulful solo with the
Allman Brothers Band in Rincon, CA, 2009.

RL: *You just adjust to it like an old Explorer neck. So then you got a '58?*

WH: *I've been playing an authentic '58 that's on loan to me. It's not officially mine.*

RL: *That's quite a responsibility.*

WH: *Yeah, but it sure sounds great! I've been playing it only in the Allman Brothers. In Government Mule I play my Signature guitar and Custom Shop Firebirds and stuff like that.*

RL: *Did you work with Edwin Wilson, Pat Foley, and Mike McGuire?*

WH: *Yes, I worked with all those guys and with Rick Gembar, who has been a very big supporter. I have a great relationship with all of them. My situation at Gibson is wonderful. It feels like family there. They had been talking to me about a specialized instrument for quite some time. I was never comfortable with the idea because, at that time especially, I didn't own a real '58 or '59 to copy. I felt there was nothing really that different about the guitars I was playing. It took me a while to wrap my head around that, because I always thought, "There's a Les Paul and I'm not him. Why should I take credit for something Les designed?" It took me a few years to finally figure out that the one we came up with is unique, and has its own thing. Now I feel more comfortable with it.*

Eventually we started going through different pickup configurations and replaced the bridges with TonePros bridges. Even then, I didn't feel that was a big enough difference to make a specialized instrument. Then one day I was talking to John Cutler on the phone. He and Peter Miller had done a lot of work for Jerry Garcia with his guitars, effects, and rig. Cutler was telling me that they had just designed a new volume pot that, when turned down, the tone didn't change. I thought that was cool, but at the same time, I got a lot of my favorite sounds by turning the volume down and getting the tone a little darker. I really like that, so I asked if I could have it both ways. "Sure," he said, "I'll just put a little switch in there and you can activate it or not." So the biggest feature about my guitar is that switch. If I'm playing with the guitar turned down really low and it's duller than I want it to be, I can flip the switch and all the top end comes back.

RL: *Gibson calls it a Unity Gain Buffer preamp.*

WH: *Yeah. And it's cool too because, at any moment,* you can compare the sound—wherever your volume and tone is set and whatever pickup setting you're on—with or without the buffer preamp.

RL: *So it brings back the fidelity with a lower volume.*

WH: *I was never a fan of coil taps and stuff like that. To me, this is a much more palatable, useable feature. It's really subtle. When you're playing through an amp at a small volume, you don't notice a huge difference. You notice a much bigger difference at a loud volume. In the studio, for example, if I'm looking for a particular sound, it gives me other options. I've gotten real spoiled with it. It's something that has become part of my everyday performances now.*

RL: *They call it a CAE sound. You also like that old '58 finish but you put your own colors together?*

WH: *They gave me a book of all the sunburst finishes and said, "Pick out what you want." Looking through that book of all those gorgeous finishes, I narrowed it down to two. I think one of them was called honeyburst. They sort of mixed the two together and called it "Haynes Burst."*

Brian Farmer, my tech, was really active in that, because he is so much more knowledgeable about all that stuff than I am. It was tough, because there are so many great finishes. They wanted to do a plain top first and possibly do a flame later, which was cool with me, though most of the ones I'd been playing were flame top. But I thought the plain turned out beautifully.

RL: *It's gorgeous. The TonePros bridge locks down. Is it easier in case you break a string, or do you like the sound of it, too?*

WH: *I like the sound of it. I think it's a step up. We were never completely happy with the bridges. When I say "we," I'm mainly referring to Brian Farmer, who's responsible for maintaining the guitar. He always said, "These bridges could be better. Why don't we put the TonePros on there?" At first, Gibson didn't want to deal with that, but we talked them into it.*

RL: *Your "Inspired By" model also has the Burstbucker 1 and 2 pickups.*

WH: *Yeah, that's what they call it, Burstbucker 1 and Burstbucker 2. TonePro bridge and the circuitry we talked about. And it's kind of a combination '58/'59.*

RL: *How would you sum up your love of the Les Paul guitar?*

WH: *It's my favorite electric guitar as far as being able to get the sound that's in my head, the sound that I'm trying to utilize in order for me to sing through my instrument. It's the one that lets me do it.*

RL: *What would you say to the younger players out there about playing guitar and grasping that sound?*

WH: *You have to find the sound that lets you be yourself. There's something about the chunkiness, the depth, that a Les Paul has. You can dial in a great guitar through a great amp and have a great sound. Then you unplug that guitar and plug in a Les Paul and it's even greater! (laughs)*

Joe Bonamassa, riding the crest of the new blues frontier

I had the great fortune to see 14-year-old guitarist/vocalist Joe Bonamassa perform for Leo Fender's Tribute concert. Then at the Belly Up Tavern in Solana Beach in late 2007 I witnessed him turn in a blistering set of red hot blues with a very receptive audience. Hailing from Utica, New York and starting out with a little Chiquita at age 5, he was later influenced by British blues guitarists like Rory Gallagher, Paul Kossoff, and early Jeff Beck. Young Joe opened for BB King when he was 12 years old. He became a protégé of the late Danny Gatton and, later, Robben Ford before finally touring and recording a number of top blues records. In 2000 Tom Dowd produced his first solo album, *A New Day Yesterday. Blues Deluxe* and *Had to Cry Today* were other favorites. His heavier blues-laden 2006 album, *You and Me*, debuted at number one on the Billboard blues charts. His *Sloe Gin* album took off in 2007 as his career continued to soar. In summer 2008, Gibson released a limited edition Joe Bonamassa Goldtop that quickly sold out. Ten were sprayed red and ten more in blue over the gold basecoat to a beautiful candy apple variety.

We did this interview on July 31st, 2008, just minutes before a lively performance in Norway. Joe shared his knowledge of tone and guitars and told us of his great affection for the crown of Gibson solid-bodies:

Robb: *You once told me that your dad had a music store.*

Joe: *Yes, my dad had a music shop and I got into collecting guitars and stuff like that. It was really an addiction more than anything.*

RL: *What attracted you to the Les Paul guitar?*

JB: *Everybody has an ideal sound in their head, a tone they strive to achieve. And what is the easiest guitar? For some people, it's a Tele or a Gibson SG, or a 335 or a Burns of London. For me, when I played the Les Paul with the humbuckers I always found it easy to achieve that mid-rangy kind of human voice quality that I was hearing in my head. I experimented by using Strats and Teles and SGs and 335s. It seems to me that the Les Paul has the most throaty, gutsy, extremely human-voice-like quality. It was easy to roll the tone off any amp and just achieve that. The higher output pickups drive the front end of any amp and you're pretty much there, so I was really attracted to the Les Paul Standard. It was less strident than the Custom and had a bit more character, in my humble opinion. The Les Paul Customs were pretty bright with the ebony necks, especially the '70s ones.*

RL: *Yes, because of the ebony fingerboard and maple top.*

JB: *It's debatable for a lot of guys. John Sykes was a huge hero. He played that black Custom; he still does. Clapton played a triple pickup Custom, so the Custom had validity, but it was more and more a rock guitar than anything. The bluesier players dug the Standard because of Bloomfield and Cream and Peter Green and Paul Kossoff, who was one of my favorite players. He was one of the most wonderful players, his personality and simplicity and the way his vibrato and tone interacted—it was like an extension of him.*

RL: *Exactly. So what was your first Les Paul?*

JB: *My dad had a 1974 Les Paul Standard sunburst that I would borrow. We had everything from 52s to 55s and 68s. The first one I remember playing was a 1974. It was pretty light. It had a really strange Standard plaque on it written in small letters. It was a two-piece top almost like someone's attempt to make a '58 Burst. It had a bigger neck than a '70s. It didn't taper. It was a single-piece neck. It was maybe an employee's guitar, a one-off that someone did for themselves. It was kind of beat and had feel. I put real PAFs in it because I bought a trashed Les Paul SG that had been flooded, cracked, burned—everything possible had been done to it. We put the PAFs in there and I played that forever. I loved that guitar. I wish I still had it.*

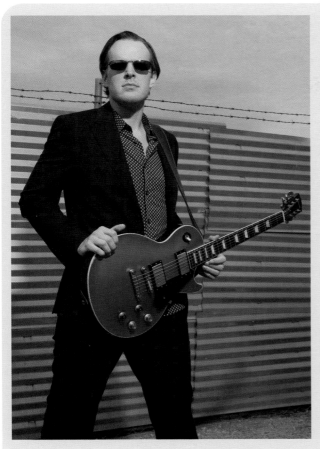

Joe Bonamassa posed with his "Inspired By" signature Les Paul Goldtop. *Courtesy Rick Gould, 2008*

RL: *How did you hook up with Gibson?*

JB: My relationship with Gibson started in 2000. I always played the Les Paul. I switch between the Tele, the Strat, and the Les Paul. Those are my trio of guitars every night. And I played at their factory down in Memphis where they build the 335s. They have a really nice Gibson club that's a beautiful venue. They said, "We have this Classic we'd like you to check out. You could have it if you like it and play it." Well, I don't want to take anything if I'm not going to play it. I played it and it had a big '59 kind of neck, and a lot of output. It was cherry red, a really cool guitar. I played that for a while and then I got a couple more '59 reissues that I bought from them, just started a relationship with them very organically. I met a guy named Pat Foley about five years ago. He and I kept in touch. By the time the end of 2007 rolled around, I'd gotten a bit of notoriety and was playing 100% Gibson at that point in time. I did a couple of records that were quite a bit thicker guitar sounds. I was pretty much playing 99.9% Gibson Les Pauls onstage. They asked me if I would be interested in doing a signature

model Goldtop. I said, "Let me put my head around it and see what I can come up with."

I remember a guitar that came through my dad's shop, a '55 Goldtop. It had been routed with humbuckers and painted black in the back. It had been cracked so many times they just Krylon-ed it for aesthetic purposes. It was all beat up and everything was wrong about it, but everything was right about it. I remember I couldn't afford it and dad had to pay the bills at the shop. The guitar slipped through my hands, but I always loved it. When Gibson asked me to do a Goldtop, I said, "I think I know something that would be kind of fun and interesting." We got them to change the placement of the logo to early correct '57. I wanted to do an early '57 black back Les Paul with black parts. I always dug the look of those and had bought some Les Paul Custom parts and made one of my Historic Goldtops into that already. We did that and put the bumblebee caps in it, and got the Grovers and the nylon saddles on it, so it really takes the treble out of it. The Grovers are really critical and the thickness of the headstock to me is really critical to getting that weight and tone. When you plug into an amp, the Les Paul is dark and it's thick. You can always add treble if you want, but it's easier to add treble to a sound than it is to take it away. That's how the Bonamassa Les Paul got started. They did a limited edition of 300 of them and we sold all 300.

RL: *Wow! Pat Foley is an old friend of mine.*

JB: Pat's a guy who always believed in me a long time ago. He said, "When the time is right, we're going to do something." He was absolutely correct about that. When they did the Bonamassa Goldtop, my records were starting to catch on and things were happening. I was in with Eric Clapton at the Royal Albert Hall playing "Further Up the Road." The Les Paul signature guitar is probably on par with the greatest honor I've ever had in my entire life, and probably ever will, to have my name associated with such an iconic piece of musical equipment. When I first started playing Gibsons back when I was five and six and seven, I never dreamed that I would have a Les Paul that said Bonamassa on it.

RL: *You made the headstocks a little thicker?*

JB: I've had 20 really good Les Pauls. You notice on |the Les Paul, when some are thicker, they sound heavier and more like Paul Kossoff. Others sound more strident. *You start looking at the differences. They go from really thick to thin. I took the thickness of my ES-345 headstock and measured it, and used it for my guitar. I think that makes a big difference, as do nylon saddles. I like the sound of the wound strings on the metal bridge saddles and the sound of the unwound strings on the nylon, so that's why I split them. I think the Grovers make a big difference. I can tell the difference between the feel of a Les Paul with Grovers on it. To me it's a feel thing and it's a weight thing. You get a thicker sound out of it.*

RL: *The aging on your guitar is done at Gibson?*

JB: *Yes, it's done in-house, not by Tom Murphy. I think they did a great job. They are all different. I've seen probably 100 of the 300. The fans bring them to the gigs. It's really cool because each of them is different. My intention in aging them—I know some guys don't like the aging and there's a debate about it—was to prevent the guitars from immediately being put into a closet with all the seals and strings and cellophane on them, never used or touched. People boast, "I have one in mint condition," and go trade it like furniture. I wanted a guitar that, if there was a ding put on it, who cares, it's already beat up. Bring it to the club and play it. Take it to your gig and play it. Play it at rehearsal. Who cares if you sweat on it and make it more worn than it is. I've been playing mine for over a year and you play them, they look more and more like the authentic ones by the day. It's not trashed, but it's enough to say, "Go play it!" I wanted it to feel welcoming to play warm and comfortable. I wanted people to reach for the Les Paul. I want them to play my guitar. That was my intention.*

RL: *When did your Goldtop become available?*

JB: *It debuted at Summer NAMM in June 2008. I got the first prototypes in April, and we sold through the line by Christmas. It's all sold out.*

The Recreation of an American Legend: Michael Bloomfield's Signature Model

Brilliant blues guitarist Michael Bloomfield came to prominence in Chicago in the early sixties. His inspired musicianship was the result of years of research into local bluesmen, such as Howlin' Wolf and Muddy Waters, who played in the South Side clubs. Michael recreated the authentic licks and phrases of masters like John Coltrane with a soulful twist of his own that mixed jazz and Indian ragas. After being discovered by John Hammond, he began performing with the Paul Butterfield Blues Band (recording *East-West*), Bob Dylan (Newport Folk Festival and *Highway 61 Revisited*), and the Electric Flag (*A Long Time Comin'* and *The Trip* soundtrack).

Bloomfield experimented with various Les Paul models early in his career (see our interviews in Volume 1) and later extolled the virtues and drawbacks of each in his *The Wizard of Waukesha* film interview. He settled upon the one guitar that gave him everything he needed in a Gibson solid-body—a 1959 sunburst Les Paul Standard. (His amp of choice was the original Fender Twin Reverb.) This Les Paul guitar was heard with majestic lead tones on the landmark blues double-LP selection *Super Session* and shown on the album cover. These remarkable recordings and his incendiary live performances had a great impact on many guitarists worldwide.

This author had the rare pleasure of playing Michael's guitar on a few occasions in the seventies. It was a workingman's axe and showed it. I even offered to clean up the dirty grime around its bridge, but he wouldn't let me, for fear of losing its precious vibe. I concurred! Then one evening at the Troubadour, Michael told me about leaving his favorite guitar behind as collateral at a Canadian venue. Being a die-hard blues audio/videophile, he had crossed back into the States to watch a special TV show and ended up missing the gig. Years later, I encountered the Vancouver club owner's two sons at the Anaheim NAMM show. They told me they still had Michael's guitar in their possession. One morning in February 1981, drummer Jeffrey James called to tell me Michael had died of a drug overdose in San Francisco. We were deeply saddened by the loss.

Years passed and the Gibson Signature series of Les Paul guitars got going as Michael's posthumous popularity was still growing. Eventually his guitar was sold at auction to a private collector for an undisclosed amount and therefore wasn't available for scrutiny. Gibson's master techs Edwin Wilson and Pat Foley studied numerous photos and consulted with Dan Erlewine (the previous owner) and Michael's son Alan Bloomfield before crafting Michael's beloved Les Paul Sunburst.

As an Entertainment Relations professional at Gibson, Pat Foley has been a key player in the "Inspired By" series of guitars:

> *Robb: I think you guys are doing a great job with the new Bloomfield guitar.*
>
> *Pat: Like the Johnny Winters Firebird, that was an instance where we felt it was time the artist was honored for his influence on generations of guitarists. We knew it wouldn't be a huge seller, but he was a really important guitarist. A lot of people's influences can be traced back to Mike Bloomfield. His brother Allen was a real joy all the way through it, so that was a fun project.*
>
> *RL: It's really a magnificent instrument, the way it came together, though you guys didn't get a chance to actually see his guitar.*
>
> *PF: We got input from a lot of sources and did the best we could working from photographs and the personal recollections of people who had worked on the guitar. It was pretty successful and the aged ones were very sweet, the ones Murphy worked on. Dan Erlewine, who actually sold the guitar to Michael, was a great source of information.*
>
> *RL: With both pickups on, they sound quite a bit like Michael's guitar from the Super Session album.*
>
> *PF: I think they do. Jimmy Vivino was also a big help in creating the guitar because he was a big fan and is very knowledgeable about Michael. He helped quite a bit on it. It was fun.*
>
> *RL: I am thrilled to see Michael's signature guitar come out. It seems like they are selling quickly, too.*
>
> *PF: It has done very well.*

Enter the "Inspired By" Bloomfield Les Paul Model

With amazing expertise, the Custom Shop recreated a remarkable version of the guitar that inspired many to take up the instrument. Small details, like the original styled thin plastic toggle switch and reinforced brass jack plate, were used, along with the Grover kidney-buttoned tuning machines previously put on by Dan Erlewine. The slightly larger, more pronounced C carved profile, '58

NAMM show display prototype of the Michael Bloomfield Signature Les Paul with Tom Murphy's special aging.

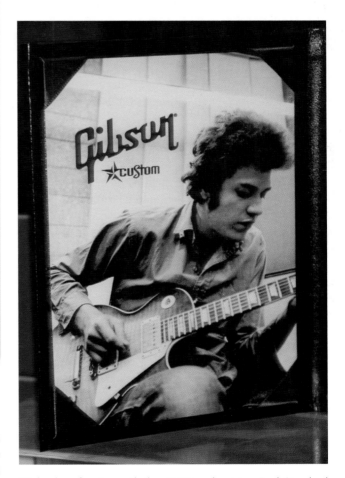

Michael performing with the 1959 sunburst Les Paul Standard that is pictured in the Custom Shop display booklet.

style neck gives added tonal mass, along with the Grover's inherent ringing brightness. A lightweight solid mahogany back and long tenon neck joint were employed in the construction. Electronically, CTS potentiometers and "bumblebee" capacitors complement the Burstbucker 1 & 2 rhythm and treble PAF-styled humbucking pickups. With non-potted coils and slightly mismatched windings, these authentic reproduction pickups greatly help recreate a mix of rich tones with stinging lead-position highs. The in-between setting nails Michael's *Super Session* tones wonderfully.

On close examination, it is apparent that much attention went into the finish details of this model. The sunburst has a unique faded coloration and shaded edge pattern. Featuring the thin "pure tone" nitro finish, this limited signature model is sprayed with the authentic "Bloomfield Burst" colors that faithfully recreate the legendary guitar. An open and resonant acoustical sound is achieved with this thinner nitro finish.

The aged Murphy versions have a vintage mojo character without being over the top. Part of the modern distressing includes three distinctive dings on the top, including the discolored E-string divet near the stop tailpiece. Specially tarnished nickel parts for this series give both versions a nice overall vibe. They have the aged nickel hardware, lightweight aluminum stop tailpiece, and include the worn/blackened screw top. Michael's guitar

Michael Bloomfield VOS #114 Les Paul Standard showing 3-D maple figuring and the distinctive Bloomfield Signature thin nitro finish. Note the gold polepieces on the humbucking pickups. *Courtesy Chuck Kavooris*

This Bloomfield model #155 weighs merely 8.1 pounds and sonically sings both acoustically and when plugged in. The aged hardware and Grover tuning machines give it the finishing vintage touch. *From the Kavooris collection*

had a few replaced control knobs, including a sixties reflector top and early fifties speed knob added. Serial numbers on the 100 Murphy versions have the name Bloomfield across the top, with the number below; the 200 VOS examples simply have MB and the number. The first two prototypes went to Allen Bloomfield and Jimmy Vivino.

Woods for the maple tops were hand selected to be slightly upward chevron patterns as on Michael's guitar, while many are even or somewhat reversed. A slightly tighter flame was also sought for these Bloomie models, unlike the wider flames on the Duane Allman series. Many of the Murphy aged examples, and some VOS models, have the wide third ribbon flame maple tops.

Overall, the guitar is a great package for the Bloomfield aficionados and a real treat for vintage reissue fans. It is also a great investment and a fitting tribute by Gibson to honor a leading blues exponent of our time.

Jeff Beck Signature "Oxblood" 1954 Les Paul

Many people know of Jeff Beck's incredible prowess on the electric and acoustic guitar from his early work with the Yardbirds, before his own sensational Jeff Beck Group—with Rod Stewart on vocals and Ron Wood on bass. During those formative years of the British Invasion, Jeff first wielded an Esquire Fender guitar, then a beautiful '59 Gibson Les Paul Standard sunburst. Soon the powerful and ripping sounds of the Gibson solid-body guitar created his memorable and groundbreaking majestic solo music on the albums *Truth* (1968) and *Beck-Ola* (1969). After a few years with the versatile Fender Stratocaster (due to Jimi Hendrix's advice), Jeff moved back to the Les Paul guitar. He wanted to fatten up the sound of his Beck, Bogert & Appice trio and, while recording in Memphis, located an old refinished Les Paul from Buddy Davis who worked at Strings & Things Music. Jeff bought the guitar for $500 and first used it with Tim and Carmine in BBA. Shortly thereafter, his monumental instrumental album *Blow by Blow* with this Les Paul guitar set a precedent, carving his epitaph of tone for future guitarists to enjoy.

Although Beck gravitated back to the Fender camp for ergonomics and the versatile vibrato tailpiece he has mastered, Jeff has used Les Paul guitars in the studio for years for the fuller tonalities. In 2008, Gibson's Custom Shop engineer Edwin Wilson and artist relations man Pat Foley left for Sussex, England to visit Jeff and scope out the "Oxblood" Les Paul wonder. They scrutinized the instrument, which was in a state of serious disrepair, and painstakingly recreated a true legend of rock guitardom. Gibson considers this "Inspired By" 1954 Jeff Beck Oxblood Les Paul to be the most detail-precise reissue they've done to date. Similar unofficial '54 reissues were built from the mid-nineties with humbuckings, the stop tailpiece, and a deep black/cherry finish made primarily for Japanese orders. They sold some in the States to fans and those discerning player/collectors who enjoy the sustaining sound quality of the naturally resonant stop bar tailpiece when coupled with the big humbucking pickups.

The new Jeff Beck Les Paul guitar is an amazing knock-off, right down to the inset neck screw and Schaller machines on the sunburst headstock back. Even Beck was astonished at how accurate the color was, especially after the Gibson guys went back and forth on the perplexing color.

Pat Foley tells us the story:

Robb: You mentioned you and Edwin were going to see Jeff Beck and took off for England.

Pat: Yep. We did the inspection of the guitar. We went to his house in Sussex and then we built a couple of different prototypes. Then I took a prototype to him and he approved it. Then I went over with a whole roomful of guitars and he did the signing. He was absolutely wonderful. He really enjoyed it, and it worked out well.

RL: I think it's fabulous that he can enjoy endorsements with you guys and with Fender.

PF: This was a limited edition of only 150. We took 50 guitars to London and we met there. He came in for the afternoon and played every one. And signed off on them.

RL: The one at the NAMM show that said #1, was that the very first prototype?

PF: That was the first one he approved. There was one before that we had to make some adjustments to.

RL: Was he paid per guitar to sign them and play them?

PF: Like anybody else he got a royalty, but then he got an additional payment for each one that he signed. He actually got a lot more money than most, but there were reasons for that. Number one, he's Jeff Beck. And two, Gibson had been making those bootleg copies, for lack of a better word. They've been making copies of his guitar for a long time, so it only seemed fair that he get a decent royalty on it.

RL: Buddy Davis first got the guitar from Robert "Butch" Johnson in Memphis, who found it at Gruhn's. I heard it was black and was sold to Strings & Things. Eddy Voorhees came in and had it done in a brownish color. Tommy Stinson said that Terry Paige had painted that guitar and they called it deep cherry at the time.

PF: I asked Jeff about the oxblood idea, that name and where it came from. He said he didn't know, that's just how people have always referred to it. He thought it was black. Looking at our prototype, the guitar is actually browner than people realize. The oxblood has a very brownish tint.

The first 50 of these historic guitars are specifically aged—slightly dinged and scratched instead of weather checked—at Gibson to closely resemble Jeff's original, with many of the nicks and onstage battle scars. The neck is custom tailored to precise specs (slightly thinner at the 4th and 5th frets), with added Schaller machines, and a long neck tenon. It even has an embedded screw with putty near the heel on back from an earlier repair. Lightweight one-piece mahogany is used for the body, which averages 8.5 pounds, with an exceptionally accurate top arch achieved. Due to the misplaced lead pickup's closer proximity to the bridge, a part of the cream surround is partially carved away to facilitate easy high E string changing. The uncovered Burstbucker 2 and 3 special wound pickups (with gold adjustable polepieces and height adjustment screws), nickel-plated aluminum "wrapover" stop tailpiece bridge, and thin nitrocellulose lacquer finish give it the final touch of authentic tone. The original's feel and vibe match the sound and oxblood finish to give the world Jeff Beck's modified Les Paul a reality all its own. Some owners say the long sustain and harmonic feedback of the original comes through the new guitar with magic emotive powers anew.

RL: *Exactly. The guys in Memphis and Buddy Davis called it chocolate. Jeff signed Buddy's 25th anniversary of* Blow by Blow *shirt "Love the Chocolate."*

PF: *It does look more chocolate. The previous knockoffs that we did for years looked like a midnight cherry of some sort. But his original guitar was really trashed and couldn't be played. I don't know what kind of shape it was when he got it, but it had the neck broken off and screwed back on: there's a big screw right through the back below the heel there. It's got the original strings on it. When we did our reproduction of it, we aged it and we beat the hell out of it, but we didn't go quite as far as we could have. I thought, "I'm not sure the people are going to want a guitar quite that badly beaten up," so we controlled ourselves a little bit on it.*

RL: *I first saw it in '73 when I met Jeff in San Diego. Then I saw him play it on the* Blow by Blow *tour in New York when Les and I went to the show to meet Jeff. It's wonderful that the replica is on the market.*

PF: *Jeff has made some great music on that guitar. He told me that he did in fact play it on the* Blow by Blow *album, and what songs he played on it. He had a pretty good recollection of it. That was nice. It was used on a couple of solos on the album.*

In addition to the 50 hand-signed and played guitars, 100 were made available in Vintage Original Specs (with a VOS pickguard sticker), guaranteed to put a smile on many faces. These have the word BECK and the serial number of 100 built on the back of the sunburst headstock. Cream back plates accent the oxblood finish. A Custom Shop black OHSC case has maroon lining that complements the guitar's color. The first signed model was shown at the winter trade show and is pictured on the next page. It is a great player with lightweight mahogany and perfect frets and nut. It exhibited majestic tone acoustically, with lots of mids, killer lows, and brilliant highs.

Considered by many guitarists to be the greatest rock guitarist in the world, Jeff Beck has enjoyed a longtime lucrative endorsement with Fender—and now a limited "Inspired By" signature Les Paul model with Gibson… to have his chocolate cake and eat it, too!

(Top Left, Above, and Bottom Left) The "Inspired By" Jeff Beck Oxblood Les Paul 1954 model #1, displayed at the NAMM convention in Anaheim.

INSPIRED BY SERIES

JEFF BECK LES PAUL

(Above) Stage shot of Jeff playing his old 1954 Oxblood Les Paul.

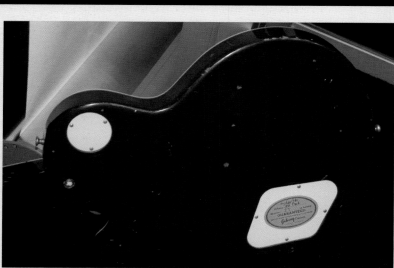

Billy Gibbons "Pearly Gates" Les Paul Model

In collaboration with the Reverend Billy Gibbons, Gibson's Custom Shop has recreated the "Pearly Gates" 1959 Les Paul Standard heard on all those glorious ZZ Top records. You may wonder why his guitar is nicknamed Pearly Gates. According to the legend, the band had a big 1930s Packard automobile and loaned it to an aspiring actress girlfriend to go to Hollywood. She auditioned for a movie and got the part. Believing the car had special powers, the band named it Pearly Gates. The girlfriend sold the car to a collector and sent the money back to Texas. Just as the check arrived, Billy found a Les Paul Sunburst made in 1959 with tight flame maple and "A Voice from God." He bought the guitar with the money from Pearly Gates. The name stuck onto the instrument that became the band's icon—it was pictured on the center of their original record, *ZZ Top's First Album*, and used for many years onstage. It has graced every ZZ Top album and is featured in Volume 1 of *The Les Paul Legacy*.

Billy Gibbons standing with a dozen new "Inspired By" signature Pearly Gates Les Paul Standards he signed and played. The "Billy Burst" finishes and tight maple figuring are very accurate in this series. Note some fingerboards are lighter rosewood. *Photo courtesy Pat Foley*

Built to exacting details of the original guitar, it recreates the distinctive colorations, complexity of deep 3D curly pinstripe maple, and approximates the light 8.5 pound weight. The Custom Shop achieved the more comfortable rounded '59 neck specs and utilized Billy's favorite Seymour Duncan special Pearly Gates pickups and CTS pots with bumblebee caps—all to capture the angelic qualities and Texas tones of the grail. It is shipped with the string-over stop tailpiece setup that Billy prefers, and with his signature full-body guitar sock.

Produced in three varieties for a total of 350 guitars, 250 are made clean to VOS specifications. Tom Murphy specially prepared the rest at his Guitar Preservation shop in Marion, Illinois. Fifty of those 100 were signed and played by Gibbons and feature a more extensive aging process. A few LP forum members were perplexed to buy an aged model since at first Tom wasn't mentioned on the Gibson website.

Tom had these reflections on the project, still in progress at the time of the interview:

Robb: What was your input on the new Pearly Gates?

Tom: *I'm doing the aged guitars. I did two color samples of the top, which were shown to Billy Gibbons. The Les Paul forum and the Gibson site were also helpful, because there was a picture of Pearly Gates lying next to the color sample. Positive comments were posted on the sites. Then I winged it, basically working from memory and the vibe I carry in my head of what Pearly Gates would look like*

now, presently, and my guitar, which I tried to emulate. I was able to accomplish a smoother, worn-looking edge and the stuff I was aiming for. Pat [Foley] told me that Billy had seen a guitar that didn't look good and commented that we were getting dangerously close. To me, that meant he didn't like it, and was only being nice. Pat and Edwin [Wilson] said, "You need to go to Houston and look at the guitar." I said, "Okay, we'll go," so they sent me to Houston.

RL: What details did you discover when you saw the guitar after all those years?

TM: *By the tailpiece there are three worn spots about the size of a pencil eraser, worn all the way to the wood between the strings, behind the bridge. Little things like that. The consumer wouldn't have any idea how they got there. I was able to get a feel by holding the guitar, playing La Grange a bit. So Billy really liked the next guitar. Then we moved forward once he signed a batch. Guitar Center got a batch of unsigned guitars. Then we have a small detail of what I do, that doesn't exist on the unsigned ones. So for those consumers, the signed ones are right. Those are now floating through the market. I haven't heard yea or nay, good or bad, anything. Everybody pretty much lets me know if they buy one and if they really dig it.*

You can imagine what his guitar looks like. It's checked all over. That probably is not even a focal point. I've never done that on a guitar before—really tight checking front and back, sides, neck, and everything. I did

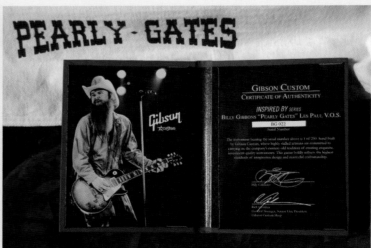

Gibson Les Paul Standard "Pearly Gates" VOS model #BG 022 with the Custom Shop certificate booklet and portion of the novel guitar body sock. *Courtesy Guitar Center Sherman Oaks*

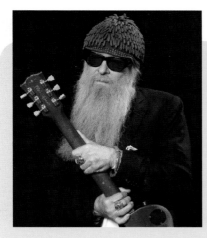

The Reverend Billy shows his signature on the back of #8 Murphy aged Pearly Gates model. *Photo by Gene Kirkland courtesy of Gibson*

that and made it one of the features of his guitar for the first time ever. I don't think Billy sees, but he knows it's there. For him, it's the radical belt buckle wear that has contoured the body at the waist. The edge is totally worn off, all the way around and beat pretty bad, mostly from him gun-slinging it on his leg. And the trademark wear on the lower, treble side of the neck from the 13th fret back to the 4th fret is not smoothly worn, but real jagged through the finish, probably from his rings. And then the trademark arm wear and some incidental, real smooth round ball bearing type dents. That's from jewelry, too. And finger wear, right above the E string, is on every guitar. I applied those things specifically. I probably could have left the radical checking off and saved time in producing those guitars, but it's there. It's cool to see. If people appreciate that as one of my trademarks, then you get it on a Pearly Gates signed one, that's for sure.

Having seen the guitar really up close a couple times in 1970 when that band was just getting started in Houston, and knowing the reputation of the guitar achieved over the years, I am thrilled to have the opportunity to do this. That kind of top with real deep, fiddle-back stuff has been my favorite. I told Edwin [Wilson], "If you did a replica, I would want you to get me that type of wood, undeniably, no question." I want the wiggle like that. But why would I want the worn stuff to decrease the beauty and potential value of that guitar? If it wasn't Billy's, it would just be a beat-up old Burst; it has character because it was his. Yes, it belongs in the Hall of Fame. If you're making a Pearly Gates, you don't have to do all that stuff to it. That won't fly in today's market. It was much more attractive to me years ago than it is now, with the weather

checking and the wear. It's really, really beat. That guitar is played to death. The frets are worn. Edwin says Billy still uses it in the studio and takes it on a real close gig maybe.

RL: *I've seen the VOS models and much of the wood is very similar. There are little blank spots on the tops too at certain angles. The color is really nice.*

TM: *I've been happy with what they're doing with the color. I get asked to do that stuff and then I take a totally different seat. I don't mind that at all on the coloration of these projects. I painted the prototype for the Bloomfield guitar and the color sample for the Pearly Gates. Now I'm not involved with painting; they just send me guitars to age. I hope the consumer understands that. Yes, I'm involved and, yes, I touched this Pearly Gates guitar, but I can't paint them anymore and I don't. The guitars play great and work great. They're still wonderful.*

Billy at the Custom Shop inspecting the production run on Pearly Gates Les Paul models. *Photo by Sandy Campbell courtesy of Gibson*

This sacred marriage with Gibson, Les Paul, Reverend Billy G, Tom Murphy, and the original '59 Pearly Gates is a heavenly gem!

Modern Historic Reissues

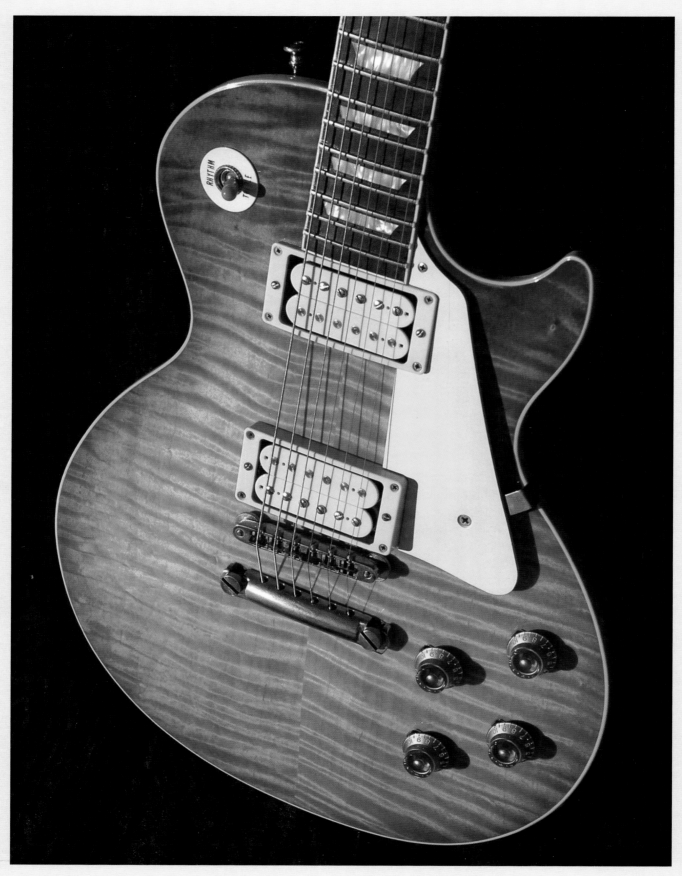

Joe Ganzler's very flamed 1994 Les Paul Standard 1959 reissue #9 4150 with a faded sunburst by Tom Murphy. As Tom was working on the instrument, German guitarist Gregor Hilden bought it and had this particular finish done. Joe later purchased it due to its striking resemblance to his old '59 "Gladys" (in Volume One) and tonally optimum 8.75-pound weight. *Courtesy Joseph Ganzler, 2006*

Gibson's Historic Custom Division

The tradition of custom-ordered instruments by the Gibson company goes back to its inception, with wonderful variations on their pioneering models, radical electrics from the thirties, and custom-colored instruments from the fifties and sixties. Kalamazoo had their "custom department" firmly established by the late fifties. Soft tooling enabled them to easily accommodate small productions of special-edition store models. Chuck Burge did marvelous custom one-offs in his downstairs custom workshop beginning in the late seventies. As production shifted to Nashville, artist specials and dealer limited-edition production runs were done in their in-house custom department from 1982 into 1988 by Phil Jones and Matthew Klein. By 1992, these elaborate orders, with their unusual woods and spectacular finishes, finally led to a separate building and the beginning of their official Custom Shop designation for Historic and Art Division. By 1993, it was well under way, with an expanded staff and a clear direction to make the finest Gibson could offer outside of their regular production.

The Les Paul Standard 1959 Sunburst R9 Historic Reissue Arrives

By late 1992, the final ascent to the top of the highest solid-body mountain (reissue vintage perfection) was near. Reaching this guitar summit was a long time coming for the Gibson company, eager players, and avid collectors. Akin to the yellow brick road on the way to the Emerald City, painstaking care, with much time and expense, resulted in the ultimate duplication of Gibson's past grandeur. After prototypes were evaluated in-house and by a handful of regional experts, the glowing reports were sent back to Nashville. The stage was set and the 1993 Winter NAMM show in Anaheim became the official debut of the soon-to-be-revered R9 flametop sunburst.

With the release of this truly accurate 1959 Les Paul Standard, Gibson attained a remarkable reissue, approaching the finest level of the original all-hallowed models. It was the final culmination of exhaustive research, examining many of the shortcomings and positive attributes of the last of the maple top solid-bodies of the late fifties. Borrowing vintage guitars from nearby Nashville guitar dealer/writers George Gruhn and Crawford White, Gibson's engineers discovered slight flaws, many inconsistencies, and myriad variations that were present in the older hand-built instruments. After

researching the many variations of details, a common-ground consensus was determined and physically achieved on the R9 Historic 1959 Les Paul Standard.

Spearheaded by the talents of project coordinator Edwin Wilson, engineer Lynn Matthews, and finish specialist/vintage expert Tom Murphy, along with a host of others in Nashville, a generalized medium was attained by taking in all the parameters and building a concise "best of" replica of the famous and highly-valuable Les Paul guitar.

First presentation of the ultimate Les Paul CE59 Flametop reissue models during the 1993 NAMM show in Anaheim.

By the spring of 1993, Tom Murphy brought one of the first prototypes to a Texas guitar show to get some feedback and generate interest with this remarkable guitar. Tom said to me, "Robb, I want to show you the finest Les Paul we have ever come up with. I think you will be very impressed. We spent a lot of time and money to finally pull this together. I respect your expertise along with a few other guys here and want to get your opinion before we officially release it. So here it is. Tell me what you think."

Tom handed it to me as I looked on in astonishment, almost thinking I was looking at a mint 1959 Sunburst. I'd seen years of "almost" accurate versions, but nothing prior to this even compared to the vibe and feel of the gem I was finally holding and about to play. The colors were beautiful—top and back, the flame and grain patterns were amazing, the arch was finally perfected, the original-style binding and edges were there, and the neck shape and fingerboard details were accurate. I strummed a few power chords and played some classic blues riffs with a serious note bend and singing vibrato. Behold! It rang out and chimed—acoustically and harmonically. It sounded and looked virtually like a freshly unplayed great old Les Paul. Even acoustically, without an amp wailing, this was the real test in my mind. I was finally impressed with a Sunburst reissue! It took great strides to achieve and it was well worth the wait. My hat was finally off to Gibson… and I was personally quite astonished.

"You guys did it, Tom!" I exclaimed, "I can hardly believe it, but it's finally here. The guitar sounds great and plays fantastic!!" Tom said, "I thought you would be impressed. All the others who have seen it were, too. I'm glad you approve. We're quite excited about this project." That lasting impression stays fresh in my mind even to this day. Thanks for the vivid experience, Tom! I knew then that they were finally onto something big. In my mind and in the minds of many others at that guitar show, a true renaissance of solid-body Gibson endeavor was achieved.

Gibson's new Historic Collection models were soon unveiled during the '93 NAMM show and, with their beautiful '94 catalog, released that fall. The R9 was the true top-of-the-line model and was priced accordingly, listing for a whopping $11,000! This full-color, heavy stock, lavish Historic Collection catalog set a precedent with its informative pages of their history of innovation, quality and craftsmanship—plus a nifty historical investment chart (in sunburst) of a 1960 LP Standard priced up to only $25,000 at that point. It featured '56 and '57 Goldtops (in antique gold with brass sourced from the original supplier), Custom "Black Beauties" from '54 and '57 with various pickup combinations, and Bigsby vibrato tailpieces. Items such as the new '57 Classic "Patent Applied For" humbucking were introduced after consulting with featured artists Joe Walsh and Dickie Betts.

With this catalog, the two especially accurate and beautiful sunburst Flametop Les Paul Standards had finally arrived. One sported the fuller neck profile of 1959, and

1994 Les Paul Standard R9 (9 4330) with its Custom Shop certificate.

One of the first Historic R9 Les Paul Standard models (#9 4014) finished by Tom Murphy in 1994. This early version features the gold Gibson Historic split-diamond headstock emblem behind the neck. *Courtesy The Knack's Berton Averra, 2007*

238

Tom Murphy at the 1994 NAMM show, helping introduce the new flametop '59 Historic reissues.

1994 Historic catalog featuring the first true reissue Les Paul Standards.

'59 and '60 Les Paul page from the 1994 catalog.

the other, a slim "fast action" 1960 neck. Both were available with either a Heritage sunburst or Heritage darkburst. These beauties really struck a chord with vintage guitar buffs (who couldn't quite afford the real McCoys) and for those who needed a great guitar to play out while leaving the expensive one at home. Many connoisseurs quickly installed real PAF pickups to get even closer to the real deal.

Gibson's new Custom Shop was just getting started with these fine Les Paul recreations of their illustrious past. Here is the comparative weights of the reissue models:

Les Paul back blanks (weight code)

R9, R0	8 or less
R8	9 or less
GT	9.6 or less
Bs	10.6 or less

During the first few years of the official Historic Custom Shop production, Tom Murphy would have his initials written in the control cavity (sometimes in a pickup routing) when working his finish magic. In hindsight, this was a good way to prevent forgeries. Others workers likewise would initial their routing work. The model number (R9, etc.) was also boldly stamped in black ink inside.

By the end of the first year, Tom had decided to temporarily retreat from in-house work at Gibson to toil in his home shop in Illinois. He stopped doing the first series of Murphy Les Pauls on November 2nd, 1994. Tom estimates he personally did 180 to 200 instruments during 1994, though there could be a few more that were in process before numbers were applied. Gibson states there were exactly 349 R9 models produced that year. LPR9 #9 4260 (later redone by Tom) was stamped on Nov, 27, 1994, showing that approximately five a day were produced. Since Tom departed, many people had their Historic LPR models refinished, some of which were done in the violet-tinged 1959 Brockburst coloration. Tom continued on as a consultant and currently maintains his liaison with a steady roster of Artist models.

With the growing exclusivity of the endangered and embargoed exotic Brazilian rosewood, Gibson finally reverted to the use of this superior wood for fingerboards with a number of guitars built during 2003. The desirability of the feel and tonality led to its reemergence. As the forests were depleted, Indian rosewood began during the late sixties, while Madagascar rosewood has been a staple since 2000.

This 1998 Les Paul R9 solid flametop in caramel shading is one nice Burst! *Courtesy the late guitar enthusiast Michael J. Parker, 1999*

1996 Les Paul R9 (#9 6370) with spectacular shattered glass maple and orangey coloration. *Courtesy David Robinson, 2006*

(Below) Close-up of a darkburst 2002 Les Paul R9 with full cream coil humbuckings. *Courtesy Norm Harris, 2003*

Inside and Out.

What does that really mean? Let's start with the inside. First off, we only use original Gibson pickups. Always have, always will. These pickups use only the finest magnets, feature vintage wiring schemes, and full wax potting to eliminate microphonic feedback. Next we use CTS potentiometers(pots) in all of our historic Les Pauls. CTS started making pots for us in the early '60s. They feature a solid carbon glide that gives you a more accurate taper for better signal response and smoother performance. Add to that the "Bumble Bee" capacitors that we've commissioned just for us and you have the most accurate reproduction parts available anywhere.

And the outside? We got it right there too. Just look at the headstock. We use Holly head veneers as opposed to fiber. Push-in bushings adorn the tuner placement, which is now in a straight line like they used to be. We changed the truss rod routing of the headstock to be more historically accurate too. It's more rounded at the top giving you better access to the truss rod.

The neck shapes are correct. We're once again using Brazilian Rosewood for the fingerboards on selected models. We're rolling the fingerboard binding like they used to, which makes for a more comfortable guitar. The inlays have been revised and feature sharper points on the corners and a more historically accurate "swirl" pattern.

The body features historically accurate, thin binding, switchwasher, and jackplate. Using the thinner material allows the pieces to form to the contour of the body much better. We also silkscreen "Rhythm" and "Treble" on the switchwasher, just like they used to. And don't forget the body carve. Despite first impressions, not all carves are alike. A historically accurate carve is actually flat at its top which allow us to position the lightweight aluminum tailpiece closer to the body.

All in all, these are the most historically accurate Les Pauls ever offered. Now you can own a piece of the magic that has turned early Les Pauls into museum pieces for a fraction of the cost - only from the Gibson Custom Shop.

1959 Les Paul Standard

(Right) A specially ordered 2001 cherry flametop Les Paul R9. *Courtesy Matt Preble, 2004*

Great flier discussing the new reissue Les Paul R9 series.

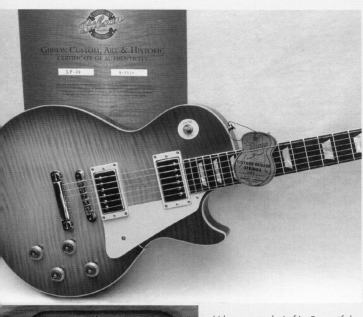

(Above and Left) Beautiful 2003 Les Paul Standard R0 #9 3216 and its control cavity showing the reissue "bumblebee" capacitors. *Courtesy Martin Miller, 2005*

1959 Les Paul Reissue AAAAA Killertop

HISTORIC COLLECTION

SPECIFICATIONS:

Pickups:	Two "57 classic reissue PAFs
Controls:	Two vintage volume, and tone controls, 3-way switch
Hardware:	Nickel
Scale/Nut Width:	24 ¾" / 1 ¹¹/₁₆"
Fingerboard/Inlay:	Rosewood 22 fret / trapezoid
Binding:	Body, neck
Bridge/Tailpiece:	Original ABR / stop bar
Materials:	Carved maple top, mahogany back, one-piece mahogany neck, holly head veneer
Finish:	Heritage cherry sunburst, Heritage dark sunburst

(Above) 1994 Les Paul Standard R9 with strong reverse chevron curl in Heritage Cherry sunburst. *Courtesy Steve Kinkel, 2005*

(Left) 1999 Les Paul Standard flier showing a 5A top.

(Left) This amazing 2001 super flametop R9 Les Paul reissue was wrangled away from Norm Harris by Matt Preble!

(Right) The 1998 Les Paul R8 with nice flame maple shows the typical faded honey sunburst standard on the 1958 reissue. Note the bridge pickup/pickguard gap apparent on '98 guitars. *Courtesy Norm Harris, 2003*

The fire is still burning on this quilted flametop 2003 LPR-9 #931224 with Brazilian rosewood fingerboard. *Guitar courtesy Don Breeze; photo by Martin Miller, 2005*

(Left) Striking 2001 LPR-9 Standard
#9 1340 at Instrumental Music.
Courtesy Jim Schwartz, 2006

Pretty cherry sunburst left-handed Les Paul R9 with some deep purple coloration near the switch.
Courtesy Norm Harris, 2003

Tight fiddle-back curl graces this R-8 Les Paul Cherry '58 reissue flametop.

A most unusual Merlot Grape Burst R8 reissue Les Paul model (#8 2951). *Courtesy Guitar Center La Mesa, 2005*

1958 reissue R8 Standard #8 2313. *Courtesy Paul Manoogian, 2006*

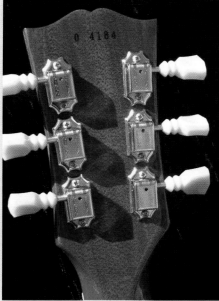

Sensational combination of curly maple and great coloration grace this magnificent 1960 Les Paul Reissue R0 #0 4184 on tour with the Gibson Custom Shop trailer in 2005. *Courtesy Danny Hoefer and Gibson*

Spectacular faded cherry R9 quilted maple Les Paul Standard #9 6070 with stunning matched headstock. *Courtesy Saul at Centre City Music, March of 2006*

This section features a series of specially chambered 1958 and 1959 (CR8 and CR9) Historic reissues. The recent "Chambered Series" Les Paul was originally the brainchild of Dave Carpenter at Music Machine in Seattle, with input from his wife, Connie, and customers. Dave collaborated with Mike McGuire, Edwin Wilson, and Rick Gembar at the Custom Shop to build the original Music Machine Stinger guitars in 2003, and eventually their Cloud Nine series. The Stinger name came about because some of Dave's vintage Gibson guitars (and his customers' orders) featured black headstock backs. "Cloud Nine" is basically a descriptive term for a euphoric state of mind. The factory refers to them as the Chambered '59 and '58 reissue models, thus the CR serial numbers.

This collaboration between Gibson engineers and Dave Carpenter (with his customer Jon Schwartz) at Music Machine created the guitars' unique attributes. Dave's Guitars in La Crosse, Wisconsin and Wildwood Music in Colorado also shared in the sales commitment to successfully distribute the series. After playing the chambered prototype in Nashville, the three store proprietors quickly realized the potential of the overall concept. They share together the sales, marketing, and promotion of the Cloud Nine CR series.

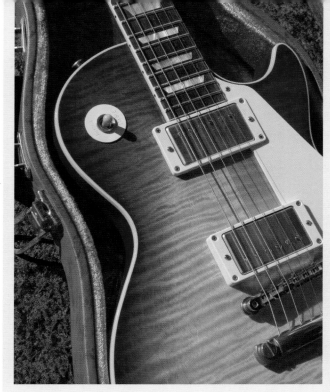

2007 chambered R8 Les Paul Standard #CR87100 nicknamed "Superman." *Courtesy Matt Preble, 2008*

2007 chambered '58 model in a faded tobacco sunburst similar to Billy Gibbons's '59 Pearly Gates. *Courtesy Matt Preble, 2008*

Beautiful deep cherry 2007 chambered 1958 reissue Les Paul Standard #CR87257. Owner Matt Preble is a big fan of George Harrison's cherry top.

Chambered Les Paul reissues are remarkably light, weighing in at just over seven pounds. They distinctly differ in construction from other "weight-relieved" and LP Elegant models. The maple top is attached to a "tonally carved mahogany bowl with strategically placed stress blocks between the back and top." Exact specifications for this model are not revealed to the public. Players feel the unique construction creates more tone with extra vibrations that adds to the feel of the instrument. Currently the series includes the Vintage Original Spec Custom, Goldtop, and Sunburst versions. Edwin Wilson's magnificent Historic Les Paul creation, coupled with Mike McGuire's brilliant internal tone chambering and Rick Gembar's sensible corporate push enabled the innovative series to come to fruition.

This 2003 Music Machine Les Paul Custom is their third production guitar made: #CS30929/MM CCQ 03. It was done in beautiful natural amber to show off the super curly maple magic. (Also shown on the front cover.) *Guitar courtesy Matt Preble*

Gorgeous 2004 chambered '59 flametop Les Paul #CR94041 with a deep, slightly faded antique sunburst finish by Tom Murphy. Matt affectionately calls this the "Wild Burst."

Danny Hoefer's sweet Cloud Nine CR9 Les Paul Historic reissue #CR94032.

Enter the Aged Les Paul

With the expertise of the talented Tom Murphy of Marion, Illinois, a new era of purposely antiqued instruments evolved. In 1999, Gibson's Custom, Art and Historic division released the Aged Figuretop 1959 Les Paul Reissue with such success that a complementary Aged 1957 Goldtop Reissue followed in 2000. Both were considered to be "a tribute to its heritage," with the look and feel of being broken-in. After a culmination of ten years of repairs and finish restoration by "Father Time" (as Gibson calls him), this time-consuming aging process was finally pioneered on new instruments. Tom's efforts of perfecting this arduous job of finish-work on vintage guitars carried over into the Les Paul range with great success.

Murphy will explain how it's not done—revealing only that he doesn't leave them outside nor chemically treat them. This hand process entails recreating weather checking, some slight dings and chips, and simulating an older patina. Other signature models actually require copying large wear-patterns across the backs. With so many years of vintage practice, he simply expanded on his simulated techniques to the modern production of new guitars—on a limited basis.

Some are wondering why this even came about. The enormous popularity of vintage instruments, mostly with playing wear and climatic effects evident, gave savvy musicians a need for that special feel and warmth of being played that is not found with a mint and shiny-new guitar. With the scarcity of vintage guitars and the growing demand for somewhat-worn reissue instruments—their West Coast competitor's Relic Series had already been gaining some steam in the marketplace—Tom embarked on doing an entire guitar to satisfy that need. Just prior to the advent of this series, he showed this author two totally refinished vintage instruments that were perfectly "aged and worn."

Originally spending months to age a guitar, with Gibson's help to expedite the process, they now have shortened the time involved. In reality, a great amount of handwork is still done. Normally, aging over time is dependent upon the degree of elemental exposure from ultraviolet, radical temperature and altitude changes, expanding and contracting (hygroscopic effect) of the woods, and hardening of the lacquer (which also adds to the finish checking).

Altogether, the look and feel simulates an older vintage guitar that has seen some usage. This whole affair has a psychological effect due to its overall vintage vibe compared to a mint and pristine guitar. I must say, however,

2001 Les Paul R9 (#9 1124) Tom Murphy aged model. Great curly top with a fade look and some weather checking. *Courtesy Jeff Lund, 2005*

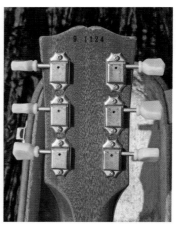

some of us who are long used to vintage guitars in slightly worn conditions often gravitate to the newer ones that are still clean—without the dents and checking, but with aged parts and slightly dull finishes only. Gibson's in-house experts also help in the process and do varying degrees of "Custom Authentic Aging" on other instruments. Tom Murphy's celebrated collaboration with Gibson gives this unique opportunity to those aficionados who relish the spirit of a vintage guitar.

Special Murphy 2000 Historic R-9 Les Paul Standard #9 0436 with aged parts and added vintage PAF pickups. Beautiful flame and great coloring make this a real keeper! *Courtesy Bill Feil, 2006*

Deep chatoyant effect present with this superb 1998 R9 Historic Murphy #9 8007 from virtually any angle. "Old Flame" courtesy Electric Lloyd Gala, Rochester, 2008

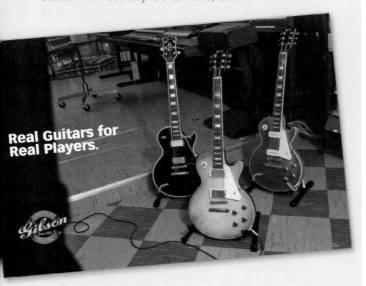

2004 Faded Les Paul Standard R0 (60 4148) with the dulled finish. *Courtesy GC La Mesa, 2004*

Real Guitars for Real Players.

Custom Authentic flier.

R8 with pickup routing exposed. *Courtesy Martin G. Miller*

Custom Authentic Models

Touting the slogan, "Real Guitars for Real Players," Gibson unveiled a new series of Custom Authentic and Artist Authentic models in 2001, recreating the "after-market" broken-in Les Paul. Starting with three basic models and two artist guitars, they simulated the effects of light player's wear with dulled topcoat finishes and nickel hardware. Not nearly as aged as the special Tom Murphy creations, the overall finishes were slightly dulled (without weather checking and scratches), while the metal parts were weather-simulated. Some tried to polish these instruments to a shiny luster, but to no avail. Since they were true Custom Shop items, the high-quality reissue construction and detail is superlative for each model, including the high playability and tonal factors. Given that the vintage craze has been going on for years now, others have gotten in on the aged look. Their professional efforts with this series can be somewhat compared to Fender's "Closet Classic," as opposed to their scratched and worn "Relic" series. These Les Pauls all feature the carved maple top with mahogany back and neck, with the original long neck tenon design for great authentic tones. And with the aged effect already in motion, Gibson urges the guitarist to "Get one and play it hard. That's what we make 'em for."

Covering a small spectrum of vintage reissues, they first released a 1956 Goldtop with aged antique gold finish and P-90s, a 1958 Standard with "aged" butterscotch finish and a 1968 Les Paul Custom in aged ebony black finish (with deeply imprinted serial numbers, e.g., 030695) but without the customary gold hardware. All feature early-fifties rounded (fairly large size) neck contours, aged nickel Grover tuners (as many guitarists added in the old days), and Burstbucker two rhythm and three treble humbuckings on the '58 and '68 models. As on the Historic Collection models, they have the original truss rod routes, holly headstock veneers, accurate vintage trapezoid fingerboard markers, CTS pots, and "bumblebee" capacitors. With their solid mahogany body construction, weights fall into the moderate 8.5 to 9.5 lb. range. The listed price on the '68 Custom is $4,500 and sells discounted for $2,900.

An Artist Authentic Dickie Betts 1957 Goldtop is premiered featuring '57 Classic Humbuckers and Tom Murphy's "Ultra-aged" finish treatment. The Master Magician's work gives the gold finish and tarnished nickel new meanings of mojo-ness. Also included in this first foray of Artist Authentic models is the Andy Summers 1960 ES-335 model in aged faded cherry finish, as on his favorite performing vintage red dot inlaid guitar. At a distance, all these guitars could almost fool an expert.

Dave Amato of REO Speedwagon sits with his vintage Les Paul collection (featured in Volume One), flanked by his flametop sunburst '58 Historic reissue LP with Bigsby vibrola, circa 2005.

Frankie Sullivan of Survivor posing with a new VOS vintage reissue Les Paul at California Vintage circa 2008. Their hit, "Eye of the Tiger," performed with fellow guitarist Jim Peterik, provided memorable moments in movie and rock history.

Jimmy Vivino getting ready to do the *Late Night with Conan O'Brien* show at NBC studios and holding a factory-customized cherry flametop Standard. His Bigsby preference carries over on the Les Paul SG Custom. Thanks, Jimmy, for a memorable afternoon!

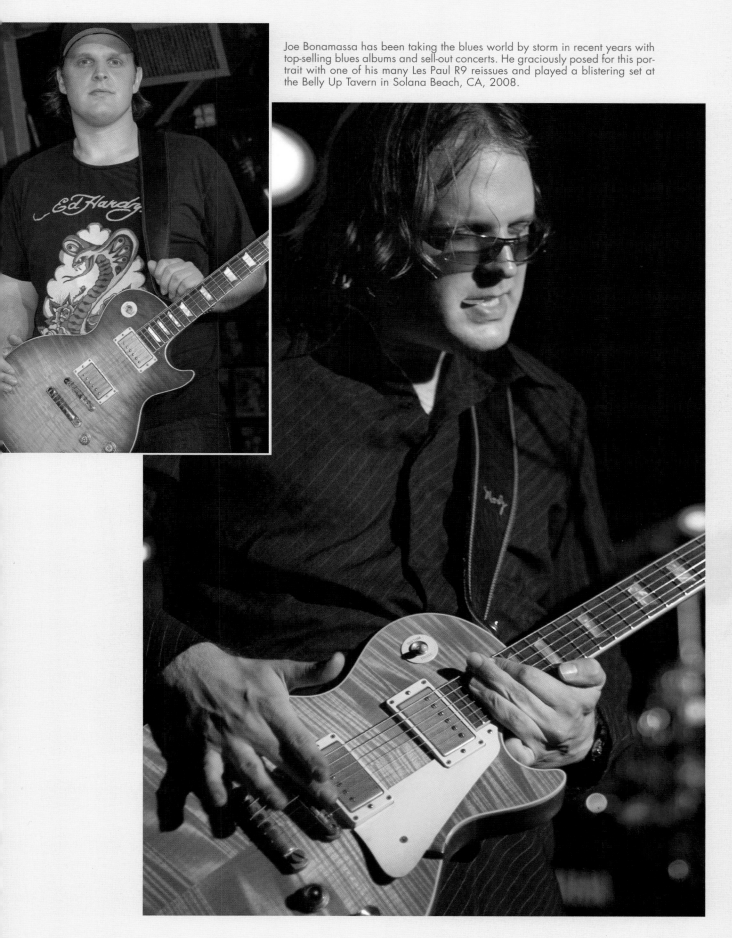

Joe Bonamassa has been taking the blues world by storm in recent years with top-selling blues albums and sell-out concerts. He graciously posed for this portrait with one of his many Les Paul R9 reissues and played a blistering set at the Belly Up Tavern in Solana Beach, CA, 2008.

Expanding the Vintage Line

In 1998, Gibson released a classy black-and-white catalog with a textured cream cover embossed with Historic Collection and a Super 400 headstock. Both the '98 and '99 catalogs had floating instruments against simulated curtains, reminiscent of the vintage 1956/1957 guitars leaning by a real curtain. An array of authentic Goldtop reissues soon evolved, including the original 1952 model (still with the old neck angle?!) on up to the 1957 humbucking-equipped version. '54 and '56 P-90 equipped versions were available with their accurate stop/stud and Tune-O-Matic bridge combinations. A special edition '54 Oxblood model was featured with exposed '57 classic PAF humbuckings. It was inspired by guitarist Jeff Beck's Les Paul from his 1975 *Blow by Blow* days being previously modified by Strings & Things in Memphis, Tennessee. Stinson and Keckler referred to the color as black cherry at the time. They were primarily made for the Japanese market and some were sold in the United States. 1957 Tune-O-Matic versions of it were also available. An attractive Mary Ford tribute '58 goldtop model with the royal treatment of cream ES-295 plastic appointments was added to the line. It has not been ascertained whether or not Mary actually owned and played the original 1958 version, with the added floral armrest, it was patterned after.

Tidy display case of a 1968 Reissue Les Paul Custom in dark tri-burst coloration. *Courtesy Hollywood Guitar Center, 2007*

(Above) Catalog page for the 2000 Les Paul Custom figured top.

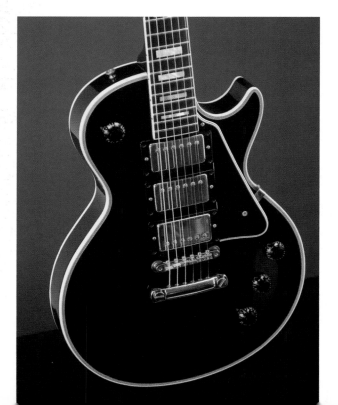

(Left) The always-regal "Black Beauty" Les Paul Custom Historic model. Some were shipped with gold Bigsby tailpieces too. This is the rare 1957 Mickey Baker version #7 3587 with three volume knobs in a straight line and a single tone control in place of the toggle switch. *Guitar courtesy Fretted Americana, 2008*

The Mary Ford Les Paul Standard R8 (#8 7248) made in 1997. This has the arm guard and floral cosmetics of the old ES-295. *Courtesy Mikey Wright, 2003*

This striking humbucking-equipped R-4 Goldtop lights up with true brilliance in the La Jolla sun. *Courtesy Mike Tilly, 2007*

Close-up of the Custom authentic 2003 Les Paul Standard R7 (brand new) with faded nickel hardware. *Courtesy Norm Harris, 2003*

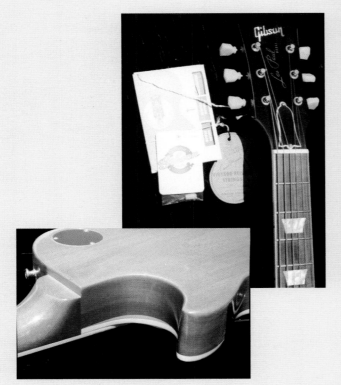

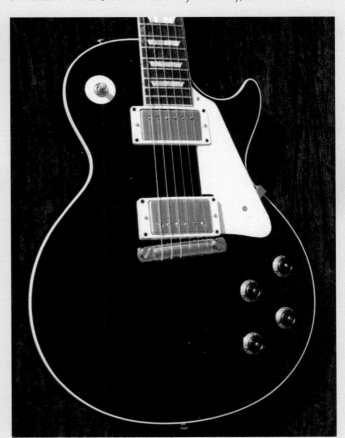

This dark-colored 2003 Les Paul Standard R4 (#4 3101) with Schallers is based on the old goldtop guitar Strings & Things, modified in a deep black cherry color that Jeff Beck bought. He used it for many years. It was known in guitar circles as the "Oxblood" Les Paul guitar. Mikey likes the sound of this one!

(Above and Top Right) Exotic flamed koa top 2008 LPR-9 Standard #9 8025. *Courtesy Saul Frank at Centre City, 2008*

A sparkle orange Custom Shop Historic 1958 Standard #CS88376, new in its case at California Vintage, 2008.

Rare one-pickup 2004 Goldtop R4 much like Billy Gibbons's single pickup model. *Courtesy Mikey Wright, 2003*

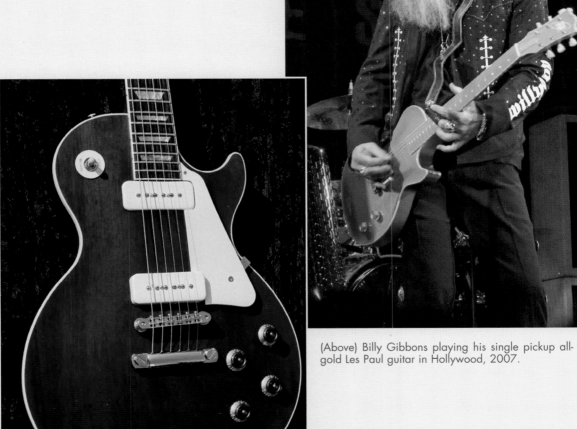

(Above) Billy Gibbons playing his single pickup all-gold Les Paul guitar in Hollywood, 2007.

(Left) A very rare 1999 mahogany Les Paul Standard (#2 9006) in vintage cherry with P-90 pickups. *From Mikey's collection, 2003*

The Music Machine Les Paul Stinger catalog showing some of their special orders. The green JB R4 is stunning. It comes stock with Brazilian rosewood fingerboards, bumblebee caps, and fancy colors.

STINGER '58, '59 & '60 LES PAUL

Special wood pull, Four necks sizes, Original electronic specifications, Dozens of exquisite finishes, Factory special certified.

Pickups: BB1 (R), BB2 (T)

Fingerboard: Brazilian

Bridge: ABR-1

Neck: Extra, '59, Vintage Flat or Slim

Back Wood: One-piece Mahogany

Top Wood: Eastern Maple

Caps: Bumblebee

Pots: CTS

STINGER '54 JB LES PAUL

Special wood pull, Burstbucker pickups, Five finishes, Unique tone & sustain with a one-piece wraparound bar, Factory special certified.

Pickups: BB2 (R), BB3 (T)

Fingerboard: Brazilian

Bridge: One-piece wraparound bar

Neck Profile: '59, Vintage Slim

Back Wood: One-piece Mahogany

Top Wood: Quilt, Figure

Caps: Bumblebee

Pots: CTS

STINGER '56 LES PAUL

The first time in history that the electronics, Brazilian fingerboard and special taps were able to come together to make this stunning '56 Les Paul.

Pickups: P-90

Fingerboard: Brazilian

Bridge: ABR-1

Neck Profile: '59, Vintage Slim

Back Wood: One-Piece Mahogany

Top Wood: Plain, Quilt, Figure

Caps: Bumblebee

Pots: CTS

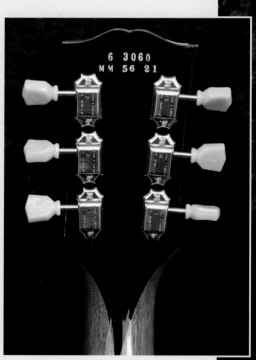

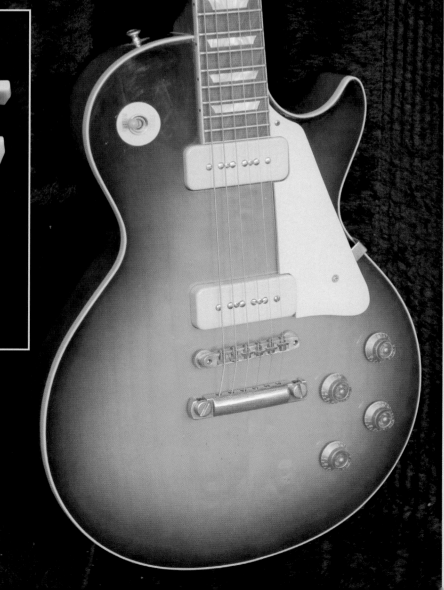

This rare bird flew to England after Music Machine sold it. The Stinger '56 Les Paul Standard #6 3060 (built in 2003) is finished in Cremona sunburst with P-90s for that vocal honkin' tone. *Courtesy Vintage Guitar Emporium, London, 2005*

A beautiful Heritage faded sunburst '56 Historic 2006 Les Paul Standard R6 with great flame maple. *From the Chuck Kavooris collection, 2007*

This very accurate 2000 Les Paul Standard R6 Goldtop (#6 0195) conforms to its catalog description and appears in mint condition... a very solid player and investment for the owner.

50th Anniversary Les Paul Models

The 50th Anniversary Les Paul guitar celebrations began in 2002 at the Historic Division with the reissue of the original 1952 LP Model. Gracefully aged to collector's vintage condition, the 52 limited production models featured Les Paul's signature on the pickguard. The model was released 50 years to the very day Gibson first sent one to the Geib case company. An additional featured instrument that year was the exquisite composite of fine woods and fancy appointments on the ultra-deluxe 50th Anniversary Les Paul Custom. Koa and flame maple was used extensively with colorful pau shell cloud inlays, wooden knobs, '57 reissue PAF pickups, and gold deco Grover Imperial machines.

A beautiful flamed koa top with maple body and neck grace this 2002 50th Anniversary Les Paul Custom, one of 50. *Courtesy David Brass, Fretted Americana, 2008*

Next on the birthday bandwagon was the 2007 edition of the Golden Anniversary Gold Les Paul Custom and Standard models to celebrate the addition of the heralded 1957 humbucking pickup. All 157 special-built editions have gold hardware, Grover "Kidney" tuners, and gold-plated metal pickguard and headstock cover (later 2008 version sans the metal headdress). This richness, coupled with its regal antique gold finish, prompted the sales line,

"A guitar fit for King Midas himself!" Concurrently, another 50th anniversary commemorative all-gold '57 Standard model was produced. It seems Gibson unknowingly brought back the mythical all-gold, PAF Les Paul Golden Anniversary collectors item after all these years. Salute!

Gleaming all-gold 50th Anniversary 1957 reissue Les Paul Custom models #57C 151 & 139, featuring gold-plated pickguard (not shown) and cast metal headstock covers, Grover heads, and the accompanying certificate booklet for #139 of the 157 built in 2007. Gibson produced a limited run of 157 reissue 1957 Les Paul Custom models celebrating the golden anniversary of the first year of Seth Lover's humbucking pickups. *Courtesy Guitar Center Hollywood, 2009*

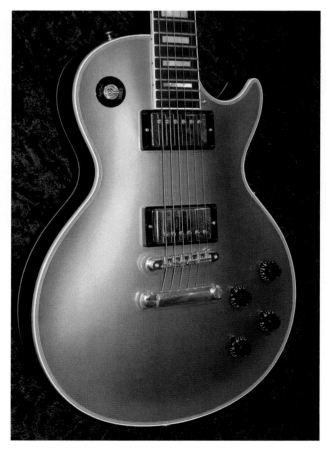

Sweet recreation of the 1958 Les Paul Standard in sunburst for Gibson's 50th Anniversary series. *Courtesy Guitar Center Hollywood, 2009*

50th Anniversary of the 1958 Les Paul Standard #8 8353, discreetly aged by Tom Murphy. *Courtesy Guitar Center Hollywood, January 2009*

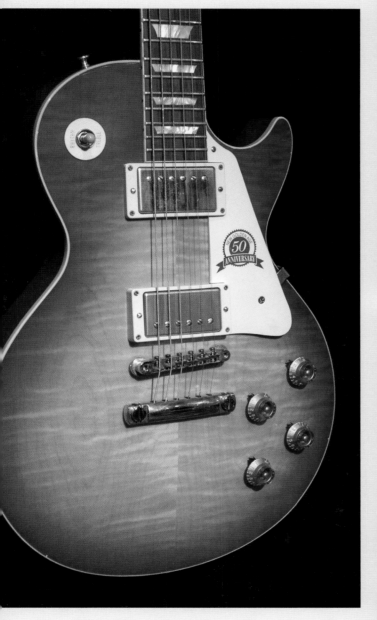

A bevy of 50th Anniversary 1957 and 1958 Les Paul models at Hollywood's Guitar Center Platinum showroom, January 2009. Thank you Olivia Niles for your kind assistance.

Continuing with the Anniversary Les Paul models for 2008, the Custom Shop released a 50th Anniversary 1958 LP Standard Flame Top guitar, specially aged by Tom Murphy. It celebrated the very first year of the original Sunburst Les Paul model, one of the most coveted of all electric guitars. The instrument came with a spare pickguard emblazoned with a gold emblem, "New Golden Age 50th Anniversary." Only 200 limited editions were available, featuring the current "original spec" carving of the figured maple top, a lightweight aluminum stop tailpiece, vintage specification Kluson-style tuners and electrical components (modern old-style CTS pots, bumblebee caps) and collared tulip grip tuners, with original

Gibson's amazingly accurate 50th Anniversary 1959 Les Paul Standard #4 Pilot Run NAMM Show special. Over 20 separate changes took place to totally dial in the final vintage specifications for this year's guitar.

All this leads to the ultimate crowning creation of electric guitar, the 50th anniversary of the highly coveted 1959 Les Paul sunburst. Manufactured to exacting specs in late 2008 into 2009, the instruments offer great feel, perfect weight, and superlative deep cherry red sunburst colors—as close to the real thing as it could possibly be. There are myriad bursts to pick from in their special commemorative models, with colors like amber honey, faded persimmon, sweet southern tea, faded lemonburst, golden orange tea, cognac, burnt wheat, and golden cherry burst. These superlative instruments recreate Gibson's holy grail to new heights of craftsmanship to deliver the ultimate aesthetic of vintage glory. I was thoroughly impressed gazing at the row of them hanging at the Gibson booth during NAMM 2009. Beautiful colors, perfect details, truly a renaissance of American ingenuity.

style pushed-in grommets. The especially thin sunburst finish was described as follows: "Nitrocellulose lacquer continues to evaporate, ensuring the thinnest possible finish that will never dampen vibrations and supports complex musical waveforms!" Afterward, guitar artisan Tom Murphy carefully does his handiwork with fine weather checking and aged nickel parts, still in well-maintained condition. As with other celebrated anniversary models, this '58 reissue is sure to be a collector's item.

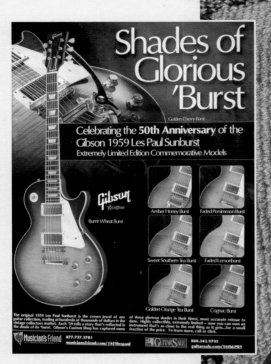

(Above) Tasty Musicians Friend/ Guitar Sale/Guitar Center ad for the 50th Anniversary 1959 Les Paul Standards in their beautiful shades of sunburst. They are the only company in the States allowed to advertise the Gibson guitar selection available to the public.

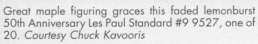

Great maple figuring graces this faded lemonburst 50th Anniversary Les Paul Standard #9 9527, one of 20. *Courtesy Chuck Kavooris*

Gibson president Dave Berryman with one of the flagship 50th Anniversary 1959 Les Paul Standards during the 2009 NAMM convention in Anaheim.

The Class V Series

Designed along the lines of the 1959/1960 original Standard, the Custom Shop finally stepped forward in January 2001 with a new and innovative Class 5 model (based on the figured woods). It brought the refinement of an R9 model, but with weight-relief cavities (17 holes, to be exact) and a variety of striking color-schemes. Sporting twin Burstbucker pickups and great colors over figured maple that include three translucents (amber, blue, and black) as well as two burst variations (tangerine and sierra). The popular 1960 slim tapered neck with a long neck tenon continued the easy feel and extra tone desired. Following the Standard fittings, cream binding and bezels, nickel ABR-1, stopbar and tulip Klusons tuners completed the package. Cutting excessive weight with hidden inner relief routings (almost a full pound) was a welcome feature of the Les Paul. This also enhanced the acoustic qualities to a degree that was beneficial for more tones.

To commemorate the historical significance of the September 11 terrorist attacks, a limited collectors' series of Les Paul Class 5 American Flag models was constructed in 2001, with proceeds donated to the Red Cross. Thirty were built that first year, with blue-colored backs and 091101 serial numbers and handwritten sequential numbers added. In 2002, the Custom Shop built versions based on this 9/11 limited-edition guitar with red backs and normal numbers, while ten were accented with silver backs in 2003. A Custom model was also built for Joe Perry; Gibson USA made up a few 9/11 Standards as well. More were done in 2005, but due to unforeseen difficulties, the silver back production was completely redone. These patriotic 9/11 models were built for a charitable cause and were also featured on the national news. They are sometimes referred to as "Flagtops" or "Stars & Stripes" Les Paul models.

Highly figured maple was placed in the AAAAA class (once the AAA rating during the late nineties). By 2003, the quilted class arrived with sensational wood patterns: "One of the Custom Shop's best just got better." Stores could also order special colors like chablis (a light pink orange) in addition to the cranberry option. Still a popular model, the Class V remains in a category of its own for many enthusiasts.

2004 catalog description of the Class 5 models, showing the quilted version.

A very sweet 2002 Les Paul Class 5 (CS21362) in sierra burst with tight fiddle-back maple. *Courtesy Martin Miller, 2003*

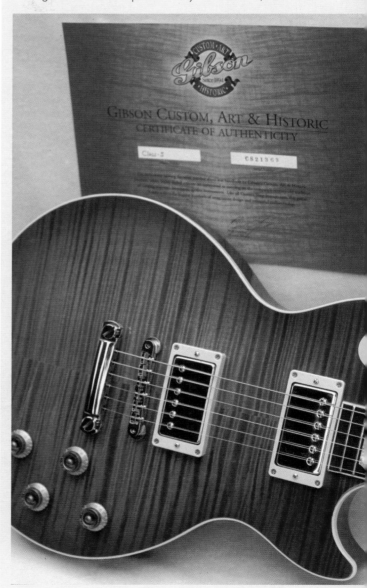

This is a 2000 Les Paul Class V(CS50077) specially ordered for a Gibson rep. It boasts a violet-hued blue and Brazilian rosewood fingerboard. *Courtesy Bart Whitrock, 2005*

Set against Malibu's Big Dume beach, this blue 2001 Class 5 Les Paul (CS10678) with a flamed mahogany back is beautifully complemented by the Pacific Ocean. *Courtesy Bonnie Ember, 2003*

Inside the Custom Shop and
Custom Art Models

Mike McGuire

Mike McGuire is a guitarist from Los Angeles who taught lessons for many years. He founded Valley Arts Guitar store, along with Al Carness, in 1975. They were virtually the main store for Los Angeles session players like Larry Carlton, Lee Ritenour, Mitch Holder, Steve Lukather, et al. The first International L.A. Vintage Guitar show was held there in 1979. Mike had one of the best repair shops around and also built a player-oriented custom guitar line that Gibson now sells. With all their experience in music retail, repair, and building, he and Al eventually hooked up with Gibson to help make the world a better place for guitarists.

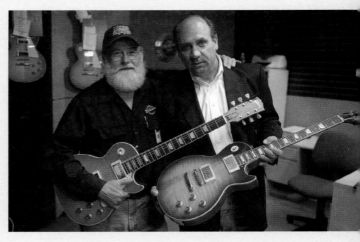

Mike McGuire and Rick Gembar in the display room of the Custom Shop, holding the long-scale LP R9 and the first Duane Allman reissue model, 2004.

Robb: When did you sign up with Gibson?

Mike: *October '93. I was doing that thing with Samick—you know Valley Arts was with Samick—and part of my deal was to be a consultant for them for several years. I was in Korea, where had to spend six months out of every year. I'd do a month in the states and a month over there. Part of what I did for them was to talk to their buyers, whether it be Rudy Schlocker from Washburn or Dave Berryman from Gibson. Back in those days, Dave Berryman was the guy coming over for Epiphone, actually, not Gibson. I had known Dave and Henry for years. I used to do some artist work for Gibson at the store, so we had a pretty good relationship.*

On one of my trips to Korea, Dave asked me how things were going. He said they were getting ready to open a Custom Shop here in Nashville, and for me to come see him when I got back from Korea. So I did. This was an empty building at the time, but I came down and checked it out. Dave asked me, "Do you want to take it over?" And I said, "I'd love to!" I've been here ever since. Now we've got close to 100 people working here. Back in those days, the Custom Shop was doing only a couple of guitar models. Basically they were using plant stuff, but they didn't really have a full-blown Custom Shop.

RL: And it expanded from there. He was actually trying to promote the true historic Les Paul.

MM: *The historic program became as successful as it is because of Edwin Wilson's tenacity, I think. He really and truly has a love for the historic product and will not compromise. That's what it took to get the program to where it is today. Right here in Nashville we've got probably the best engineer in the country as far as guitars go. Lynn Mathews has been with Gibson forever and ever. She's an absolutely incredible lady. Matthew Klein is great, too.*

RL: They took all the best attributes of the Les Paul Sunburst and made a point of concentrating on refining it.

MM: *Well, you know—probably more than anyone else, because you've studied the Les Paul so thoroughly—that the older Les Pauls were all over the map, in terms of neck shape and everything else.*

RL: From production batch to production batch… even within a given production batch.

MM: *Sure. Those old guys up there did such heavy drinking, who knew what the guitar was going to be that day? So basically Edwin took kind of the middle of the road and evaluated many of them and came up with what we got.*

RL: Now you have the finest Gibsons ever.

MM: *Yes, the program has done very, very well.*

The entrance to Nashville's Custom Shop Gibson factory, 2004.

Mahogany blank routed for switch wiring, with dowels for the maple tops to be glued.

Stacks of flame maple waiting to be glued together.

Presses for gluing maple tops.

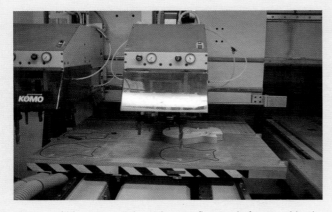

The incredible CNC machine doing a flame relief Les Paul body.

The Custom Shop Factory Tour

Old friend Mike McGuire graciously takes us for a tour of the Custom Shop facility and discusses the process of building their famous Gibson guitars.

Robb: *We're now in the wood room.*

Mike: *Yes. This is the rough mill. This is where we get all the wood in. And we'll grade it. Right now we're going through maple tops. We will lay them out for R-9s, R-8s, whatever. An R9 is really a '59 reissue. That's our top model. Then we will grade the backs and glue them together. Once we get done with them over there, then we book-match them up. Then we glue them together to go on the back. We put two pin dowels in here so when we glue the top on it won't slip. It maintains our center-line. This will give us our center-line.*

RL: *Is this specifically an R-9 plank with the rout for the wires and the weight marked?*

MM: *Yes. We have a weight restriction on all the reissue guitars. An R-9 has to be less than nine pounds top and back. These will all be goldtops. These are all nine pounds.*

RL: *And the goldtop is okay to be heavier.*

MM: *Well, they're supposed to be over nine pounds. The lightest wood they have on the mahogany is going to go on the R-9, because it's the most expensive guitar.*

RL: *And it's the most resonant.*

MM: *Probably because of that.*

Bound bodies with freshly-attached binding drying.

273

RL: *There's a Les Paul Sunburst right there.*

(As we walk and look, the sound system is playing "Time Is on My Side" by the Rolling Stones.)

MM: *We're doing a 3-D carving on a Les Paul with the flame.*

RL: *That's an amazing machine.*

MM: *Every neck is hand-rolled. That's what he's doing here. So there are going to be differences in feel in every single guitar. This is where we bring an artist if we're doing a guitar for them. We let them feel the guitar as he's rolling it. That way they can take off a little more cheese, make it a little flatter in the back, whatever they want to do.*

RL: *They're going for the feel. That's the real deal.*

MM: *Absolutely. This is Dave Lindsey. He does all the fretting and puts on all the head veneers. He binds the necks right here, too. It's a big job. How long have you been with the company, Dave?*

Dave: *Sixteen years.*

MM: *Imagine how many frets he's put in, in 16 years.*

RL: *Great job. You do the dressing, too?*

DL: *No. Installation.*

RL: *You don't hammer them in old-style, you press them with the press?*

DL: *Yes, in an Arbor press one at a time. We start with the press on the whole fingerboard, then each one is individually pressed. Then we look at it and make sure there are no high spots. If there are, then we repress to make sure they are seated against the fingerboard. Then we glue them and start filling the fingerboard out from there.*

RL: *Then you put the binding on.*

DL: *We taper the ends to the final taper. Then we put a t-slot in the head on the board as it gets binding. Our binding goes inside that slot. Then we trim the binding down with a little trimmer and sand the back of the fingerboard to the right thickness. Otherwise, our side dots are going to be off-center. Then we drill the side dot holes, put in the side dots, and put the location pins in for the neck. Then we glue it on the neck.*

RL: *I see. May I take your portrait?*

DL: *Sure!*

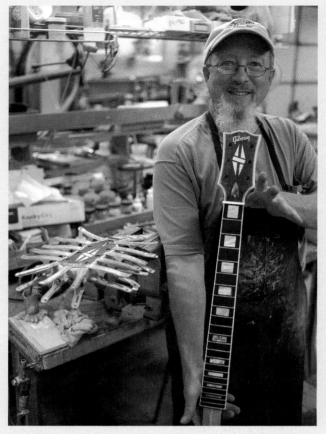

Here's the smiling fret man Dave Lindsey showing a Les Paul Custom neck in progress.

This is how they do the very important sanding of the final neck profile.

The fret leveling is done in this department.

We move on to the spray department. You can hear the big reverse blower fans going full-blast.

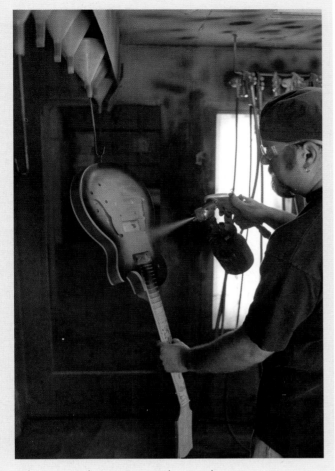

Mike's son Mickey McGuire is the main burst sprayer. Here he's doing a tobacco burst.

RL: *Mickey, Mike's son, is doing the sunburst.*

MM: *After scraping from the color, they go to the clear line. Depending upon how porous the wood is, we determine how many coats we have to put on it— a minimum of eight to ten, I think. Here are some of those diamond ones we introduced at the show.*

RL: *Amazing. Beautiful.*

MM: *Mickey's doing that chameleon thing on there. He started doing the bursts in '93, so everything that's come out of here since then, he's done. A lot of bursts there, buddy!*

RL: *Wow! I'd say. That's amazing. Do you notice that when it's more humid the blacks turn into a little greenish or gray like they did in Kalamazoo?*

MM: *Actually, we have that problem here in the summer, because that's when we have the humidity. In the winter, we're too dry, so we run sprinklers in here. We have a misting system. I don't know if you can see it up there. We have to keep the humidity around 45 to 50 percent.*

(We spot a vivid green Les Paul model.)

MM: *I don't know whose that is, but it's a custom order.*

RL: *Green and P-90s, too!*

MM: *Get a picture of that!*

The final once-over on a fine R9 by Steve Vause in the set-up department.

The rack of completed Custom Shop instruments awaiting shipping. Note the Zakk Wylde guitars that stand out.

Edwin Wilson

Having discussed the evolution and personnel of Gibson's embryonic Custom Shop of the prior decade, Edwin Wilson picks up with the Les Paul story as it began during the 1993 Historic era.

Edwin: *The Custom Shop started was with a handful of us—maybe five people. We did custom-ordered guitars at that time. Jimmy Wallace (Southwest Music) was ordering guitars. He was a Gibson dealer and he wanted some hand-picked tops on Les Paul Classics. "Maybe the shoulder is a little bit more square," Jimmy would say. Some of the details weren't that easy just to tell the guys in production, so we would take the guitars to a point where production would stop. Then we would pull them into our area and work on them, then get them back to production. They would work on them some more. It definitely was a joint thing, to make it more like a fifties Les Paul.*

Robb: *Thus, the collaborative versions we see with Custom Shop decals and large numbers or imprinted numbers. I understand afterward you gathered a number of vintage Les Paul guitars from Gruhn's shop to scrutinize.*

EW: *We got several guitars from Gruhn's. Crawford White in Nashville had a number of 1960s guitars that we went through. That was really the first time that they had put the R & D into it. A lot of times in the past Gibson would go off of what people were telling them: "The guitar needs to look like this and it needs to be like this." And they would make it like what they were hearing instead of what they were actually trying to recreate.*

RL: *It was a long road from the dealer specials to the point when Tom showed me the '93 final version.*

EW: *Oh, yeah, it was a very long road. It was a lot for production to take in. They had to change the way they thought. They were used to short neck tenons, which were very easy to neck fit. They didn't have to remove as much material when they were neck fitting it, so they could do a lot of guitars in a day. For long neck tenons, they had to remove a lot of material when they were neck fitting, so it was a very different animal for them.*

They also had to change the way they were sanding the tops out after they were carved. They were used to real deep, real wide spaced marks from the cutters in the machine that carved the tops. The only objective at that point was to get the marks out. It didn't really pertain to a shape because the machine put a shape in it, so a lot of times on standard production Les Pauls the tops were a little too domed in the middle. On the Historic guitars, they had to make sure they maintained a shape that was carved into it. There were a lot of things about it.

RL: *I understand you ran a topical examination of a number of tops.*

EW: *Yes, we did, and we still do. At that time, we used a coordinate measuring system that we made that wasn't digital. It consisted of taking measurements every sixteenth of an inch, up and over, up and over—both vertical and horizontal—so there are thousands and thousands of points on that guitar. This was all done without the assistance of a computer. You get that information and put it together, then you have to figure out how to get it into a program. This then tells the machine what to do to make a template.*

RL: *Time consuming and expensive.*

EW: *Very. A lot of hard work. That's how the first ones were done. Now we have a laser scanner. When we have original fifties guitars in there, a lot of times what we'll do is drop the pickups down, take the rings and stuff off. We'll put it up on the machine and go through and scan it. We'll be able to use that information to see how close the tops are. We see there are discrepancies in some of them, many from flat-belting. It's real cool, but you have to keep on doing it so that the tops can stay good.*

RL: *What about the necks? Everyone now is getting used to the new '59 kind of bulky neck, whereas, in my experience, a lot of the original '59s weren't that big. Some were, though.*

EW: *One of the biggest difficulties in manufacturing, at least at Gibson, is that the guitar is a 3-D thing. It takes a lot for someone to see into warp 3-D versus something that is 2-D, so all the necks are shaped by hand. When we get a neck, it is band-sawed out, flat on the top, flat on the back, flat on the sides. Then we put it on a CNC and it will do an initial cut across the face of it to make sure that it's flat. It will drill a couple of locating holes for a fingerboard and it will come off that part of the fixture and go onto another part. It* will go on the back and will sort of carve a section where the heel is. It will go flat on the back and the headstock. At that point you have something that is a dimension where the neck is a thickness which would be at the nut .9, and one inch at the 12th fret. Then it goes onto another fixture face down where it actually starts a carving process. It will cut out sort of a rough carve for the heel. Then it will do a rough carve for the profile of the neck. But there are still carving marks that are in there. At that point the neck is a real good shape. But then, once the fingerboard gets glued on, the guy goes to sand the neck. He's got these big wide belt sanders, and they'll hold the neck against the sanders and they blend in the heel and they have to blend in the headstock. And a lot of times that's where things go awry because...

RL: Because they might not press as hard as they did before.

EW: Right. When they sand that profile on the back of the neck, they are sanding to meet the edges of the fingerboard. The fingerboard is smaller than the width of the neck, so they sand to try and bring that in. They interpret the size of the neck as the dimension at the nut, which is 1.683. Then they interpret it as the dimension from the top of the fingerboard to the back of the neck, but what they don't pick up on is that the shoulders is where you play and it's where you feel. Most of the time when the player says it feels big, that's what they're talking about. It's really the cheeks on the neck and the guy rolling it is talking about the thickness from the top of the fingerboard to the back of the neck. So you say, "I need the neck smaller." Then he'll reduce that dimension so it no longer will be .9 at the nut, it will be .86 at the nut. You can take a neck that is .9 at the nut, and you can take some of the shoulders off and it will feel like a small neck. What we've noticed about the fifties Les Pauls is that typically they have less shoulder on them than we put on ours, so our necks do feel a little chunkier.

RL: ES-355 and Custom binding was more rounded, too.

EW: The binding starting out on a fifties Les Paul is about 40/1000 thick on the fingerboard. Beginning with the Les Paul Customs it was 62 or 63, so it was a little bit thicker. Coming from someone who's done it, you're thinking, "This is 63, so I have a little bit more room. As I blend this in, if I hit a little bit of the binding, it's not that big of a deal." That's how it starts

out. They get thin on Customs just as they do on Les Pauls, but it starts out from a sanding thing. It is a standard size for the thickness of the material, so I think it's the same thing.

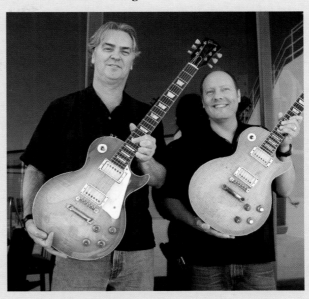

Pat Foley and Edwin Wilson in Texas—by the pool with two very special vintage Les Paul guitars, 2008.

RL: Have you dialed the ledge out on the fatter necks?

EW: Some of the necks that come through feel absolutely great, and some of them still feel a little too chunky for me. I don't inspect every guitar, but I go through production and pick up guitars and try to do spot checks on certain things to try and keep the Historic program together. If some necks feel a little thick, I'll go back and talk to the guy who's doing the sanding, to try and find out what's going on and get him to tone it down a little bit so they don't feel so big. He does a lot of guitars every day.

RL: That is a lot of work. I understand—since wood is of primary concern, and you're searching for the ultimate tone—finding the aged, old-growth wood has become difficult. Have you made an effort to build guitars out of older seasoned wood?

EW: Old is a subjective thing. I'll call one of my mahogany vendors and ask, "Do you have some old mahogany?" He'll say, "Yeah, I've got some mahogany that's 80 years old." I say, "Great! Where is it?" "It's sitting here. It just came in," he says. From the lumber guy's standpoint it's all old, because the trees that we get the mahogany out of need to be old-growth trees. The size to get a one piece back out of, for a tree to be that big, especially to be flat sawn, has to be a very large tree. Some of the trees that we get mahogany out of have a diameter of six or seven feet. They are very, very old mahogany trees. As far as stuff that's just been sitting around, that's not been used, that's already been cut and dried and processed, that's been hanging out for 50 or 60 years, the stuff doesn't exist. You might find a few pieces, but not enough to keep a manufacturing facility going.

RL: Do you have some wood set aside that is aging specifically?

EW: *All of our wood is kiln dried, and kilning is definitely an art. Most of the maple we use is hard and soft, Eastern and Western. Most of the Eastern we use is silver maple or sugar maple. On the West Coast it is just big leaf maple. Usually what we find is that guys who want a guitar truer to a fifties Les Paul will like the Eastern maple or maybe some of the flat-sawn*

Edwin Wilson holding a choice 50th Anniversary 1959 Les Paul Standard at the 2009 NAMM show.

Western maple. That's typically what they were using because it was softer. One of the dealers that we used to have said, "There's always a good angle of a curly top. You might have to look for it, but there's always a good angle." But a lot of guys just like straight quarter-sawn. It's pretty wood but it's not traditional looking for a fifties Les Paul. Most all of the fifties guitars that I've ever seen, all the wood that they ever used was flat into rift, or rift into flat, something

like that. Very seldom did they use straight on quarter. I think with setting the wood aside and letting it air dry, it would have to air dry many years to be able to use it.

RL: And get that aged tonality. So you bring it down to what percentage?

EW: *It's a subjective thing. We run our mahogany backs at about 9 percent. And hard maple is around 11 percent moisture content, and soft maple is around 9 percent content. You get some variations on that with the density of material and stuff like that. It's different for different areas. If we lived in Arizona and were making guitars, it would be different because if we did them at 9 percent, they would split and crack. You have to do for whatever your average humidity is in the area that you're in. First is what the wood's equalized moisture content would be, in its natural environment. There are charts and tables that you look at to make sure the moisture is right when you are starting a manufacturing process.*

RL: It's fascinating, the science of retro-engineering.

EW: *It definitely is. The engineering aspect is the coolest thing about guitars.*

RL: They look great, too! It's a renaissance of American craftsmanship.

EW: *Indeed! The best thing about it is that we don't do everything on a machine. We have guys who show up every day and use their hands to make stuff. We do a Neal Schon model guitar that has a scarfed heel on it. There's not a program that does that scarfed heel. It's a guy with a file and chisel and he goes back there on every one of those guitars and he shapes it down with a chisel, and then he takes a file and blends it in, and he takes sandpaper and he does it. The Neal Schon is our first entry into doing that cutaway heel on any kind of production level. We weren't really sure how many guitars we were going to make. We didn't set up for a lot of tooling on it. We're getting ready to introduce a new guitar… the All Access model.*

Pat Foley

Pat Foley picks up the conversation at this point. He has spearheaded the artist relations department to coordinate the guitarist's conceptions into marketable instruments with exacting specs. Pat came on board through the Mapex and Slingerland drum divisions at Gibson in Nashville and soon migrated to a position in artist relations, ultimately becoming head of Entertainment Relations with a base in London, England. In 2003 Foley returned to Nashville, where he has continued to play an important role as liaison to Gibson's top artists, with a specialty in developing signature and "Inspired By" models.

Pat and Edwin have a great time holding Gary Moore and Peter Green's 1959 Les Paul Standards in Dallas, summer 2008. *Guitars courtesy of Eric Ernest, Abalone Vintage.*

Pat: *Gibson acquired Slingerland and started building Slingerland drums. Because of my experience with Paul Jamieson, I was intimately familiar with Radio Kings—the solid maple drums and all that. The Gretsch snares and Slingerland Radio Kings were the holy grail for drummers, because that was what Gene Krupa played, with all these solid maple, steam-bent shells. I like to remind our pal Edwin here that when we were getting started, it was about the time he was moving from the factory into the new Gibson Custom Shop. Slingerland shared the building with the Custom Shop. When we commenced setting up our production, the Custom Shop consisted of a pallet in the middle of the room, parts and bodies and things. These guys followed us in there very shortly, so they*

divided the building in two. The Custom Shop started with banjos. There were just a couple of benches in the corner. This was on Massman Drive. Then these guys began moving their stuff in and taking over more of the building and eventually they crowded Slingerland out. That, in turn, is how I ended up at Gibson. Along with my responsibilities in Slingerland production, Rick Gembar, who was running the Custom Division, had me help out with some finish work at Gibson. I used to come in on weekends and spray guitars. They had always been my first love. Drums were kind of a digression that I went through for a number of years out of necessity and my experience in Los Angeles. To fast forward, after a few years with Slingerland, I was asked to move to Gibson, where I took over artist relations. I moved to London and ran the program from an office on Denmark Street, along with Juliette Avery, who is still with Gibson in the UK.

Robb: *You stopped finish work. No more fumes.*

PF: *No more fumes for me. It was funny because I was kind of dragged, kicking and screaming, from Slingerland into Gibson. Slingerland was a smaller world and we had more control of it. Then Henry, the owner and CEO, insisted, "You're good with artists and you know people. I need you at Gibson," so I made that transition. I started with Slingerland division in late 1993, originally as a consultant, and then went full time in March 1994. It was just about the time you (Edwin) were making that transition, too. I've done artist relations work since about 1998. And of course Edwin and I have worked together on a lot of the artist projects. I moved back from England and have been doing Custom Shop related stuff. I do other things, too. We did the Paul McCartney Epiphone Texan. I do some projects for other divisions, but mainly my focus is the Custom Shop. We've done together all of the Pete Townshend models, several Jimmy Page models, Eric Clapton Crossroads 335, and the Bob Marley.*

Interview from summer of 2008 picks up again in July 2009.

Pat: *We've just done Billy Gibbons's Les Paul. It's great to add new stuff. Pearly Gates is one of the guitars that is most often requested as an "Inspired By" model. Of course, any of Jimmy Page's guitars are always of interest. We are currently working with*

Jimmy to recreate his number two Les Paul with the four push/pull knobs and the switches under the pickguard. This is the fourth electric we have done with Jimmy, the others being his number one Les Paul, double neck SG (EDS 1275), and the three-pickup Custom with the six-way toggle. We now have a long-standing relationship with the greatest living guitarist/composer of his generation. Jimmy is in a class by himself.

Pat Foley enjoying himself with Jeff Beck during his signing of the new Oxblood Les Paul models. *Photo by Dean Fardell, courtesy Pat Foley*

RL: *How did the Black Beauty come about, with that new toggle switch?*

PF: *During the development of the various Jimmy Page models, Jimmy spoke about his original 1960 Black Custom, and how he felt that it should have been able to access more pickup combinations. That was always the drawback of that guitar. It had three pickups, but you could only get the rear pickup or the rear two or the front pickup. That became the starting point for the Page Les Paul Custom guitar. We approached the first prototype like a Peter Frampton, where it had a normal switching but then you had the middle pickup on a master volume control where you could bring it in with any combination. He didn't like that at all and asked, "Why couldn't it be a toggle switch that hits them all?" He didn't want extra switches on it. We got in touch with a company in England that made a six-position toggle switch.*

Chris Swope, one of the builders at the Custom Shop, wired it up so that when it's in the front position, when the toggle switch is forward, it's like a normal three-pickup Les Paul. When you flip it backward, there are two more positions that add in the center pickup and the last one [6] is the outside two, so you can effectively get every position except the middle pickup alone. Then we added the push-pull knob that actually splits the coils for the rear pickup, makes it a single coil or a humbucker. Jimmy played the first prototype less than two weeks before the London gig and called to say, "It really is good! It's just perfect." He played it at the 2002 Led Zeppelin reunion and has since mentioned that he thought it had just about the best sound of the night!

RL: *What is the story of the "Inspired By" Jeff Beck guitar?*

PF: *In the case of Jeff Beck, Ralph Baker, who was his manager, was amazingly helpful. It's always a matter of developing credibility with the artist, first and foremost. They have to trust you. It has to be something he's happy with. How we presented it was that this was not trying to steal him away from Fender, not trying to rewrite history, but celebrating a milestone in his career and the birth of a genre of music with Blow by Blow and with fusion music and the way he approached instrumentals. He finally agreed that it was worth celebrating.*

RL: *The first ones from the nineties had a dark finish with cherry tint.*

PF: *Yes. They were doing an oxblood that was basically a black finish with a coat of cherry over it. It created a midnight cherry, for lack of a better term.*

RL: *How does the new guitar compare?*

PF: *Oh, completely different. We mixed that right from the ground up. It was funny because Edwin and I went and looked at the original guitar and pho-*

tographed it. Photographs can be very deceiving. You look at them and unless you have something to compare it to, the camera is going to alter the look with the lighting. It's very difficult to reproduce a guitar. You take pictures, but then you have to know in your mind what it looks like. So we actually worked with Mick, our painter, in the room and kept adding brown until it had that chocolate look. I took it to Jeff. When he looked at the first one, he immediately said, "I can't believe you matched the color." He approved the color. It was kind of a flat look, too. The color doesn't really have a 3-D look to it. It's just dark brown.

RL: *With a little tint of maroon in it.*

PF: Yes, it does have a maroon tint to it. It would best be described as a milk chocolate color, really. That was a surprise, because I had always been told oxblood. I think of oxblood as a shoe polish, but it's not that color at all. It's more chocolate. That probably was a surprise to people who saw the guitar in the store. The back of the headstock was interesting because it's sunburst. When you look at the tuners, it's mahogany, and there's just a dark sunburst. The back of the neck was almost black, not the same color as the guitar.

It was a very small number we actually did. The entire run was 150 guitars. I think we did 50 signed, aged guitars and then 100 aged guitars. It was more to have the association with Jeff. Strategically, it was a good move because it reminded everybody that Jeff did some of his best work on a Les Paul. And in a lot of cases, that's what it's about. It's about reminding people we're a part of that history.

Tom Murphy

Guitarist and finish restoration expert Tom Murphy is world renowned for his magnificent guitar finishes and the art of distressing a guitar to make it look vintage and aged from years of playing. We spent time performing together onstage and gave a lecture together at the Dallas guitar show in fall 2008 when I did my first book signing at John Kinnemeyer's JK Lutherie booth. Here are portions of our 2009 interview regarding the current state of Gibson's efforts to get back to the basics and add a bit of antique magic to the instrument.

Tom: *When I started at Gibson, the back of a Les Paul was sprayed red with Heritage Cherry after the filler was put on it.*

Robb: *Was the filler red?*

TM: Not when I was there. The filler was natural and they would spray just so much red. If you look at them, even the reissues, they're virtually opaque red. I thought, "I wonder when that started? When did they quit using stained filler?" They must have encountered the same thing we have now at Gibson, that the powder to stain the filler can contaminate your whole area real quickly. It was worth it for the effect you get on an SG or a Les Paul, of course. Those are the things as we think back on, "Why did they quit this? Why did they do that? Why did they quit silk screening the logo?" All the things that someone said, "This thing keeps breaking or this thing keeps messing up, but we have to keep making this every day. Can't we do it a different way?" That's exactly why they got away from things, and all we've always wanted was the way they did it. We want to try to relive it one time to see what the effect was.

RL: *It's like collecting nostalgia, "Let's get back to roots." Gibson and Fender are both living that reemergence, like the retro thing with cars, too.*

TM: And clothes and all kinds of stuff now. They know those things cause a good feeling about the quality of items and it's because if it looks like that, it must have been made before, almost like we really don't want to own up to the stuff we make now. If you try and explain why guitars have changed and why there is such a big deal about an element of a guitar today, or a reissue series of any kind or a reissue of any clothes for instance, it is because we as consumers drove the change.

RL: *We just want to put on our old jeans!*

TM: Exactly! What person has not been upset the day they finally blow the crotch out of their best jeans. If someone came up and said, "You don't have to worry about it. I'll make you a pair exactly like those are today," you'd be really happy. We didn't trust Gibson and Fender manufacturers to know what we wanted and what we had latched onto. The natural progression was for us to demand they go back. And they were saying, "What, what? No. What are you saying? You don't run the company. We know what we need to do here." They were going in an opposite direction than we were going.

It dawned on me that, with the guitar, there were very

few restrictions. Just draw or trace around an old one and we'll start from there. I think they had never done that. Tim Shaw implied that they didn't really take an old one and try to reproduce it. I've explained to people that Gibson responded many times to outside requests for the same thing: Guitar Trader, Leo's, Strings & Things, Jimmy Wallace. Every one of those guitars is different and none of them are like a '59. But until the factory itself decided to take it on as a project, it wasn't going to happen. They were just responding, "What's this guy want?" One guy on the line would know only one thing, not know anything but what he was told to do. Until the Historics happened, I don't think Gibson got onboard. They finally agreed to let me pile up as many elements as I could in one place and let us try to do them all at the same time.

I'll tell you one of the coolest things that ever happened. One day I said, "Can we go to each department and talk to them? We can't just lay this on them and not explain it." We got department after department to come into the cafeteria. We explained to them what they were going to have to adhere to and change and do exclusively on this model of guitar. At the same time I explained to them why it would be necessary, that an original guitar like that was 20 or 30 thousand dollars. We want to make guitars just like it, that everybody could buy. They all said, "Alright, just tell us what we're supposed to do." Now they did have problems. The guys gluing on the holly veneers said, "Wait a minute. This isn't going to work." And they left them thicker for a while. But I said, "No, they've got to be thinner," because they would split when they pulled them out of the press. Not to mention the logo. You have to paint the head veneer instead of staining it because they used to have that black fiber, so all of a sudden we're painting black head veneers. They said, "How do we keep the logos clean?" You have to clean the logo off or mask it off while you paint it, so there are always different systems devised to do this stuff. Nobody even knew how to do it. The serial number was different. That never happened, I guarantee, in Kalamazoo when they tried to do the Guitar Trader and those others. A couple of guys probably got a kick out of it, but that was it. They pulled off what they could. I would say Guitar Trader was the most notorious, and probably the most internal Gibson effort was put forth on it. I thought it was funny, that in Gibson to me, I think their actual attempt was the Heritage Series.

RL: Yes, but the body was shorter.

TM: Then they had wacky three-piece necks, and the quilted tops, and the brown sunburst and the Grover tuners.

RL: They were getting there. Chuck Burge tried to talk to everybody at stations, too.

TM: Today the proof—it's not just Gibson and Fender by any means—is there that you need to attend to that stuff. If I owned a company, I would be a little disturbed if people wanted only what was made before I came there. "Can't we innovate?" I think Gibson is doing a decent job of that, too.

RL: They are doing both.

TM: I saw the Dark Fire guitars. You pick them up off the rack and they tune themselves. If I were a kid, why would I want something that was built in 1959 when I could have this thing? But if there are elements of aesthetics and structural design that can be passed on and used, go for it!

It didn't all stop with the sunburst Les Paul. That became an icon of our culture and the music we were all enthralled with. As long as you're looking at the guitar, you aren't going to see one much prettier than that. I always thought as I stared at the picture, "Wow, that looks like it was built to play rock 'n' roll." It actually wasn't, but what else would it do? Rock 'n' roll is younger people, that guitar is smaller, old people play those big guitars and this one looks cool. It's got those two pickups there. It became a symbol for the high end of rock 'n' roll when matched with the Marshall amp.

RL: Exactly. The Les Paul is really built for tone. And it is a jazz guitar, as Peter Green said.

TM: When I'm playing a gig, if I'm not able to open it up a little bit with my amps, then the Les Paul is being choked back. When it's free to do its thing…

RL: When you get out the Les Paul, you're breaking out all the horses.

TM: I have two different 2-12 cabinets, so there are some speakers in the other one, and I'm listening to two different 2-12 cabinets. I've taken this amp to only one gig and we were already getting bitched at. I'm using my Super Reverb with plexi-glass in front, or I'm using Blues Juniors or whatever. Golly, I want to use this but I don't want to turn that amp down and turn my Les Paul down, too.

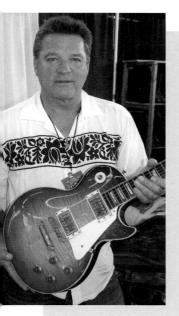

RL: *When your guitar checked from the cold in Colorado, did that inspire you to get into finish work?*

TM: No, not at all. It intrigued me in that I caused something to happen to the guitar that wasn't at all pleasing. Weather checking did not make a guitar look cooler, so I wasn't digging that because it was something I wasn't in control of and that I couldn't put back. That's not to say that, prior to that, I hadn't messed with finishes on guitars. I have no idea why I took the finish off every single guitar I bought while I was in Houston. I guess I wanted to know something else about the guitar and nothing was really special about a gold top on a '68 Les Paul. It's not an old guitar. I had no way of putting the finish back. My dad taught industrially, taught wood and is a craftsman in that regard. I didn't do any of that kind of work with him, per se, but it must be in the blood that I fiddled around with things. But I almost never really wanted to know how to do some of the stuff he did.

Ultimately, I totally backed away from it as a player because I respected the guitars so much and the people who knew about that. I would have other guys change nuts and frets because it was way too technical for me. I didn't even mess with guitars until the eighties when a '55 Junior fell off the strap while I was playing it. It hit a monitor and put a dent in the center of the back of the neck. I had done furniture work at a store in Nashville, and when we would deliver a piece and have a small dent we would steam it out. I did that on the back of the '55 Junior. It also caused a larger area of the finish to be marred, and that took me a year and the spot got about four or five inches long. While I thought I was improving it, I was really making it worse. I became obsessed with figuring out how to repair that, so I talked to guys at Gruhn's. They didn't know how to fix it and make it look like it never happened, but I really got into it. It drove me crazy that I'd made a mockery of this one little dent on this original old vintage guitar, so I worked at it and painted some grain and I probably cut a few very subtle lines in there. I was satisfied with how it turned out.

When I was working at Gibson, I bought a refinished Junior, which I hung in my garage in a makeshift booth. I bought a spray gun and a compressor to paint this guitar. On the last pass, I spun it on the hook it was hanging on. The hook came loose and the guitar spun off and landed headfirst, breaking off the headstock, which flew across my garage floor. That's the first guitar I ever painted. I went to Gibson and said, "How do I glue this headstock back on?" Phil Jones and I messed with epoxies and I got it where it would actually stay together. I tried to touch up the crack and eventually put strings on it and sold it. At that time I thought, "Man, I don't have any business doing this."

A year later I was doing so much repair and hand touch-up that they moved me to the paint department. One day a kid asked me to paint his Les Paul Reissue. I said, "What if I paint it like this," and I tried to fade it. That's how the whole thing started. Then it expanded into them asking me to be in the other Custom area. I was obsessed with trying to make things the way I wanted them. I thought, "If they're not going to tell me not to, I'm going to do them my way. I bet there are a lot of guys out there like me that would like to see another Pelham Blue Firebird," or a whatever I was into, especially the sunburst on the Les Paul. It was too abrupt and too monotonous, monotone and not enough of the character of the wood was showing for me. That expanded into the vintage thing. Then the next step was, "Can we change the structure of the guitar?" That was '92 and—oh my gosh—what have I gotten into? I tried to savor the time, and make the most of it. It wasn't that big of deal to anyone else. I knew it was potentially going to mean a lot to the guitar people. That's how it all happened.

The aging thing was an accident, not meant for commercial use at all, but it expanded into that. That's the chapter we're into now. It started in 1999 because Gibson wanted to participate. They said, "We don't think it's real practical, but we'll try it." It's what was necessary in the market and people want it to be there. We've further expanded with the artist models because they need it and other techniques of aging. Hopefully, we've done some stuff that people will enjoy and keep talking about and may look back at in the future, like we had old guitars to look at. They'll have different elements of all this stuff to appreciate. Some will look back and say, "That was sort of goofy!" But others will look back and say, "Wow, that was really cool!"

Gibson Custom on the Road

Danny Hoefer and David Perris working the Custom Shop trailer in Les Paul style.

Danny Hoefer, Gibson Rep

Guitarist Danny Hoefer started when I was 14 and bought his first Les Paul in 1964, an unusual orange top '56 with Bigsby. He paid $96 for it. He's owned many Gibsons over the years and, like many of us playing in the sixties, learned from the great records of the Bluesbreakers, BB King live at the Regal, the Electric Flag, Butterfield Blues band, and Hendrix. Eventually, Danny joined the Tower of Power group after Bruce Conte left. Later he got into retail music store business that lead him to work for Gibson guitars. We got together on August 24th, 2005 when the Custom Shop trailer was in Van Nuys, California.

Robb: How did you hook up with Gibson?

Danny: In 2003, I was working at American Music in Seattle. For most of the time I was there, our rep was Vic Russelavige. He was being promoted and wondered if anyone was interested in a job with Gibson. I said, "Sounds like the job for me." I had loved Gibson guitars since the day I started playing. I knew a lot about them. I came on as a regional sales manager and had 11 states on the West Coast. They changed our title to business development manager, which it's been for about a year now. A lot of things changed at Gibson at that time.

RL: And now you're doing the roving display.

DH: The roving display! It's funny. This is the first time I've done the Custom Shop trailer working for Gibson guitars. I've done a few with the Montana trailer.

RL: They're a great team.

DH: I think the acoustic guitars and the electric guitars we've been making for the last 10 to 15 years are some of the best stuff Gibson has made.

RL: *They brought in the right people, like Mike and Ren.*

DH: *Oh, absolutely! Rick Gembar, Mike McGuire, and all those guys are doing a fabulous job.*

RL: *What are your favorite innovations that they've done with the Les Paul guitar?*

DH: *I like the reissues—the '59s and the '58s, and the '57 Goldtops. Those have always been some of my favorite guitars. Now that they are making them like the originals, they've got the vibe, they've got the feel, they've got the sound. I love all that stuff.*

RL: *What's been the popular Les Paul model?*

DH: *Probably the '59 or the '60, depending upon what kind of neck they like. The '57s and '58s are great. Some people like the two-pickup '57 Custom. That's a great guitar. The Johnny A guitar has been pretty popular. Guys like its longer-scale length. It gives you a bigger and a snappier sound than the shorter scale. Plus, it's amazing with a body that doesn't have a block in there. It doesn't seem to feedback. It's got a great sound, I think.*

RL: *Do you find a lot of guys like the P-90s?*

DH: *Yes. They're a bit noisy, but they're real vocal-sounding. They have a great sound.*

RL: *How is it with Gibson? Are you happy with your job?*

DH: *It's been good. I like representing a product that I believe in, which I really do with the Gibson guitar. It's not without its challenges, that's for sure. It's a challenging industry, but business is good. We're selling everything we can make. So you can't complain too much about that. (Laughs)*

RL: *What's the big seller?*

DH: *In Custom Shop I'd have to say Les Pauls, but since the movie The School of Rock we're selling tons of SGs now. More than ever before, I think. The Jimmy Page guitar has done really well.*

RL: *Thank God, the Les Paul guitar is still alive.*

DH: *It's amazing—they ever quit making it. (Laughs)*

A portion of the Custom Shop trailer exhibit of Les Paul models.

The Les Paul Custom Art Models

The Gibson Company has taken great pride in their fine heritage for over a century now. From time to time through the decades, Gibson created their fancy Presentation models for special occasions. In recent times, theme-oriented creations depict people and important events. One of the main objectives of the modern Gibson Historic and Art Division has been to produce some of the finest hand-crafted Art instruments the world has ever seen. This carried on the expertise of their founder Orville Gibson and past artisans. Contemporary times brought about special themes to commemorate, such as the diamond-studded Centennial Les Paul Black Beauty. There is an astounding amount of effort that goes into each original work, and it ultimately makes a major investment and future legacy. The buyer brings home a piece of history that can be cherished, now and in future generations. Under the guidance of Phil Jones in the Custom Shop, many great instruments have been hand-designed; his specialty is fine marquetry that is expertly done. One creation is his Les Paul "Art Piece" to showcase the gamut of their capabilities.

Various art exhibits have featured Gibson's special creations such at the Art of Guitar I and II events. The latter was held at the Animazing Gallery in SoHo NYC on November 9th, 2001, with Bruce Kunkle, Rick Garcia, Bill Sienkiewicz, and other Gibson artists. Also in attendance were talk-show host Conan O'Brien, his guitarist Jimmy Vivino, and the Custom Shop's Rick Gembar.

Among the many great artist/luthiers who have graced the halls of Gibson Nashville, the talented artist/musician Bruce Kunkle is responsible for many fine Gibson Art guitars. His family is steeped in a true woodworking tradition that comes from the Black Forest of Germany. His father noticed his carving skills as a boy and, over the years, primed him to learn the fine techniques of creating 18th-century furniture masterpieces. After banjo lessons from Roger Siminoff, building an F-5 mandolin to his specs, and teaching himself alongside great luthiers such as Bob Benedetto, Bruce and his family moved to Nashville; he is also a songwriter. His background in musicianship, fine woodworking, carving and design all led up to his approaching Gibson.

When Dave Berrymore saw his work, he gave him a hefty assignment: to recreate the traditional carved Bela Voce, Florentine, and All-American banjos for Gibson's Centennial Celebration in 1994. During his tenure at Gibson, he was responsible for a number of Art Guitars and historic releases mentioned in this book, such as the Old Hickory, the Slash Snakepit, the Corvette model and Indian Motorcycle LP, the incredible Art Deco series, and tributes to Elvis and Chet Atkins. The four seasons were depicted in Les Paul guitars with carved and inlaid leaves for the Autumn model, bare trees with birds and snowflakes for the Winter version (with white P-90s), faded sunburst with inlaid pearl butterflies and Bigsby on the Summertime Les Paul Florentine. Bruce spent ten years with Gibson and eventually left on good terms to pursue his own acoustic instruments. He still does contractual art pieces for them, such as the painted Flying V of Jimi Hendrix.

Gibson's 1995 NAMM display of the Centennial Custom.

The baseball Les Paul model #PCA 98. *Courtesy Saul Frank, Centre City Music, 2007*

The Corvette Les Paul Models

The Les Paul guitar icon meets up with the American Chevrolet Corvette sports car icon in a creative blend to commemorate the 35th anniversary of the 1960 classic. It was specifically designed to showcase their outstanding innovations and to share the tremendous impact both have had on American history. Stylized cues from the '57 to '62 Corvette's celebrated side coves (scoops) are re-liefed into the maple top with decorative chrome strips. Other features include the original script style "283" number engraved on the pickup covers (signifying the cubic-inch capacity of the engine of the car) and "Fuel Injected" on the stopbar tailpiece (which would make it the top 315hp 11:1 $484.20 optional CS version). The bound headstock has the colorful Corvette crossed racing flags logo inlaid with Gibson in abalone. This logo is also engraved on the chromed switch back plate. Corvette (a French high-speed sailing vessel term) is inlaid in pearl on the ebony fingerboard. Binding and pickup bezels are white to match the cove paint. Grover tuners, ABR-1, and stopbar tailpiece all in chrome complete the hardware.

Authentic Corvette color options of the era were used, in-cluding Tasco turquoise 504A, Roman red 506-A, ermine white 510A (with a Inca silver cove), tuxedo black 503-A (with sateen silver cove) and horizon blue 502A—all sanctioned by GM in their collaboration on the project. Corvette VIN style serial numbers are sequential from 001 to 200 with the number five through seven to designate the year (e.g., VIN5157 = 1995): Cases were deluxe black leather covered and emblazoned with the SS chevron racing flags.

At the 1995 Winter NAMM show, auto-motive artist extraordinaire Harold Cleworth was on hand, greeting the crowds with his fine 1958 Corvette portrait displayed. One turquoise ex-ample was shown in the trunk of a 1961 Corvette. A special print of his came with each guitar sold, along with accompanying paperwork. Incidently, the featured Corvette of the popular *Route 66* TV show was a 1960 model. This exclusive Corvette Collection col-laboration produced 200 highly valu-able collectors' items.

A 1963 Corvette "Split Window" Sting Ray model was also immortalized with a Les Paul SG model later that year. It had the rear fastback carved into the top of the instrument, with chrome split-window pickguards. This limited edition featured original '63 silver, black, and red colors, a stop tailpiece with one P-100 pickup, and Sting Ray pearl inlaid in the fingerboard.

By 2003, Chevy had teamed up with Gibson again for the Corvette's 50th anniversary. Premiered at the Summer NAMM show in Nashville, it was displayed in the arena with a matching 50th Anniversary Corvette. Based on the double cutaway 24-fret DC Pro Les Paul with two P-90s, this special edition of 50 guitars featured the smooth lines of the engine exhaust vent carved onto its top. Strings were rear-loaded and had a varied distance to the Tune-O-Matic bridge. The newly-mixed 50th Anniversary red color was standard and Corvette was inlaid in pearloid across the fingerboard. List price was over $9,000 and came with a wall-hanging display.

Billy Gibbons and ZZ Top were on hand in Nashville to do a sizzling concert set, performing with the new guitar for two tunes. It was in the Rolling Stone exhibit and finally rested in the Rock and Roll Hall of Fame. Special pins also commemorated the release of the instrument. One Corvette/guitar lover's reaction was, "Corvettes and Les Paul Gibsons… it doesn't get any better than this!" Another wondered if it's mandatory to play the guitar as fast as possible!

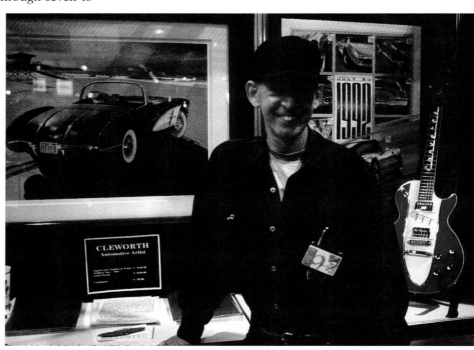

Harold Cleworth, automotive artist on hand at the 1995 NAMM show. His painting of the 1958 Corvette is displayed with Gibson's new Les Paul Corvette models.

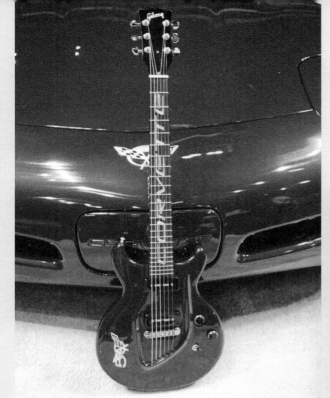

Gibson's 50th anniversary was celebrated with the Corvette Les Paul DC and displayed at Summer NAMM 2003 with the 50th anniversary Corvette in matching colors.

A pristine example of a 1995 Les Paul Corvette (VIN 5095) in cascade green. *Courtesy David Robinson, 2006*

The Old Hickory Limited Edition Model

In April 1998, a 275-year-old tulip poplar tree that once provided shade for President Andrew Jackson at his famous Tennesee Hermitage was violently uprooted by a tornado. Luckily, the home was spared as hundreds of trees were devastated. Gibson's Rick Gembar responded by teaming up with the estate to create a limited edition of 200 "Old Hickory" Les Paul models. The tree held the state record in age and size and was already quite old when Jackson was lived there from 1804 to 1845. With the help of CS luthier Bruce Kunkel, in-house specialist Gene Nix, and Michael Hill of Appalachian Hardwoods, a large section of the felled tree was carefully harvested and milled on the grounds to create a Custom Shop special.

The bodies and neck (with LP Custom appointments) were constructed of the poplar wood with a special hickory wood fingerboard from another felled tree near the grave of Jackson's wife, Rachel. Pearl inlaid portions included "Old Hickory" on the fingerboard and the image of Andrew Jackson on the headstock, while the pickguard had a portrait of the Hermitage. Three special versions featured a long inlaid pearl banner across the guitar, with historic Jackson dates engraved. The first one was presented to the Smithsonian Institution. A portion of the guitars' proceeds were presented for the Hermitage tornado recovery fund.

Vice President Al Gore and Chet Atkins were on hand for the unveiling ceremony with Gibson officials at the historic estate on July 12th of that year. The Rain-forest Alliance also certified the instrument as a Smartwood Gibson model. Gibson CEO Henry Juszkiewicz was quoted as saying, "Mother Nature has truly tested our resolve, and we can think of no better way to respond than by creating the Old Hickory guitar... We hope the guitars will always symbolize the boundless courage of the people of Tennessee and the undaunted American spirit that has been so prevalent through the many natural disasters of the last year."

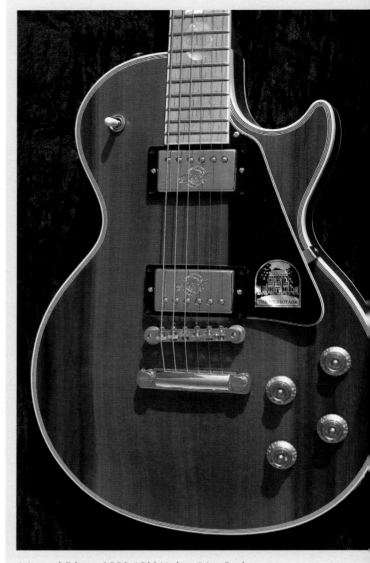

A Limited Edition 1998 "Old Hickory" Les Paul.
Courtesy Guitar Center Hollywood, 2005

Indian Chief Les Paul Model

In 2002, Gibson guitars delved into the two-wheeler realm with the Indian Motorcycle Corporation to come up with a roadworthy Custom Shop Indian Chief Les Paul model. Both companies have over 100 years of classic design history. The famous Indian company was celebrating their new Chief's PowerPlus 100 V-Twin engine and collaborated with the Gibson boys to incorporate their sleek, inspired curves from their first Chief motorcycle from the twenties and the smart color schemes. Throw in some '57 Classic pickups and the chromed cast war bonnet with Indian engravings and you have a limited run of 100 guitars. Guitarist Kenny Olson (from Kid Rock's band) endorsed this Les Paul model from his love of these motorcycles and the Gibson solid-body he uses onstage most often.

The instrument was introduced at Daytona Bike Week 2002 with much fanfare from the motorcycle world and rock enthusiasts. For promotion, prototype #2 is on loan to Kenny from the motorcycle company. He's performed with the guitar on the tour with Kid Rock and for the Aerosmith tribute on MTV Legends. He felt it sounded like "a well-seasoned Les Paul with a fat bottom and perky highs" and was glad to be a part of the promotion.

The guitar came in black combinations of cream, red, silver, and copper; blue/silver, crimson/cream and solid black, silver, and red. Included is the leatherette case, embossed strap with Indian concho attached, and a photograph backdrop inside the lacquered display cabinet. I can picture an Indian motorcycle enthusiast revving up their Les Paul Indian guitar, taking a break while cruising Mulholland to the Pacific Coast Highway!

Indian Les Paul model with the famous chief headdress emblazoned. *Courtesy GC Hollywood, 2004*

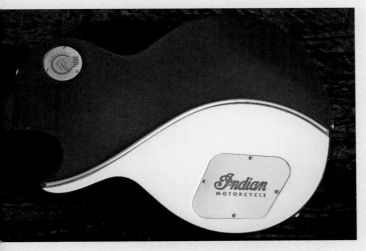

Les Paul Indian back.

Les Paul Indian fingerboard inlay.

Les Paul Tribute Guitar

Rick Gembar encouraged Bruce to create numerous themed instruments for the permanent Gibson collection. Naturally, a special tribute to Les Paul was done to top off the series. Bruce Kunkle set out to carve Les Paul's epitaph into wood from three different important eras of his life. With the front showing the persona of young Lester with his first guitar playing the harmonica to Les with his signature Goldtop during his hit parade with Mary Ford. The back has Les in the forties, swinging with his old Epiphone electric.

The cover is quilt maple for Gibson's Custom Art and Historic flier. Bruce Kunkle is shown carving the Les Paul Tribute model, with his sketches nearby.

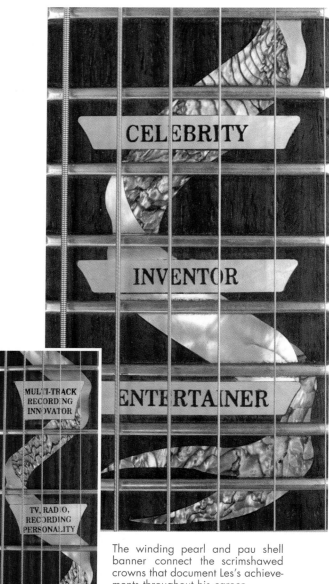

The winding pearl and pau shell banner connect the scrimshawed crowns that document Les's achievements throughout his career.

Great torch and banner pearl and abalone inlays with "One of a kind" on the truss cover.

The Gibson Les Paul Tribute model, with Les playing his new Goldtop and a young Lester in his sailor outfit and harmonica. Les signed the pickguard appropriately. *Courtesy Mike McGuire, Las Vegas, 2001*

The back relief has Les Paul swinging away in the late forties and the famous signature logo inlaid in abalone. Matching mahogany backplates complete the historic instrument.

Les Paul: 1968 to Today

Les Paul: 1968 to Today

After kicking back for a few years, something stirred in the air. The Les Paul guitar had been discontinued but Les was still tinkering on some new electronics. By late 1967, Les renewed his Gibson ties, which was truly a godsend for the guitar world. Due to overwhelming popular demand, the company was finally ready to reissue the original-style guitars. These were unveiled in late 1968, restarting the whole phenomenon. Concurrently, Les released *Les Paul Now* on London Records as his first on their Phase Four Stereo recordings. Its fold-out sleeve included great pictures from his studio, control, and editing rooms. Les's buddy Zeke Manners wrote two cool tunes for the record ("Los Angeles" and "The System"), and Les did some wild contemporary fuzz guitar with radical string bending. He also wrote an unreleased book that was geared toward guitarists in the studio.

Gibson was also quite excited about his secret hi-fi guitar pickups, which were unveiled in 1969. The low-impedance pickups were what his pure guitar sound was all about, so it was time to share it with the world. His amazing LP-70 contact pickup (that could be used on any instrument, including piano, cymbal, or drums) was never released. It can be heard on Joe Bushkin's album *Play it Again… Joe.* Les proved his point with the pickup by setting up in a busy spot in Manhattan to record a band. There were pickups on the guitar, bass, piano, drums, and cymbals attached with a special adhesive tape—with no leakage of outside sounds. It sounded as though you were listening with your ears to the instruments. It was shelved and never released to the public. Meanwhile, Les was promoting the guitars and doing small endorsement concerts.

Les suffered a broken right eardrum in 1969 when Gibson rep Tiny Timbrel innocently cuffed his ears and said, "Guess who?" to surprise him. This unfortunate occurrence "blew his woofer" and created a series of ear operations that set his hearing back for a while. His previous hand injury and subsequent bone-grafting also started an arthritic condition that began to flare up from time to time. Being the perennial trooper, Les carried on despite these physical maladies.

(Above) The *Les Paul Now* Phase Four London LP with a twin-pickup LP SG Custom on the cover.

(Left) Decca's sixties re-release of Les Paul's 1940s swingin' mood instrumental material, including "Guitar Boogie," "Blue Skies," "Dark Eyes," and "Steel Guitar Rag." The flip side featured the best of his "Hawaiian Paradise" material.

This 1968 Gibson *Gazette* article was instrumental in re-introducing Les Paul to the new guitar world.

The letter from Les to Julius Bellson.

Les Paul

July 19, 1972

Mr. Julius Bellson
Gibson, Inc.
225 Parsons Street
Kalamazoo, Michigan 49001

Dear Julius:

This is to introduce Robby Laurence, who is writing a book on the development of the guitar.

I wrote you, but in the event the letter doesn't reach you in time I would appreciate any help you can give him.

Thank you.

Cordially,

Les

In early 1972, old friend Bucky Pizzarelli asked him to fill in on a standing gig that George Barnes had departed. Bucky had been playing with Goodman and as NBC's staff guitarist for a number of years and his chordal sense was impeccable—a perfect fit for Les. They started playing, with Les unannounced, and were an instant hit. Many celebrities frequented the St. Regis cabaret and marveled that Les was back in action. The response was great, stirring up feelings in him like the old days.

Visiting with Les Paul

In the summer of 1972, Steve Rodriquez and I traveled the country on our American guitar history safari. We visited with Les Paul and Wally Kamin on July 19th to conduct our first interview. Les graciously welcomed us into his Mahwah, NJ home and showed us around. We jammed and had a great time talking about everything to do with guitars and guitar players. He played some recordings, too. The following day, we came back and took pictures of his amazing guitar collection.

After visiting also with Harry West and Jimmy D'Aquisto, we headed to Kalamazoo to visit Gibson for the first time. Les had Wally Kamin type a letter of introduction to Julius Bellson. Off we went to see where Gibson guitars were built.

Les at his original "Monster" console with the big knobs, playing his Gibson classical guitar. Note the prototype low-impedance Les Paul thin body hanging on the wall.

297

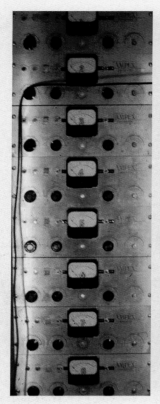

(Above) The original "Octopus" stacked eight-track recorders, given that name by W.C. Fields.

(Right) Les pickin' and smilin' on a beautiful day.

The Monster board in its heyday (1972), before Les upgraded.

(Right) The Ampex recorder with the extra playback head.

(Above) When Les broke out the old headless aluminum guitar, it became apparent how much work it took to keep it in tune.

McCabe's

In 1973, Les came out to L.A. to gig at McCabe's Music store concert venue. Les had made arrangements to play with the renowned West Coast bassist Leroy Vinnegar—"Master of the Walking Bass"—with Tom Bruner on back-up guitar. Les played a cool set of his favorites with the guys and we all had a great time.

Les having fun playing his recent Recording model in this early 1970s concert.

Les Paul performing at McCabe's Music in Santa Monica, CA, 1973. The great Leroy Vinnegar is on bass with Tom Bruner on guitar.

Bring the Boys to Mahwah

Our road trip across the USA and living with Les

Les invited me to come to the East Coast with him the following year and stay a while so I could engage publishers for my book on American guitars. Les and his son, Bobby, came by our home in San Diego to pick me up for the long journey. My parents could see how congenial Les was and later told me how comfortable they felt because he was so nice. They could tell I was in good hands for a new life journey, one that would carve a new niche in my life.

In early February 1975, we took off for a memorable trip across America. Normally a five-day drive at a reasonable moving pace without the sightseeing stops, we made it in three days! Our first night layover was in Tucson, AZ, where we met guitarist Harvey Moltz and Cathleen McDonough in the morning before departing eastward. Then we drove all day across scenic New Mexico and into the night through the wide expanse of Texas.

After a sleepover in the middle of nowhere, and another long drive, we finally got into Memphis. Les had just woken up as I was pulling into a small convenience store parking lot to get some refreshments. As we drank some pop, Les groggily said, "I'm going to drive now," so he took over and I got in the back seat. Next thing I knew, he was pulling out in front of a line of cars coming from the right while making his left turn. As we barely made the turn out of the driveway, we heard tinkling glass breaking behind us as the cars skidded to avoid us. Then, within a block, we hit the expressway and got out of Dodge. We still laugh about the incident from time to time.

We reached Cincinnati at dusk, and it looked like the sky was a hellfire red. We finally got into New Jersey early the next morning. As we drove down the main road toward Mahwah, Les said, "Nearby is where Edison had his laboratory for many years." Moments later, we pulled into his driveway off Deerhaven Road and soon settled into the house.

I stayed with Les, Wally, and his son Bobby in the Ramapo Mountains for four very interesting months. In my bedroom, I often played the original old Les Paul Custom, modified with Wally's special pickups. I think

this is the TV show guitar that had Doc's vibrola on it before. It was an interesting guitar to play, with the Bigsby tailpiece and strangely ground-down frets, as if someone (Wally, no doubt) just filed them without crowning and polishing them. When Les told me he liked them like that, too, I shook my head in wonder. Even though I would almost scrape my fingers across the frets, I thought it sounded incredible through his big studio amp.

After dinner, Wally would go in the office and type things while Les was on the phone. Bobby and I would jam in the studio, with him on drums and me on guitar or bass.

Driving in New Mexico before the long trek across Texas... that took almost 24 hours!

I used to play the unfinished Les Paul Triumph bass that was kicking around in the other office. It sounded quite amazing through Les's big low-Z Monster amplifier. I noticed that the amp would be uncontrollably loud with any normal guitar—even with his old Telecaster—because of the high pre-amp gain.

Les would eventually come down into the studio, plug in, and play some guitar with us. It was mostly blues stuff, of course, but we worked up a few tunes, too. This went on for a few months, along with lots of late-night popcorn. Later, Les played occasional local gigs, with Bobby on drums. I always thought Bobby was a very talented musician. Guess it runs in the family.

Hanging every day with Wally Kamin was also a special treat. He played with Les and Mary all those amazing years while married to Mary's sister Carol. I wish I'd recorded all the great tales he had to tell. The story about him wearing mismatched brightly-colored green and fluorescent-pink socks during concerts was priceless. Les would do a skit about it and everyone would laugh at his neon socks. Wally also told me how he would take a hot screwdriver to gouge holes into the guitars for the big low impedance pickups for Les. They were all covered over with big pickguards anyway, so it didn't matter. I told him it was a lot easier with a hand-held Dremel router. I still can't believe such things happened to vintage guitars.

We would take off for the grocery store every so often. Once, we were walking down the aisle and I saw some Listerine and said, "Do they still give you free Listerine?" Les replied, "Not anymore. They did for a while after the TV show stopped."

I would always pick out vegetables, rice, pasta, and various healthy things since I was a young vegetarian. Sometimes Les would take me to the health food store, too. He'd say, "You and my Mom and all this health food stuff!" But then he added, "You know, Robby, when I was young, eating all the natural foods and our homegrown vegetables with my Mom and taking naps regularly, a lot of things came into my mind about what I was going to do later. I did my clearest thinking back then and actually

thought of many ideas that later came to pass." I'll never forget that conversation.

While I was staying there, I would get inspired and write a few pages here and there on the different Les Paul guitars. Then one day Les and I sat down in the living room to write some notes with an outline on what he thought should be in the book, including various types of guitars and different guitarists to discuss. A few weeks later, we went into Manhattan to see his manager and called on a publisher. They were interested, but didn't want to publish a full-color book. The waters hadn't been tested yet.

One day Les asked if I wanted to see some more of his old guitars. This time I got to get a better look at what today he calls the "clunkers." There was a row of old Epiphone Zephyrs with removable backs. Each one had a different pickup setup, with either metal or plex-glass platforms with various controls and Doc's Vibrolas. I knew there was a lot of history in those boxes. Then I saw a dusty old Maccaferri Selmer guitar. Les informed me that was one of Django's old instruments that Django had given him. It was in a state of disrepair—there were no strings and an extra hole had been cut out of the top for a pickup.

An avid guitarist/collector friend, Phil Pierangelo, told me about a mint 1953 Les Paul Goldtop he just got and asked if Les might want to have it. Les said he was interested, since all of his were worked over. Phil sent it out to us and Les really liked it. He offered a trade of loads of guitar parts and Phil agreed, since he loved Les and could always use the parts. Les and I proceeded to go through the basement looking at various drawers full of amazing goodies. There were old PAFs, P-90s, load of rings and knobs, original unused pickguards, and a short-scale Standard fingerboard. I boxed up the stuff and sent it to California. At the time it was a good trade for both of them, but today the guitar is worth many times what the parts are worth.

The box of Les Paul's vintage parts he traded for the mint 1953 Goldtop. *Courtesy the late Phil Pierangelo, 1975*

Carnegie Hall

Les Paul officially came out of his retirement in style when he performed at the prestigious Carnegie Hall in 1975. On the bill was classical master Laurindo Almeida and jazz guitarist George Benson with his new protégé, a young Earl Klugh.

While riding the bus uptown from the Village, I struck up a conversation with a distinguished-looking fellow who was a jazz buff. I told him I was going to a concert to hear Les Paul. He commented, "Les is a great guitarist! His popular material with Mary Ford was amazing… but he's not really a jazz guitar player anymore." I was shocked at first and remembered, "He played plenty of jazz before to win those *Downbeat* polls. The pop material they did later certainly charmed the world." He said, "You're right. I'm a basically a jazz purist, though. I like the Charlie Christian and Carl Kress recordings and the way Barney Kessel plays today. I'm sure Les Paul is still a wonderful guitarist. Go enjoy yourself. It should be great tonight!" He got off the bus and in a few stops I disembarked near the concert hall. As I was walking, I reflected on the conversation and how artists often have to get into the popular trend to have commercial success. I was still very excited, anticipating Les Paul's first big comeback concert.

I arrived in plenty of time. Les soon introduced me to George Benson and Earl Klugh, then I took my seat just before Laurindo Almeida opened the show. With his tasty bossa nova jazz feel that mesmerized the audience, he was a master of nylon-string guitars. George Benson followed with the smooth and jazzy instrumental Verve material he was becoming famous for, showing his tasty Wes Montgomery octave styling. He then introduced Earl Klugh, who played his electrified nylon string beautifully. George came back out and they did a great duet together.

They wrapped it up as George introduced Les to the stage where he received a standing ovation. Bucky Pizzarella came out to accompany him. Being the consummate showman, Les immediately captivated the audience and continued playing a number of classics—from early hillbilly tunes to Bing Crosby. He recounted some past times, throwing in a few funny lines. Bucky once again did a superb job backing Les with his seven-string guitar. Les also included some jazzy stuff I knew he could do. For the finale, they all got up together across the stage and shared solos, hitting more than a few crescendos. What a night!

"Blow by Blow" Jeff Beck Concert

When Jeff Beck's landmark instrumental album, *Blow by Blow* (produced by George Martin of Beatles fame), was released, I made a point to play it for Les. He remarked that one cut especially reminded him of Roy Buchanan's playing (which was what Jeff had in mind). I told him Jeff was playing at Avery Fischer Hall in Lincoln Center with the Mahavishnu Orchestra soon and that he should see these monumental guitarists and meet them. Through John McLaughlin's office I made arrangements for passes and Bobby, Les, and I went to see the show. Beforehand, we saw Rick Derringer and Johnny Winters sitting nearby in the audience.

Jeff played beautifully that night, with Max Middleton on keyboards, Bernard Purdie on drums, and Clive Chaman on bass. He used the dark maroon '50s Les Paul guitar from the album cover and it sounded absolutely great. Afterward, we all went backstage to say hello. Jeff had told me in 1973 how much Les had influenced him and that he would love to meet him someday. When I said, "Jeff, I'd like to introduce you to Les Paul and his son, Bobby," Jeff did a double-take and almost fell over. He was overjoyed to meet his favorite guitarist in the world. Les told him how much he enjoyed the new album and they had a chance to get acquainted. This was the beginning of their long friendship.

Then I introduced Les and Bobby to John McLaughlin on the other side of the room. John was pleased to meet Les and was quick to point out, "Look! I'm playing one of your guitars," as he showed us his faded 1959 Standard on the table. John's custom double-neck had mysteriously fallen and broken recently, so he was doing shows with an old Sunburst. He mentioned he had been playing a Les Paul Custom (late '60s model) with Mahavishnu, too.

Hanging Back in L.A.

Les came to L.A. every few years for various things. He would call beforehand to let me know what's shaking. Often we would visit Del's home and studio and Mike Durloo's home video studio, or hook up with Zeke and go out to a delicatessen to enjoy great food. I also made a point to take Les to various recording studios to meet guitar players and producer/engineers. He very much wanted to be in touch with the music scene in L.A., too. We went to the Village Recorders studio in Santa Monica, the Record Plant, and Sound City where Carlos Santana was recording with Keith Olson. Carlos even gave him a vintage surround camera.

We also visited the Studio Instrument Rentals Sunset Stages rehearsal and rental building on the old Gower Gulch movie lot. This is at the Beachwood Street entrance on Sunset Boulevard, at the foot of the Hollywood sign. A lot of entertainment history was made for many decades at the original Columbia Studios. While we were in the back parking lot near Gordon Street, Les pointed out the house where he lived with Virginia and the kids when they first came to L.A.

Les checking out my 1960 cherry Standard, Hollywood, 1979.

Les in late 1978, enjoying playing Eddie Lang's favorite 1929 Gibson L-5.

Chester and Lester

While Chet Atkins was playing with Arthur Fiedler in New York, he and Les had the opportunity to jam together at the Warwick Hotel. Their performance sparked Chet to consider the possibility of doing an album with Les, something that could be very special. Roy Horton thought it would be great for them to do a record and had previously mentioned it to Chet. He was a music publisher and knew their playing together would be exceptional.

Les and Chet had met briefly many years before while Chet was tracking at an old radio station where Les had played with Wolverton. Les had also performed for years with Chet's half-brother Jimmy. Through the years, Chet (known as "Mr. Guitar") had become a legend himself, making numerous records of great guitar music. He also became the head of RCA Records in Nashville. Merle Travis was an immense influence on young Chester, who had developed the amazing Travis-style fingerpicking style to a new level of artistry. Chet also idolized Django and Les from growing up listening to the radio. He was fascinated with the verve both possessed. Now he and Lester were finally going to do their first album together in Nashville.

Les and Bobby flew to Nashville in early May 1975, just after the Carnegie Hall gig. The sessions took place over a period of several days and included many live takes of some of Les's favorites—"It's Been a Long, Long Time," "Caravan," "Avalon," "Deed I Do," and "Moonglow/Picnic." On much of the record, both did melodic lines together. They left in much of the banter between themselves. "Sounds good, Mary," said Les. "Why, thank you, honey," replied Chet on "It Had To Be You." At the end, Les said, "Do you know Mel Bay?" Chet retorted, "Let's send for it!" Chet used some of his harmonic melodies and gorgeous chording on that one, too. Les threw in all his tricks and Chet came right back at him with his own. Chet said he had to play faster as he ripped into "Avalon" and Les kept right up with him. Then

Cover for the GRAMMY®-winning album *Chester & Lester*, 1976.

they yakked while the bass and piano did their thing. Les hollered, "Leave it in. Two dirty old men. Massage parlor. You and I," as they all laugh. Some truly priceless exchanges were caught on tape that week.

Les used his 1958 white Custom LP with the Low-Z electronics and Chet used his signature Gretsch guitars. On some tracks, Chester had some chorus/flanging effects going on while Lester had his echo thing happening. Chet displayed some classic fingerpickin' on "Someday Sweetheart" and "Lover, Come Back to Me." Les and Chet were both in truly good form. Some of Nashville's best musicians were there to play on the tracks and had a hoot in the process. The rhythm section was so smooth it's worth listening to repeatedly. Only "Caravan" and "Lover, Come Back to Me" were overdubbed. The rest were live.

It was a fun experience that translated directly onto the recording and charmed everyone, including the NARAS folks. The jazzy album had a distinct country flavor that appealed to many for its warmly pleasurable listening experience. When released in February 1976, *Chester & Lester* did quite well. Chet came to New York for their interview on NBC's *Today* show. The truly spontaneous interplay, high-spirited jamming, and sheer magic between the two transpired into a GRAMMY® a year later, when they received the award for Best Country Instrumental Performance in February 1977.

They got together for another album, *Guitar Monsters*, the following year. Some of the more memorable tunes included "Over the Rainbow," "Brazil," "Limehouse Blues," "I Surrender, Dear," and "It Don't Mean a Thing (If It Ain't Got That Swing)." Chet added "Hot Toddy," which he'd done years before. To promote the record, Chet and Les did two sold-out shows at New York's famous Bottom Line nightclub. The album was released in June 1978 and rose to #13 on the *Billboard* Country charts.

Their second effort, *Guitar Monsters*.

Mary Ford

In 1968, Mary Ford married Don Hatfield, an old school sweetheart who was in the construction business. They lived in El Monte and then in Monrovia, CA. She occasionally played out and did some recording. She even made a promotional album sold in Ford dealerships, *A Brand New Ford*. Things had smoothed out between her and Les and she called the house from time to time. I had the pleasure of talking to her while living with Les. I told her about our wild trip and how much fun Bobby and I were having staying with Les. I'll never forget her wonderful speaking voice. I can hear it in my mind today.

Bassist Red Wooten had married Mary's sister Eva in the late 1950s. Red had played with the Woody Herman Orchestra and done some gigs with Carol and Bob Summers locally. Red also played on *Melody Ranch*, Gene Autry's television show, in 1965. After the divorce, Red eventually gigged with Bob and Mary, doing some of the Les and Mary hits. Red mentioned how much he enjoyed their records, but missed hearing a normal bass. So he got a real kick out of doing their popular material with Mary and Bob, adding his solid bass backing. Red remembers, "Mary, bless her heart, recorded a few of my compositions [never released]. She did an excellent job, as always."

Mary developed diabetes in her later years. After a problem with her insulin regimen and blurry vision, she was taken to the Arcadia hospital in a diabetic coma. The Summers family played music to Mary in the hospital, hoping to wake her. But Mary never woke up, and died of complications from pneumonia. The local El Monte newspaper ran the following obituary:

Singer Mary Ford Dies at 53

Singer Mary Ford has died after a lengthy bout with pneumonia after weeks in a diabetic coma, a hospital spokesperson said Saturday. Miss Ford, 53, the singing and guitar-playing partner of Les Paul on a string of silky harmonized pop hits in the 1950s, died late Friday, said Marilyn Morrison of Arcadia Methodist hospital. "She died after being here 54 days," Mrs. Morrison said. "Her cause of death was the insulin reaction that brought on pneumonia." Miss Ford, a diabetic, was admitted to the hospital in a diabetic coma August 8. Though she had retired from performing after her divorce from Paul in 1964, letters and phone calls poured into the hospital from people who remembered such Paul-Ford hits as "How High the Moon," "Vaya Con Dios," "Mockingbird Hill," and "The World's Waiting for the Sunrise."

An album Mary did for the Ford Motor Company in 1967.

Beautiful portrait of Iris Colleen "Mary Ford" Summers from 1951.

Mary Ford's gravestone in Forest Hills Cemetery, West Covina, CA.

Les Paul is interviewed for *The Wizard of Waukesha* movie.

Les with Wally and Eleanor Jones at home in Northridge, CA.
Courtesy Gail Bellows

The Wizard Movie

A New York film student named Catherine Orentreich had an assignment for her class project. She contacted me through Les Paul to collaborate on a modern documentary about Les called *The Wizard of Waukesha*. Catherine visited California to review some material and discuss the most important things to cover about Les Paul's career and the guitar's history. She had planned to do a 30-minute short, but it turned out to be a one-hour film. Preliminary arrangements were made for her film crew to visit Kalamazoo and shoot the guitar-making process

I asked Michael Bloomfield to do an interview with me about his relationship with the Les Paul guitar. Meanwhile, Catherine interviewed Rick Derringer in the studio and did a location shoot with Rich Friedman and Ace Frehley at the We Buy Guitars store on New York City's 48th Street.

Then Catherine and her crew headed out to Gibson to show the factory making Les Paul guitars. This footage is a highlight of the documentary. It is totally amazing to see if you're a Les Paul guitar devotee.

In California, I set up a filming session at record producer Norman Dayron's home in Mill Valley. Since Michael had recently left his '59 Standard at a club in Canada, Robbie Dunbar graciously loaned Michael his 1960 Flametop. Michael gave a wonderful description of how he became aware of the Les Paul guitar and its players, and how the sounds were different between the older Goldtop models and the sunburst Standard that he championed. The film was released in 1980.

Bypass Surgery

By 1980, Les needed to have his heart fixed. He sought out the best cardiologist team in the country to do his bypass surgery, and discovered one at the Cleveland Heart Clinic who agreed to take him. He was discharged six weeks later with flying colors. Les called and said everything was all right and that he was coming to California to visit Wally Jones and his family.

Wally's daughter, Gail Bellows, remembers, "When Les arrived, he had just had his surgery and was very weak. My parents took him home and nursed him back to health. My mom cooked special meals and had the correct food for him with the Atkins heart diet. It was about a six-month recovery while he got his strength back. Robby and my dad walked him around, which helped a lot. When he left back home, he was in excellent condition."

At Home with His Guitars

In 1981, concert photographer Neil Zlozower was asked by Japan's *Young Guitarist* magazine (*YMM Player*) to do a photo session with Les Paul in his home in Mahway, N.J. Neil headed out from L.A. and went up to the Ramapo Mountain retreat. Les broke out some noteworthy guitars, showed him the studio, the old cutting lathe, and took some portraits.

Lester with his disc cutter (lathe) machine.

Local audiophile Ralph, who spent much time up at the house with Les during the seventies and eighties.

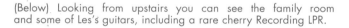

(Below) Looking from upstairs you can see the family room and some of Les's guitars, including a rare cherry Recording LPR.

Les showing a slew of guitar cases in his bedroom… the plight of many a guitar collector!

Les with his old L-5 next to the 1930s portrait with his first L-5 and harmonica rack.

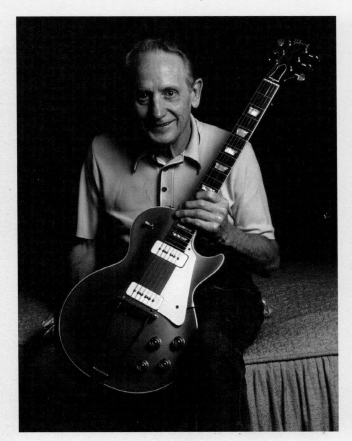

Les sitting on his bed holding the 1953 mint Goldtop I found for him, 1981.

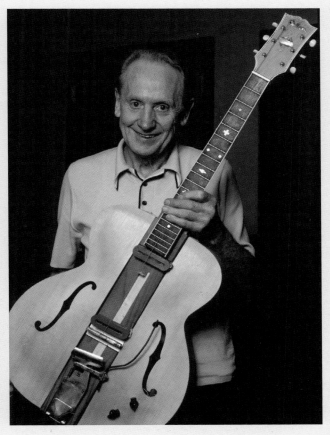

Les proudly shows one of his "Log" guitars—with the stripped L-12 neck, Epiphone body, and red fiber pickups.

Rock 'n' Roll Tonite

In late March 1982, Les called to say he was coming to L.A. to play with Jeff Beck. The show was to be at the old Raymond Theatre in Pasadena, known then as Perkin's Palace. He told me Jeff was flying in, as well as Billy Squier from Boston. Billy loves old Les Paul guitars, and when he arrived, he was quite excited to play with Les. The show was actually a television concert series called *Rock 'n' Roll Tonite*. Our rehearsal downbeat was the day before the taping. As I arrived and got Les's rig together and helped him dial in the Fender Twin amps, drummer Rick Jaeger and guitarist Jim Kreiger (both from Dave Mason's old band) showed up. Rick told me Mike Finnegan (keyboardist on *Electric Ladyland*) was also on the bill as I saw the Hammond B-3 being set up.

Jeff Beck arrived with his traveling assistant, Allen. As we all caught up a bit, I noticed Jeff had a big wrap around his left wrist. He proceeded to tell the story of slipping on a wet pavement on the way from his Corvette to a call box. He evidently passed out from the pain of falling on his wrist. He awakened to find his wrist in terrible pain, but not broken. A few weeks later, he was on the plane to L.A. for his first performance with his favorite guitarist, Les Paul.

Les had his trusty '58 white Custom with added Low-Z pickups and I got him plugged into a few Twins to be able to keep up with Mr. Beck. Les asked me to put his mock Paulverizer on the Bigsby tailpiece. It looked like he was switching on his old backstage contraption… but actually it was the empty box, since the PA guy had a Revox reel-to-reel ready to start Les's playback previously-recorded tracks. I wasn't to tell anyone, of course. Reggie McBride was getting set up and doing his fancy "quick lick" (like he's turning a magazine page) with his bass licks. Marty Grebb got his sax out to warm up a bit, filling out this kick-ass band for Les.

Billy Squire played his Telecaster during the sound check with Les and Jeff. Later, he and Les posed for me backstage in an interview room full of beautiful Les Paul guitars supplied by vintage dealer Frank Lucido.

During the show, while Les and Jeff were trading scorching leads, Les reached over and unplugged Jeff's guitar. Jeff simply laughed, kept going and soon tried to detune Les's guitar! Teching this show was great fun, with one of Los Angeles's best backup bands ever.

Les and Billy Squier sat down together afterward. I snapped a few photos as they made a number of crazy expressions.

Les lets loose and starts tearing it up as Jeff looks on in amazement—a sight most fans haven't seen since his days with Mary.

Things are starting to heat up with Les and Jeff.

Billy gets his solo going as Les and Jeff look on.

Billy Squier, Les Paul, Jeff Beck, Marty Grebb, and Jim Krieger performing at the
Rock 'n' Roll Tonite show, Perkin's Palace, 1982. *Photo by Neil Zlozower*

Billy Squier gets saddled up with his Telecaster and Mike Finnegan
has the B-3 cooking.

Les Paul and Jeff Beck rehearsing the day before the concert. It was
quite a special moment to see them sparring for the first time.

Les holding his own with the pros.

The New LP Trio & Fat Tuesday's

After great jams at home and a Staten Island show, left-handed jazz guitarist Wayne Wright got Les interested in gigging regularly. Gary Mazzaroppi was already on board as bassist for gigs. Instead of a cushy hotel setting, Les wanted an easy-going, intimate atmosphere. Through the grapevine, Fat Tuesday's owner Scott Alderman had heard that Les and company were looking for a venue. He thought the new Les Paul Trio would be a perfect fit for his club.

Fat Tuesday's was located in downtown Manhattan, on Third Avenue at 17th Street. It had a southern Louisiana flavoring of merriment, with good food and good music for one and all. Les checked it out and thought it was a perfect environment for being close to his audience. It was a crowded basement-type atmosphere he could thrive in. Scott gave the trio a Monday night slot that normally would be a slow night, but that could become something else entirely with the right music.

On March 26th, 1984, Fat Tuesday's hosted the first "Return of the Living Legend." To attract patrons to the initial show, Gibson got in on the act by having a contest with a free give-away Les Paul Studio guitar. Soon the word was out and the house was filled with lots of excitement and anticipation for the two shows, at 8:30 and 10:30 p.m. When Les came out of the backstage room, a standing ovation ensued as he walked through the audience, shaking hands on his approach to the stage. The shows were electrified that night as he played his sets, interspersed with great anecdotes that delighted the audience. The owner spontaneously announced (almost as a question to Les) that they would be regulars on Monday nights. Everyone roared and Les agreed right then.

It soon became almost like the old Club Rounders gigs in Hollywood. Les was now holding court in Manhattan for the whole world to come see him play—and boy did they come. Everyone who was anyone dropped in and had a play. The sign at the entrance said, "Come and hear the truth. See the Living Legend Les Paul on Monday nights!" Guys like Tal Farlow came up from Seabright, Barney Kessel would make an appearance

when he was in town, Lenny Breau, Paul McCartney, Jeff Beck, and Jimmy Page—the who's who of guitardom arrived and paid homage to the master. And of course his birthdays were something very special, with free champagne and cake for everyone. The most amazing musical guests would show up for the occasion. Eventually, Wayne left and Les asked Lou Pallo to fill in. He and Lou had played at Molly's Tavern near Mahwah when he was just starting to play again after his surgery. Lou had impeccable timing with his comping chords and also sang very smoothly.

Hollywood's Rock Walk Induction

In November 1985, Les took part in Hollywood's Guitar Center Rock Walk induction, the rock 'n' roll version of the nearby Graumin's Hollywood Theatre with hand and shoe imprints. We attended the function together

Twenty years later, Les Paul's handprints and signature are forever enshrined at the GC Rock Walk.

and met Robin Williams, Martin Mull, Jim Marshall, and Bill Ludwig. Loads of rock musicians also jammed the building. This was the first time Les had met Jim and they had an interesting time together.

Guitar Center's big new store on Sunset Boulevard was just a few blocks from Curson Street where Les had his famous garage studio. Les took Jim, Bill, and GC A&R man Dave Weiderman up the street to stand near where the original magic happened (was a Chevrolet dealership). With all the glitterati and hoopla, Les and the others put their hands into the cement alongside the other music and industry notables. That night, everyone partied and we listened to funny stories by both Robin Williams and Martin Mull.

Les signing his name at Guitar Center Rock Walk.
Courtesy Dave Weiderman

Strand Beach Show

Les, Gary, and Lou headed to California for a gig at the Strand nightclub in Hermosa Beach. The son of composer/comedic screenwriter Sid Kuller was running the club and had booked them to play. We did the sound check and had dinner upstairs as the room filled up. The first show was quite good and many stayed for the second set. Afterwards, I organized the fan line and Les came downstairs to sign autographs for everyone. Here are a few pictures from that show. Zeke, Bea Manners, and the Kachers were there, too. "It was a romping great job," Del remembers.

The Les Paul Trio playing the Strand nightclub in Hermosa Beach, CA.

Rock and Roll Hall of Fame

Les was inducted into the Rock and Roll Hall of Fame on January 20th, 1988. The gala event was held at New York City's famous Waldorf Astoria hotel. Fellow inductees included the Beatles, the Supremes, the Beach Boys, Leadbelly, the Drifters, Bob Dylan, and Woody Guthrie. Ahmet Ertegun began by praising Les and Jeff Beck. Jeff then presented the eight-inch bronze statuette award to Les in front of the stellar crowd.

> *Ahmet: Les Paul is an inspiration to a world of guitarists for his playing, for the instrument he created, and his multiple-track recording innovations. Without him, it is hard to imagine how rock and roll would be played today. Of the many guitarists who love Les Paul, not the least is one of my favorite all-time musicians, the great Jeff Beck, who will present our next inductee.*
>
> *Jeff: Thank you. I guess that I've copied more licks off of Les than anyone else. I showed him the speech that I was going to read out and he said that's worse than a United Airlines meal, so I won't bother. Suffice it to say, he's given me 33 years of inspiration and just general good vibes. So I'll hand you over to the man himself, Les Paul. [Everyone cheers, and the Letterman band plays "How High the Moon."]*
>
> *Les: I have less to say than what Jeff Beck had to say. To tell the truth, I happened to be driving by the Waldorf and I thought I would stop by to see what was happening here. (everyone laughs) I'd like to tell you I'm very honored. This is the first time anything like this has ever happened to me, that people have put together to give me something that's this nice. I have been credited with inventing a few things that you guys have run across that a few generations are playing with out there. About the most that I could say is: "Have a lot of fun with my toys!" Thank you.*

Then the 45-minute all-star jam started, featuring Neil Young, Bob Dylan, Mick Jagger, Billy Joel, Julian Lennon, Arlo Guthrie, and Bruce Springsteen. George Harrison did "I Saw Her Standing There" while Les got out front and played some guitar with George.

The concept for the Rock and Roll Hall of Fame originated in 1983 and the original museum was founded in Cleveland in 1986. Noted architect I.M. Pei later designed the amazing glass pyramid dome overlooking Lake Erie in 1995. Among the guitars displayed in their unique building is Duane Allman's Hot 'Lanta 1959 Les Paul, Dickey Betts's 1957 Goldtop, and Carl Perkins's '56 ES-5 Switchmaster. The extensive Les Paul and Mary Ford exhibit includes their wedding photo and a picture of Les's mother at 100 in 1985. It also features a video of the personal, technical, and musical aspects of Les Paul's life.

He Changed the Music

A 1988 Cinemax Sessions movie was made from a great concert called *Les Paul & Friends: He Changed the Music.* The show was held at the Majestic Theatre at the Brooklyn Academy of Music after three days of rehearsals. Guitarists included B.B. King ("Everyday I Have the Blues"), Steve Miller (who played a great rendition of "God Save the Children" on his Goldtop), Carly Simon ("It Happens"), David Gilmour (played a great solo with

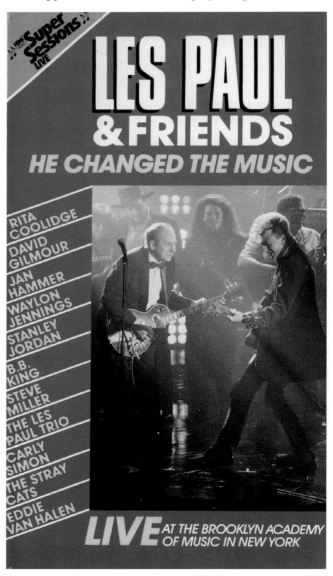

Video cover for *Les Paul & Friends: He Changed the Music.*

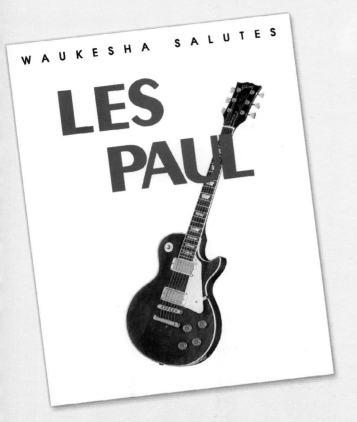

Program for the Waukesha event, saluting Les Paul and Evelyn's 100th birthday event.

Les at the 1999 TEC Awards with that year's Les Paul Award recipient Sting. *Photo courtesy of the Mix Foundation, photo by Alan Perlman*

his Stratocaster on "Deep in the Blues"), Jan Hammer, Stanley Jordan ("Georgia on My Mind"), Brian Setzer and the Stray Cats, Eddie Van Halen ("Echo Tribute" and "Back Pain Boogie"), Rita Coolidge, Waylon Jennings and his wife Jessi Colter. Les with his trio did "How High the Moon," "Lover," "Over the Rainbow," and "It's Been a Long, Long Time." It was a four-hour show, condensed for the video release and aired a few months later. It's a fun tribute concert to watch. Jan Hammer and Gilmour took it into the stellar reaches.

Waukesha Tribute

Lester's hometown of Waukesha, WI had a special event to show their appreciation. Les Paul's mom, Evelyn, was the special focus for her 100th birthday on March 30th, 1988. The party was held at the ballroom of the Country Inn near Pewaukee. The nearby park band shell where he used to perform as a young man was renamed the Les Paul Performance Center. Over a thousand people attended the big hometown event, including some of Les's oldest friends whom he grew up with. A proclamation for Les Paul Day was declared on Evelyn's birthday, even though it was her day. Les, Lou, and Gary did a few sets and Les told some funny stories about his old friends Harold Vinger and Claude Schultz. Many people danced, ate, and had a good time in Waukesha.

TEC Awards Hall of Fame, LP Award

A special Les Paul Award was created 1991 by the Mix Foundation (*Mix Magazine* and David Schwartz) for individuals or institutions that have set the highest standards of excellence in the creative application of recording technology—a fitting tribute for Les Paul. The Technical Excellence and Creativity (TEC) Awards are bestowed annually to recognize the achievements of audio professionals.

Since 1991, these Les Paul awards have been presented to various artists and producer/engineers including Bob Ludwig, Clair Brothers, Power Station, Bob Clearmountain, Peter Gabriel, Herbie Hancock, Alan Parsons, Brian Wilson, Stevie Wonder, Neil Young, Sting, Paul McCartney, Steely Dan, Robbie Robertson, Bruce Springsteen, Jimmy Jam & Terry Lewis, and David Byrne. Gibson has been sponsoring the awards since 1995. Sting and others were presented with a Gibson Les Paul guitar.

315

Les Paul: The Legend and the Legacy Box Set

In 1991, Capitol Records released the ultimate collectors' edition of Les Paul's career, spanning his early "New Sound" material and a great wealth of recordings with Mary Ford. It's quite entertaining and a good feel into the pop melodies of the day, featuring the sound of Les's slick studio trickery. Included are a few memorable TV show episodes, including the first—"The Case of the Missing Les Paulverizer," with Mary's great multiple-voiced skit—and a few commercials for Robert Hall clothing and Rheingold beer. A down-home take on "Walkin' and Whistlin' Blues," complete with footsteps, is also featured. *Guitar World* photographer John Peden provided some great pictures of three vintage Les Paul guitars and the Log for the CD and tape covers. The accompanying booklet is jam-packed with great artwork from Capitol's archives of their fabulous hit parade. This four-piece box set provides hours of Les and Mary music for your enjoyment, all beautifully remastered. Les made it out to California for this Capitol release and did a public appearance to sign autographs at Tower Records in Hollywood.

Back side of the box set, with Les and Mary behind the song titles.

Box set cover for Capitol's *Les Paul: The Legend and the Legacy*, released in 1991.

John Pedan's fine guitar photography is displayed on the booklet cover, CDs, and tapes for this special box set. Note Bryan Brock's '59 Les Paul Sunburst Standard.

Christopher Guest and Les Paul rehearsing for the Dennis Miller taping.

Cameraman Richard Ocean shoots a close-up of Les as the band grooves.

Capitol's 50th Anniversary

Les had a double-header whirlwind lined up for us this time. First we went to the KTLA studios for the Dennis Miller show taping. Actor/musician Christopher Guest, better known as Nigel Tuffnel of Spinal Tap fame, was also featured on the show. Chris's lovely wife, actress Jamie Lee Curtis came along. Chris brought his 1955 Goldtop and they did a run-through. Les graciously signed Chris's guitar and Jamie Lee strummed a few chords on Les's. Rusty, Del and Eiko Kacher were there, so we all sat together during the taping. Les was sharp-witted and congenial to host Dennis Miller. Christopher wore his Scottish kilt to play with Les and the band.

Les is interviewed by Dennis Miller.

Christopher Guest smiles as Les signs his 1955 Goldtop Les Paul.

(Left) Nigel Tuffnel arrives in his kilt to sit in with Les and the band.

317

After the taping, we piled into the limo and headed to the famous Capitol Records circular building for the label's 50th Anniversary gala party—with artists and alumni, live music, and dancing. Les—along with other artists like Anita O'Day and Kay Starr—was sitting in with Ray Anthony's big band. We were invited upstairs to see where *The Legend and the Legacy* four CD/tape box set had recently been mastered. I was amazed to learn that they used Formula 409® cleaner to stop the popping noises from the old 78 recordings.

When Les finally went onstage to a packed room of well-dressed guests, he played some great stuff and was wailing a few heavy lead notes when a string broke. Del remembers, "It was a very big celebration and it seemed everyone had a momentous time. Everybody who was anybody attended that party." As we left, they gave everyone copies of the Capitol 50th Anniversary book and CD collection.

Les wails away with the big band. What a night!

(Left) Many past and present Capitol artists pose for the camera. Les is on the left side.

Ray Anthony playing his trumpet with Les Paul.

Badge for the Capitol 50th Anniversary festivities.

AES (Audio Engineering Society) Speeches

In their heyday, Les and Mary were already doing octave-transposed tracks and tape-echo effects. Les first addressed the AES convention in 1952, announcing that multi-tracked tape recording was on the immediate horizon. He also pleaded for higher quality audio equipment and explained that someday a system would be developed that eliminated tape noise.

The Audio Engineering Society invited Les Paul to give another speech in the banquet hall at the Marriot Hotel in Manhattan. Stevie Wonder and Les were the guests of honor. Les gave a brilliant and funny speech, opening with, "It's great to be here tonight with all you folks… here on earth." The audience cracked up!

A nice warm moment on the stairwell with Les and Eiko Kacher. *Courtesy Del Kacher*

Les talked about his career and related several recording studio anecdotes. Most folks had thought it was going to be a boring old man talking. Instead, he knocked everybody on their ear, speaking for 45 minutes to an appreciative audience. The AES wanted to reprint it. Afterward, there was a party in the guest suite with Stevie Wonder and the guests. "It was a great night!" said Del Kacher, who had come out from Los Angeles with his wife Eiko.

Guitar Legends in Seville

Prior to the 1992 Olympics in Spain, a series of Guitar Legends concerts was staged at the La Cartuja Auditorium in Seville, the host city for Expo '92 Guitar Festival. Concerts began on October 15th and ran for five nights. They featured an array of artists that included B.B. King, Bo Diddley, Robert Cray, Stanley Clarke, George Benson, John McLaughlin, Larry Coreyll, Jack Bruce, Keith Richards, Bob Dylan, Steve Cropper, Dave Edmunds, Phil Manzanera, Brian May, Joe Satriani, Steve Vai, Nuno Bettencourt, Joe Walsh, Nathan East, and Brian May. Cozy Powell and Steve Ferrone played drums, and Paul Rodgers sang.

Each concert featured five artists doing a short set. Les Paul played on the night of October 18th, along with Roger McGuinn, Richard Thompson, Robbie Robertson, and Roger Waters. The backup band included Bruce Hornsby on keyboards, Manu Katche on drums, Tony Levin on bass, and Snowy White on guitar. Les performed "Brazil" and "How High the Moon." Each show lasted over two hours and was broadcast all over the world. An in-depth documentary on the guitar was also produced and shown during the events. The televised film shows the warmth of Les Paul's personality and the depth of his involvement with music. The Olympic-themed concerts were put on by Tony Hollingsworth's Tribute Productions and were intended to act as a preview for the following year's exposition.

Les Paul captured in Barcelona, Spain. *Courtesy Michael Morris*

319

The Living Legend of the Electric Guitar **Film**

In 1991, guitarist Jeff Baxter hosted a Showtime Networks Special on various significant guitar players. He interviewed Hank Marvin in Perth, WA via satellite and also included an interview with Les. This led to a 1992 film that begins with a brief overview of Les Paul's career and features 12 performances from a Fat Tuesday's set, interspersed with Jeff doing short interviews sections.

Allman Brothers/Jeff Healy

While in L.A. during 1993, Les asked me about going to see Jeff Healy, a talented blind guitarist from Canada that he had been talking to on the phone. Healy was playing with the Allman Brothers at the Verizon Ampitheater in Irvine. Les, Rusty, and I drove down and visited with Jeff in his dressing trailer just after his performance.

Then we all went backstage where I informed the Allman's tour manager I had brought Les down to visit. He quickly told the guys between songs, Dickey said hello and brought Les out and introduced him to the audience—to a standing ovation. The crowd was estatic and the energy was wild. Later I introduced Les to Greg, Woody, and Warren Haynes and took their photo. A rockin' good time was had by all.

Cover for *Les Paul: The Living Legend of the Electric Guitar* video.

Les with the late bassist Allen Woody after the show.

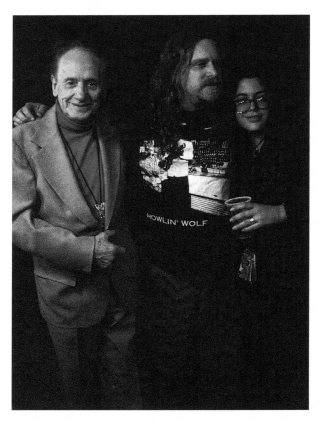

Les shows his illustrious smile with Warren and Stephanie Haynes.

Dickey Betts meets Les Paul onstage at the Verizon Ampitheatre, Irvine, CA.

The stage set-up, with "Muy Linda," vintage Les Paul guitars, and memorabilia for the event.

Gene Autry Museum/ Les Paul Day/TJ's Heart of Music Award

The T. J. Martel Foundation for leukemia, cancer, and AIDS research put on a series of events in May 1993. It was their 11th annual Rock and Charity Celebration featuring a Rock 'n' Bowl, baseball game, etc. There was also a special event at the Gene Autry Heritage Museum for Les Paul Day on Friday, May 21st. Included in the festivities was a Western party and dinner, a silent auction, an all-star jam, and a Les Paul birthday sing-along. Gibson, Guitar Center, and Capitol Records helped sponsor the show. Integral personnel included GC's Dave Weiderman, Gibson's Gypsy Carns, Capitol's Sujata Murthy and Clark Duvall, TJ Martel's Linda Archer-Weinstein and Scott Weinstein. Peter Huggins helped me with an extensive Les Paul stage display that touted our memorabilia and vintage guitars. I was honored to write the Les Paul Day Proclamation that Mayor Bradley signed for the event.

The Western party in the courtyard included movies in their theatre, a tour of the museum, and a great dinner. Wally Jones and family attended, along with the Zeke Manners family. Mary Ford's brother sat with us during dinner and related interesting stories of growing up with Mary. He also told us of his '59 green sunburst Standard flametop that he ordered new.

Then, out on the expansive lawn, the stage activities began. Les called me to the front of the stage for an intro-

duction to the audience, to thank me for the stage display and for helping organize the show. Then TJ Martell came onstage and presented the Heart of Music award. He read my Les Paul Day Proclamation and we all sang "Happy Birthday" to Les as they brought out the big cake. Mr. Martel and Les go way back to when he was a DJ in New York City, playing Les and Mary's records.

Les started his show with Del Kacher on backup guitar, jazz great Ndugu Chancellor on drums, and Jeff "Skunk" Baxter on bass. Les spoke highly of Judy Garland as they went into "Over the Rainbow." Their set was terrific and Del played a jumping solo chorus.

Soon the rock jam started, with Craig Chiquico and Rick Neilson on their vintage Les Paul guitars, Billy Sheehan on bass, and Ndugu on drums. Rick said, "Can anybody sing 'Crossroads'?" Guitarist Zinner jumped right up wearing his 1880s Western coat and sang a great version. He could have showed them a few licks on his '59, too. The second set was with our band, featuring Laurence Juber and yours truly on our old Les Pauls, Phil Chen on bass, Fred Mandel on keys, and Bruce Gary on drums. We did "Going Down" and then "Little Wing," to a standing ovation. TJ and Les came out and thanked everyone for coming. And of course, Les signed many autographs including Phil's jazz bass—right over the Fender decal!

The May 21st Les Paul Day Proclamation
written by this author.

The lovely Sujata Murthy from Capitol Records poses
with Les and his enormous birthday cake.

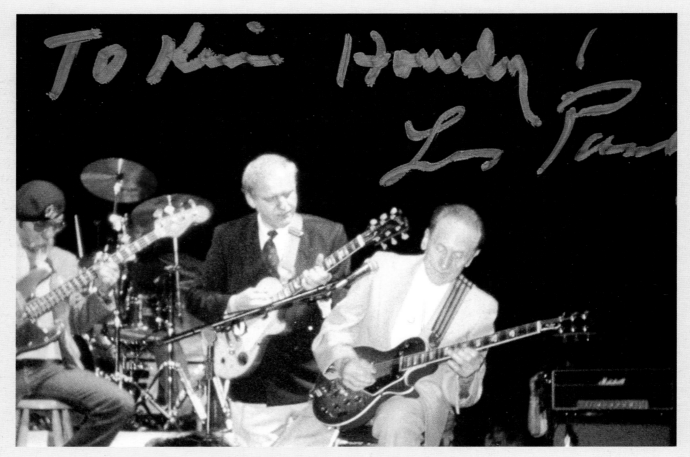

Les Paul performing with Del Kacher, Ndugu Chancellor, and Jeff Baxter. *Courtesy Kim Shaheen*

Playing Out West at the House of Blues

The House of Blues was conceived as a restaurant with music by comedian/actor Dan Aykroyd and Hard Rock Café founder Isaac Tigrett. The venture began in Cambridge, MA, and has become a chain of concert halls that serve Southern food and have a traditional Gospel Brunch on Sundays. The hit movie, *The Blues Brothers*, starring Aykroyd and John Belushi, helped spawn the idea. Other venues opened soon afterward, including Los Angeles, built on the property that formerly was John Barrymore's estate. The new building features corrugated tin roofing and sidings, as well as the dirt, alleged to be from the Missippippi juke joint where Robert Johnson played his last gig and was poisoned. Les first played at the House of Blues in Hollywood in May 1994. The first show, another tribute with an all-star lineup, was filmed for a special Time-Life/Warner *History of Rock 'n' Roll* video series.

When Les and Rusty came out to Los Angeles with the trio to play the House of Blues for the first time, many of Les's friends visited, including Zeke Manners, Wally Jones and family, Les's daughter Colleen and Mary's nephew Greg Corona. The show was jam-packed with famous musicians, too: Slim Jim Phantom (drummer from the Stray Cats), Jeff Baxter (guitar and bass), Steven Stills, Graham Nash, Johnny Rivers, Slash, Jeff Healy, Steve Vai, and Robbie Kreiger. The back line consisted of Twin-Reverbs for everyone, including the blonde Twin and Dual Showman cab for Les (for extra punch). Johnny Rivers played his sunburst '70s Deluxe through his modified Gibson GA-40 Les Paul amp that held its own with the Twins.

Throughout the evening, different players took turns coming out and playing with Les. It was quite the line-up for the ending song, "Rock Me Baby," with everyone playing. The whole show was filmed for the Time-Life/Warner special and was shown on their series, *The History of Rock 'n' Roll, Volume 7*, the following year. The last song track plays over the ending credits with Steve Vai and yours truly at the top of the mix.

The second show at the Hollywood venue was in April 1998 and featured a number of the same artists, including Jeff "Skunk" Baxter. Les's guests included KABC talk show host Ray Bream, the Kachers, Suzie Manners, and Gail Jones Bellows and her husband, Phil. Steve Vai did a splendid version of Gershwin's "Summertime" with Les, and then went into Jeff Beck's "Freeway Jam." The finale with everyone was Frankie Ford's "Roberta."

The big line-up for the Les Paul Tribute at the House of Blues. *Photo courtesy Susan Simmonds, 1994*

The Iridium Starts

In 1996, the Les Paul Trio became aware that Fat Tuesday's was closing, so it was time to find another venue. Gary Mazzaroppi had dropped out and a talented young local named Paul Nowinski had joined on stand-up bass. Wayne had other things going on with Buddy Rich, so the smooth-playing and -singing Lou Pallo joined up. Les had first met Lou Pallo, who was known in some circles as "the man of a million inversions," in 1963. The newly revamped trio soon discovered that the recently-opened Iridium club was interested in booking them. They made arrangements and started a new engagement, informing everyone of the move. The club was on its way to becoming one of the very best jazz clubs in all of Manhattan.

As you walk in front of the Empire Hotel across from Lincoln Center and Central Park at 63rd Street and 8th Avenue, you see a downstairs entrance for the popular nightclub Iridium. Now that Les and his trio had moved uptown, things started cooking again, with Lou Pallo on steady rhythmic guitar and Paul Nowinski on bass. Many amazing artists started showing up again, making the scene as happening as before. Guitarist/repairman Tommy Doyle continued on the soundboard while Rusty was still filming the shows.

The name Iridium is taken from the Latin word for "rainbow." It is an element in the platinum family and is white iridescent colored with a yellow cast. Its radiance and strength make it a great name for a classy club.

Lou is singing while Paul is keeping an eye on Lester.

Paul Nowinski's turn for a ripping solo with the trio.

The legendary LES PAUL TRIO
EVERY MONDAY

We are proud to present the legendary Les Paul trio for two sets every Monday night. One of the Jazz world's most important guitarists and innovators, Les continues to amaze his fans with his mastery of the instrument. Always the showman, Les can take his audience from the beauty of "Over the Rainbow" to a rocking "Happy Birthday". As the inventor of multitrack recording and the classic Les Paul Gibson guitar, he knows how to get a wide range of tone from his guitar. He can play a thick jazz sound and then by turning a few knobs and dials get the 50's sound that he also invented.

Musicians from all over the world flock to listen to Les and there are always celebrities on hand when he takes the stage. Les makes himself available to all his adoring fans and he's always gracious with autographs and photos. This is a must see act at Iridium that any night on the town must include.

Les having a ball playing his show-case Monday night gig at the Iridium.

Les getting serious at the Iridium, January 1997.

By 2001, owner Ron Sturm made the move over to 1650 Broadway, near 51st Street in the heart of theatre district. This visually exciting and intimate club was designed by Larry Bogdanow and Associates with split-level seating and a new Meyer sound system, Steinway piano, and recording studio set-up. The service and delicious food are world-class, too. This was a classy joint for Les and the trio to perform in regularly.

After seven years of great bass playing, Paul took a recording and road gig with Rickie Lee Jones, so Australian bassist Nicki Parrott joined the band. Her sexy style and fabulous bass playing struck a deep chord with Les and the audience right away. Her captivating and provocative performances meshed great with Les. Nicki's vocals were an added plus and she could keep the schtick going well with Les's shenanigans. As Les's arthritis got worse he hired young jazz guitarist Frank Vignola, whose Django influence was a welcome treat. He played his acoustic archtop with great verve… and just a microphone. Now, as a quartet, the band was really cooking!

Bucky Pizzarelli, the great Al Caiola, Charlie Daniels, and Al Dimeola—along with other amazing musicians— started showing up at the weekly showcase. Even Zeke Manners and Del Kacher came to pay tribute and have fun in the court of Les Paul at the Iridium.

Les and the management take great pride in the quality of their presentation, sound, and lighting at the Iridium— not only for the audience, but for the musicians, too. As with his big concerts, the complete sound check with his team is essential every Monday afternoon. This professional attention to detail is an integral part of the Les Paul experience. Les's talented musicians and crew are like family and they strive to make every show their best. Go see them when in New York. It's a truly exciting experience. No wonder the line goes around the block every week!

The new Iridium street entrance on Broadway, 2005.

Bucky Pizzarelli shows up with his seven-string to play with Les. *Photo courtesy TJ McGann*

Long-time Les Paul player Charlie Daniels sits in with the house Les Paul Studio guitar. *Photo courtesy TJ McGann*

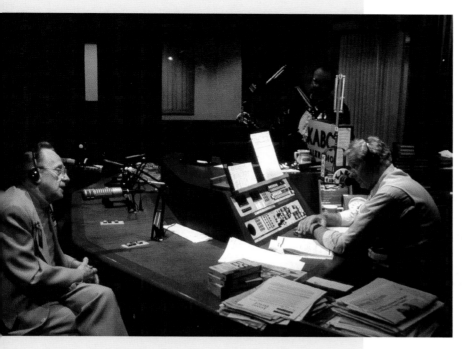

Les being interviewed by late-night talk show host Ray Bream, 1997.

Ray Bream Talk Show

Over the years, Les did several stints on KABC radio with late-night talk show host Ray Bream. During the course of the three-hour shows, Les gave informative interviews and answered provocative questions from radio listeners. One evening in 1997, a lady called from Pasadena who was actually speaking from the original Curson Street house. She told how they transported it right down Sunset Boulevard during the middle of the day.

Smithsonian, New Jersey, and Wisconsin awards

In 1996, Les Paul was awarded the John Smithson Bicentennial Medal by the Smithsonian Institution. Marc Pachter interviewed Les during the "Evening with Les Paul," discussing his career and his advancements in recording and guitar technology. The interview was filmed and also aired on National Public Radio. Numerous guitarists were on hand and Les signed guitars afterwards.

The New Jersey Inventors Hall of Fame inducted Les Paul in February 1996, for his contributions to the development of the electric guitar and multitrack tape recording. At the ceremonies, other inventors were also honored for developing the bar code, innovations in microphones, chlorinating water, and the flight simulator.

Les Paul returned to Madison, in his home state of Wisconsin, to receive the first Lifetime Achievement Award from the Wisconsin Foundation for School Music on October 27th, 2004. Being one of the most influential musicians in their history, governor Jim Doyle stated that Les dramatically changed the landscape of music and that everyone who enjoys rock music should thank Les Paul. Les hadn't been back since his mom turned 100 in 1985. He reminisced about his musical beginnings, growing up in nearby Waukesha. He told the story of how his piano teacher, Mrs. Wilson, pinned a note on him to take home that said, "This fella isn't going to make it," since he couldn't read music, even though he played music by ear.

Les is also a member of the Tau Kappa Epsilon Fraternity, founded in 1899 at the Illinois Wesleyan University in Bloomington, IL. Other noted entertainment members include Willie Nelson, Elvis Presley, Lawrence Welk, Ronald Reagan, Danny Thomas, and Merv Griffin.

Commercials: Coors/Gibson (1997)

Les went on television once again in a snappy commercial with a young man who is interested in guitar. After jamming, the guy asks Les his name and Les points at the headstock of the guitar. Toyota also did a commercial in 2005 with a vintage Les Paul Goldtop guitar, comparing it to their stereo system.

GRAMMY® Technical Award

In February 2001, Les received a special award during the 43rd GRAMMY Awards® Nominee Reception and Special Awards ceremony at the California Science Center in Los Angeles. Both Les and Digidesign received the Technical GRAMMY Award® "For individuals and/or companies who have made contributions of outstanding technical significance to the recording field." Lifetime Achievement awards were given to the Beach Boys, Tony Bennett, Sammy Davis Jr., Bob Marley, and the Who. Tony Bennett, Al Jardine, Rita Marley, and John Entwistle personally accepted the awards. Arif Mardin and Phil Ramone received the Trustees Award and both gave nice speeches and made kind references to Les Paul, as did Tony.

A series of short films was produced by NARAS®, including one on Les for which I contributed artwork. Les gave a memorable speech about his contributions to the recording world. The GRAMMY® High School Jazz Ensemble also performed on the lower level of the museum. The following night, Les went to the big show and received his award, but wasn't shown on television.

2001
GRAMMY Awards
Nominee Reception
& Special Awards
Ceremony
California Science Center
February 20, 2001

Les and yours truly with the NARAS® film production gang.

Producer Phil Ramone having a word with Les after the ceremony.

House of Blues

Anaheim/Hollywood

In April 2001, Les and his trio did a show at the House of Blues, Anaheim, near Disneyland. On the bill was Dave Edmunds, Jeff Baxter, and Eric Sardinas on bottleneck Dobro guitar. The rehearsal consisted of Eric Sardinas playing some cooking blues with his slide workout. Then Edmunds did some amazing finger-picking stuff and Les, Jeff, and Dave discussed the finale. We got Les's guitar/amp rig dialed in with Rusty and it was a go for the trio to do their run-through. The staff of the new HOB was quite gracious and bent over backwards to be helpful to us.

Les having a ball onstage at the HOB, Anaheim.

The show began with Les, Lou, Nikki and Frank. They launched into "Making Whoopie" and Lou started singing while Les did his whoopee sounds. Someone yelled, "Play it, Les!" and Les replied, "Please." Then they got "Caravan" going and Frank did a spellbinding solo. The audience ate it up! Les started talking about Bing Crosby and segued into "It's Been a Long, Long Time." Lou started to play softly and Les began to imitate Crosby and everyone laughed. Les started telling jokes while Lou played "Won't You Come Home Baby." Then they got serious and went into "Over the Rainbow," with Les doing his close-to-the-bridge picking. At the end, he took a quick look at his watch before playing the last line and everyone laughed again. They went into "How High the Moon" and Nicki did a neat bass solo while Lou comped light chords.

The next night, Les played at the Hollywood HOB. The big lineup included Slash, Skunk, Dave Edmunds, and Eric Sardinas. After the show, we headed back to the hotel and conducted an entertaining interview specifically for the Les Paul Forum. Another great experience in a day in the life of Les Paul.

Les introducing Dave Edmunds.

Ryman Auditorium Tribute Concert

For many years, Nashville's historic Ryman Auditorium was home to the Grand Ole Opry. It is downtown, just a block above the clubs and George Gruhn's vintage guitar store. Talented guitarist Muriel Anderson organized her 27th bi-annual music concert series and star-studded guitar night to tie in with a Les Paul tribute. A beautiful brochure was designed with a series of congratulations from many companies and sponsors, and a note from Muriel. The bio, proclamation, and a foldout timeline of Les Paul's career were written by this author. Leslie Turner was instrumental in pulling the whole show together for Muriel Anderson. Nokie Edwards, Hubert Sumlin, Seymour Duncan, Dave Pomeroy, Ken Lovelace, and Scotty Moore were in attendance.

The 2004 show featured the great Hubert Sumlin, guitarist for the blues master Howlin' Wolf. This gifted musician is truly a class act in the blues world today and played Les Paul guitars during the fifties. Singer David Johanson, bass player Dave Pomeroy, and guitarist/pickup specialist Seymour Duncan played with Hubert. Steve Morse and his protégé performed amazingly. Nokie Edwards and his lovely wife Judy were there. Nokie played some great stuff with Jerry Lee Lewis's guitarist Ken Lovelace. Tom Bresh (Merle Travis's son) and Muriel Anderson performed and made a presentation to Les with a proclamation. Henry Juszkiewicz made a presentation speech (written by yours truly) and had one of the old "Log" guitars from the museum brought onstage. Elvis's guitarist, the gracious Scotty Moore, attended and sat just behind us. I was honored to be the announcer for the show, help with the program, and write the proclamation.

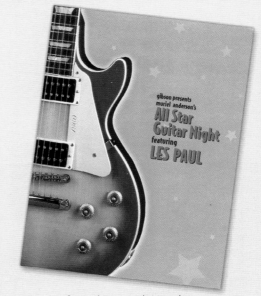

Program for Gibson and Muriel Anderson's All Star Guitar Night.

Les appreciates the proclamation presented by Thom Bresh and Muriel Anderson.

Informative Les Paul timeline spread.

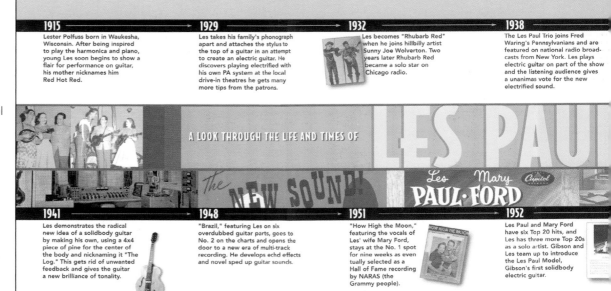

1915
Lester Polfuss born in Waukesha, Wisconsin. After being inspired to play the harmonica and piano, young Les soon begins to show a flair for performance on guitar, his mother nicknames him Red Hot Red.

1929
Les takes his family's phonograph apart and attaches the stylus to the top of a guitar in an attempt to create an electric guitar. He discovers playing electrified with his own PA system at the local drive-in theatres he gets many more tips from the patrons.

1932
Les becomes "Rhubarb Red" when he joins hillbilly artist Sunny Joe Wolverton. Two years later Rhubarb Red became a solo star on Chicago radio.

1938
The Les Paul Trio joins Fred Waring's Pennsylvanians and are featured on national radio broadcasts from New York. Les plays electric guitar on part of the show and the listening audience gives a unanimas vote for the new electrified sound.

A LOOK THROUGH THE LIFE AND TIMES OF LES PAUL

The NEW SOUND!

Les Mary Capitol
PAUL · FORD

1941
Les demonstrates the radical new idea of a solidbody guitar by making his own, using a 4x4 piece of pine for the center of the body and nicknaming it "The Log." This gets rid of unwanted feedback and gives the guitar a new brilliance of tonality.

1948
"Brazil," featuring Les on six overdubbed guitar parts, goes to No. 2 on the charts and opens the door to a new era of multi-track recording. He develops echd effects and novel sped up guitar sounds.

1951
"How High the Moon," featuring the vocals of Les' wife Mary Ford, stays at the No. 1 spot for nine weeks as even tually selected as a Hall of Fame recording by NARAS (the Grammy people).

1952
Les Paul and Mary Ford have six Top 20 hits, and Les has three more Top 20s as a solo artist. Gibson and Les team up to introduce the Les Paul Model, Gibson's first solidbody electric guitar.

Gibson CEO Henry Juszkiewicz makes a presentation with the "Log" guitar.

Henry Juszkiewicz and Les Paul during the reception beforehand.

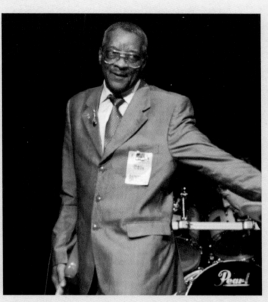

Nokie Edwards and Ken Lovelace, Jerry Lee Lewis's guitarist, backstage.

Hubert Sumlin thanks the audience after his performance with Seymour Duncan and Dave Pomeroy.

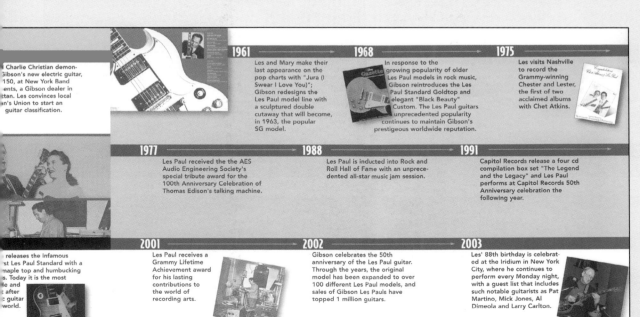

Charlie Christian demon- Gibson's new electric guitar, 150, at New York Band ents, a Gibson dealer in tan. Les convinces local n's Union to start an guitar classification.

1961
Les and Mary make their last appearance on the pop charts with "Jura (I Swear I Love You)"; Gibson redesigns the Les Paul model line with a sculptured double cutaway that will become, in 1963, the popular SG model.

1968
In response to the growing popularity of older Les Paul models in rock music, Gibson reintroduces the Les Paul Standard Goldtop and elegant "Black Beauty" Custom. The Les Paul guitars unprecedented popularity continues to maintain Gibson's prestigeous worldwide reputation.

1975
Les visits Nashville to record the Grammy-winning Chester and Lester, the first of two acclaimed albums with Chet Atkins.

1977
Les Paul received the the AES Audio Engineering Society's special tribute award for the 100th Anniversary Celebration of Thomas Edison's talking machine.

1988
Les Paul is inducted into Rock and Roll Hall of Fame with an unprecedented all-star music jam session.

1991
Capitol Records release a four cd compilation box set "The Legend and the Legacy" and Les Paul performs at Capitol Records 50th Anniversary celebration the following year.

releases the infamous st Les Paul Standard with a mple top and humbucking s. Today it is the most le and after c guitar world.

2001
Les Paul receives a Grammy Lifetime Achievement award for his lasting contributions to the world of recording arts.

2002
Gibson celebrates the 50th anniversary of the Les Paul guitar. Through the years, the original model has been expanded to over 100 different Les Paul models, and sales of Gibson Les Pauls have topped 1 million guitars.

2003
Les' 88th birthday is celebrated at the Iridium in New York City, where he continues to perform every Monday night, with a guest list that includes such notable guitarists as Pat Martino, Mick Jones, Al Dimeola and Larry Carlton.

A series of photographs of Les Paul with myriad expressions over a period of five minutes during the Ryman Tribute show.

Hard Rock Café Les Paul Pins

The Hard Rock Café is a chain of popular dining spots where fans can enjoy rock music displays in many major cities of the world. Isaac Tigrett and Peter Morton began their venture in Hyde Park, London, in 1971 and later expanded to Los Angeles, San Francisco, and elsewhere. The excellent fare is superfluous to the rock 'n' roll atmosphere, which is the main attraction. Their collection of musicians' instruments was obtained at auctions and from private owners and is the largest in the world. Much of it is now on display in Orlando, FL. Through the years, they have amassed plenty of great Gibson Les Paul models, including one of Jimi Hendrix's Flying V guitars. Their decorative and colorful pins are popular souvenir mementos and an active business with collectors worldwide.

They have since incorporated live music at many venues and host some of the fabulous Les Paul birthday parties.

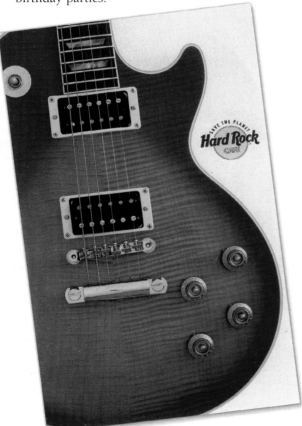

Hard Rock Café menu for La Jolla, CA.

La Jolla HRC souvenir brochure.

(Above) San Francisco Hard Rock Café menu with LP Standard Plus.

These examples of Hard Rock Café pins include San Diego, Acapulco, Las Vegas, Denver, New Orleans, and Salt Lake City.

Jim Marshall on Les Paul

With the British invasion and popular blues artists of the sixties came the inimitable tone of the Gibson solid-body turned up full through a new breed of tube (valve) amplifiers. One in particular was Jim Marshall's line of fine high-powered amplification. The Marshall brand soon caught on with the discerning players who got a big sound with their vintage Les Paul guitars.

Jim Marshall discusses Les Paul and the various musicians who used the guitar through his legendary amplifiers.

Robb Lawrence: *Jim, you told me years ago that Mitch Mitchell took lessons from you.*

Jim Marshall: *Oh, yes. Well, I had a very large drum school during the fifties. I had 64 pupils a week. That was 64 hours per week. Then I would get up at four o'clock in the morning, writing out drum scores to sell to the pupils as well. And I was very successful at it. I made lots and lots of money teaching drums. Then I decided to open a drum shop, which turned out to be a drum and guitar shop because Pete Townshend, Ritchie Blackmore, and Big Jim Sullivan (who is still one of our top session guitarists), came to see me and said, "Why don't you sell guitars and amplifiers?" I said, "Well, I'm a drummer, you know. I've opened a drum shop." But I hadn't opened it then when they tackled me with their pupils… because I taught all their drummers. So they talked me into turning it into a guitar shop as well. And it was very successful. They said to me, "If we go into the West End, we're treated like idiots because we play rock 'n' roll." In the West End they obviously thought orchestral music was going to still carry on with the big band, you know. But they were wrong, fortunately.*

RL: *So you had a successful shop and you decided to make amplifiers…*

JM: *The same people came to see me and said, "Look, we use the Fender Bassman because it's near the sound sort of thing, but not very near. We'd like you to manufacture an amplifier that would be good for rock 'n' roll." So I said, "I'll have a go." And they explained to me the sound they wanted. To me it was obvious they wanted the harmonics of the tube (valve), and that's what we worked on. First of all, we turned out six prototypes. The first five I turned down because I didn't like the sound. Number six I said to my two engineers, "That's going to be the sound of Marshall forever." Fortunately, it has been.*

RL: *This was a 1959 or 1960 Bassman?*

JM: *Oh, I don't know. They were all using Fender Bassman amplifiers, so I couldn't tell you exactly what it was.*

RL: *It was a 5F6-A circuitry with the four inputs. So you made your first amplifier in 1962?*

JM: *We started designing in 1961. It took quite a bit of time tracking down components and that sort of thing. And then in 1962, I let it loose in the shop one Saturday and we sold 23 the first day!*

RL: *Wow!*

JM: *It's true all the guitarists would come to my shop, you see, to try out guitars and whatever.*

RL: *So the Les Paul guitar was being used through your amplifier.*

JM: *Yes.*

RL: *How do you feel about that sound?*

JM: *The Les Paul guitar, to my ear, was the best sound of the lot through our amplifier. But we used the Fender Stratocaster as well. So we would know it was workable with the two leading guitars of the time. The Gibson Les Paul was definitely the leading one.*

RL: *You told me years ago that Eric Clapton originally used his Les Paul guitar through your 4-10 amplifier.*

JM: *We made the 4-10 combo for him. That was the first 4-10 combo that was made for Eric Clapton… He came in the shop a lot, actually. On this particular occasion, he said to me, "I'd love to have a 4-12 and a 50-watt head, but I'll never be able to get it in my car. I don't know what to do about that." So I said, "Let me have a go at making a combination for you." It was the first combination we made for his Gibson Les Paul. It was the first combo in those days.*

RL: *The 1961 model.*

JM: *It became known as the "Bluesbreaker" combo, but I forget the number. So I did all the cabinet work and made all the chassis and all that as I always did. And it turned out to be very good because the 4-10s carried the volume whereas the 2-12s wouldn't. They blew because they took only 25 watts each. And the amp peaks at 67 or 68—somewhere in there—so we were blowing speakers when we used 2-12s.*

RL: *Eric also had a 2-12 combo after his original one was left in Greece. Then he switched over to the 2-12 model that he used on the John Mayall Bluesbreakers album.*

JM: *That's right. I bought a 4-10 combo amplifier from Guitar Center while I've been over here this week, because I've never had a 4-10 in my museum. (laughs)*

RL: *And then Jimmy Page came along and he had his Les Paul guitar and your amps.*

JM: *Yes. He had a stack. Most of them wanted a stack.*

RL: *What are your thoughts on your relationship with Les Paul?*

JM: *We've been great friends for years. It was funny… quite a few years ago, he came up behind me and threw his arms around me. I just looked down and said, "Hi ya, Les!" I don't think he knew how I could tell by him just putting his arms around me, but he's got this bad hand, you see, and I recognized it every time. (laughs)*

When I got back from the Mexican show last year, I went to the club where he was playing in New York. He said, "Sorry Jim, I haven't got a drum kit on the stand." I said, "It's alright, Les." He said, "Could you still sing a few numbers?" I said, "Yes, by all means." I sang three or four numbers and he was very happy. (laughs) At the end of the evening, we had crowds for autographs from both of us.

José Feliciano talks with Nicki Parrott and Les Paul before performing. *Photo courtesy Chuck Burge*

Close-up of the finale with Peter Frampton, Kenny Wayne Shepherd, Lou Pallo, Joe Satriani, Steve Lukather, Pat Martino, Steve Miller, and Will Lee. *Photo courtesy Chuck Burge*

Stanley Rendell, past president of Gibson, chums with Les at the party.

The whole congregation is onstage for the finale, led by Jon Paris.

Les Paul's 90th Birthday

Carnegie Hall

June 2005 marked the 90th birthday of Waukesha's own Lester Polsfuss, known as Les Paul to the larger world. The year was full of many special events commemorating his birthday, all leading up to a gala performance at Carnegie Hall, produced jointly by Bob Cutarella of Capitol/EMI and Gibson for the JVC Concert Series. An amazing array of talented musicians lined up to perform, many of whom also played on the new release.

Naturally, everyone's anticipation was very high coming into the venue. The attendees were all very well dressed and excited about being there. The show sold out quickly, so our small party of Les Paul's West coast friends ended up being seated high in the balcony. The show began with a short biographical film that showed Les's background and his multitude of achievements. It went on to discuss his long-standing association with Gibson.

Steve Miller came out first and gave a little background on his family's long relationship with Les and Mary. He told of getting his first guitar lessons from Les, then launched into a killer rendition of "Fly Like an Eagle." Guitarist Kenny Wayne Shepherd played the soulful Texas-flavored tune "Shame, Shame, Shame." Edgar Winter with Derek Trucks did a few tunes on piano and guitar, too.

Steve Lukather, Will Lee on bass guitar, and Omar Hakim on drums formed the basic backup group. Neal Schon did a blistering blues number with the remarkable vocalist Karen "Lilias" White. José Feliciano performed a memorable song about a famous battle, using some fascinating rhythmic segments. Australian artist Tommy Emmanuel's commanding performance on "Mombassa," with the added percussive effects on his well-worn acoustic guitar, brought a standing ovation. Joe Satriani donned a Les Paul guitar on a blazing tune as well.

The second half of the concert was more laid back with the man of honor performing with his current trio (that now includes pianist John Colianni on a gold piano), much more in the jazz vein. Wonderful renditions of "Blue Skies" and "Over the Rainbow" ensued before his collaborations with Derek Truck's slide work on "Good Night, Irene." Then beautiful Madeleine Peyroux sang the hit tune Les did with DerBing, "It's Been a Long, Long Time," while José Feliciano picked up the pace on "How High the Moon." Steve Miller came out again to sing Nat King Cole's hit, "Nature Boy."

(Above) The nifty Les Paul 90th birthday button.

The show finished with a final lineup of all the artists, with singer/harmonica player Jon Paris leading the finale. Everyone's solos ensued, showing the incredible diversity of talent that came together for this special event.

Afterward, Les and guests boarded the big Gibson bus and headed to their New York headquarters/studio complex. It was quite the affair, with everyone visiting the studio and control room, and perusing the Gibson instrument showroom. A small concert hall downstairs featured live music and the big birthday cake. The jam session was really cooking, so I played several heavy blues tunes. CEO Henry Juszkiewicz got up for a few, too!

Pat Martino plays a demo Epiphone Goldtop.

The festive birthday cake, with Gene Martin's wild picture of Lester.

Michael Braunstein (Les's manager), Bob Cutarella, Bob Gagnon (Capitol rep), Les Paul, and Herb Agner (Capitol rep) pose for pictures.

Henry Juszkiewicz jams at the party downstairs!

Les performing at the Iridium for his 90th birthday party.

Les and Steve Miller enthralled with each other.

The Iridium Celebrates

The following night was the Iridium's special 90th birthday bash for Les Paul. Tommy Emmanuel, Muriel Anderson, Steve Miller, and Stanley Jordan were the musical guests for the first set that evening. Authors Michael and Russ Cochran were on hand since their new limited edition of the autobiography *Les Paul: In His Own Words* had just been released. After Les and the trio did some tunes, Tommy Emmanuel came out and played up a storm. His percussive tapping on the guitar is dramatic, much like a timbale player. Muriel did her remarkable fingerstyle material to the audience's delight. Stanley Jordan came out with the first birthday cake and everyone sang "Happy Birthday." Stanley then proceeded to show how lyrical the guitar can sound, playing with both hands, piano style.

Nicki Parrott playing her bass and having a really good time.

Steve giving Les his 90th-birthday cake.

Stanley Jordan delivers another 90th birthday cake!

Les back at it, having a good time tonight.

Multi-instrumentalist Jon Paris plays harmonica with Lester.

Les Paul and Friends

The album American Made, World Played

To bring it all together, a new album was in the works. EMI/Capitol producer Bob Cutarella masterminded the effort with co-producer Fran Cathcart, who owns Eastside Sound in New York City. With the able assistance of Marc Urselli and other revered engineers, the record proceeded with professional expertise. Rob Christie and Kevin Flaherty were the EMI A&R producers, with Phil Quartararo the executive producer. Recorded on both coasts, and with a few tracks done at the artists' home studios, this wonderful tribute to the 90-year-old Les Paul was a culmination of combined efforts on a modern technological platter.

The roster for this project included many of the world's greatest guitarists, new soulful singers, and recordings of one of the most beloved singers of our age—the great Sam Cooke. Les Paul played on every track. This album is a guitar lover's dream-come-true. Long-time friend Steve Miller wrote the touching liner notes. EMI/Capitol released the recording on August 20, 2005 to critical acclaim. It also did well in Europe. Les won two GRAMMY Awards® and has the distinction of being the only person over 90 years of age to win.

The old radio show recording of Les talking about the Paulverizer comes up and Mary is saying, "You're not going to fool with that again?" A modern hip-hop groove gets going for a new version of "How High the Moon," with Russian songstress Alsou. Also, we hear a five-year-old Steve Miller singing. Les says, "Come over, Steve. Hey, that was very good. You want to know something? You've got a good, good voice. I think you should keep singing like that. That's what I did when I was a little guy." Steve says, "The more I do it, the more embarrassed I get!" Les adds, "Steve, you're really going to go places," as the echo fades out. Then Steve's new version of "Fly Like an Eagle" starts. The song includes Gordy Knudsen on drums, Billy Peterson on bass, and Joseph Wooten on keyboards. A very fine track, recorded at Sailor Studios.

The Capitol Records building in Hollywood.

Marc Urselli and Fran Cathcart holding their gifts from Les Paul.

Producers Bob Cutarella and Fran Cathcart with Joss Stone at the Record Plant, Los Angeles. *Photo by Chris Mongiello*

Fran and Bob with Billy Gibbons, sharing a happy moment at Capitol. *Photo by Chris Mongiello*

Eastside session for "All I Want Is You," with Shawn Pelton, Bob Cutarella, Steve Zuckermand, Will Lee, Fran Cathcart, Marc Urselli, and Peter Frampton.

Photos courtesy Bob Cutarella, Fran Cathcart and supplied by Marc Urselli

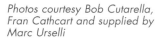

Capitol session with Vinnie Colaiuta, Hiram Bullock, Greg Mathieson, Abe Laboriel, Sr., Neal Schon, Chris Mongiello, Fran, and Bob. *Photo courtesy Bob Cutarella and Fran Cathcart*

Eastside session with Bob, Alsou, Fran, and Marc Urselli.

The man himself, signing a Les Paul guitar, with producer Bob Cutarella. *Courtesy Fran Cathcart*

Les during his recording session at Eastside Sound studios. *Courtesy Fran Cathcart*

Les laying down a track on his latest album. *Courtesy Fran Cathcart*

Visiting Waukesha

In July 2007, I made a trip to Waukesha to visit the old stomping grounds of Les Paul. First I visited the beautiful Waukesha County Historical Museum. The folks there are spearheading a much-anticipated project that will feature the exhibits of the Les Paul Experience. The various displays and interactive areas will be in the 5,000 square foot new wing of the museum. As of this writing, it is scheduled for completion by 2010. Les attended local gala events in May 2007 to help raise funds for the museum and to premiere "Chasing Sound," his *American Masters* film recently shown on PBS. The following night, his trio performed for a special fundraising banquet at the Milwaukee Marriott in Les's honor.

Next I visited the actual birthplace of Les (now a parking lot by a new Walgreens), the area of his family's home on St. Paul Avenue (now a small strip mall), and the various schools he attended. I noticed the tracks where trains used to buzz by his boyhood home, giving him primitive lessons in stereo panning and frequency shifts. Nearby is the music bandshell and Historic Indian Mounds where Les played guitar and harmonica. The park's stage area has been fitly renamed the Les Paul Performing Center.

Waukesha's original Club 400, renovated by his father George and brother Ralph in 1948, is still in business. We experienced firsthand the historic room where Lester and Marylou sat together on the stairs for their first performances together. A small Les Paul tribute area is planned for the upstairs area. As we wrapped up the book project, it was a fitting time to get a feel for Les Paul's own digs and to see where this man's path to greatness began.

(Above) Artist T. Agazzi's 2005 conceptual mural of the Les Paul Experience exhibits.

(Right) Lester and Marylou first performed at Club 400 in 1948, when Les's father George and brother Ralph renovated the 1890s train hotel. The establishment is aptly named for the 400 minutes it takes to travel between Chicago and Minneapolis.

(Bottom) This beautiful print shows Les playing a Gibson Super 400. He donated it to "Poky" at Club 400. The original invitation to the 1948 grand opening is attached.

Built as the county courthouse in 1893, the stately Waukesha County Historic Museum is a fine example of Richardson Romanesque architecture. The Les Paul Experience wing is scheduled to open here in 2010.

Wisconsin Highway 59/164 traverses the eastern and southern portions of Waukesha. It is now designated the "Les Paul Parkway."

Les, at his 93rd birthday party, smiling at John Colianni. Later while enjoying the cake, I showed Les the full color layout for this book.

The Last Birthday Bash

From 1995 onward, Les celebrated his birthday at the Iridium Jazz Club. This photo dates from June 9, 2008, the last birthday party at which Les performed. It's obvious how much he enjoyed playing at "his club" and hosting the annual star-studded jam and mutual admiration society, full of fellow players and friends.

Discovery World— Milwaukee, Wisconsin 2008

In 2008, a group of Wisconsin devotees visited Les Paul and arranged to have an exhibit called Les Paul's House of Sound installed in the newly opened Discovery World, on the shore of Lake Michigan in Milwaukee. This interactive display boasted the world's largest collection of Les Paul's artifacts ever assembled. Designed around Les's innovative, creative spirit, it charted his life—from his humble beginnings in Waukesha through to the present day, including a recreation of the Los Angeles garage, where he ushered in a new era of music and sound in the 1940s and 1950s.

Les made sure the stories were accurate, and that the House of Sound inspired creativity in every visitor. It was a fitting tribute, then, that his body lay in state at Discovery World on August 21, 2009, before the final procession to his burial site at Prairie Home Cemetery in Waukesha.

Ribbon-cutting ceremony for Les Paul's House of Sound at Milwaukee's Discovery World, July 2008. From left to right: Joel Brennan, President/CEO, Discovery World; Paul Krajniak, Executive Director, Discovery World; Kirsten Lee Villegas, Executive Director, Waukesha County Historical Society and Museum; Les Paul; Milwaukee Mayor Tom Barrett; and Oscar Tovar, Office of Wisconsin Governor Jim Doyle. *Photo courtesy Cy White*

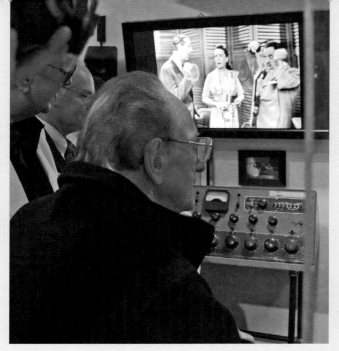

(Above) Les calls this large broadcast mixer "The Thing" and used it with the "Octopus" recorder. *Photo courtesy Cy White*

(Right) Les watches clips from his fifties *Omnibus* television show. *Photo courtesy Cy White*

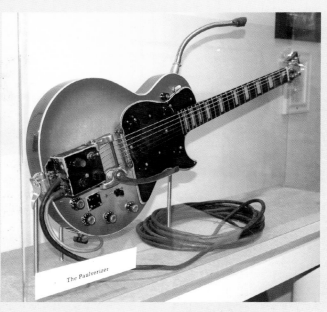

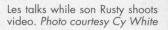

Les's original 1952 guitar, redone in sunburst, with the innovative Paulverizer attached. *Photo courtesy Cy White*

Les looks at his famous Log guitar with fans nearby. *Photo courtesy Cy White*

Les talks while son Rusty shoots video. *Photo courtesy Cy White*

The Ventures perform a few of their hit songs with Mel Taylor's son, Leon, on the drum and Bob Spaulding left of Nokie playing Bob Bogle's parts.

Rock and Roll Hall of Fame Museum — American Music Masters Series Tribute

The Rock and Roll Hall of Fame and Museum, Case Western Reserve University, and the Gibson Guitar Company honored Les Paul with a week-long series of special events in Cleveland. These included a retrospective of his life, a symposium, and an all-star tribute concert at the Playhouse Square Theatre. Along with the producers of the PBS special *Chasing Sound*, I was honored to participate in a lecture slide show that concluded with a question-and-answer segment and book-signing. The Ventures presented a lively workshop on their career and performed "Walk Don't Run."

The three-and-a-half-hour tribute concert began with Texans Billy Gibbons and Barbara Lynn playing ZZ Top's funky "Just Got Paid." Then Steve Lukather and Eric Carmen did a wonderful impression of the Bing Crosby/Les Paul rendition of "It's Been a Long, Long Time," and Steve segued into a superb instrumental version of "Over the Rainbow." Duane Eddy did his classic "Rebel Rouser" and Lonnie Mack offered a blistering "Memphis" on his Cherry '58 Flying V. Richie Sambora brought out his '58 Sunburst for "Wanted Dead or Alive," exclaiming, "Let's thank God for this... and thank God for Les Paul!" James Burton rendered his classic riffs on his signature Telecaster and fellow San Diegoian Jennifer Batten did a brilliant tap version of "Lover." Skunk Baxter received an ES-175 and swung hard on "Take the 'A' Train." Vocalists Katy Moffatt and Alannah Myles performed a tribute to

Mary Ford, singing "How High the Moon" and "Via Con Dios" with guitarist Lenny Kaye. Afterward, Slash tore it up with "Vocalise" and Dennis Coffey did his funk magic.

The grand finale was Les and his trio, with the entire cast joining in for a fitting end to an historical event. Les Paul was moved and stated humbly, "This is a wonderful night for me. Thank you so much." This would be his last public concert performance.

Richie Sambora plays his solo, up close with Les.

345

James Burton, guitarist for Ricky Nelson and Elvis, plays a solo as Les and the all-star band admire his handiwork.

(Above) Slash plays his signature Les Paul Goldtop.

(Left) Les smiles at the audience.

Jennifer Batten does her fancy work.

Les Paul's solo, November 15, 2008.

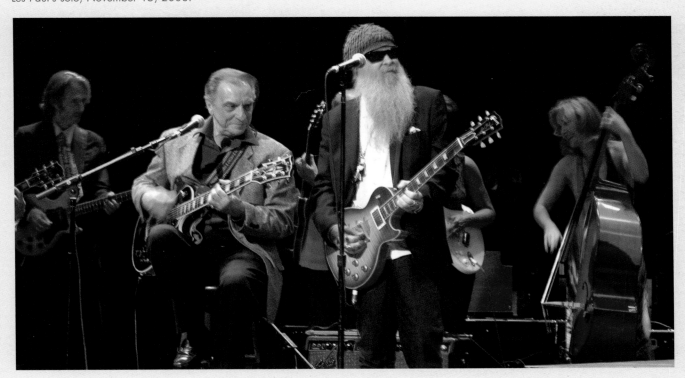

Lou Pallo watches Billy Gibbons.

(Left) Top Gibson representatives Mike McGuire (Custom Shop), Ren Ferguson (Montana Acoustic Division), and Frank Johns (Gibson USA) pose after their lecture on Gibson instruments.

(Below) Gibson President Dave Berryman presents Les with a special commemorative Custom model as he holds his precious award.

Guitarist/Singer Barbara Lynn poses with the author following their lectures at Case Western Reserve University.

With his Lifetime Achievement Award, Les leaves the stage. Except for his Manhattan jazz club residency gigs, this was Les's final public performance.

348

So Long, Lester

Playing his weekly gig at the Iridium kept Les going pretty strong. Though a limousine most often transported him, he'd sometimes resort to driving himself to the city if a ride wasn't ready. He loved to play and was driven all his life to make people happy. Within the last few years of Les's illustrious career, besides the nagging arthritis, he began having some lung congestion problems. He had smoked cigarettes during the 1930s, '40s, and '50s and this might have had an effect on his lungs later in life.

Eventually Les started running out of steam. His weekly gig began to wear him out, and he would spend the rest of the week recuperating. Having been in the hospital for a bout with pneumonia, Les missed his Gibson Amphitheatre tribute gig in 2007, and we all prayed for his speedy recovery. Luckily he resumed playing, and the last Iridium gig was the week before his 94th birthday. Bassist Paul Nowinski attended and said Les was in good spirits and told many friends how much he loved them. Within a week, though, his lungs were a problem again, so he was hospitalized. After being released for a week, the pneumonia became a real problem, so he went back to the White Plains hospital. By August 7, his condition became grave and close family members arrived to see him.

Coming home. Les Paul's closed coffin lying in state at Discovery World's digital theatre. Over 1,500 people paid their respects in Milwaukee, August 21.

Reception to follow at
Gibson Showroom
421 West 54th Street, New York

A second viewing will take place at
Discovery World
in Milwaukee, Wisconsin on
Friday, August 21, 2009 from 10:00 am - 2:00 pm

Private interment to follow at the
Prairie Home Cemetery
Waukesha, Wisconsin

Les Paul

June 9, 1915 to August 12, 2009

Funeral Services
Wednesday, August 19, 2009 - 5:00 pm
Frank E. Campbell, The Funeral Chapel

Les Paul Trio
"It's Been A Long, Long Time"

Welcome
Gary Wess, son-in-law

Gary Paul, grandson

Les Paul Trio *"Nature Boy"*

Ron Sturm, Iridium Jazz Club

Lou Pallo, long time friend and trio member

Les Paul Trio *"How High the Moon"*

Henry Juszkiewicz, CEO Gibson Guitar

Les Paul Trio
"Vaya Con Dios" (May God Be With You)

The program handed out at the New York City service, August 19, 2009. *Courtesy Frank E. Campbell The Funeral Chapel*

Lester lost his fight to live longer, succumbing to complications of pneumonia on August 12th. His family was at his side. That day, the world lost one of the most important figures in American musical history, an icon in the record-ing industry. Word spread around the world the next day like thunder and lightning had struck a big chord in the sky—a disturbance in the musical order of the universe! Our phones rang off the hook all day and many condolences came in to his family and close friends from all over the globe. It was the end of an era. Everyone in Les's immediate circles on both coasts wanted to know what to do.

A 5 p.m. service was set for Wednesday the 19th in New York, at the Campbell Funeral Home. Gibson had a special event at their headquarters on 54th street, with many entertainers performing. These included godson Steve Miller, Joe Satriani, Chad Smith, Pat Martino, Bucky Pizzarelli, Tony Bennett, Slash, Jeff Baxter, Richie Sambora, Frank Vignola, Gary Mazzaroppi, Paul Nowinski, Jon Paris, Del Casher, Sonya Hensley, Christian Howes, Andrew Nimmer (tap artist), Jay Leonhart, Lisa Parrott, and Tommy Morimoto—among others. Gibson's president Dave Berryman, CEO Henry Juszkiewicz, and others like Jeff Salmon, Jackie Martling, and Greg Ercolino joined the event with Les Paul's musicians, management, and crew.

Guitarist Lou Pallo got it started with a special speech, delivered to an emotional group. Then Henry Juszkiewicz told many stories of how Les regularly broke everyone up wherever they went. The trio's performances of "How High the Moon" and "Via Con Dios" were more moving than ever. It was quite a way to remember our Lester.

Next was Wisconsin. I made arrangements to be with the family and pay my respects to Les in his hometown. In Milwaukee, a special event was held at Discovery World's

"Les Paul's House of Sound" exhibit, with Les lying in state in a closed casket for the public to pay its respects. Video testimonies were taken of friends outside the mourning area and many poured in to experience the last of Les Paul's physical presence.

Final interment services took place at Prairie Home Cemetery, where other members of his family are buried. Nearly 80 people attended this private service, where old and new friends spoke about the good times and the effect he had on them. His irascible, humorous nature pervaded. It was a touching ceremony. Then the military honored him with a 21-gun salute and taps was sounded. Many wept as the flag was held over the casket.

Nearby, at the Club 400, family and friends celebrated Lester's life with great food and drink. Lester will forever remain in our hearts, playing his special guitars and touching so many.

Rusty Paul shared his heartfelt feelings about his father:

Many people don't know how much he touched so many, not only players with guitars and amps, but daily acquaintances, like his heart surgeon. I just got a letter from the doctor and he called twice. It was hard to talk since they all considered him a second father. He knew he had a piece of their hearts. It's hard to take. We could ask him any question, and now we don't have an answer. He took the whole world under his wing.

All he wanted to do was play and make people happy. Playing "Over the Rainbow" would make people cry, no matter how he played it. We will miss him greatly. He always hung around the right people. He just picked it up in life. He sponged it up. People wouldn't know, but he learned right from being around the right people. He not only would have electronic guys, but also others. He's seen the whole ball of wax. He had great friendships with everyone. That was important. I'm getting calls all the time from people who all knew they have the special feeling.

Les Paul's family at the Prairie Home Cemetery burial site in his hometown, Waukesha, Wisconsin.

White roses sit atop the elaborately carved casket. A gold plaque on top displays the simple inscription "Les Paul, August 12, 2009."

Paying tribute to my friend. I felt Les was looking down on all of us.

During the gathering after the service at Club 400, Muriel Anderson is fed a tasty lemon tart, a favorite dessert for Les, by son Rusty Paul.

Rusty's son, Gary Paul, and his wife, Tara.

Gary and Colleen Weiss (Les's daughter) enjoying the repast for her father.

Before they headed to the Iridium for an ongoing Monday night gig to honor Les, guitarist and singer Lou Pallo and Tommy Doyle shared their reflections on working so many wonderful years with Les Paul:

Robb: How do you reflect back on your years performing with Les Paul?

Lou: *It was a great honor and a privilege to work beside a legend in my lifetime. There is no one who will ever duplicate Les Paul's sound. He was way ahead of his time. His records from 1948 on are better than some of the new digital recordings today.*

RL: You were the brunt of Les's jokes at times.

LP: *He was very warm and humorous, too. Everyone who has worked with him has learned more from him than any other musician or entertainer. At the eulogy, I said that every time I look up at the headstock and see his name, he's always with me—and the rest of the world. I will look at it tonight, too. The last thing I said to Les at the eulogy was "God Bless You" and "Via Con Dios." Then I went onstage and played it for the last song. It was a tear-jerker for everyone as they took the casket out. And they applauded, too. Right onstage I just let it all out. When I play "How High the Moon" now, it gives me tears. I will think of it tonight.*

Tommy Doyle had this to say about his mentor and dear friend:

Robb: What do you hold fond in your heart for Les?

Tommy: *I think the man that I worked for since 1966 was more than just a guitar player and a man to me. He gave me the incentive to carry on to be what I am today. I idolized him so much and never thought I would meet him or end up working with him. As a kid, I looked through binoculars from behind his house, trying to find out where his echo and delay came from. That was in 1960, when I was 17. The day I actually met him at his front door, at first I didn't know I was speaking to Les Paul. I thought he was the carpenter, for he had a hammer in his hand, penny loafers, dungarees rolled up, and a dirty shirt. It just couldn't be*

Les Paul. I told him that I was a guitar player that Les knew, and that I was in town to stop by and see him. He said, "Really?" and led me to believe he about the shows, from flying saucers (like you guys saw in Texas) to God. So he was very open to why we are here, what is it for, and where are we going.

wasn't who he was because I still didn't know. He had been wearing tuxedos on Ed Sullivan. Some five and half years later he came to see my sister and me doing a Les Paul/ Mary Ford act. We had the Electro-Voice Concertone tape deck for echo and a 350 Ampex tape doing all the parts, along with us doing the lead. We finished "Bye, Bye Blues" and he walked over to us and said, "You kids are great!" That was

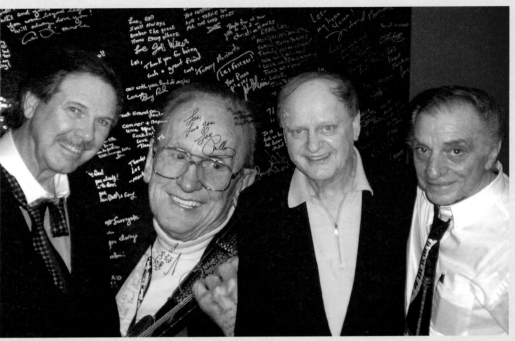

Standing before a signed mural at the Gibson party, Tommy Doyle, Del Casher, and Lou Pallo celebrate Les Paul's beautiful life. *Courtesy Del Casher*

the beginning of the relationship for the next 40 years.

I became his engineer on the shows for Fat Tuesdays and the Iridium. I would take him down to the Iridium every Monday. We would discuss afterward everything

That really is the Les Paul I knew. He was a great, great mentor of mine and I will miss him for the rest of my life.

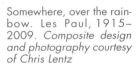

Somewhere, over the rainbow. Les Paul, 1915–2009. *Composite design and photography courtesy of Chris Lentz*

Epilogue

To chronicle the life and times of this remarkable man has been a joyous experience. From his first singing as a child to playing the harmonica, to becoming a talented guitarist and being heard on the radio during the thirties, to winning the *Downbeat* guitarists poll and having a string of hit tunes with Mary Ford, to finally endorsing the most prestigious electric guitar in the world—Les Paul turned the world on its ear and set a path for all to admire.

His life as an inventor went hand-in-hand with the music. Of necessity, Les could see what had to happen to get results. With his inquisitive nature, he had an insatiable knack for creating new equipment and for improving the old. Having such an inventive, tinkering mind led him to pioneer the backbone of today's modern multiple-track recordings with echo and reverb effects. Les used these techniques on his hit Capitol releases, first with his instrumentals and then with the lovely songstress/guitarist Mary Ford. Their crystal-clear recordings charmed everyone and amazed many young guitarists at the same time.

Les Paul witnessed the emergence of the electric guitar, while having an integral part in shaping and promoting it. He, in turn, began his own experimenting with electronics and with solid wooden-bodied guitars.

This portrait was featured on the front page of Les's hometown newspaper, the *Waukesha Freeman*, the day he was laid to rest. *Courtesy of painter and fellow Wisconsinite Tom Noll, www.creativebonesartworks.com*

Through his collaborative efforts with the prestigious Gibson guitar company, Les became a driving force with the success of this solid-body electric guitar. This combined effort resulted in the popular Les Paul signature model that today has become a true American icon, one that the world is still embracing after 50 years' advancement. It is the instrument of choice for countless artists and virtually caused the musical revolution we have today.

His historic contributions are heralded today. (It's no wonder Thomas Edison has been such a role model.) The great diversity of his career's achievements stands tall with his immense influence on American culture. Les's pioneering efforts opened the doors to a world of creative possibilities. His example of fusing technological innovation with his musical genius has inspired many of us.

Thank you, Lester! You're a guiding light to all who treasure your music, showmanship, innovative recording advancements and—most of all—the greatest electric guitar in the world!

Index

Note: Page numbers in *italics* indicate both illustrations and caption text.